The Quintessential Quintuplets

negi haruba

2

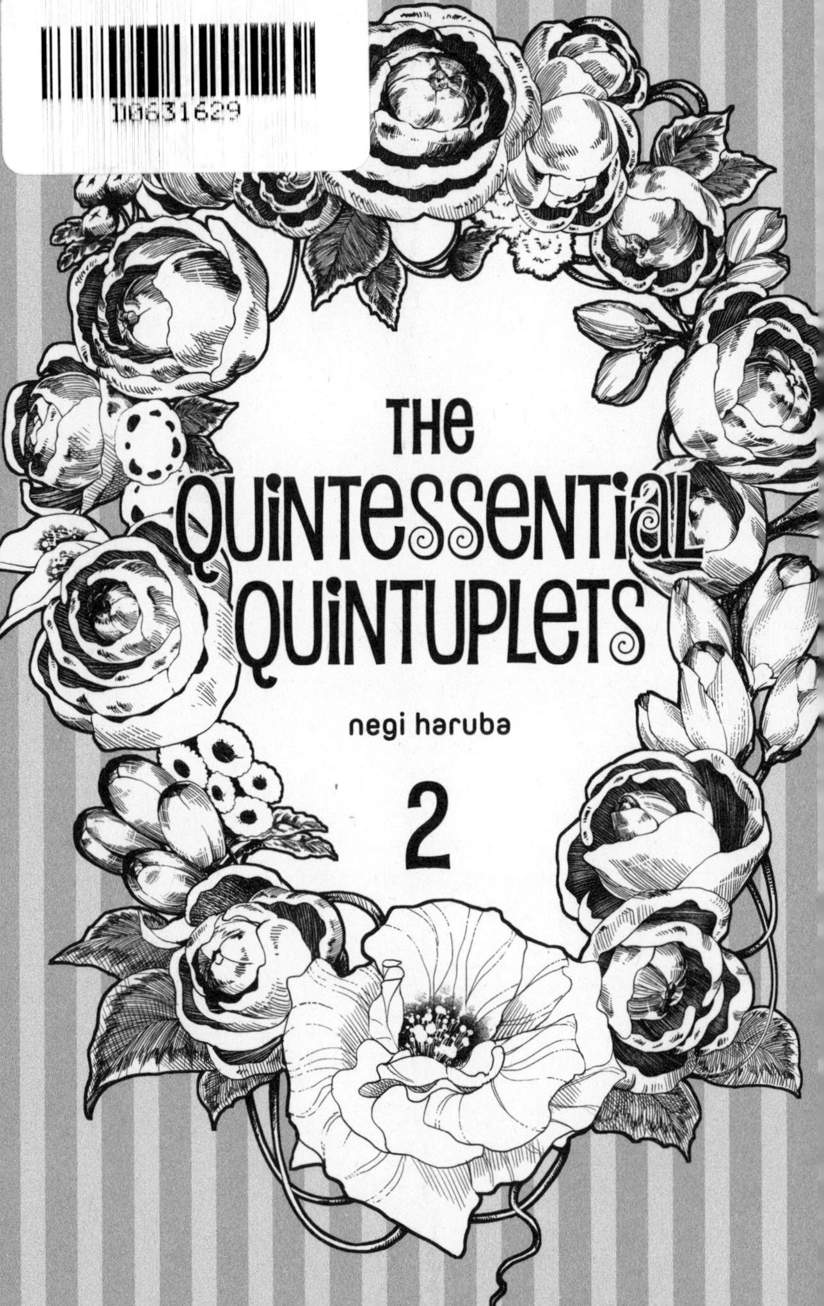

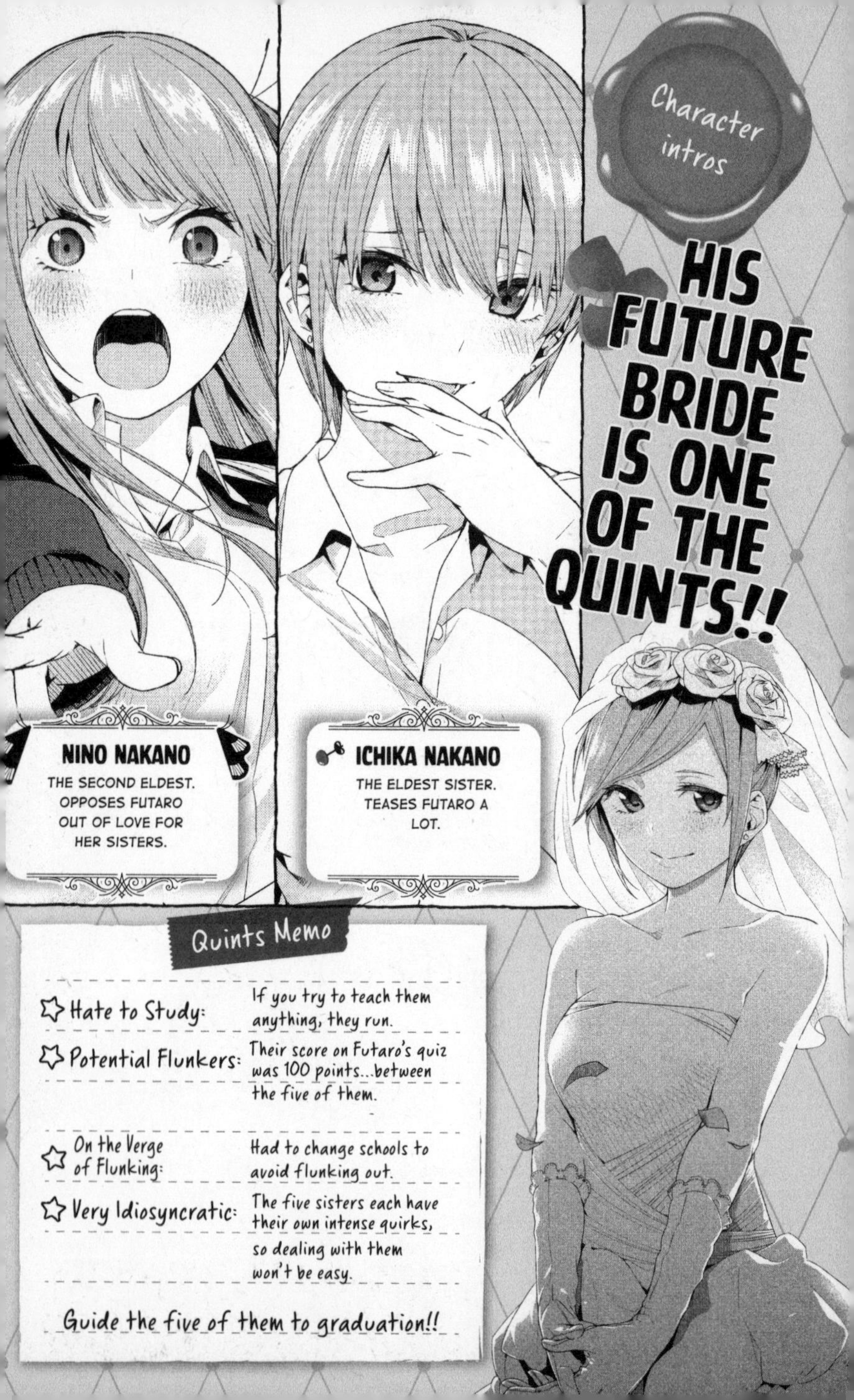
Character intros
HIS FUTURE BRIDE IS ONE OF THE QUINTS!!
ICHIKA NAKANO
THE ELDEST SISTER. TEASES FUTARO A LOT.
NINO NAKANO
THE SECOND ELDEST. OPPOSES FUTARO OUT OF LOVE FOR HER SISTERS.
Quints Memo
Hate to Study: If you try to teach them anything, they run.
Potential Flunkers: Their score on Futaro's quiz was 100 points...between the five of them.
On the Verge of Flunking: Had to change schools to avoid flunking out.
Very Idiosyncratic: The five sisters each have their own intense quirks, so dealing with them won't be easy.
Guide the five of them to graduation!!

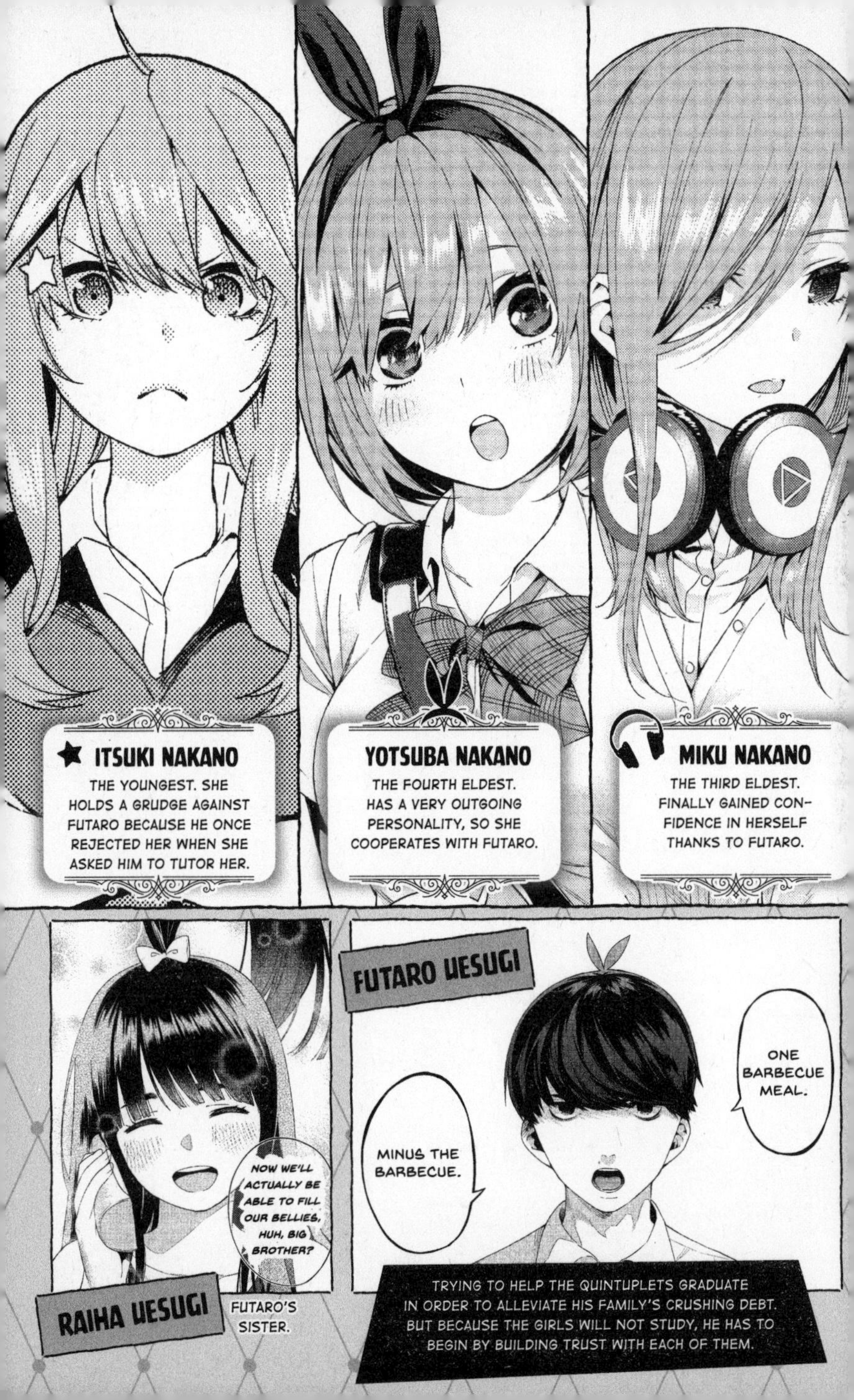
MIKU NAKANO
THE THIRD ELDEST. FINALLY GAINED CON-FIDENCE IN HERSELF THANKS TO FUTARO.
YOTSUBA NAKANO
THE FOURTH ELDEST. HAS A VERY OUTGOING PERSONALITY, SO SHE COOPERATES WITH FUTARO.
ITSUKI NAKANO
THE YOUNGEST. SHE HOLDS A GRUDGE AGAINST FUTARO BECAUSE HE ONCE REJECTED HER WHEN SHE ASKED HIM TO TUTOR HER.
FUTARO UESUGI
ONE BARBECUE MEAL.
MINUS THE BARBECUE.
TRYING TO HELP THE QUINTUPLETS GRADUATE IN ORDER TO ALLEVIATE HIS FAMILY'S CRUSHING DEBT. BUT BECAUSE THE GIRLS WILL NOT STUDY, HE HAS TO BEGIN BY BUILDING TRUST WITH EACH OF THEM.
NOW WE'LL ACTUALLY BE ABLE TO FILL OUR BELLIES, HUH, BIG BROTHER?
RAIHA UESUGI
FUTARO'S SISTER.

CONTENTS

Chapter 6 Open the Door

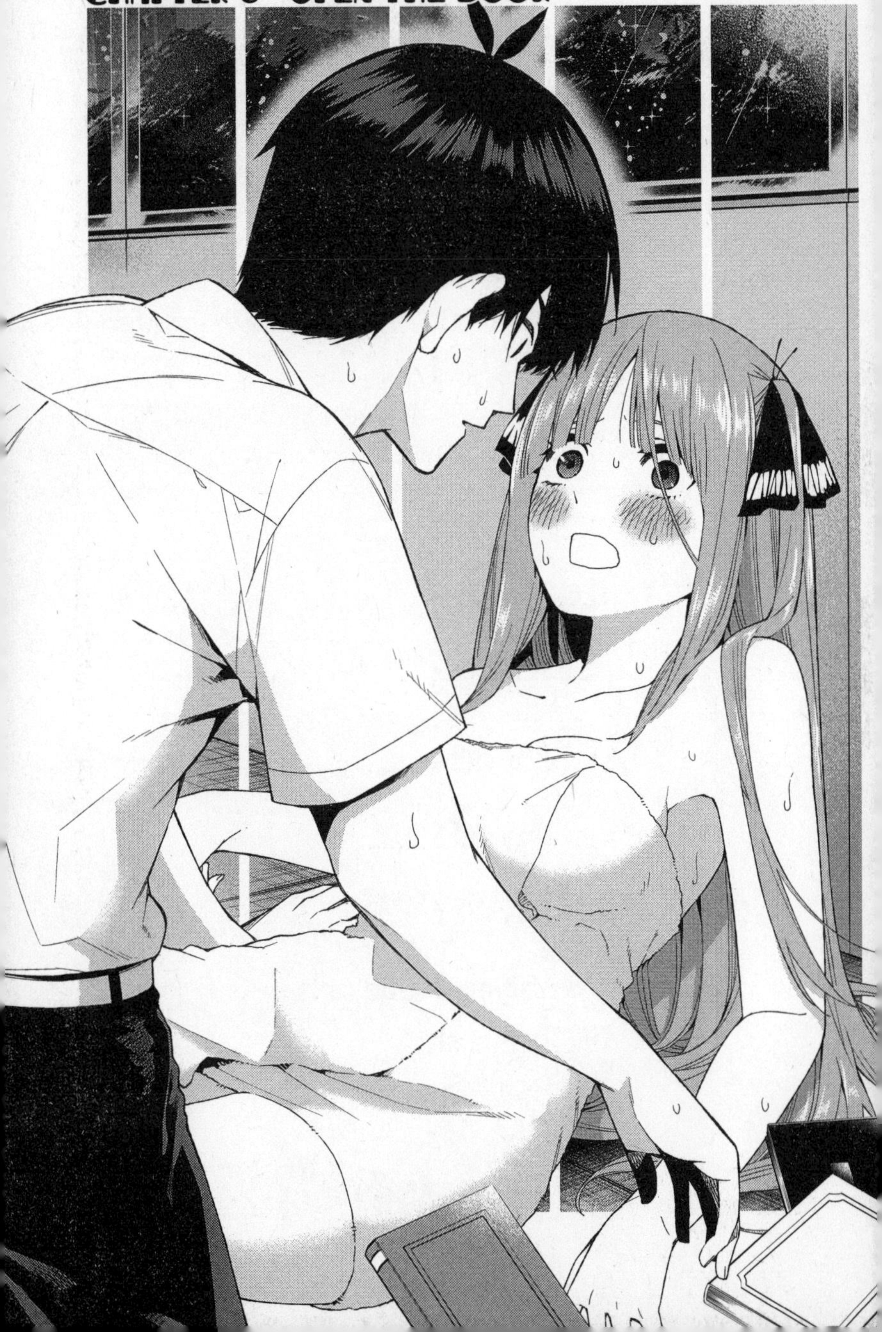

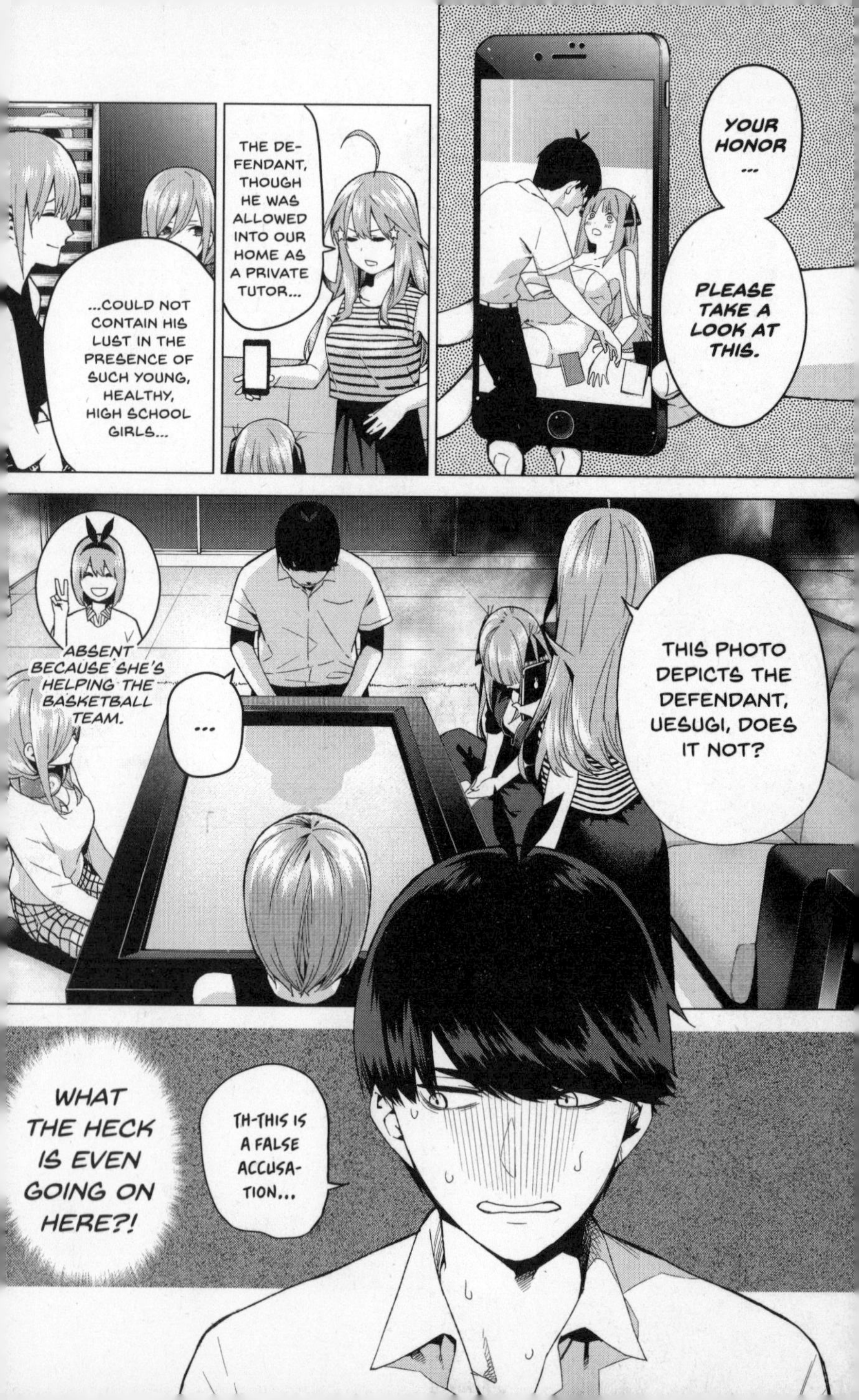
YOUR HONOR ...
PLEASE TAKE A LOOK AT THIS.
THE DEFENDANT, THOUGH HE WAS ALLOWED INTO OUR HOME AS A PRIVATE TUTOR...
...COULD NOT CONTAIN HIS LUST IN THE PRESENCE OF SUCH YOUNG, HEALTHY, HIGH SCHOOL GIRLS...
THIS PHOTO DEPICTS THE DEFENDANT, UESUGI, DOES IT NOT?
...
ABSENT BECAUSE SHE'S HELPING THE BASKETBALL TEAM.
TH-THIS IS A FALSE ACCUSATION...
WHAT THE HECK IS EVEN GOING ON HERE?!

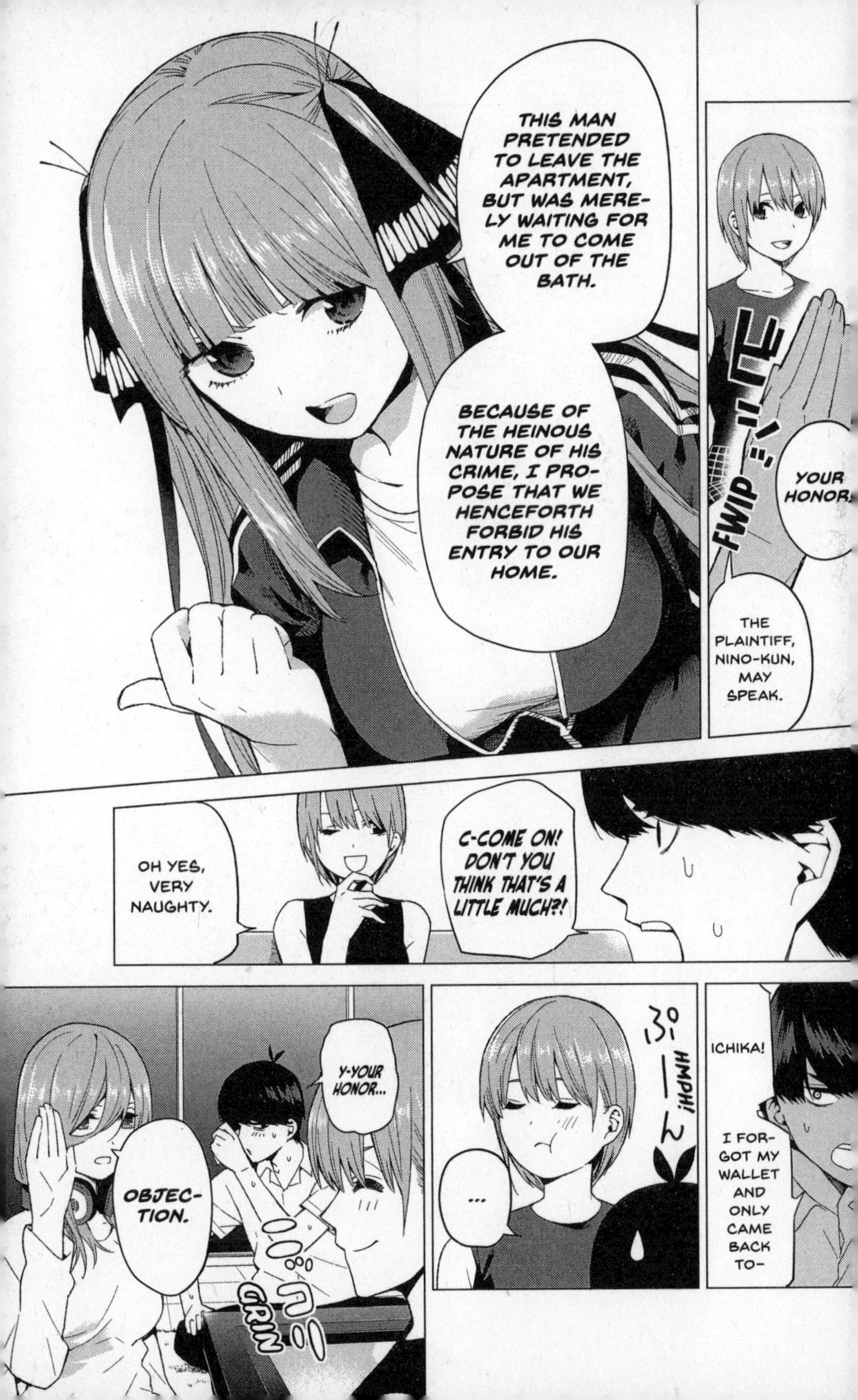
YOUR HONOR!
FWIP
THE PLAINTIFF, NINO-KUN, MAY SPEAK.
THIS MAN PRETENDED TO LEAVE THE APARTMENT, BUT WAS MERELY WAITING FOR ME TO COME OUT OF THE BATH.
BECAUSE OF THE HEINOUS NATURE OF HIS CRIME, I PROPOSE THAT WE HENCEFORTH FORBID HIS ENTRY TO OUR HOME.
C-COME ON! DON'T YOU THINK THAT'S A LITTLE MUCH?!
OH YES, VERY NAUGHTY.
ICHIKA!
I FORGOT MY WALLET AND ONLY CAME BACK TO-
HMPH!
...
Y-YOUR HONOR...
OBJECTION.
GRIN

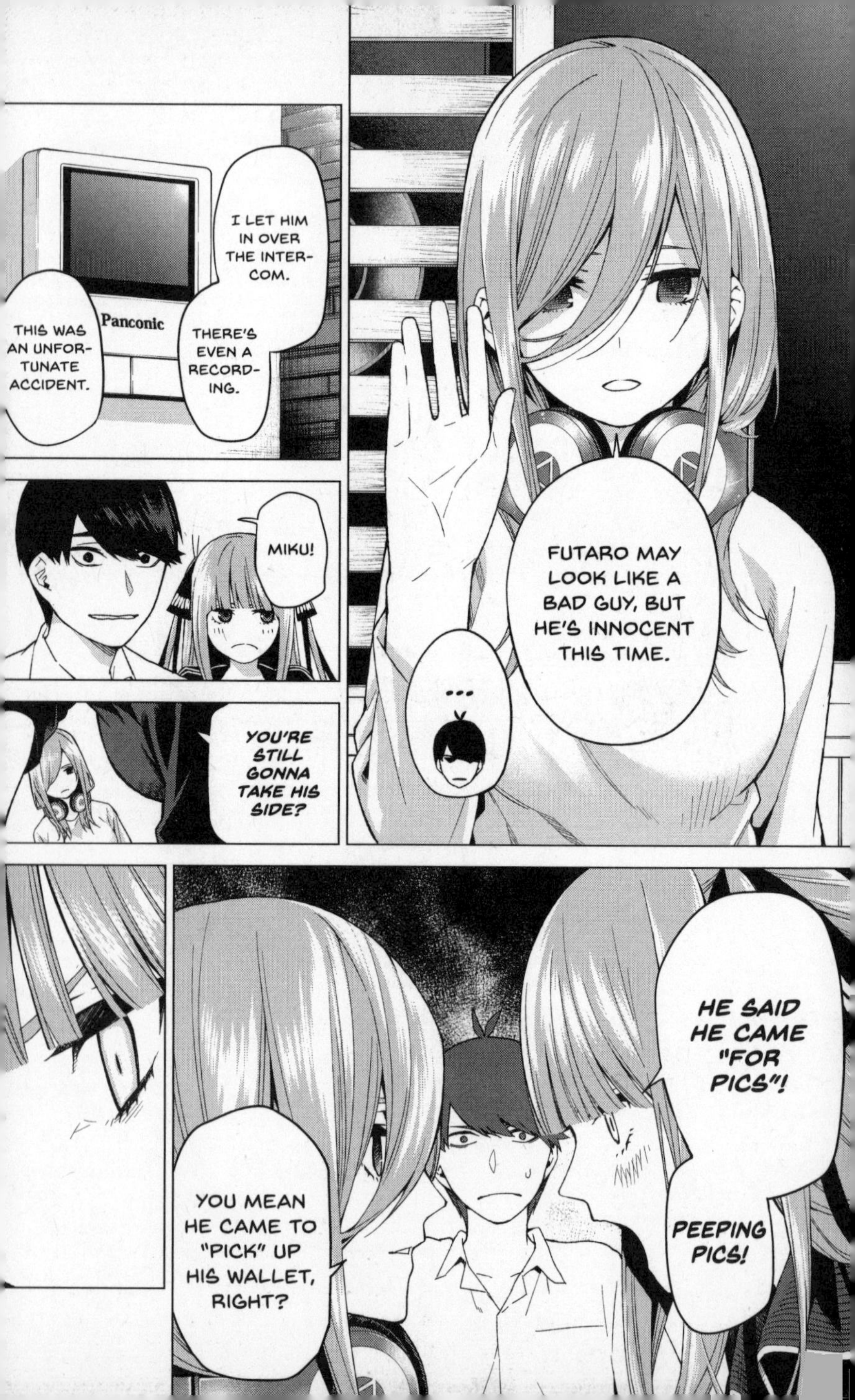
FUTARO MAY LOOK LIKE A BAD GUY, BUT HE'S INNOCENT THIS TIME.
...
I LET HIM IN OVER THE INTER-COM.
THERE'S EVEN A RECORD-ING.
Panconic
THIS WAS AN UNFOR-TUNATE ACCIDENT.
MIKU!
YOU'RE STILL GONNA TAKE HIS SIDE?
HE SAID HE CAME "FOR PICS"!
PEEPING PICS!
YOU MEAN HE CAME TO "PICK" UP HIS WALLET, RIGHT?

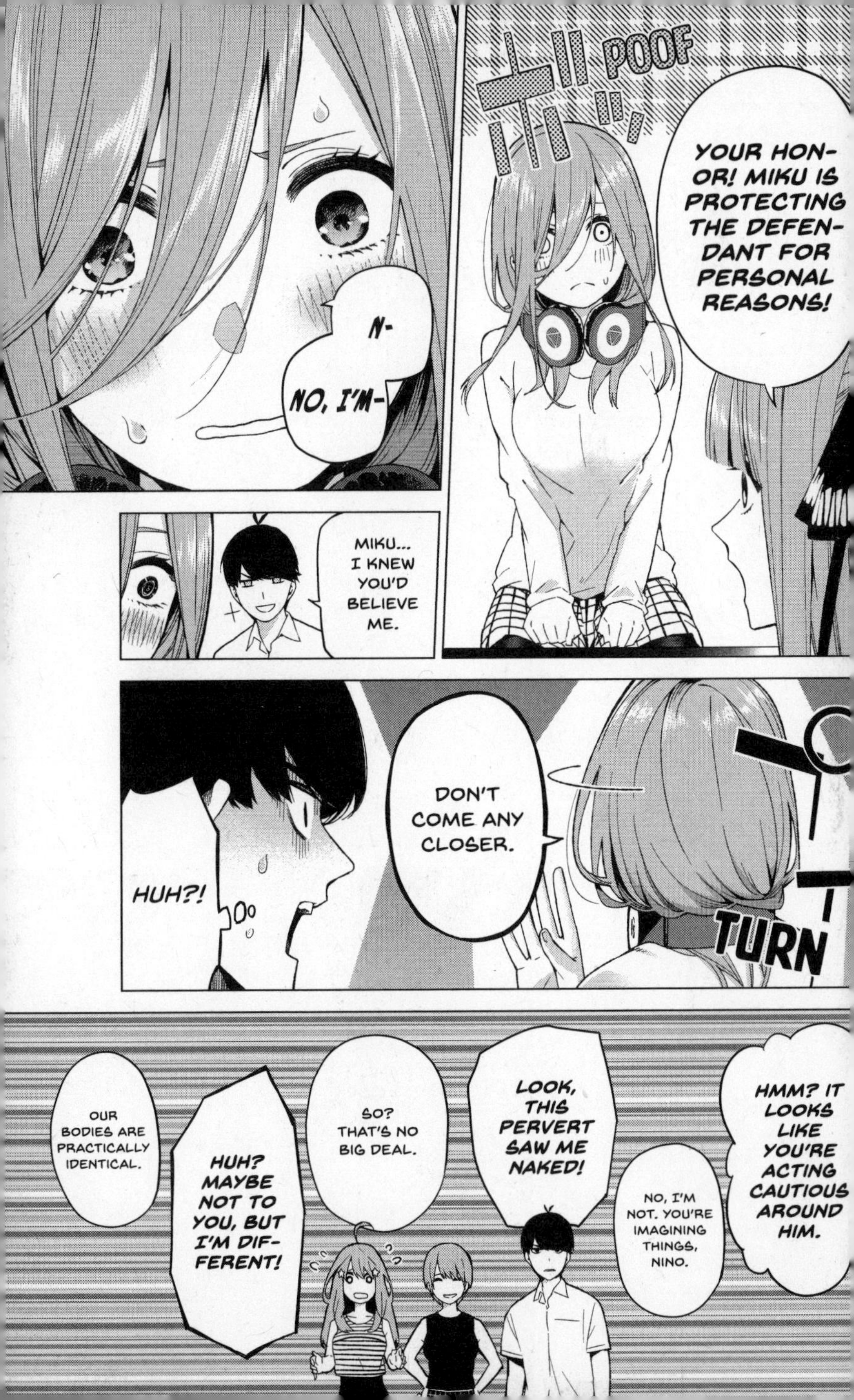
POOF
YOUR HONOR! MIKU IS PROTECTING THE DEFENDANT FOR PERSONAL REASONS!
N-
NO, I'M-
MIKU... I KNEW YOU'D BELIEVE ME.
TURN
DON'T COME ANY CLOSER.
HUH?!
HMM? IT LOOKS LIKE YOU'RE ACTING CAUTIOUS AROUND HIM.
NO, I'M NOT. YOU'RE IMAGINING THINGS, NINO.
LOOK, THIS PERVERT SAW ME NAKED!
SO? THAT'S NO BIG DEAL.
OUR BODIES ARE PRACTICALLY IDENTICAL.
HUH? MAYBE NOT TO YOU, BUT I'M DIFFERENT!

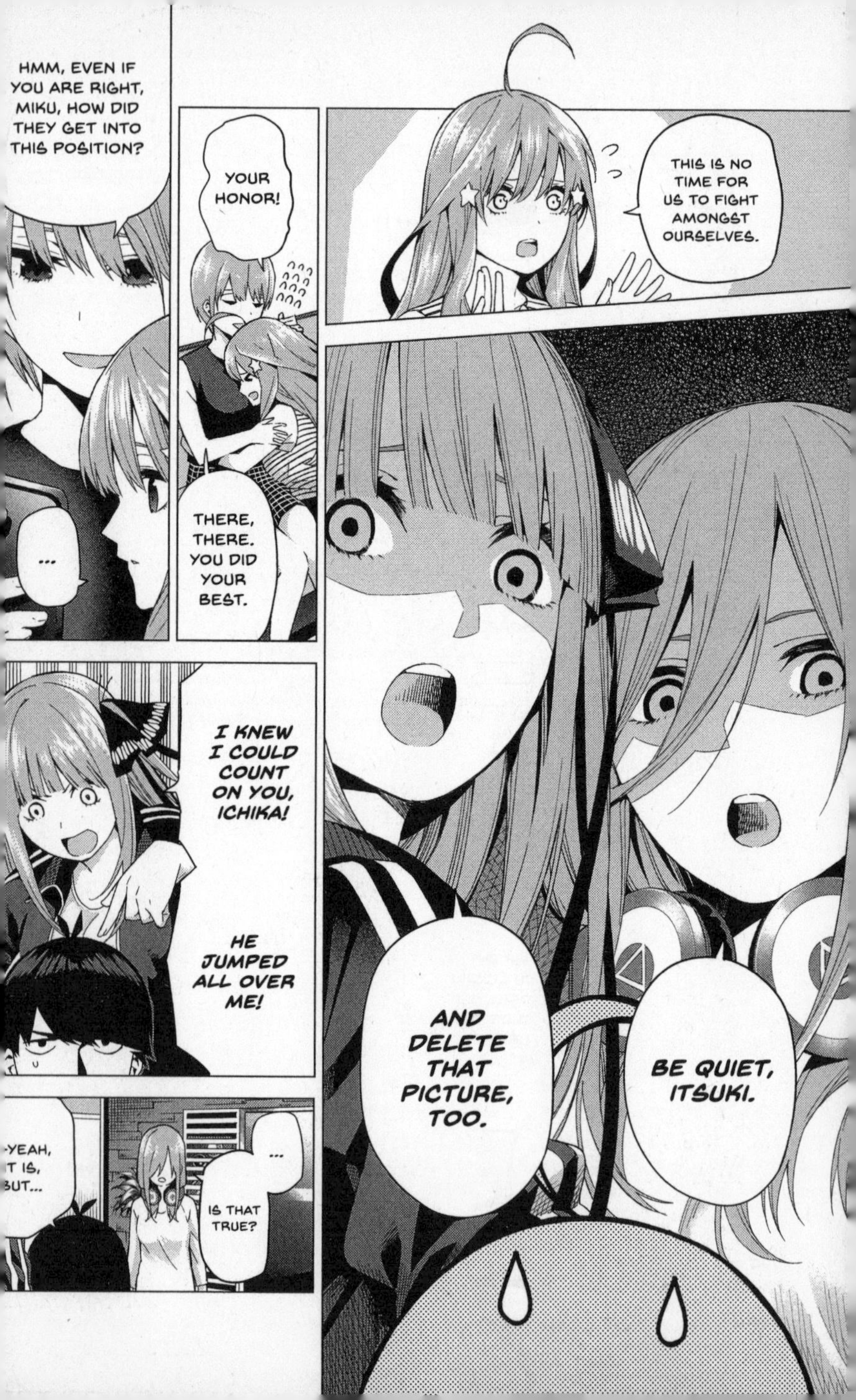
THIS IS NO TIME FOR US TO FIGHT AMONGST OURSELVES.
BE QUIET, ITSUKI.
AND DELETE THAT PICTURE, TOO.
YOUR HONOR!
THERE, THERE. YOU DID YOUR BEST.
HMM, EVEN IF YOU ARE RIGHT, MIKU, HOW DID THEY GET INTO THIS POSITION?
...
I KNEW I COULD COUNT ON YOU, ICHIKA!
HE JUMPED ALL OVER ME!
...
IS THAT TRUE?
-YEAH, T IS, BUT...

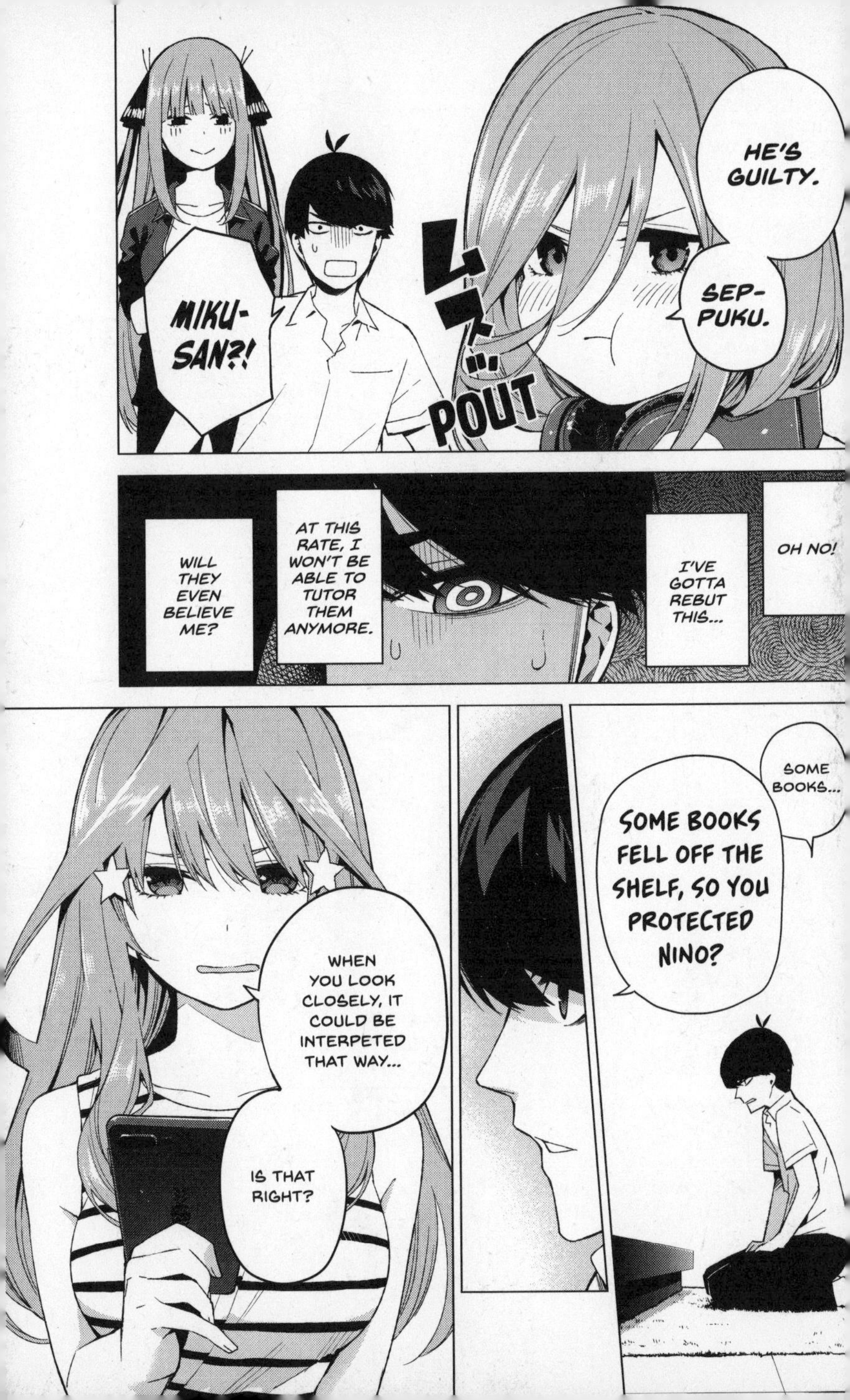
HE'S GUILTY.
SEP-PUKU.
POUT
MIKU-SAN?!
OH NO!
I'VE GOTTA REBUT THIS...
AT THIS RATE, I WON'T BE ABLE TO TUTOR THEM ANYMORE.
WILL THEY EVEN BELIEVE ME?
SOME BOOKS...
SOME BOOKS FELL OFF THE SHELF, SO YOU PROTECTED NINO?
WHEN YOU LOOK CLOSELY, IT COULD BE INTERPETED THAT WAY...
IS THAT RIGHT?

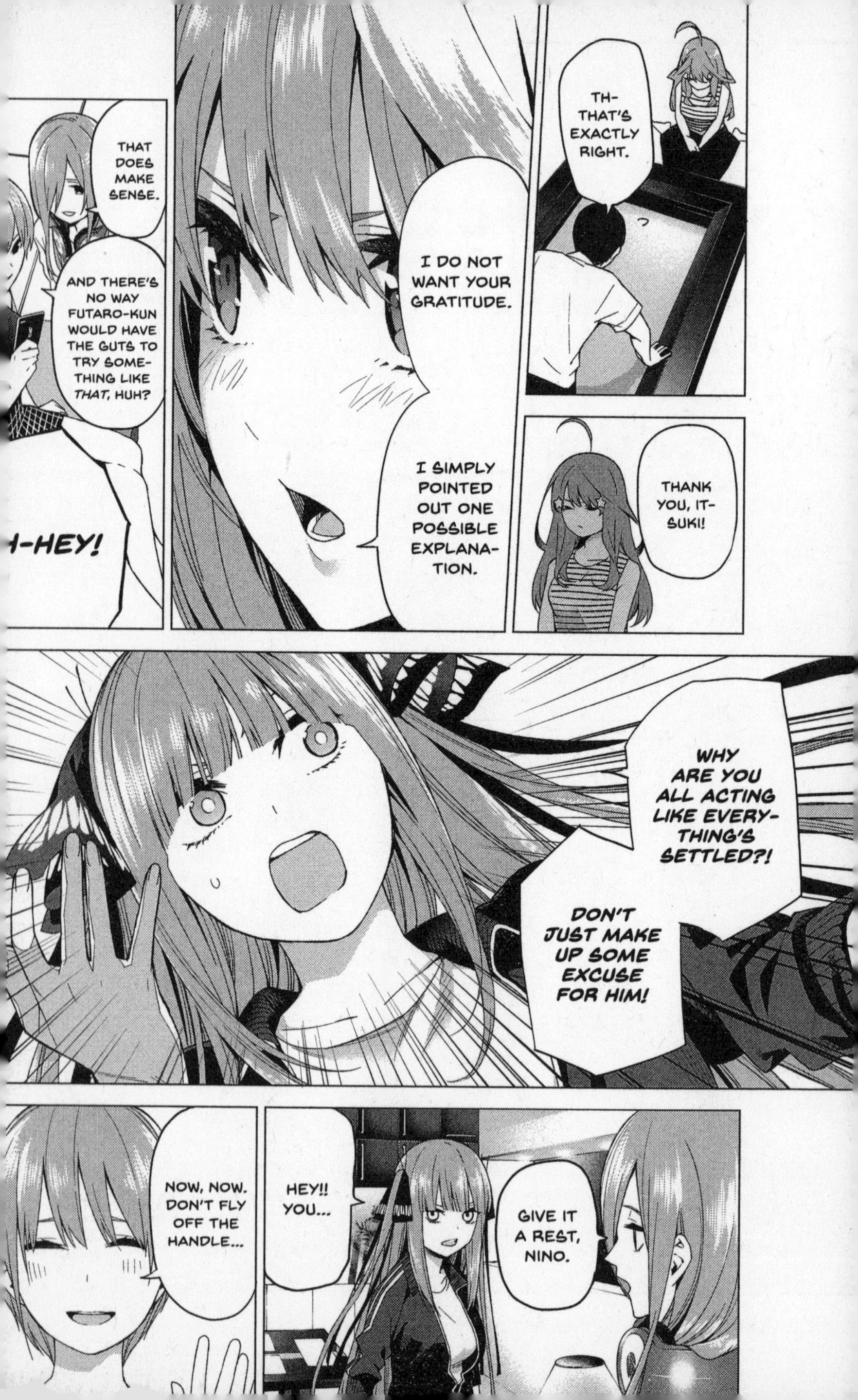
TH- THAT'S EXACTLY RIGHT.
THANK YOU, IT-SUKI!
I DO NOT WANT YOUR GRATITUDE.
I SIMPLY POINTED OUT ONE POSSIBLE EXPLANA-TION.
THAT DOES MAKE SENSE.
AND THERE'S NO WAY FUTARO-KUN WOULD HAVE THE GUTS TO TRY SOME-THING LIKE *THAT*, HUH?
H-HEY!
WHY ARE YOU ALL ACTING LIKE EVERY-THING'S SETTLED?!
DON'T JUST MAKE UP SOME EXCUSE FOR HIM!
GIVE IT A REST, NINO.
HEY!! YOU...
NOW, NOW. DON'T FLY OFF THE HANDLE...

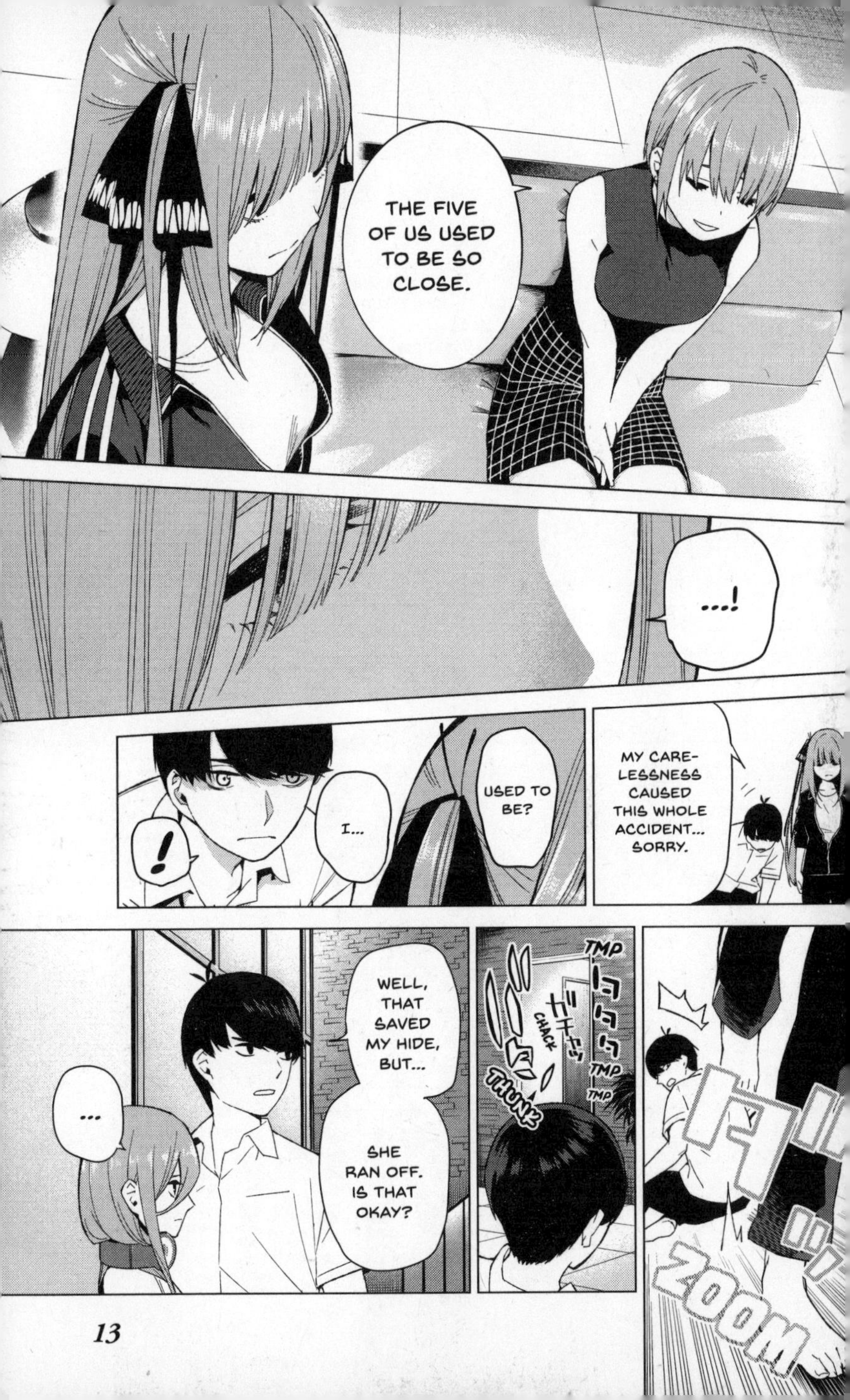
THE FIVE OF US USED TO BE SO CLOSE.
...!
MY CARE-LESSNESS CAUSED THIS WHOLE ACCIDENT... SORRY.
USED TO BE?
I...
!
ZOOM
TMP
TMP
TMP
CHACK
THUNK
WELL, THAT SAVED MY HIDE, BUT...
SHE RAN OFF. IS THAT OKAY?
...

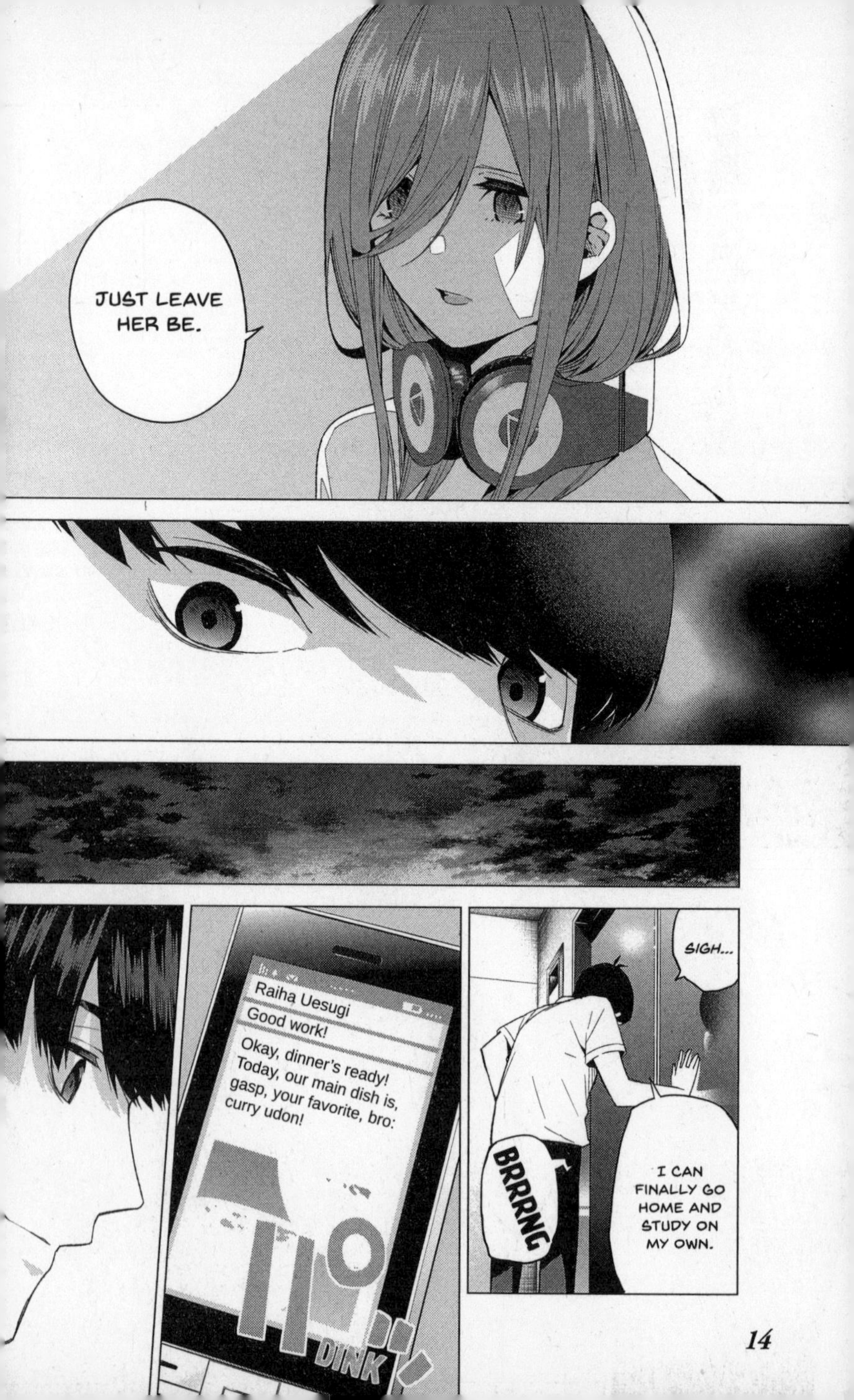
JUST LEAVE HER BE.
SIGH...
I CAN FINALLY GO HOME AND STUDY ON MY OWN.
BRRRNG
Raiha Uesugi
Good work!
Okay, dinner's ready! Today, our main dish is, gasp, your favorite, bro: curry udon!
DINK

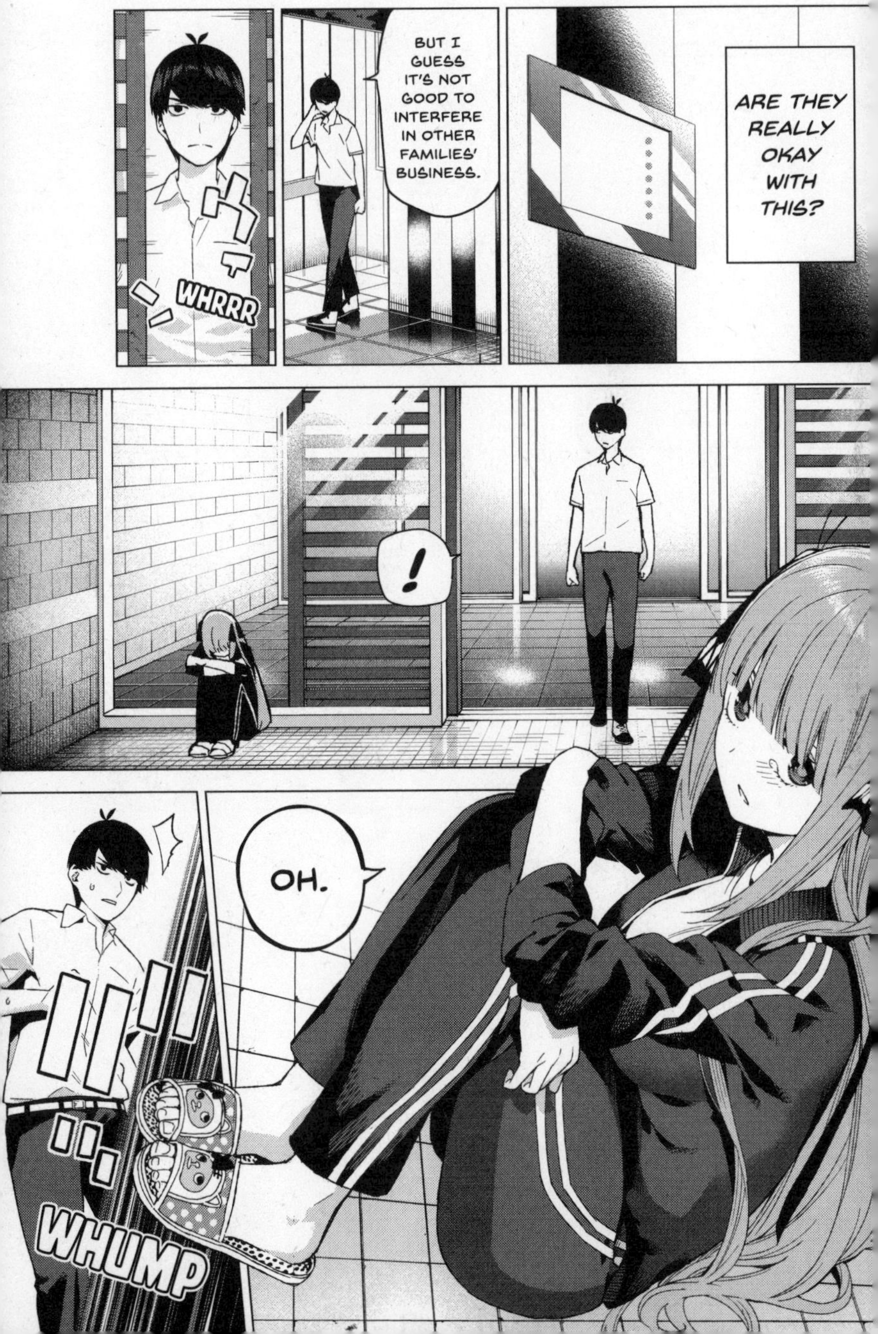
ARE THEY REALLY OKAY WITH THIS?
BUT I GUESS IT'S NOT GOOD TO INTERFERE IN OTHER FAMILIES' BUSINESS.
WHRRR
!
OH.
WHUMP

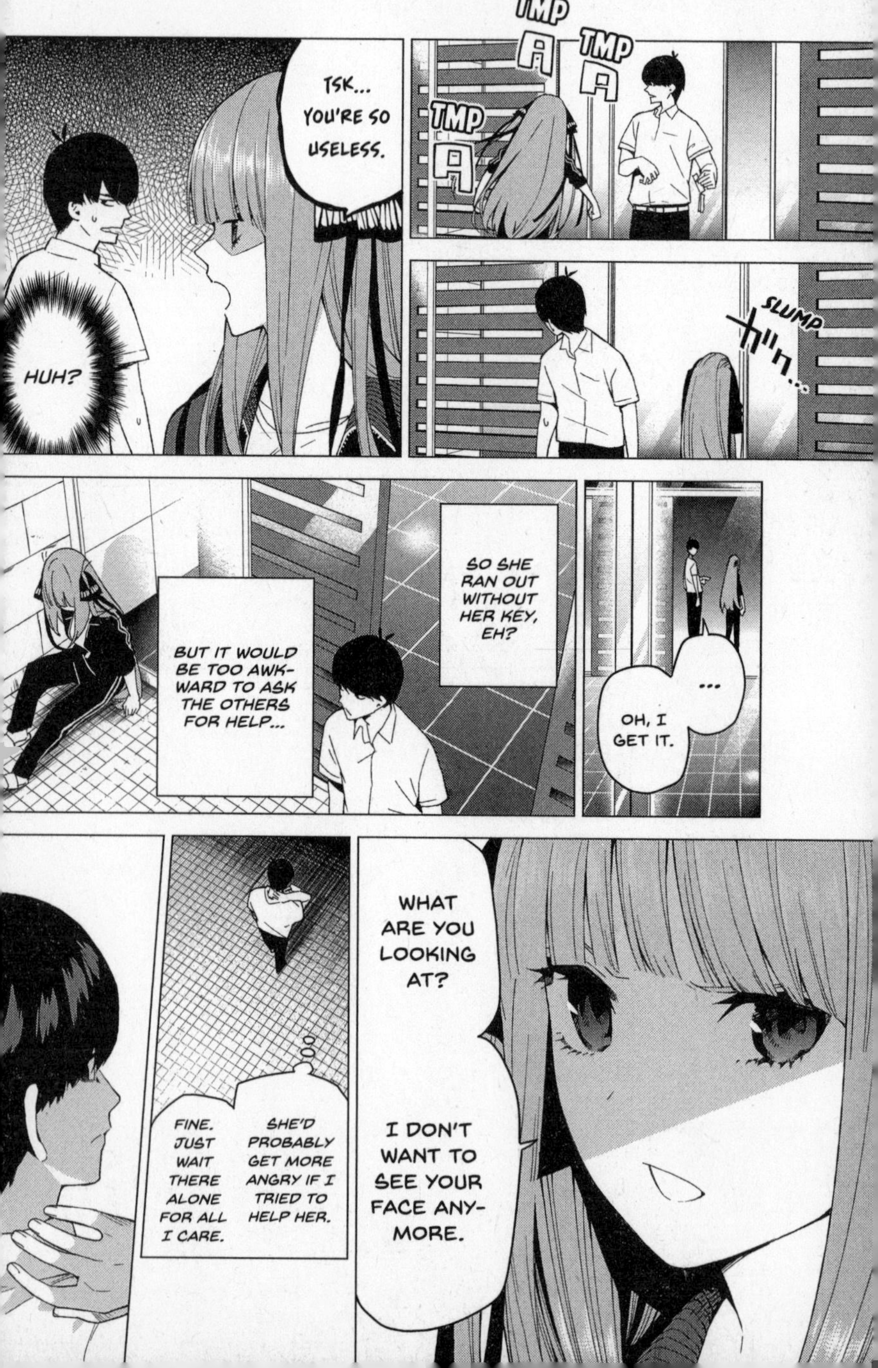
TMP
TMP
TMP
SLUMP
TSK... YOU'RE SO USELESS.
HUH?
...
OH, I GET IT.
SO SHE RAN OUT WITHOUT HER KEY, EH?
BUT IT WOULD BE TOO AWK-WARD TO ASK THE OTHERS FOR HELP...
WHAT ARE YOU LOOKING AT?
I DON'T WANT TO SEE YOUR FACE ANY-MORE.
SHE'D PROBABLY GET MORE ANGRY IF I TRIED TO HELP HER.
FINE. JUST WAIT THERE ALONE FOR ALL I CARE.

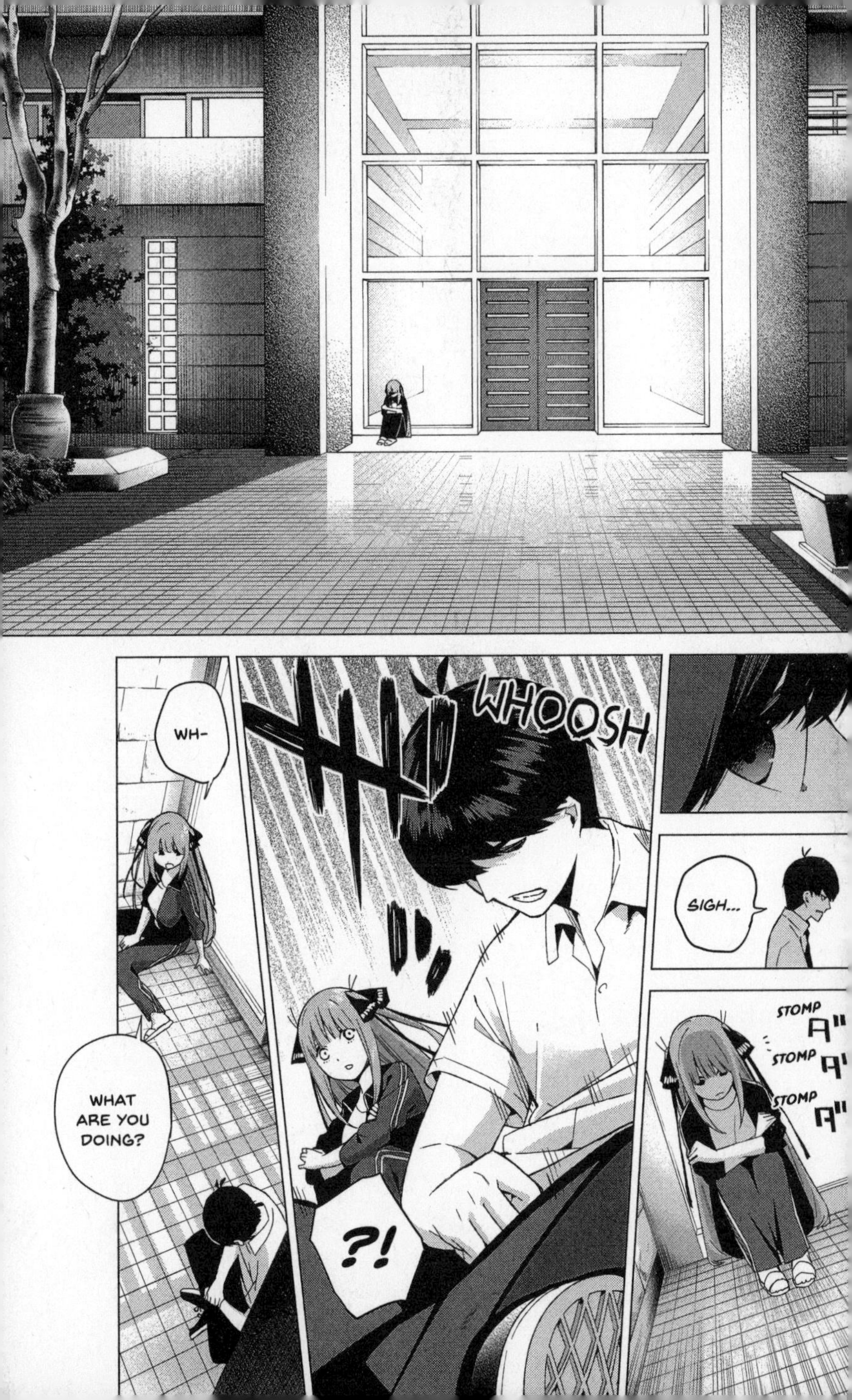
SIGH...
STOMP ダ
STOMP ダ
STOMP ダ
WHOOSH
?!
WH-
WHAT ARE YOU DOING?

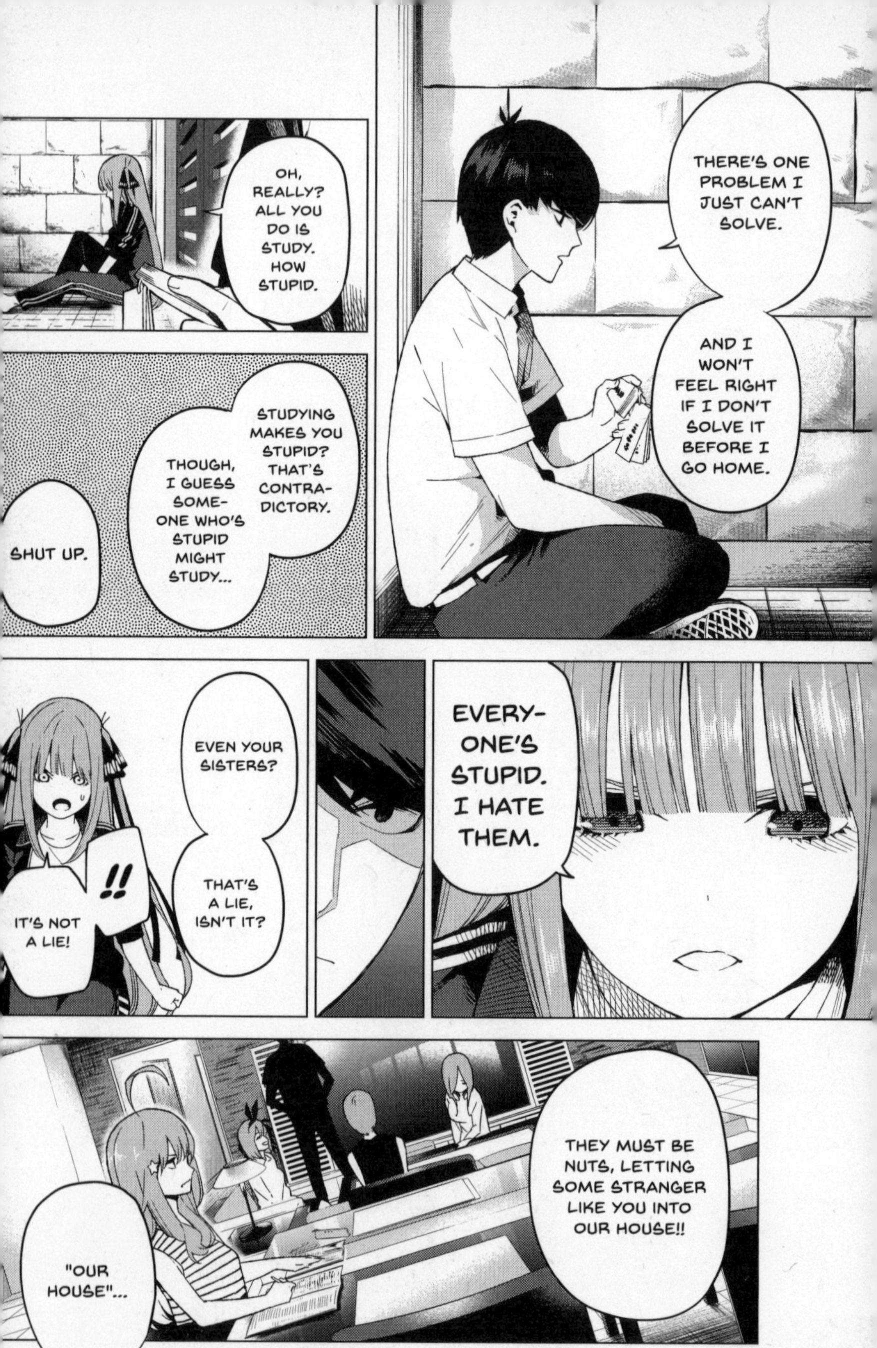
THERE'S ONE PROBLEM I JUST CAN'T SOLVE.
AND I WON'T FEEL RIGHT IF I DON'T SOLVE IT BEFORE I GO HOME.
OH, REALLY? ALL YOU DO IS STUDY. HOW STUPID.
STUDYING MAKES YOU STUPID? THAT'S CONTRA-DICTORY.
THOUGH, I GUESS SOME-ONE WHO'S STUPID MIGHT STUDY...
SHUT UP.
EVERY-ONE'S STUPID. I HATE THEM.
EVEN YOUR SISTERS?
THAT'S A LIE, ISN'T IT?
!!
IT'S NOT A LIE!
THEY MUST BE NUTS, LETTING SOME STRANGER LIKE YOU INTO OUR HOUSE!!
"OUR HOUSE"...

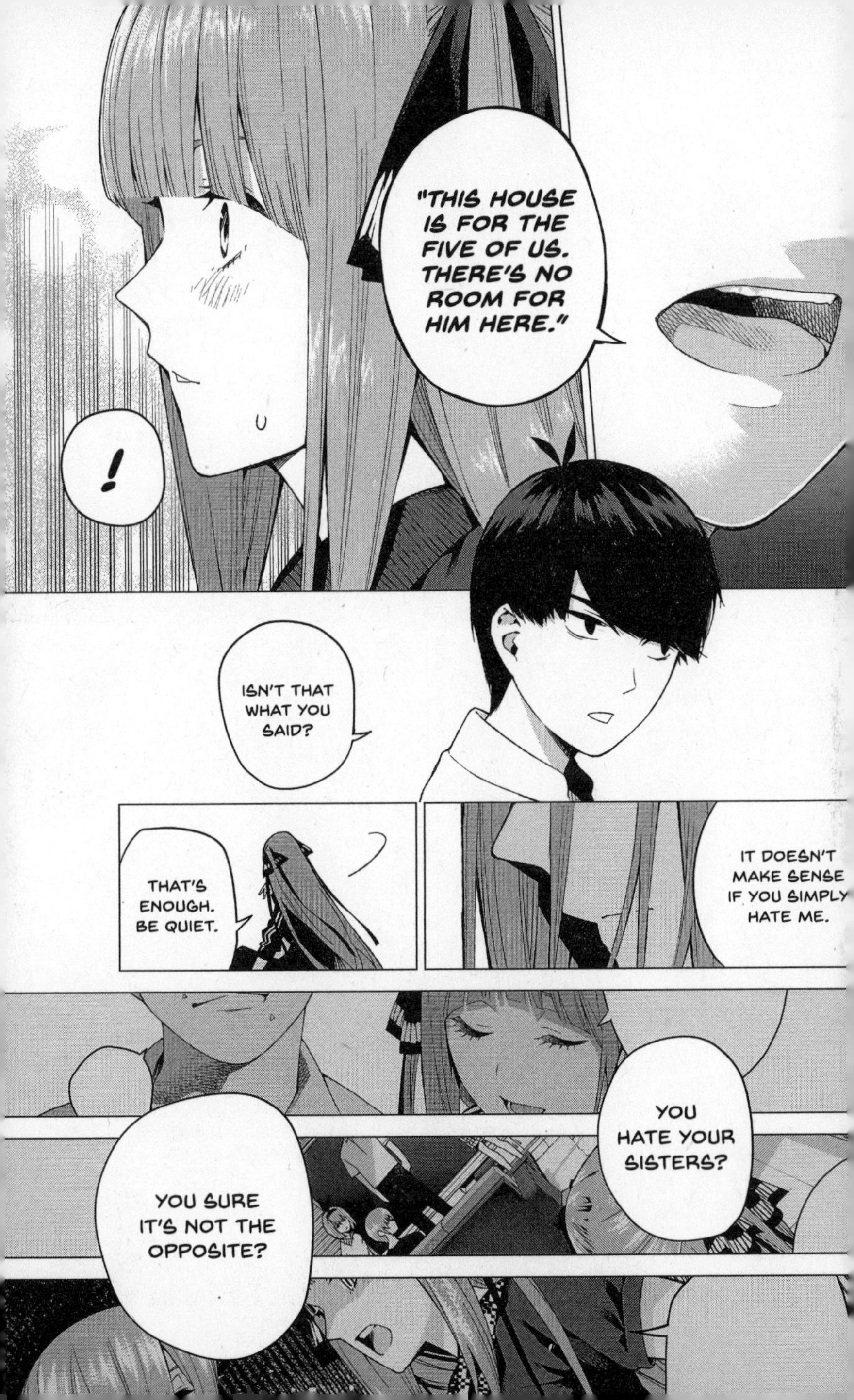
"THIS HOUSE IS FOR THE FIVE OF US. THERE'S NO ROOM FOR HIM HERE."
!
ISN'T THAT WHAT YOU SAID?
IT DOESN'T MAKE SENSE IF YOU SIMPLY HATE ME.
THAT'S ENOUGH. BE QUIET.
YOU HATE YOUR SISTERS?
YOU SURE IT'S NOT THE OPPOSITE?

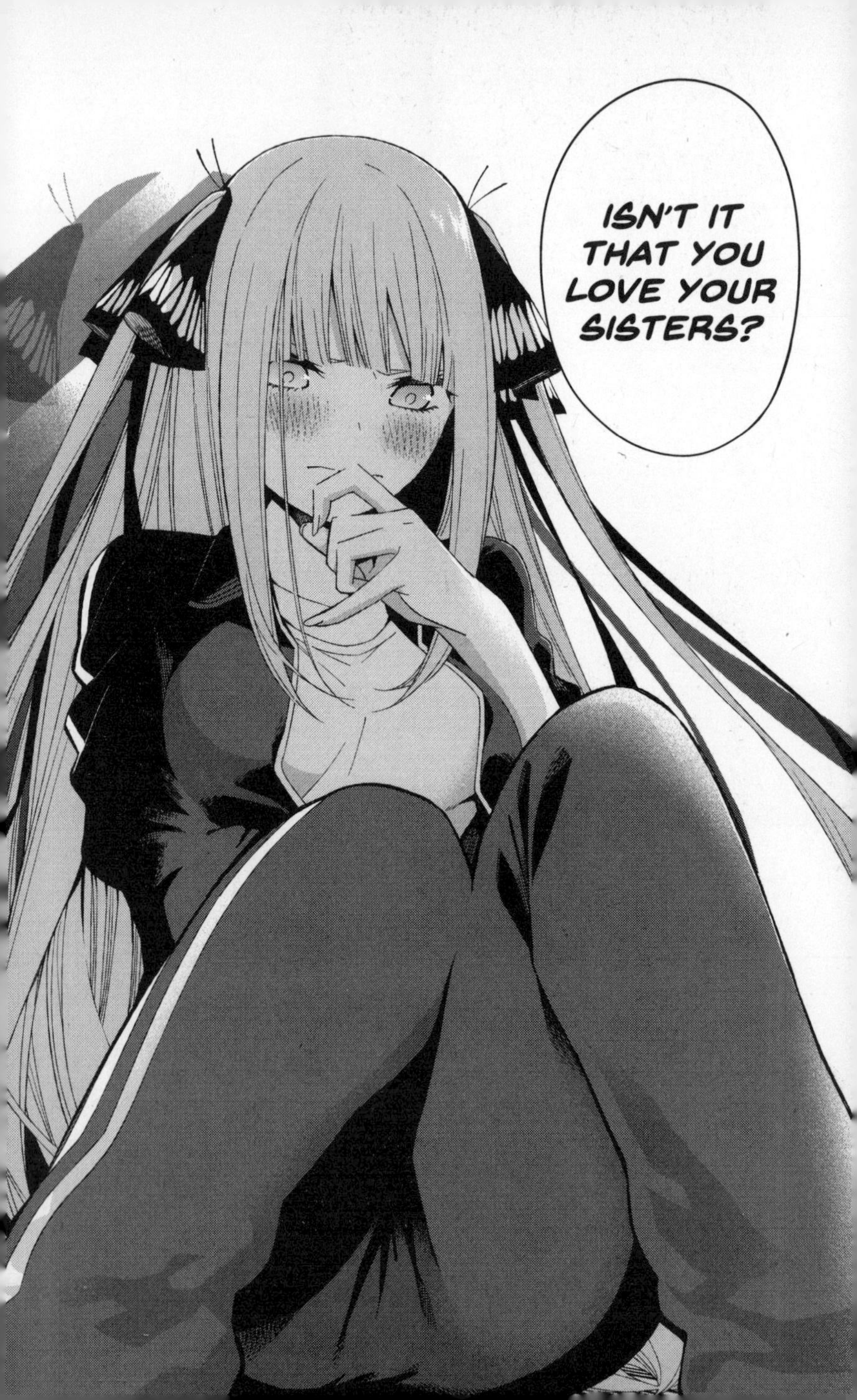
ISN'T IT THAT YOU LOVE YOUR SISTERS?

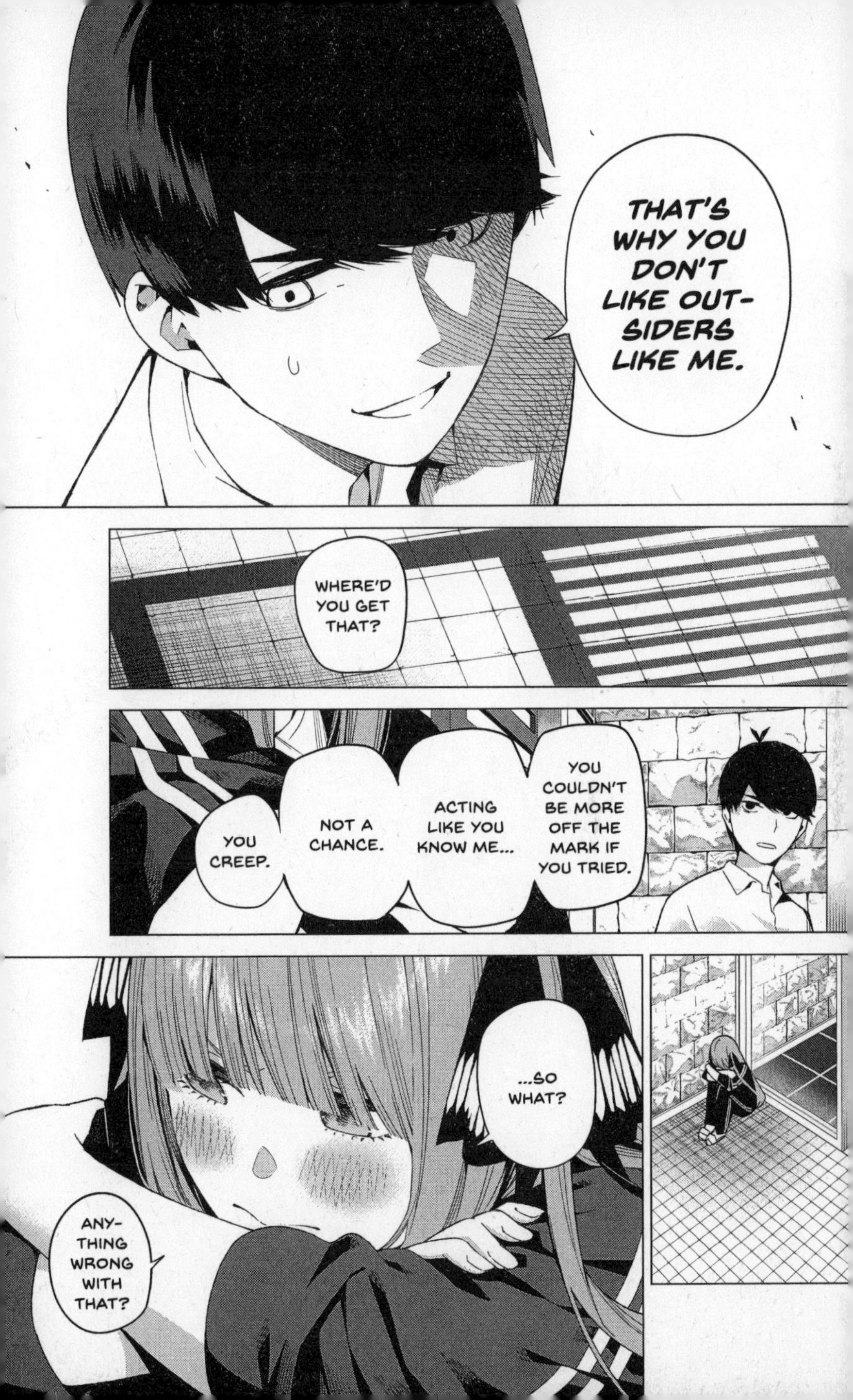
THAT'S WHY YOU DON'T LIKE OUT-SIDERS LIKE ME.
WHERE'D YOU GET THAT?
YOU COULDN'T BE MORE OFF THE MARK IF YOU TRIED.
ACTING LIKE YOU KNOW ME...
NOT A CHANCE.
YOU CREEP.
...SO WHAT?
ANY-THING WRONG WITH THAT?

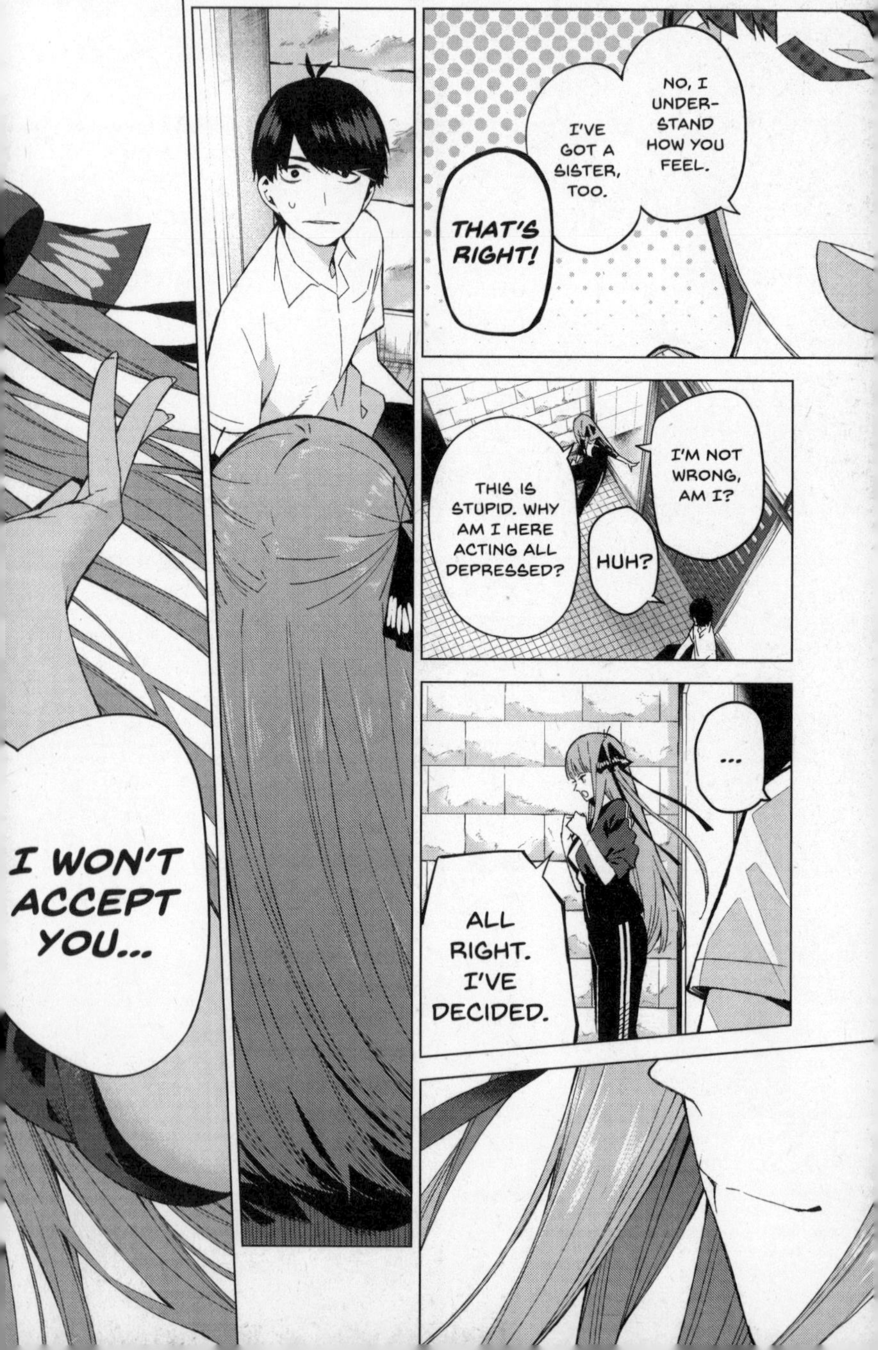

NO, I UNDER-STAND HOW YOU FEEL.
I'VE GOT A SISTER, TOO.
THAT'S RIGHT!
I'M NOT WRONG, AM I?
THIS IS STUPID. WHY AM I HERE ACTING ALL DEPRESSED?
HUH?
...
ALL RIGHT. I'VE DECIDED.
I WON'T ACCEPT YOU...

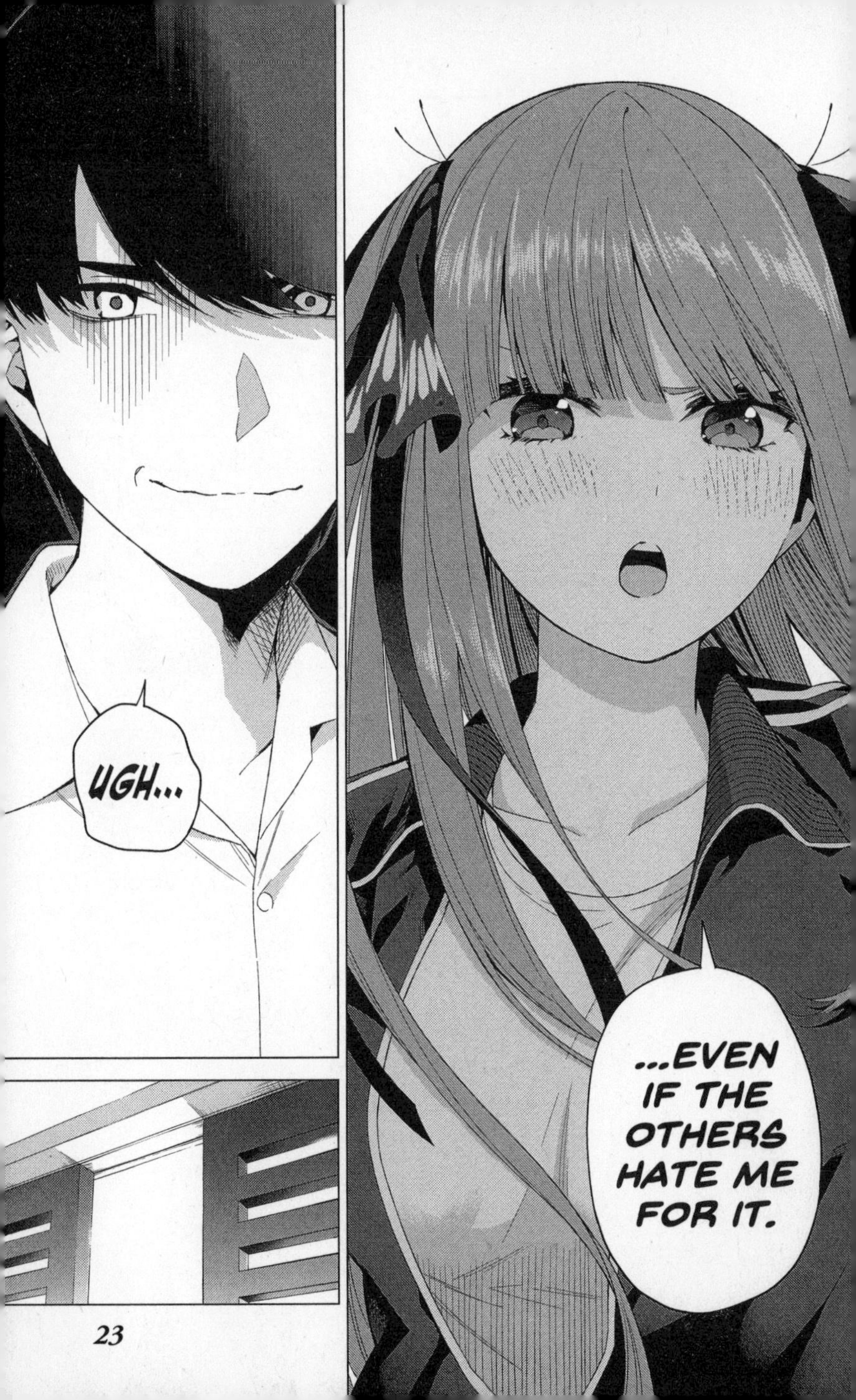
...EVEN IF THE OTHERS HATE ME FOR IT.
UGH...

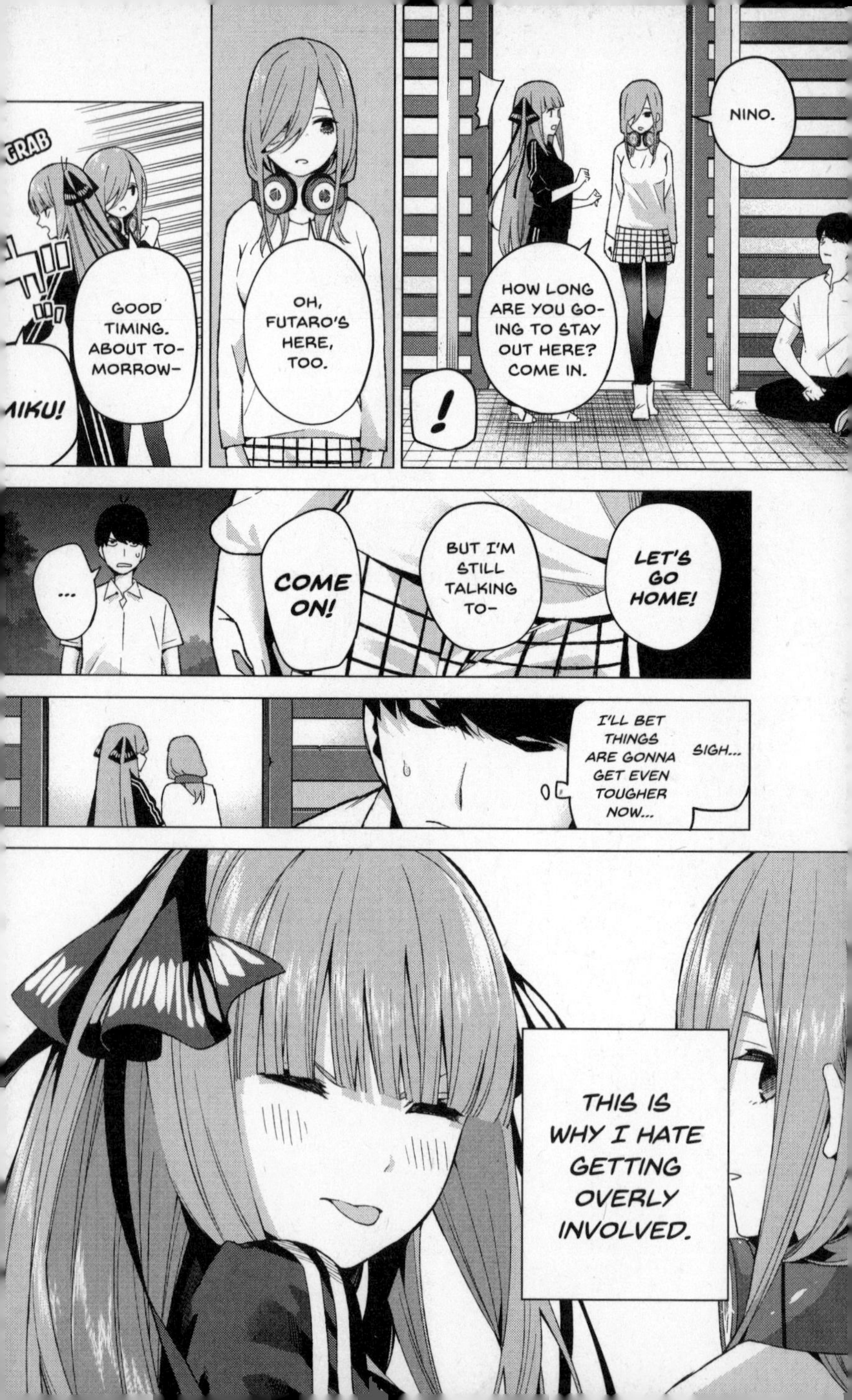
NINO.
HOW LONG ARE YOU GO-ING TO STAY OUT HERE? COME IN.
!
OH, FUTARO'S HERE, TOO.
GRAB
GOOD TIMING. ABOUT TO-MORROW-
MIKU!
LET'S GO HOME!
BUT I'M STILL TALKING TO-
COME ON!
...
SIGH...
I'LL BET THINGS ARE GONNA GET EVEN TOUGHER NOW...
THIS IS WHY I HATE GETTING OVERLY INVOLVED.

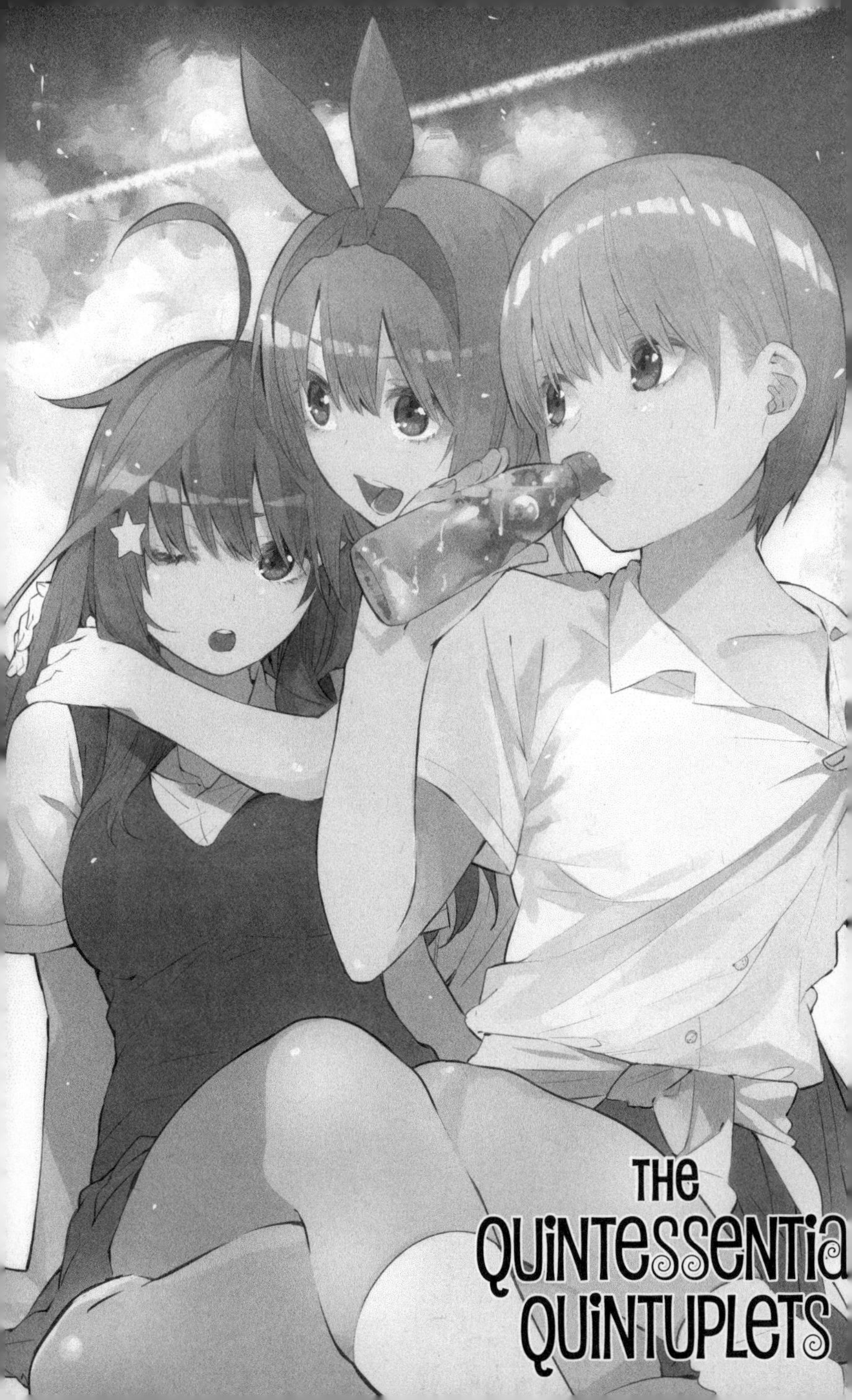
THE
QUINTESSENTIA
QUINTUPLETS

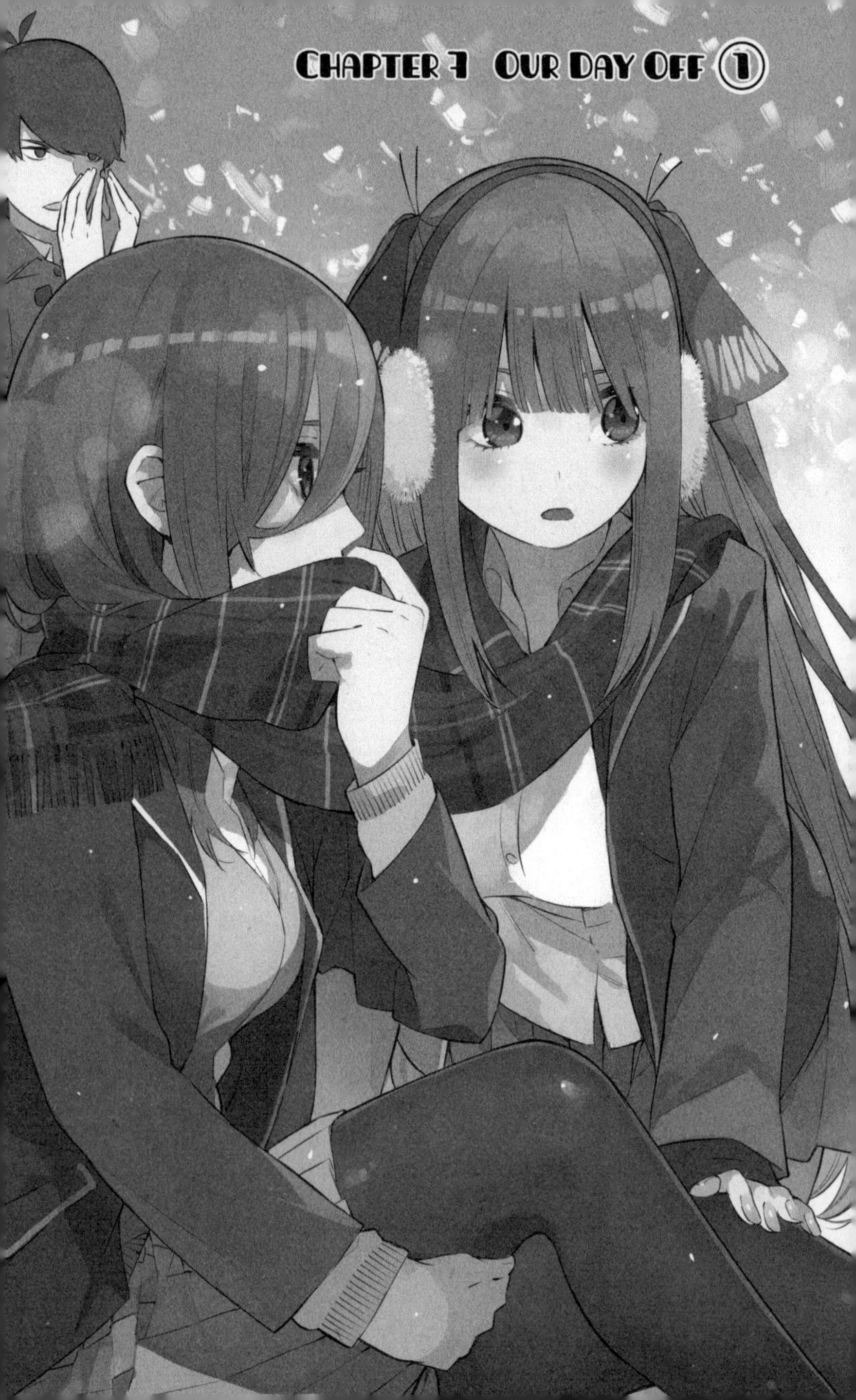
CHAPTER 7 OUR DAY OFF ①

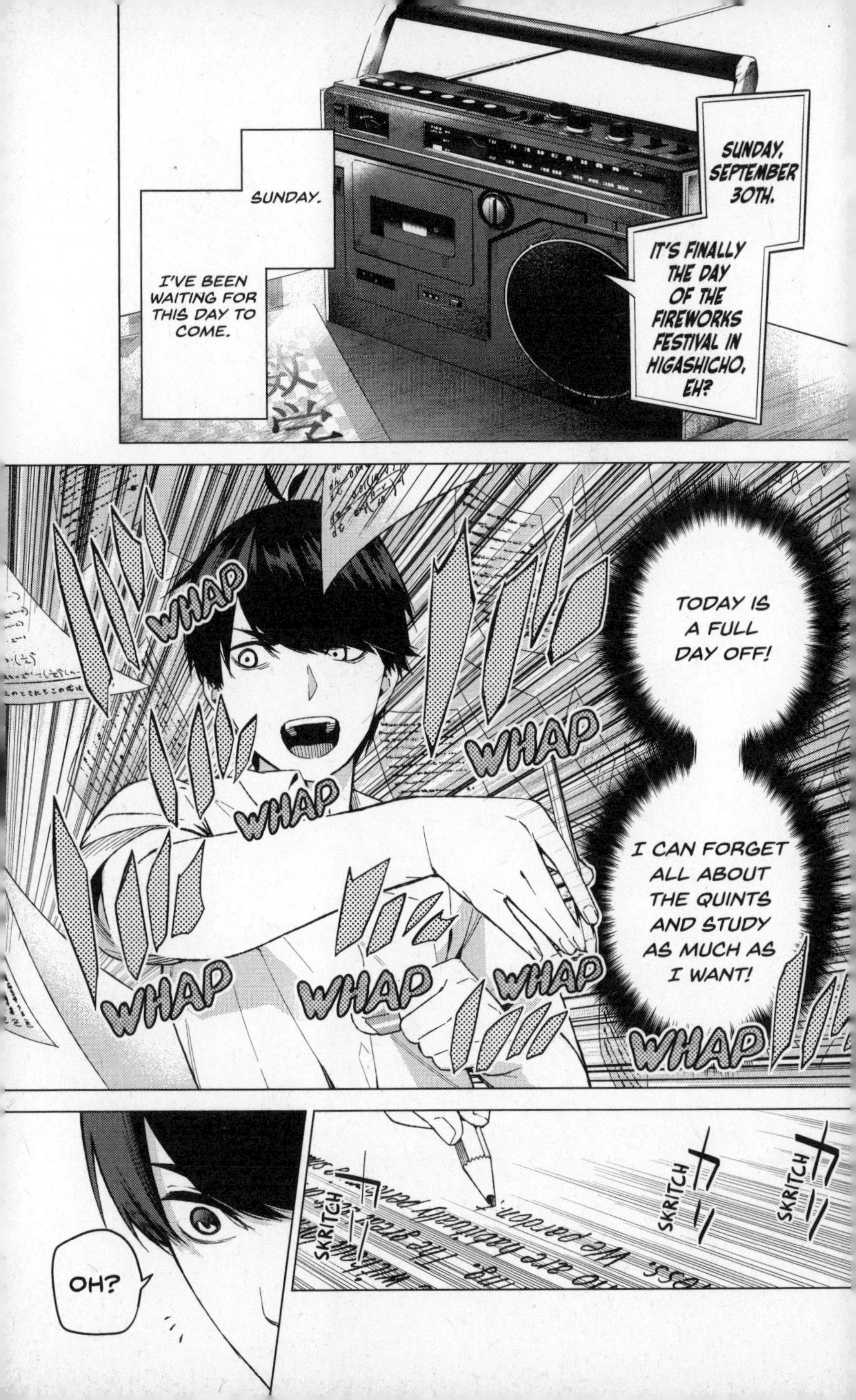
SUNDAY, SEPTEMBER 30TH.
IT'S FINALLY THE DAY OF THE FIREWORKS FESTIVAL IN HIGASHICHO, EH?
SUNDAY.
I'VE BEEN WAITING FOR THIS DAY TO COME.
TODAY IS A FULL DAY OFF!
I CAN FORGET ALL ABOUT THE QUINTS AND STUDY AS MUCH AS I WANT!
WHAP
WHAP
WHAP
WHAP
WHAP
WHAP
WHAP
SKRITCH
SKRITCH
SKRITCH
OH?

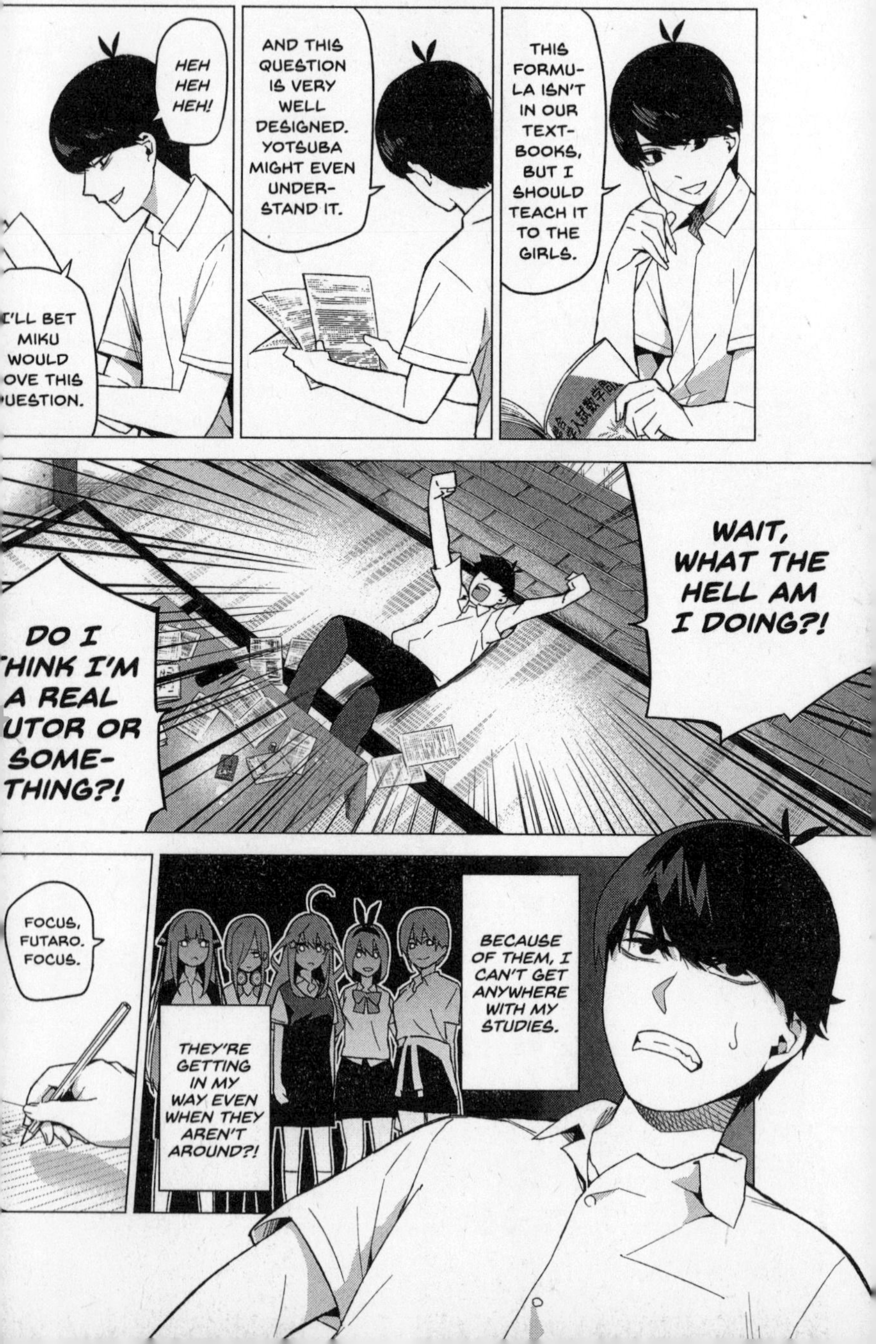

THIS FORMULA ISN'T IN OUR TEXTBOOKS, BUT I SHOULD TEACH IT TO THE GIRLS.
AND THIS QUESTION IS VERY WELL DESIGNED. YOTSUBA MIGHT EVEN UNDERSTAND IT.
HEH HEH HEH!
I'LL BET MIKU WOULD OVE THIS UESTION.
WAIT, WHAT THE HELL AM I DOING?!
DO I HINK I'M A REAL UTOR OR SOMETHING?!
BECAUSE OF THEM, I CAN'T GET ANYWHERE WITH MY STUDIES.
THEY'RE GETTING IN MY WAY EVEN WHEN THEY AREN'T AROUND?!
FOCUS, FUTARO. FOCUS.

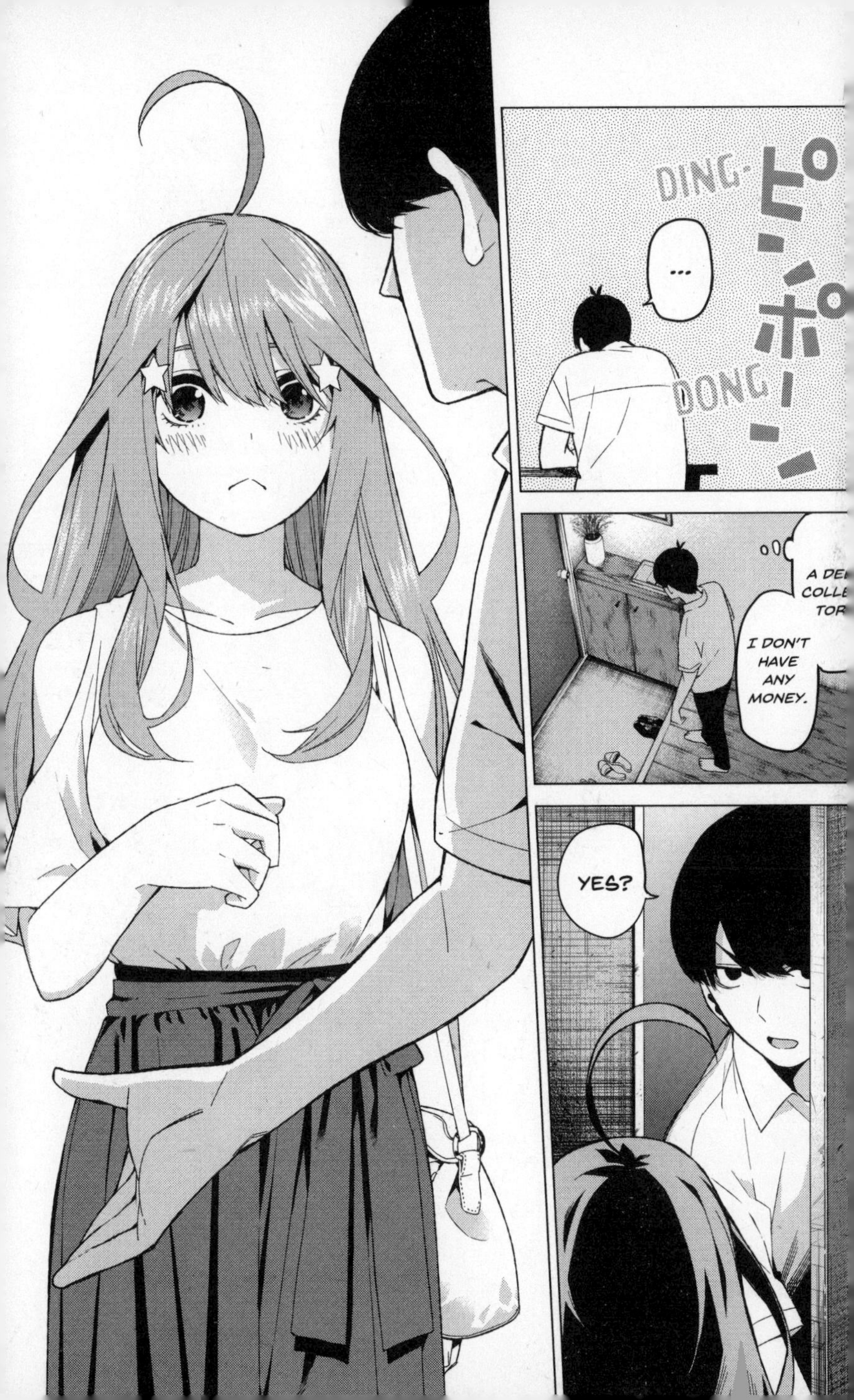
DING-
ピンポーン
...
DONG
A DE
COLLE
TOR
I DON'T HAVE ANY MONEY.
YES?

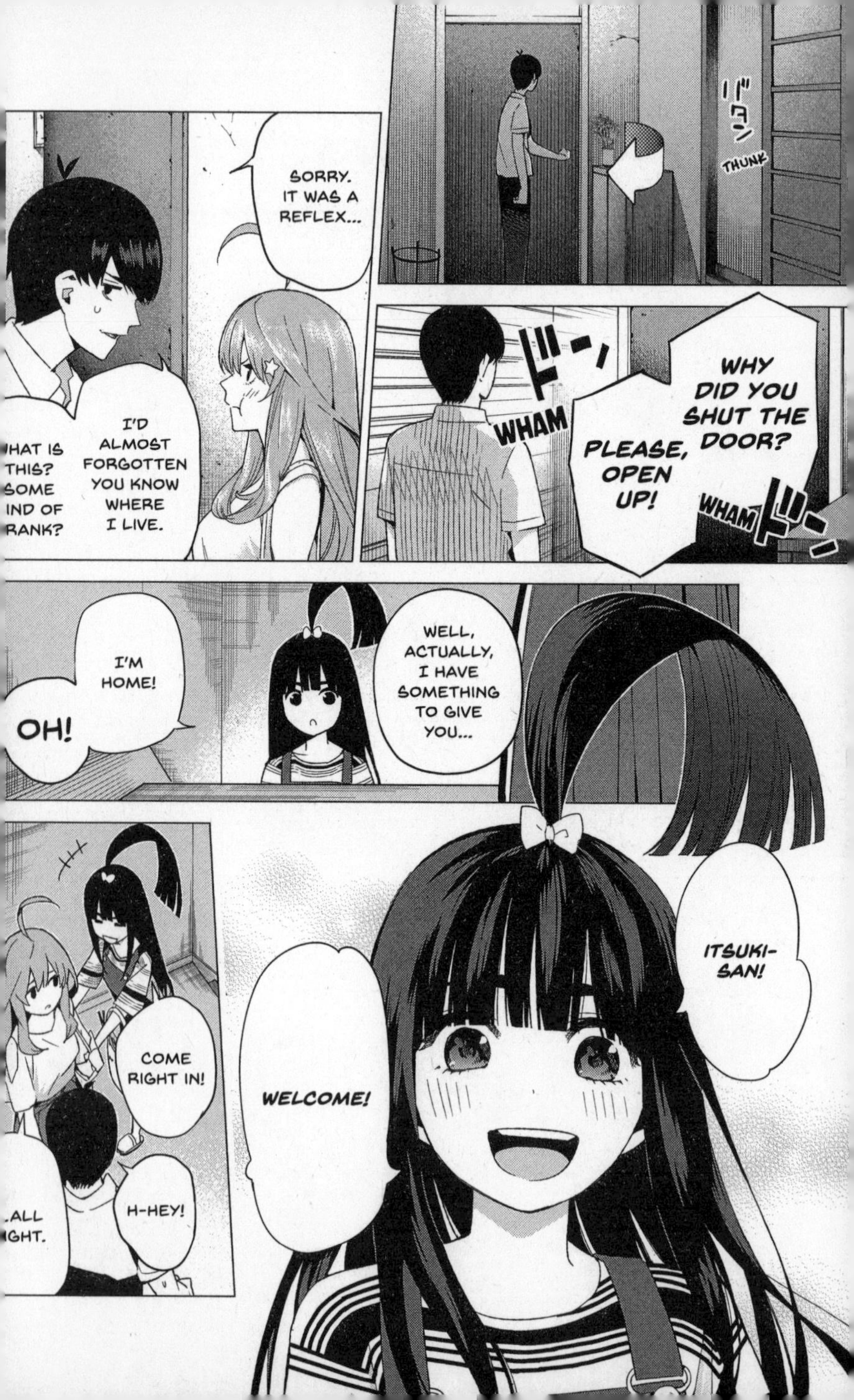
ドタン
THUNK
WHY DID YOU SHUT THE DOOR?
PLEASE, OPEN UP!
ドーン WHAM
WHAM ドーン
SORRY. IT WAS A REFLEX...
I'D ALMOST FORGOTTEN YOU KNOW WHERE I LIVE.
HAT IS THIS? SOME IND OF RANK?
ITSUKI-SAN!
WELCOME!
WELL, ACTUALLY, I HAVE SOMETHING TO GIVE YOU...
I'M HOME!
OH!
COME RIGHT IN!
H-HEY!
ALL IGHT.

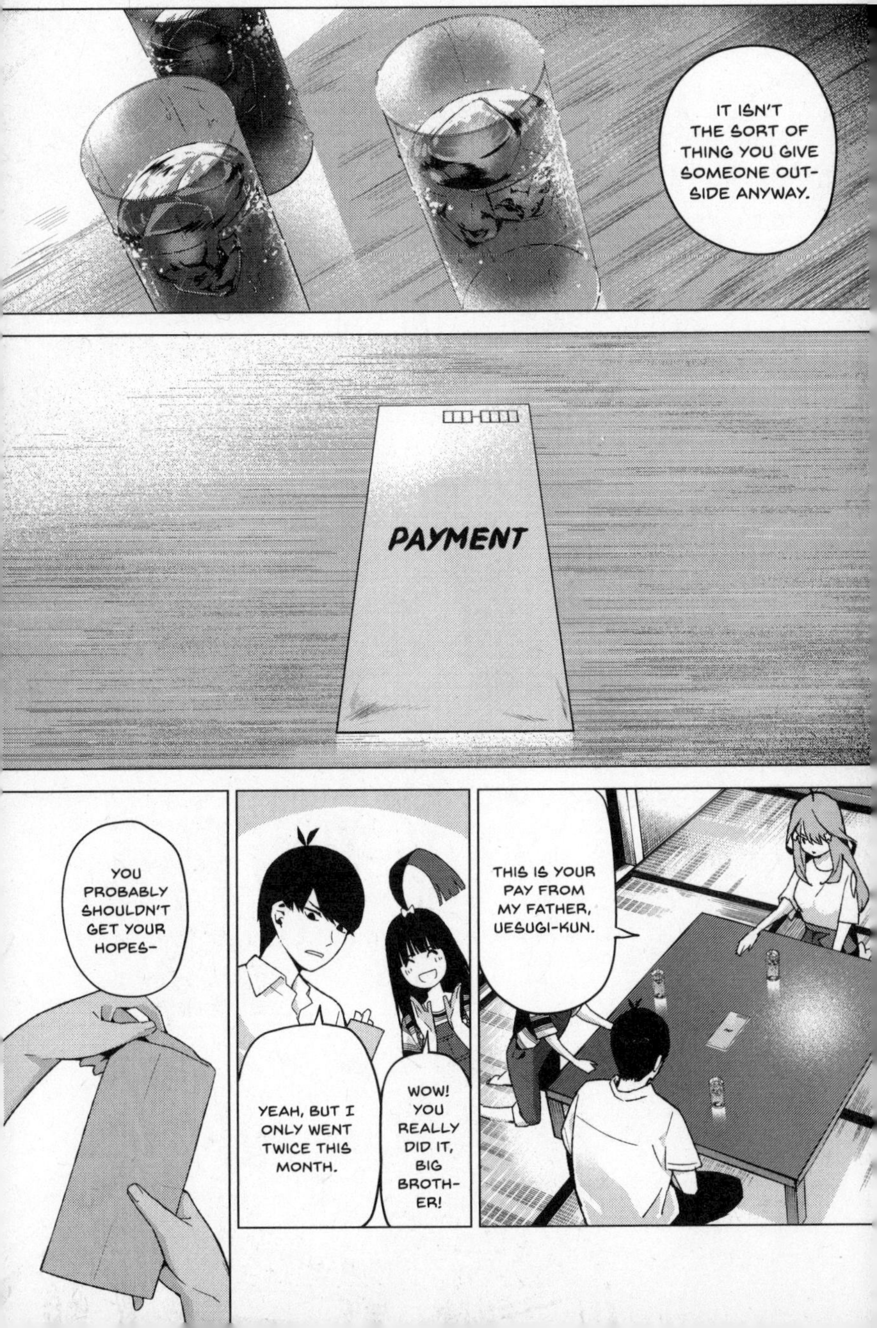
IT ISN'T THE SORT OF THING YOU GIVE SOMEONE OUT-SIDE ANYWAY.
PAYMENT
THIS IS YOUR PAY FROM MY FATHER, UESUGI-KUN.
WOW! YOU REALLY DID IT, BIG BROTH-ER!
YEAH, BUT I ONLY WENT TWICE THIS MONTH.
YOU PROBABLY SHOULDN'T GET YOUR HOPES-

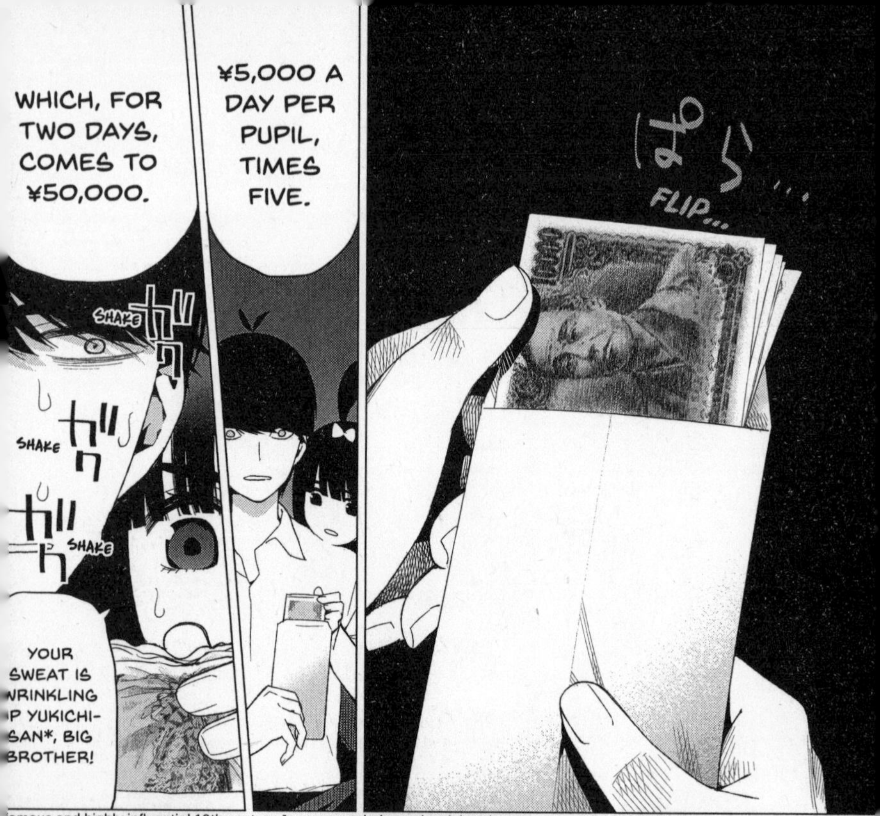
ぱら…
FLIP...
¥5,000 A DAY PER PUPIL, TIMES FIVE.
WHICH, FOR TWO DAYS, COMES TO ¥50,000.
SHAKE ガク
SHAKE ガク
SHAKE ガク
YOUR SWEAT IS WRINKLING P YUKICHI-SAN*, BIG BROTHER!

amous and highly influential 19th century Japanese scholar and activist who appears on the ¥10,000 bill.

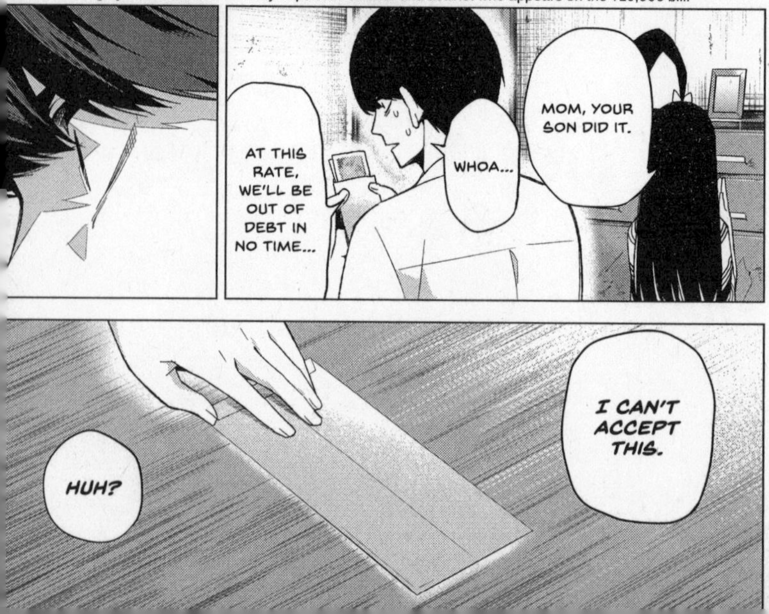
MOM, YOUR SON DID IT.
WHOA...
AT THIS RATE, WE'LL BE OUT OF DEBT IN NO TIME...
I CAN'T ACCEPT THIS.
HUH?

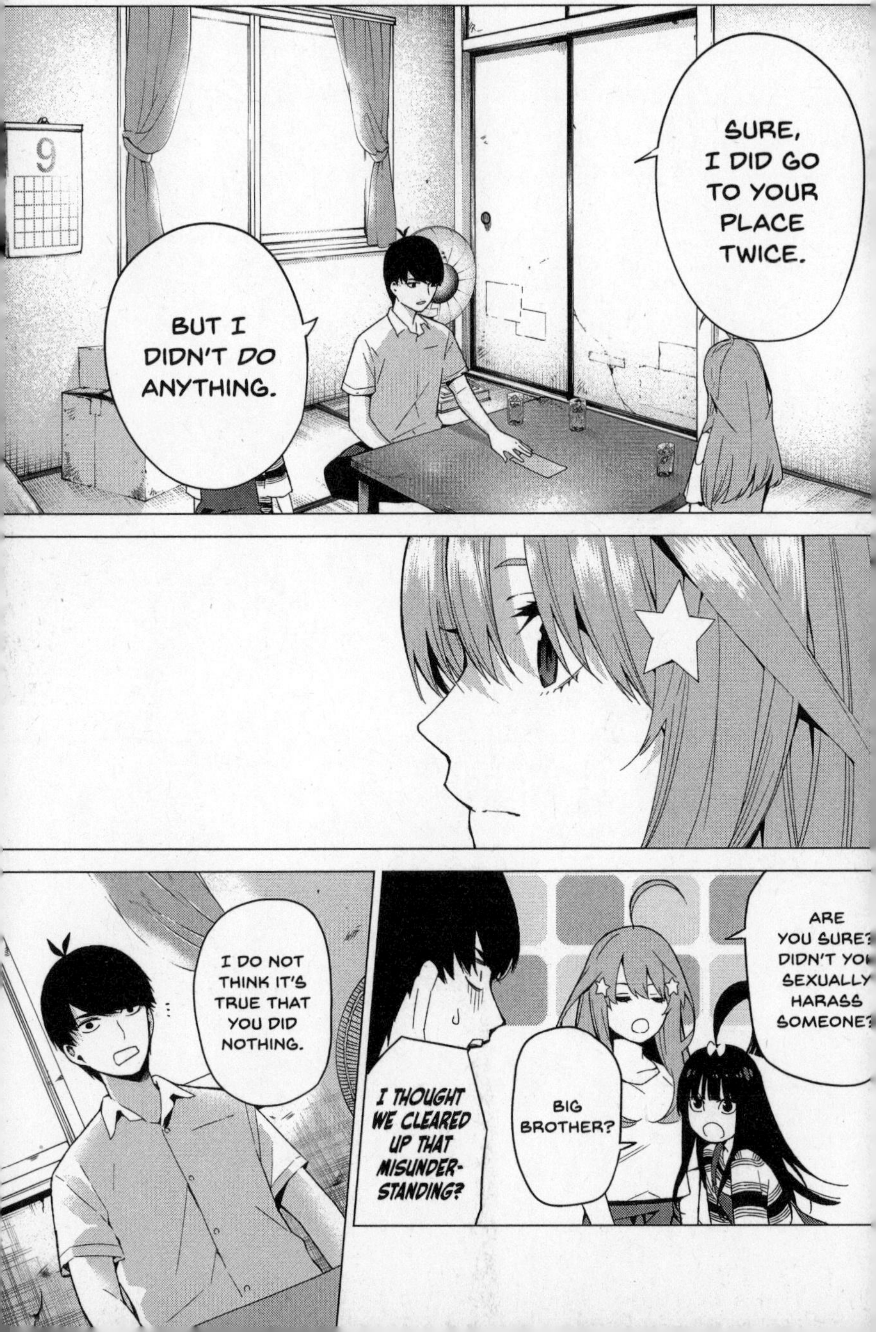
SURE, I DID GO TO YOUR PLACE TWICE.
BUT I DIDN'T DO ANYTHING.
ARE YOU SURE? DIDN'T YOU SEXUALLY HARASS SOMEONE?
BIG BROTHER?
I THOUGHT WE CLEARED UP THAT MISUNDER-STANDING?
I DO NOT THINK IT'S TRUE THAT YOU DID NOTHING.

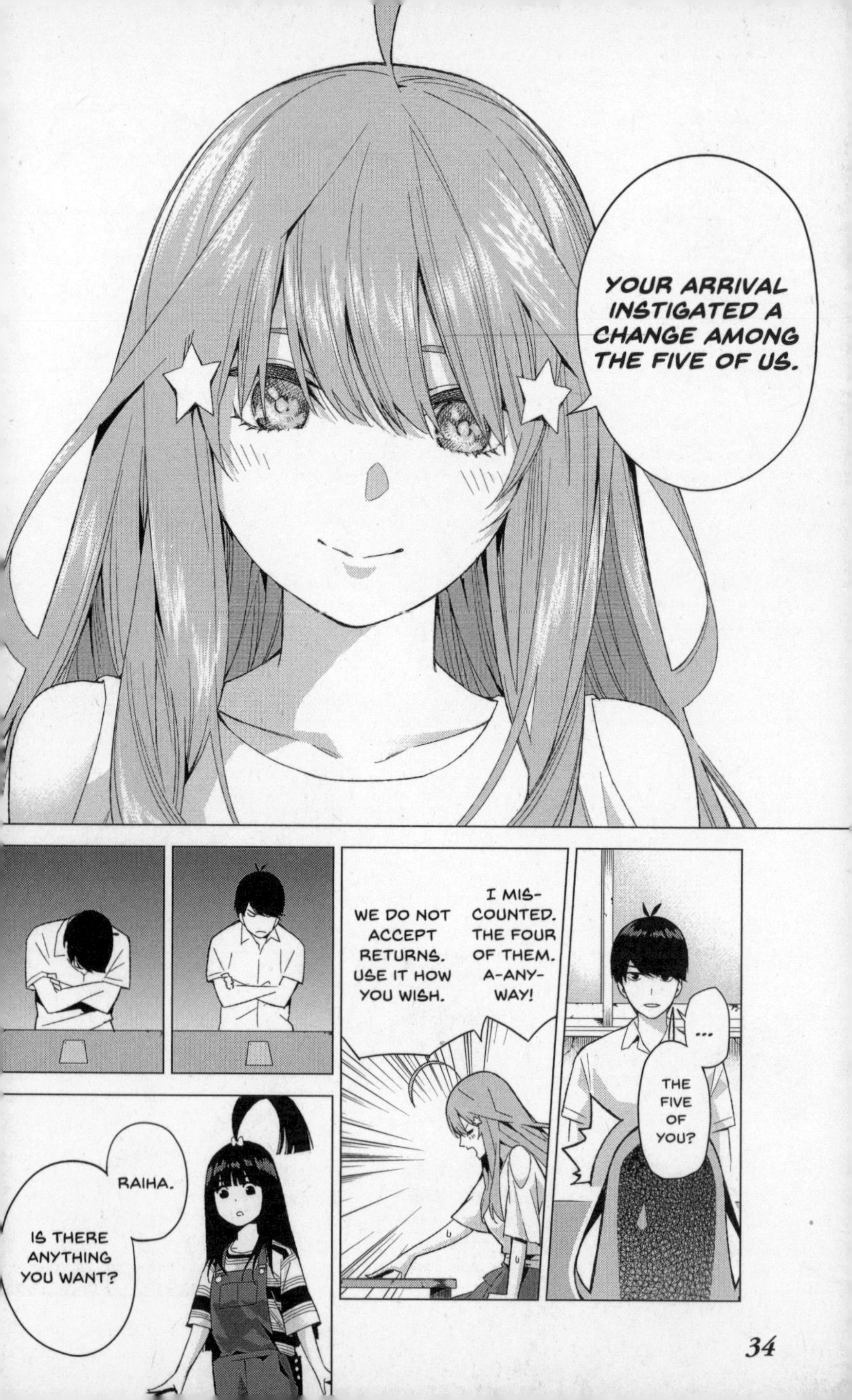
YOUR ARRIVAL INSTIGATED A CHANGE AMONG THE FIVE OF US.
...
THE FIVE OF YOU?
I MIS-COUNTED. THE FOUR OF THEM. A-ANY-WAY!
WE DO NOT ACCEPT RETURNS. USE IT HOW YOU WISH.
RAIHA.
IS THERE ANYTHING YOU WANT?

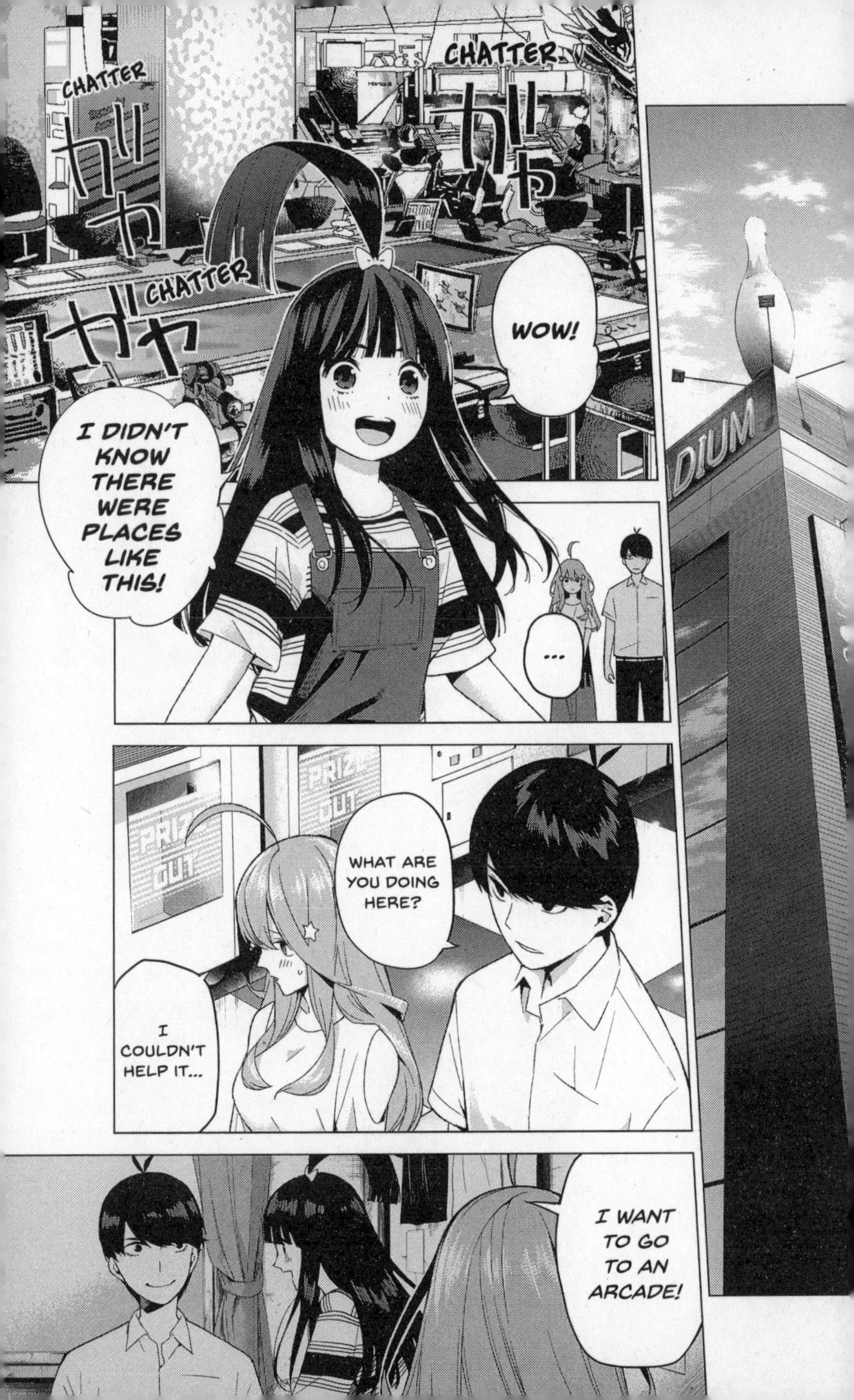

DIUM
CHATTER
ガヤ
CHATTER
ガヤ
CHATTER
ガヤ
WOW!
I DIDN'T KNOW THERE WERE PLACES LIKE THIS!
...
WHAT ARE YOU DOING HERE?
I COULDN'T HELP IT...
I WANT TO GO TO AN ARCADE!

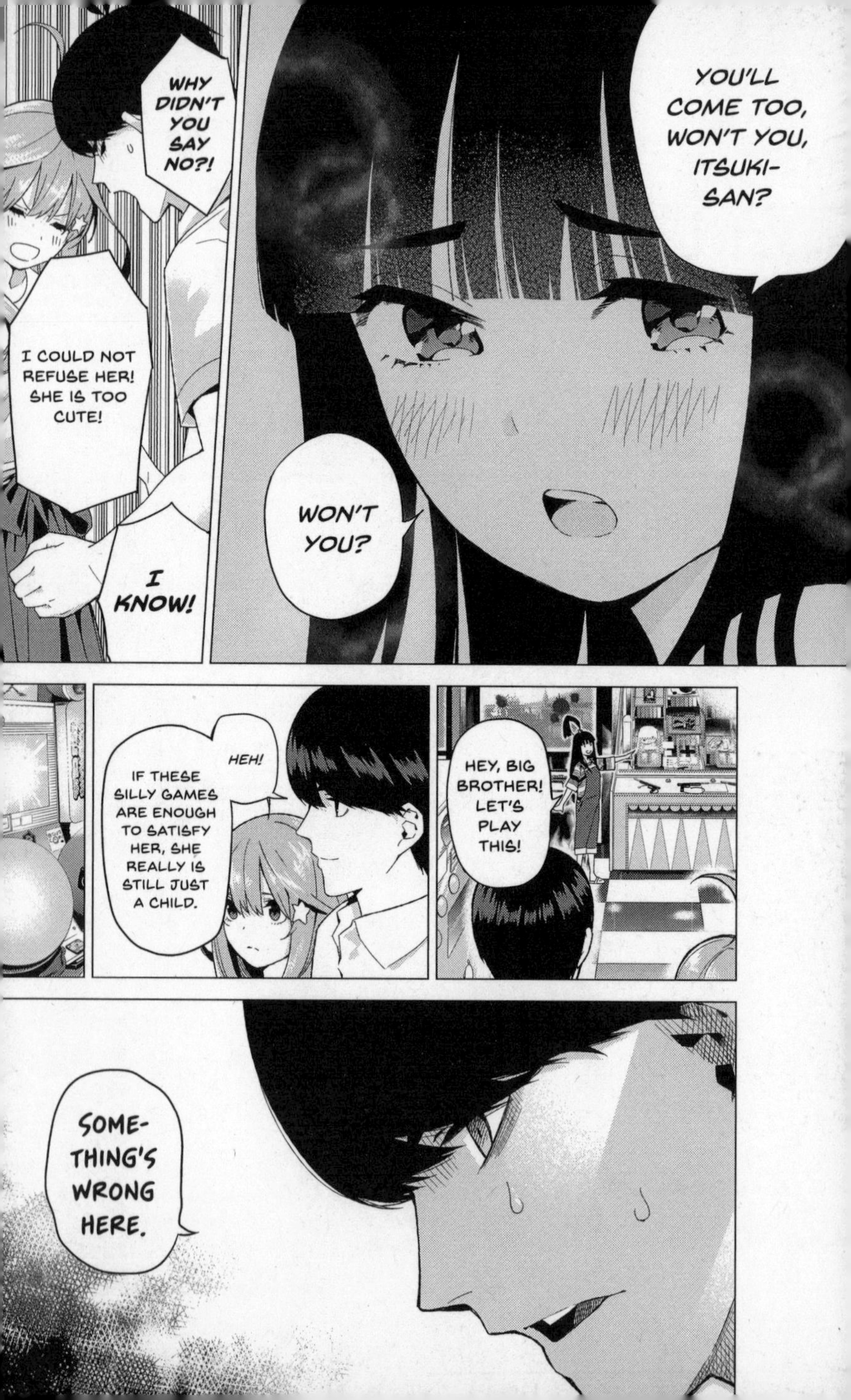
YOU'LL COME TOO, WON'T YOU, ITSUKI-SAN?
WON'T YOU?
WHY DIDN'T YOU SAY NO?!
I COULD NOT REFUSE HER! SHE IS TOO CUTE!
I KNOW!
HEY, BIG BROTHER! LET'S PLAY THIS!
HEH!
IF THESE SILLY GAMES ARE ENOUGH TO SATISFY HER, SHE REALLY IS STILL JUST A CHILD.
SOME-THING'S WRONG HERE.

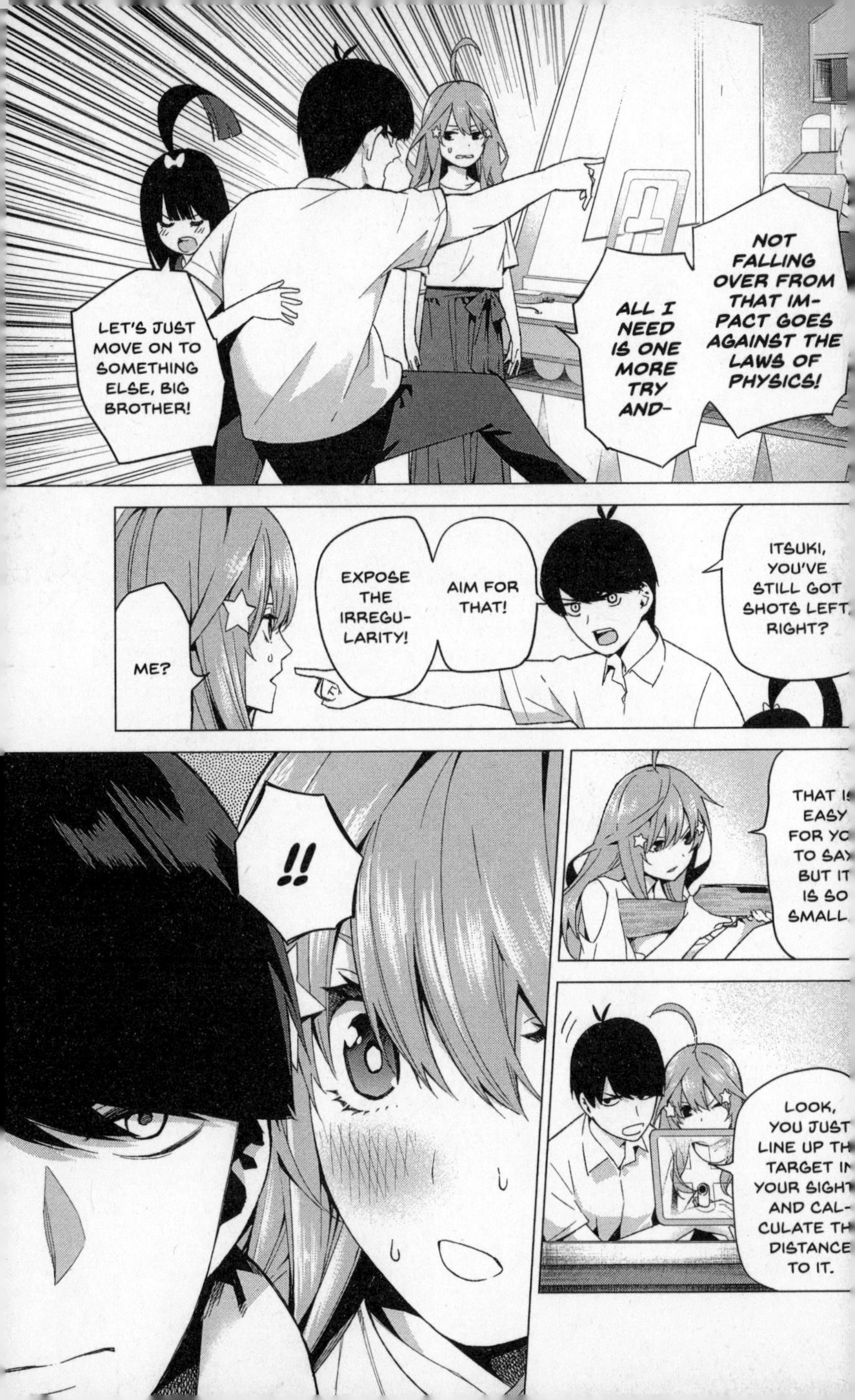
NOT FALLING OVER FROM THAT IMPACT GOES AGAINST THE LAWS OF PHYSICS!
ALL I NEED IS ONE MORE TRY AND-
LET'S JUST MOVE ON TO SOMETHING ELSE, BIG BROTHER!
ITSUKI, YOU'VE STILL GOT SHOTS LEFT, RIGHT?
AIM FOR THAT!
EXPOSE THE IRREGULARITY!
ME?
THAT I EASY FOR YO TO SAY BUT IT IS SO SMALL.
LOOK, YOU JUST LINE UP TH TARGET IN YOUR SIGHT AND CALCULATE TH DISTANCE TO IT.
!!

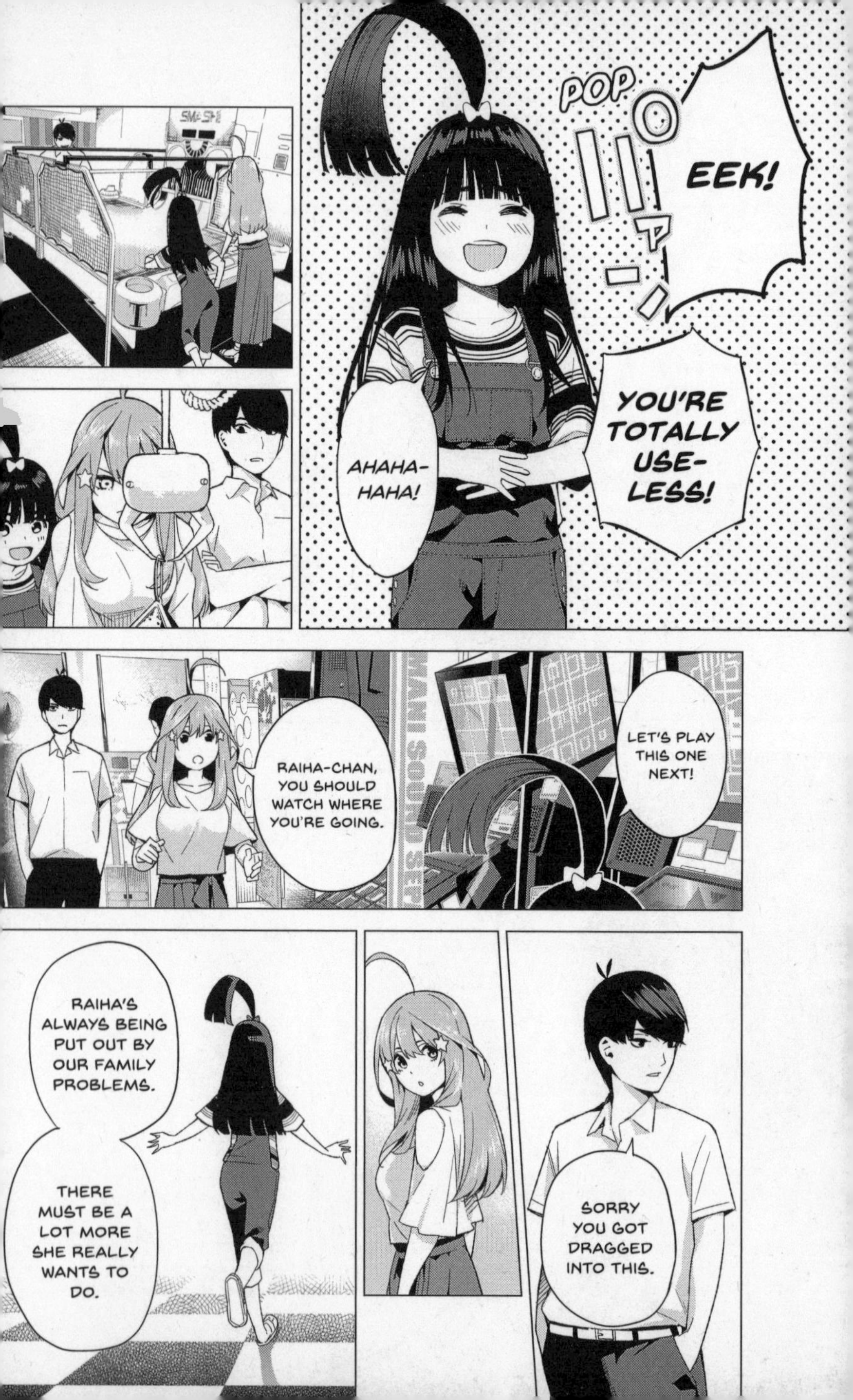
EEK!
POP
YOU'RE TOTALLY USE-LESS!
AHAHA-HAHA!
LET'S PLAY THIS ONE NEXT!
RAIHA-CHAN, YOU SHOULD WATCH WHERE YOU'RE GOING.
SORRY YOU GOT DRAGGED INTO THIS.
RAIHA'S ALWAYS BEING PUT OUT BY OUR FAMILY PROBLEMS.
THERE MUST BE A LOT MORE SHE REALLY WANTS TO DO.

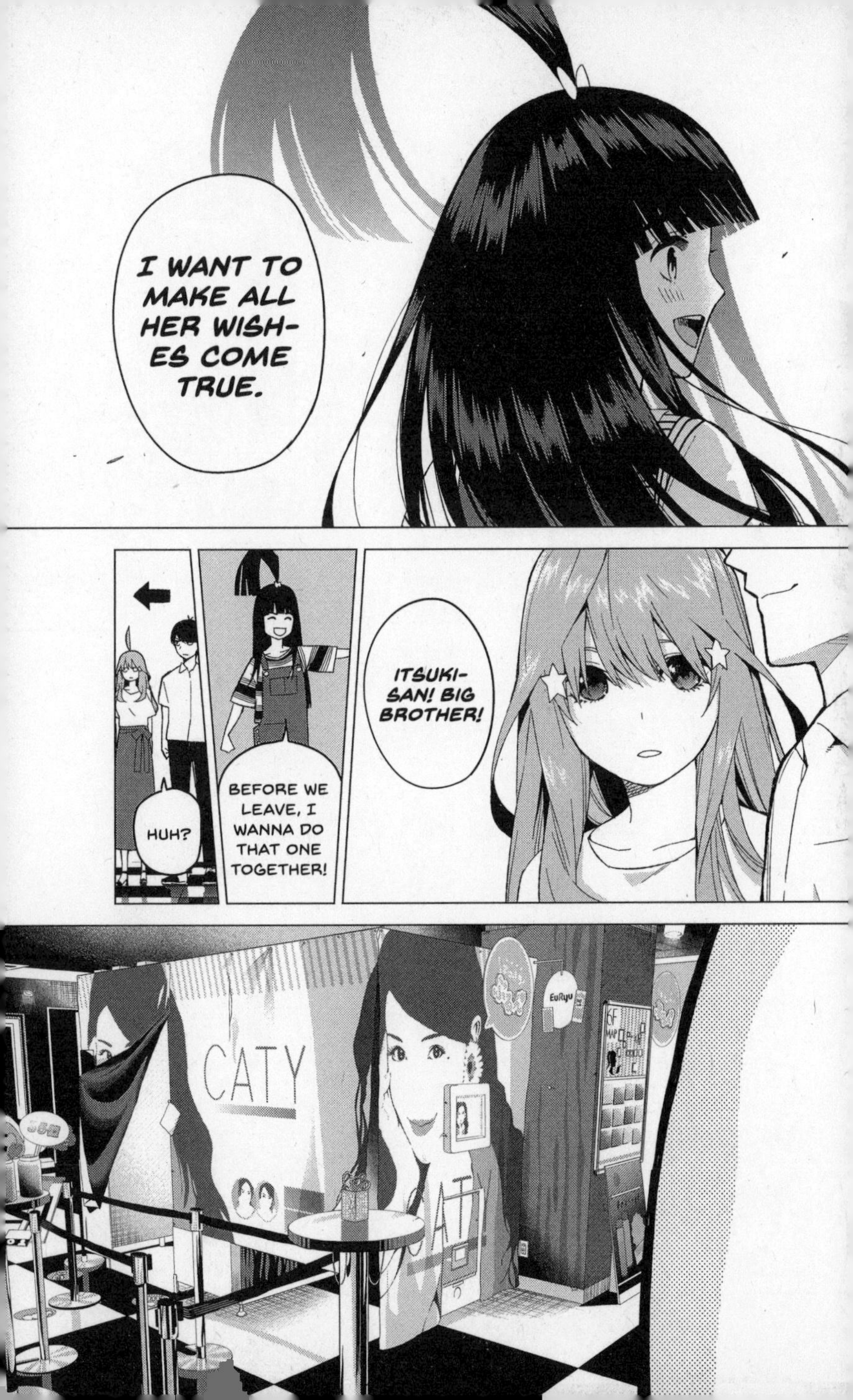
I WANT TO MAKE ALL HER WISH-ES COME TRUE.
ITSUKI-SAN! BIG BROTHER!
BEFORE WE LEAVE, I WANNA DO THAT ONE TOGETHER!
HUH?
CATY
EuRyu
6F MAP

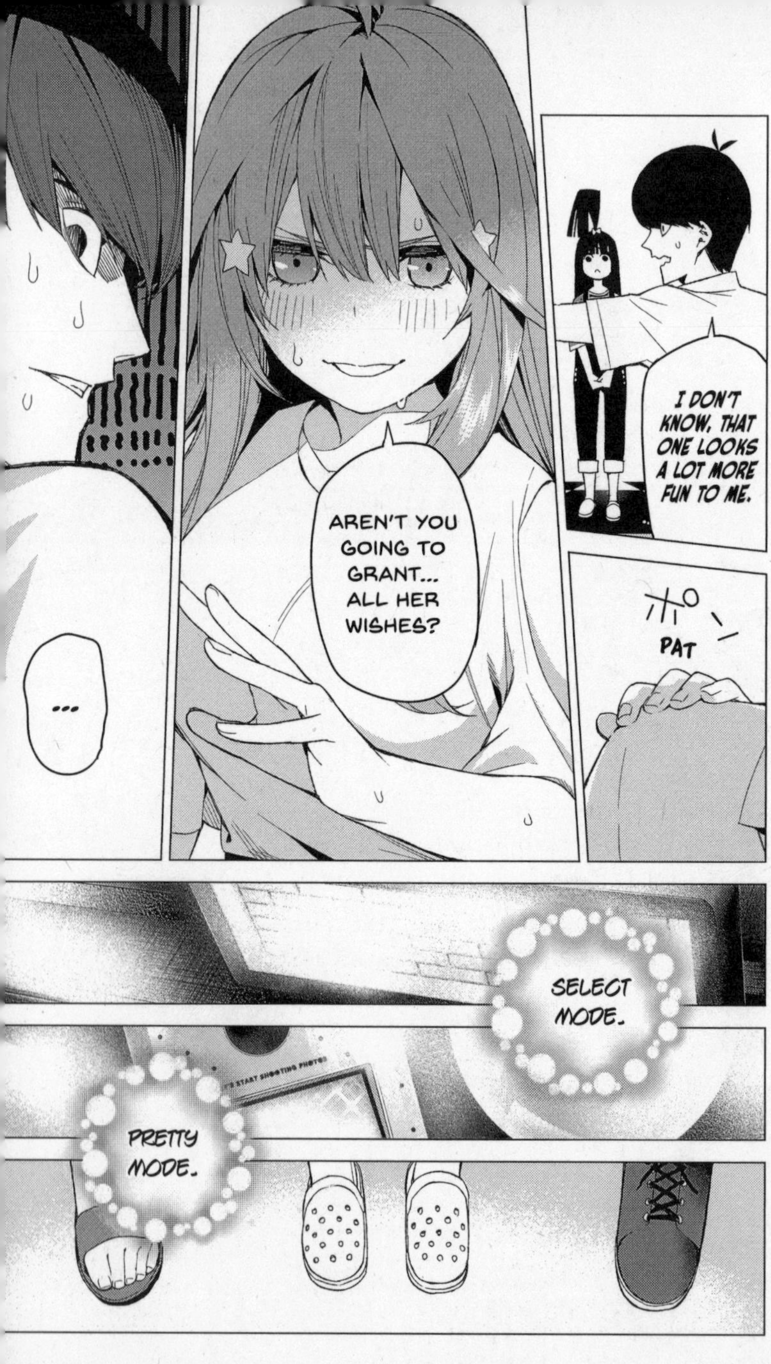
I DON'T KNOW. THAT ONE LOOKS A LOT MORE FUN TO ME.
PAT
AREN'T YOU GOING TO GRANT... ALL HER WISHES?
...
SELECT MODE.
PRETTY MODE.

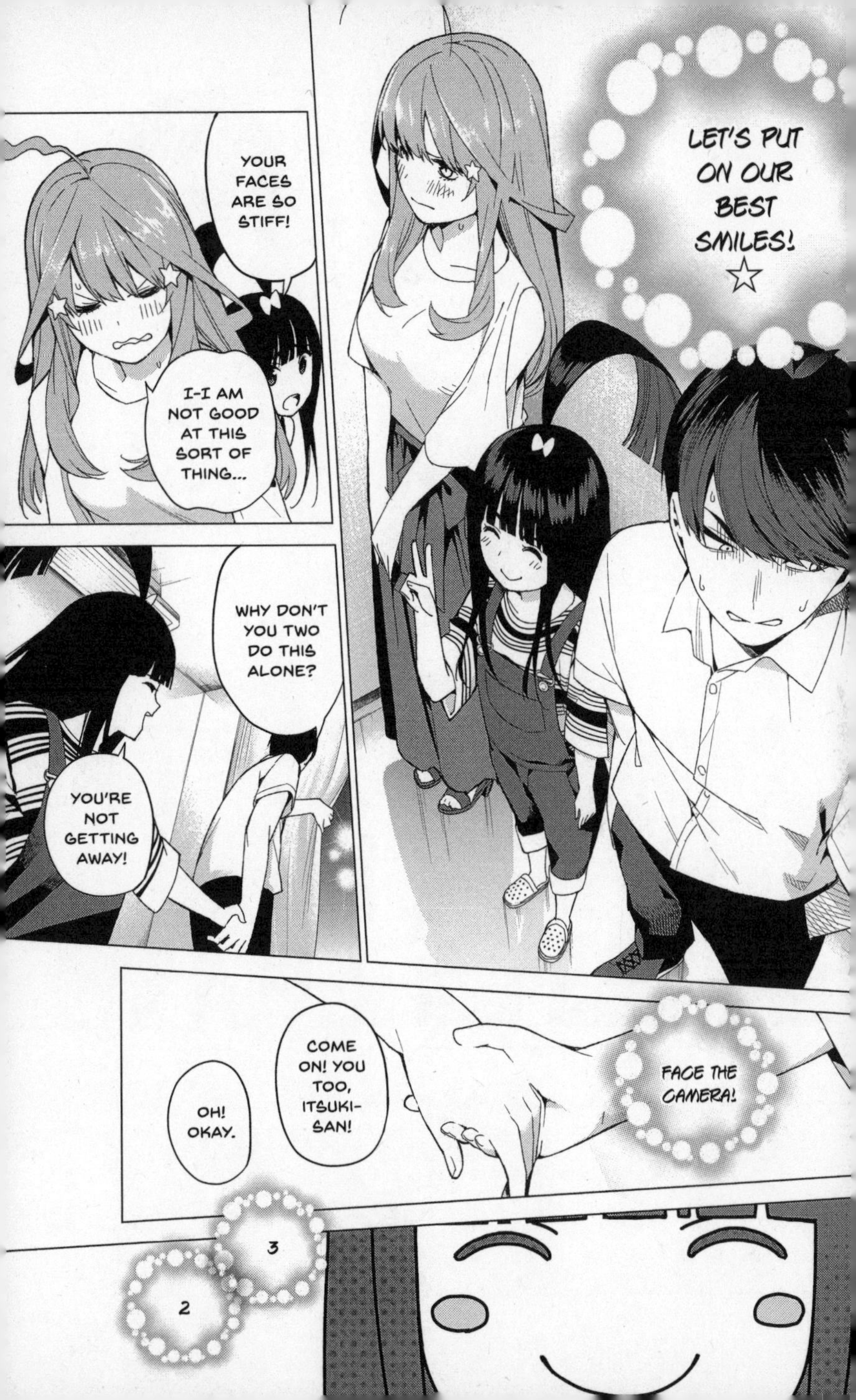
LET'S PUT ON OUR BEST SMILES! ☆
YOUR FACES ARE SO STIFF!
I-I AM NOT GOOD AT THIS SORT OF THING...
WHY DON'T YOU TWO DO THIS ALONE?
YOU'RE NOT GETTING AWAY!
FACE THE CAMERA!
COME ON! YOU TOO, ITSUKI-SAN!
OH! OKAY.
3
2

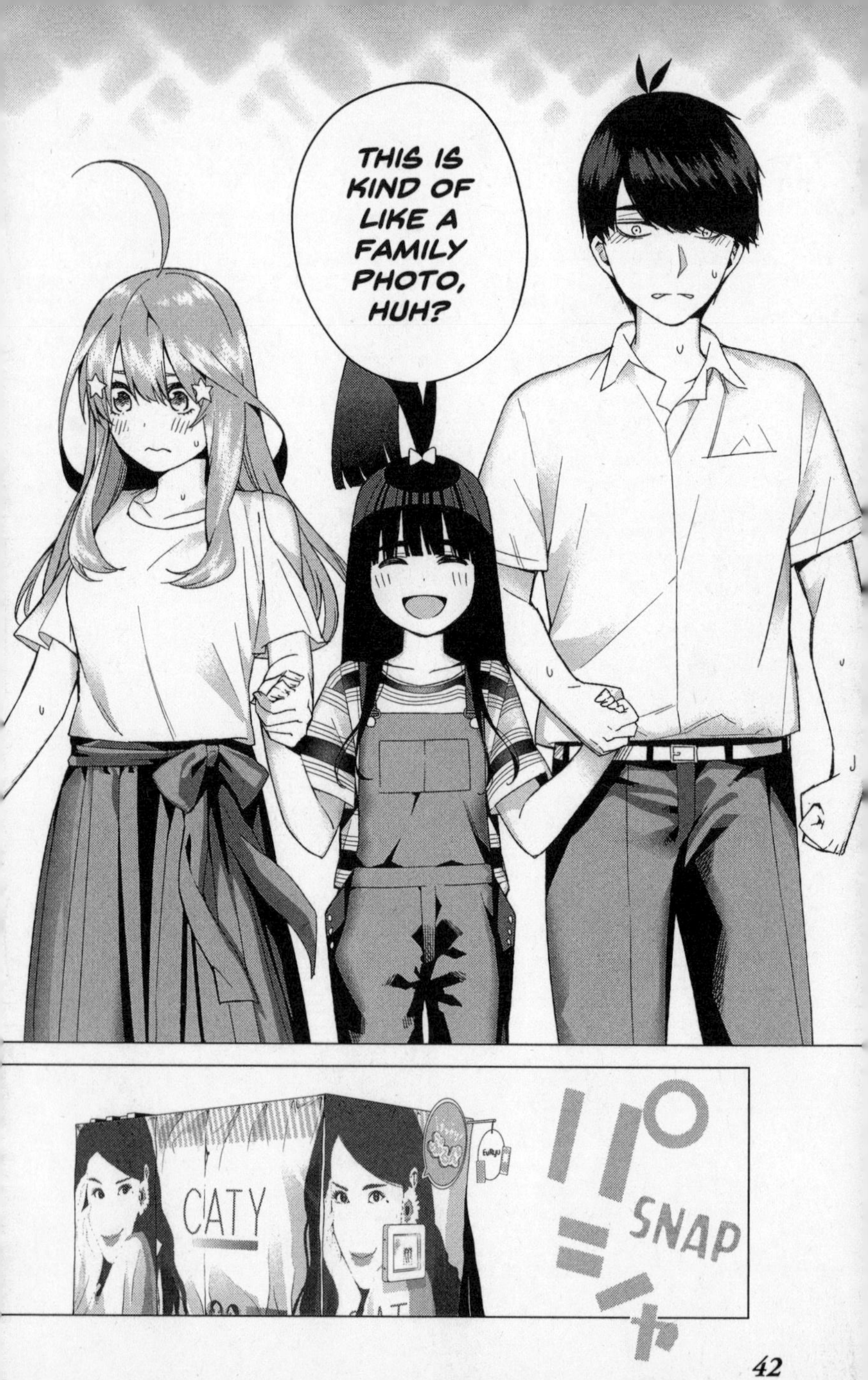
THIS IS KIND OF LIKE A FAMILY PHOTO, HUH?
CATY
パシャ
SNAP

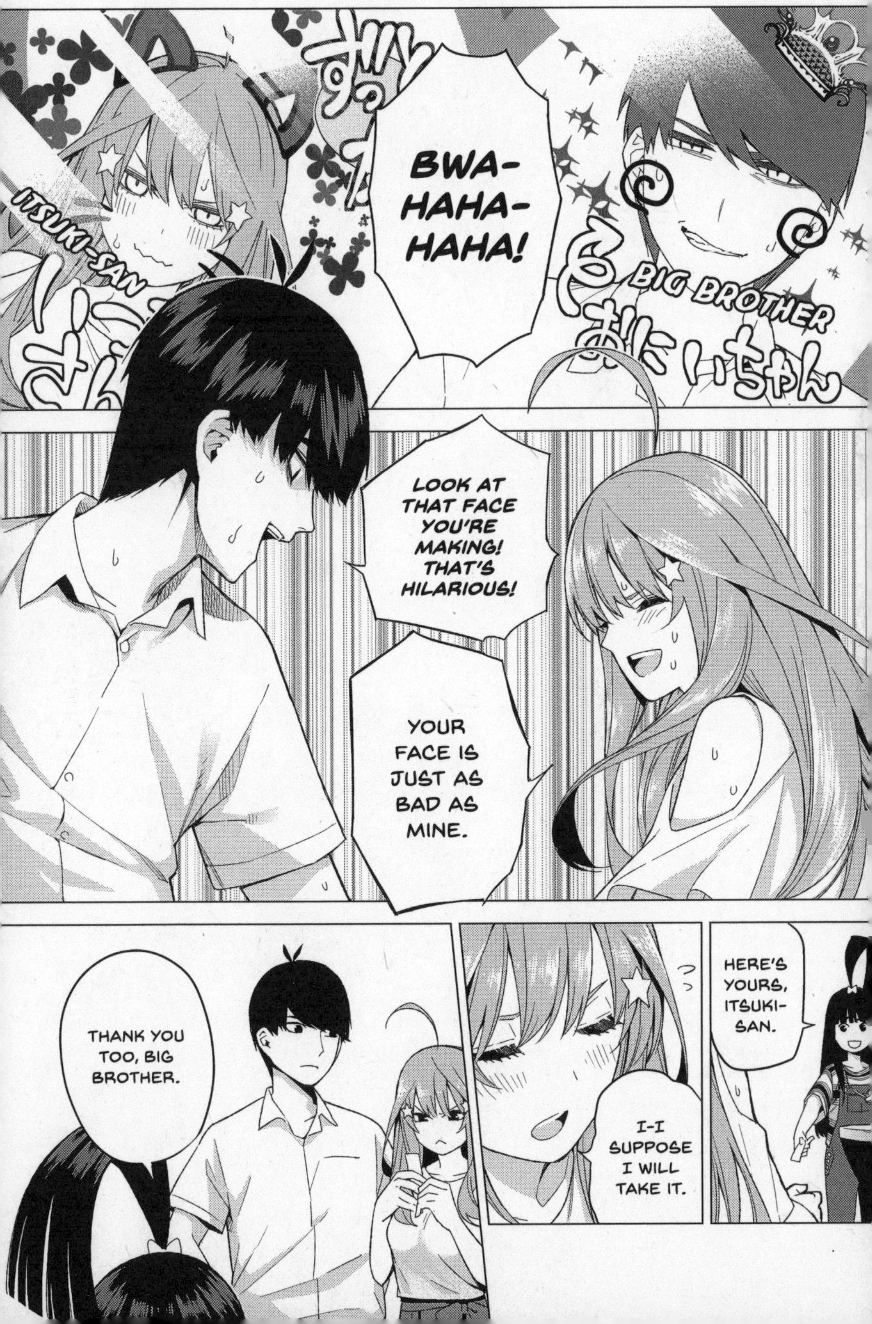
BIG BROTHER
おにいちゃん
BWA-HAHA-HAHA!
ITSUKI-SAN
LOOK AT THAT FACE YOU'RE MAKING! THAT'S HILARIOUS!
YOUR FACE IS JUST AS BAD AS MINE.
HERE'S YOURS, ITSUKI-SAN.
I-I SUPPOSE I WILL TAKE IT.
THANK YOU TOO, BIG BROTHER.

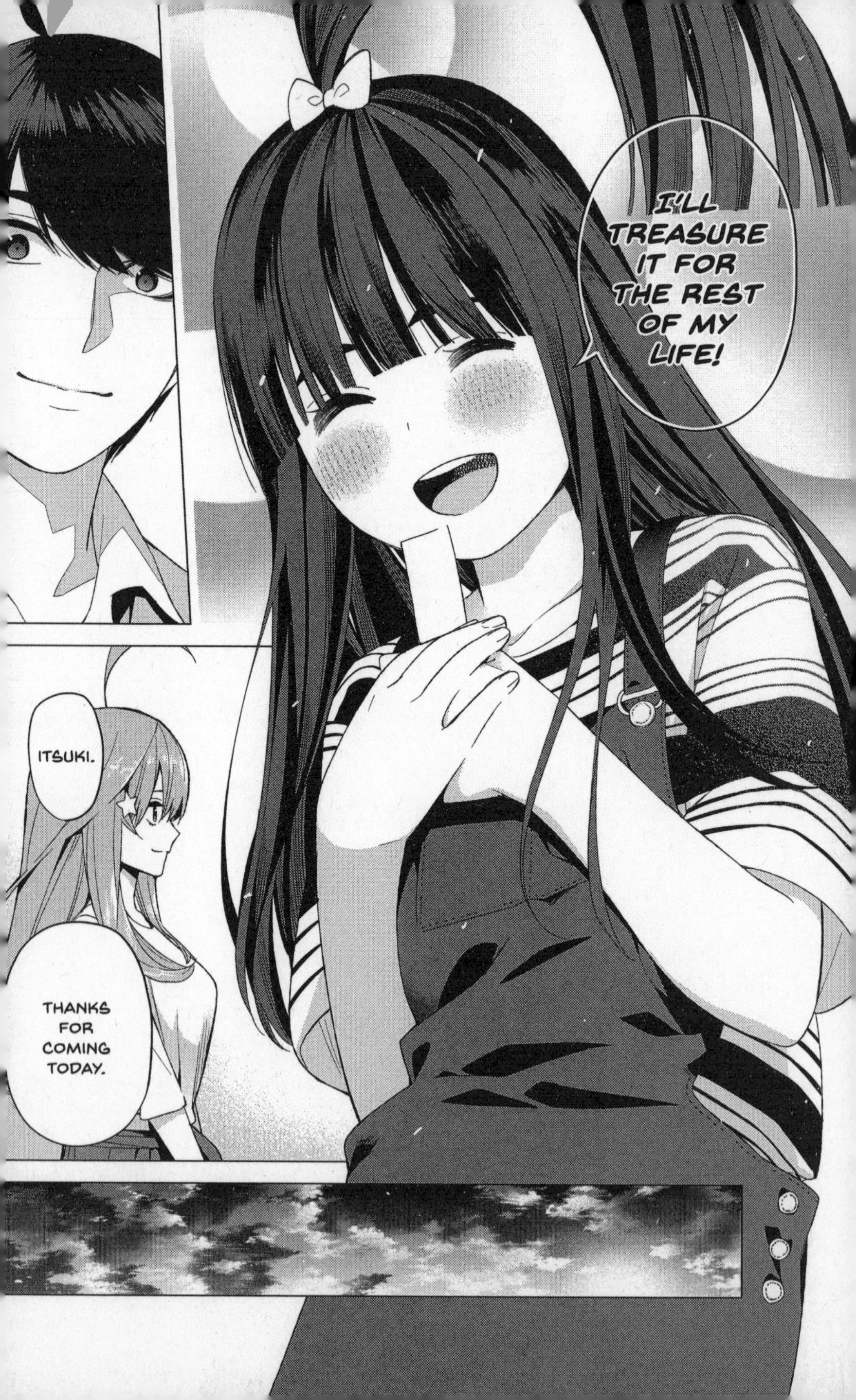
I'LL TREASURE IT FOR THE REST OF MY LIFE!
ITSUKI.
THANKS FOR COMING TODAY.

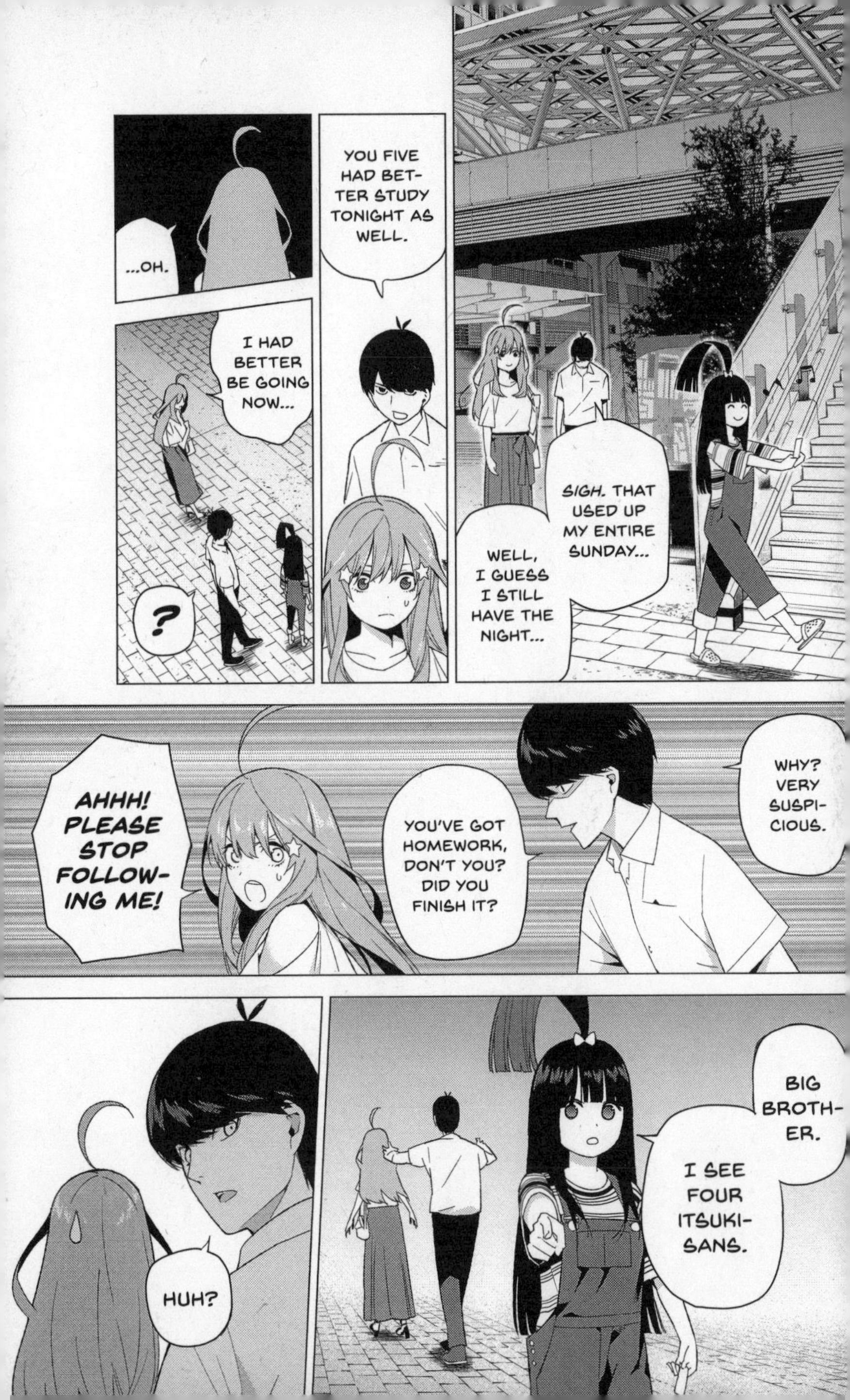
SIGH. THAT USED UP MY ENTIRE SUNDAY...
WELL, I GUESS I STILL HAVE THE NIGHT...
YOU FIVE HAD BETTER STUDY TONIGHT AS WELL.
...OH.
I HAD BETTER BE GOING NOW...
?
WHY? VERY SUSPICIOUS.
YOU'VE GOT HOMEWORK, DON'T YOU? DID YOU FINISH IT?
AHHH! PLEASE STOP FOLLOWING ME!
BIG BROTHER.
I SEE FOUR ITSUKI-SANS.
HUH?

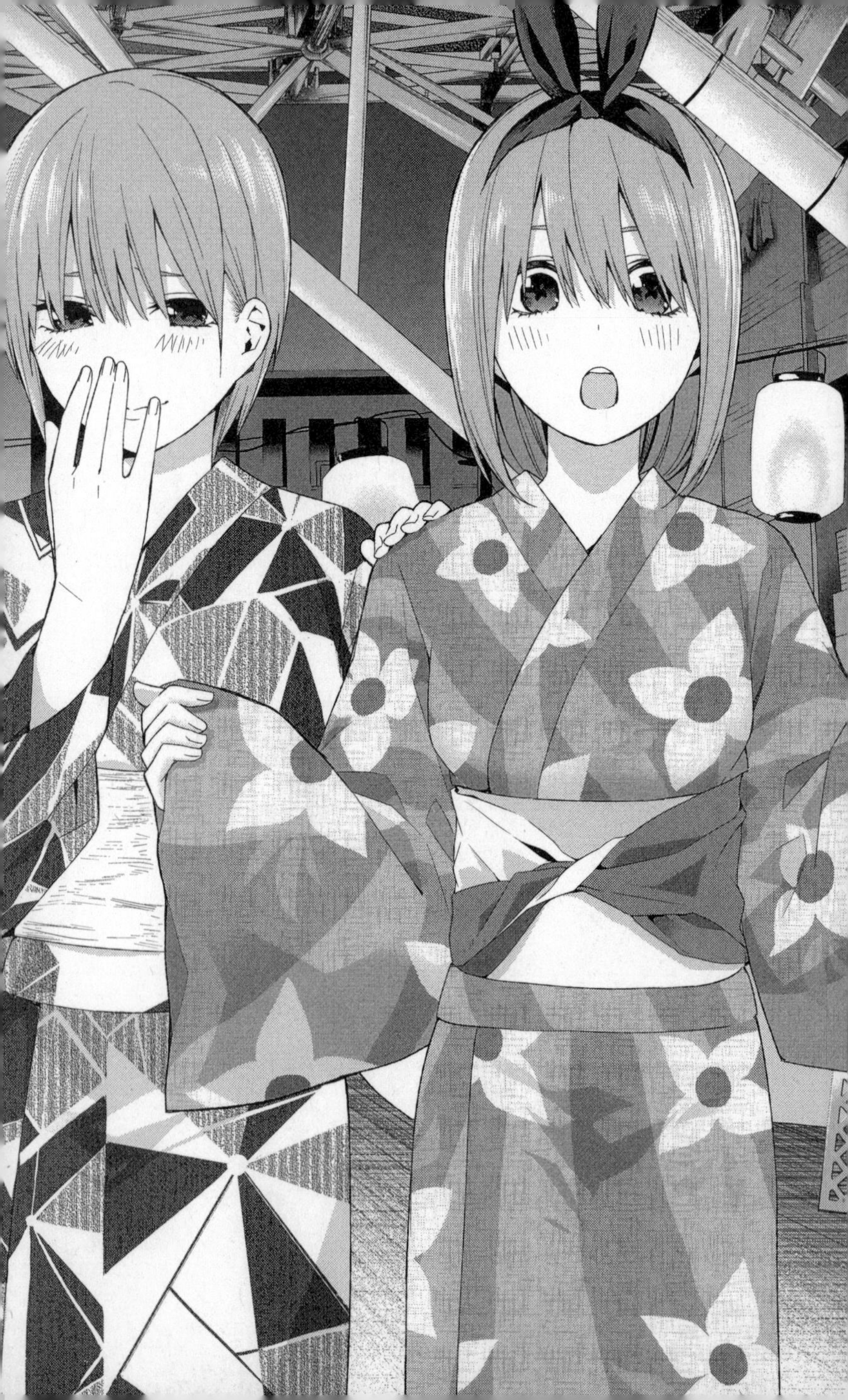

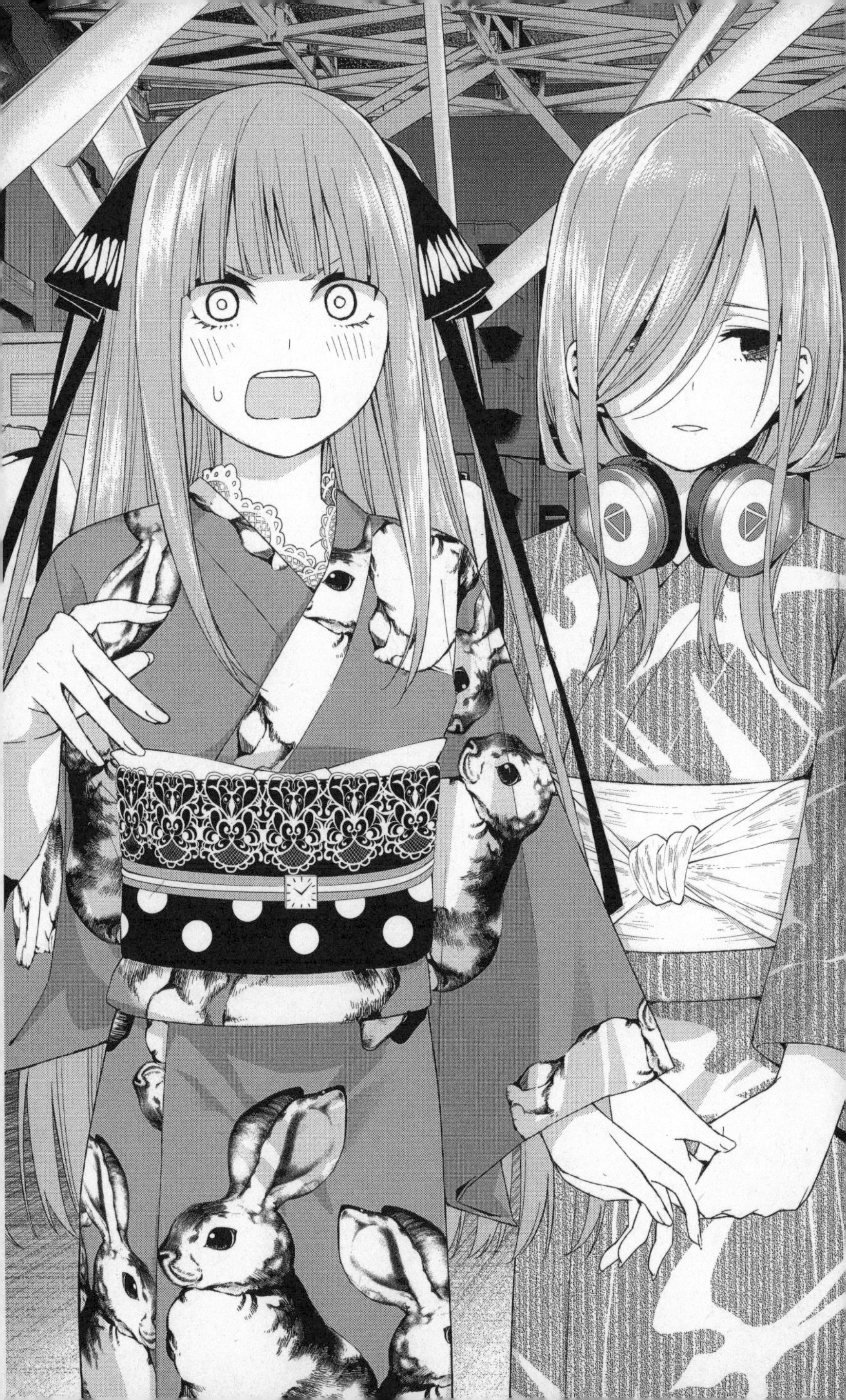

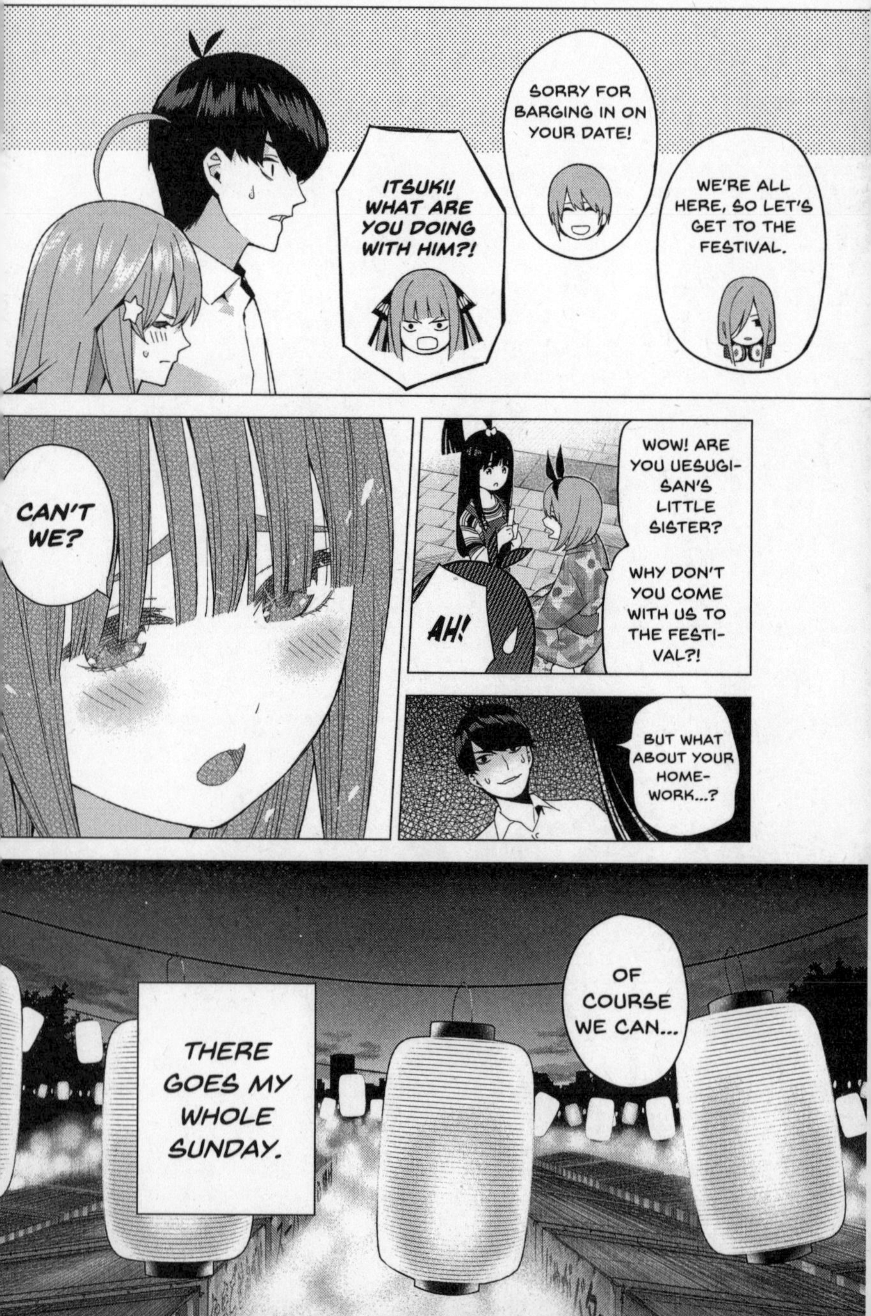
SORRY FOR BARGING IN ON YOUR DATE!
WE'RE ALL HERE, SO LET'S GET TO THE FESTIVAL.
ITSUKI! WHAT ARE YOU DOING WITH HIM?!
WOW! ARE YOU UESUGI-SAN'S LITTLE SISTER?
WHY DON'T YOU COME WITH US TO THE FESTI-VAL?!
AH!
BUT WHAT ABOUT YOUR HOME-WORK...?
CAN'T WE?
OF COURSE WE CAN...
THERE GOES MY WHOLE SUNDAY.

CHAPTER 8 OUR DAY OFF (2

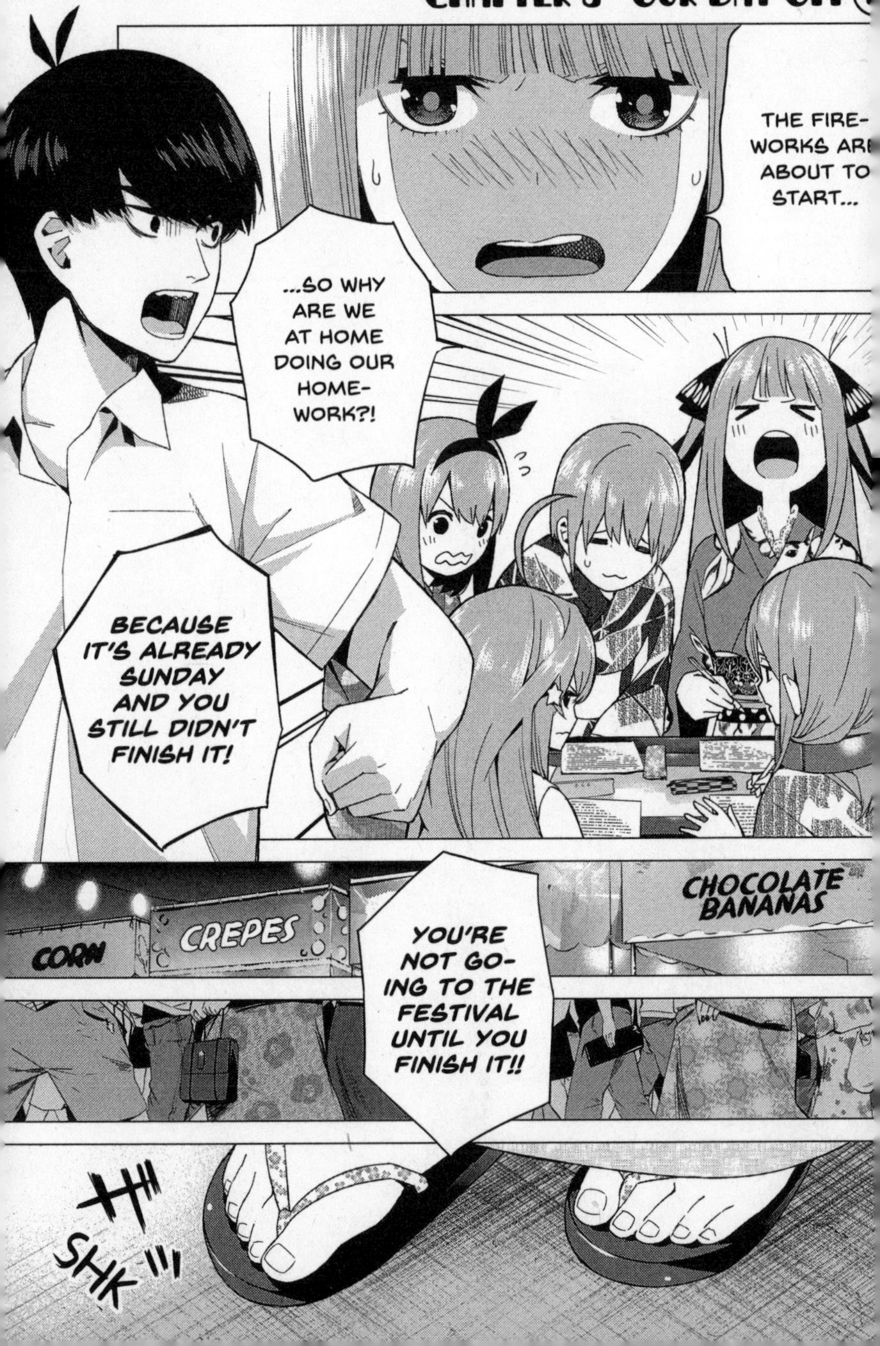
THE FIRE-WORKS ARE ABOUT TO START...
...SO WHY ARE WE AT HOME DOING OUR HOME-WORK?!
BECAUSE IT'S ALREADY SUNDAY AND YOU STILL DIDN'T FINISH IT!
CHOCOLATE BANANAS
YOU'RE NOT GO-ING TO THE FESTIVAL UNTIL YOU FINISH IT!!
CREPES
CORN
SHK

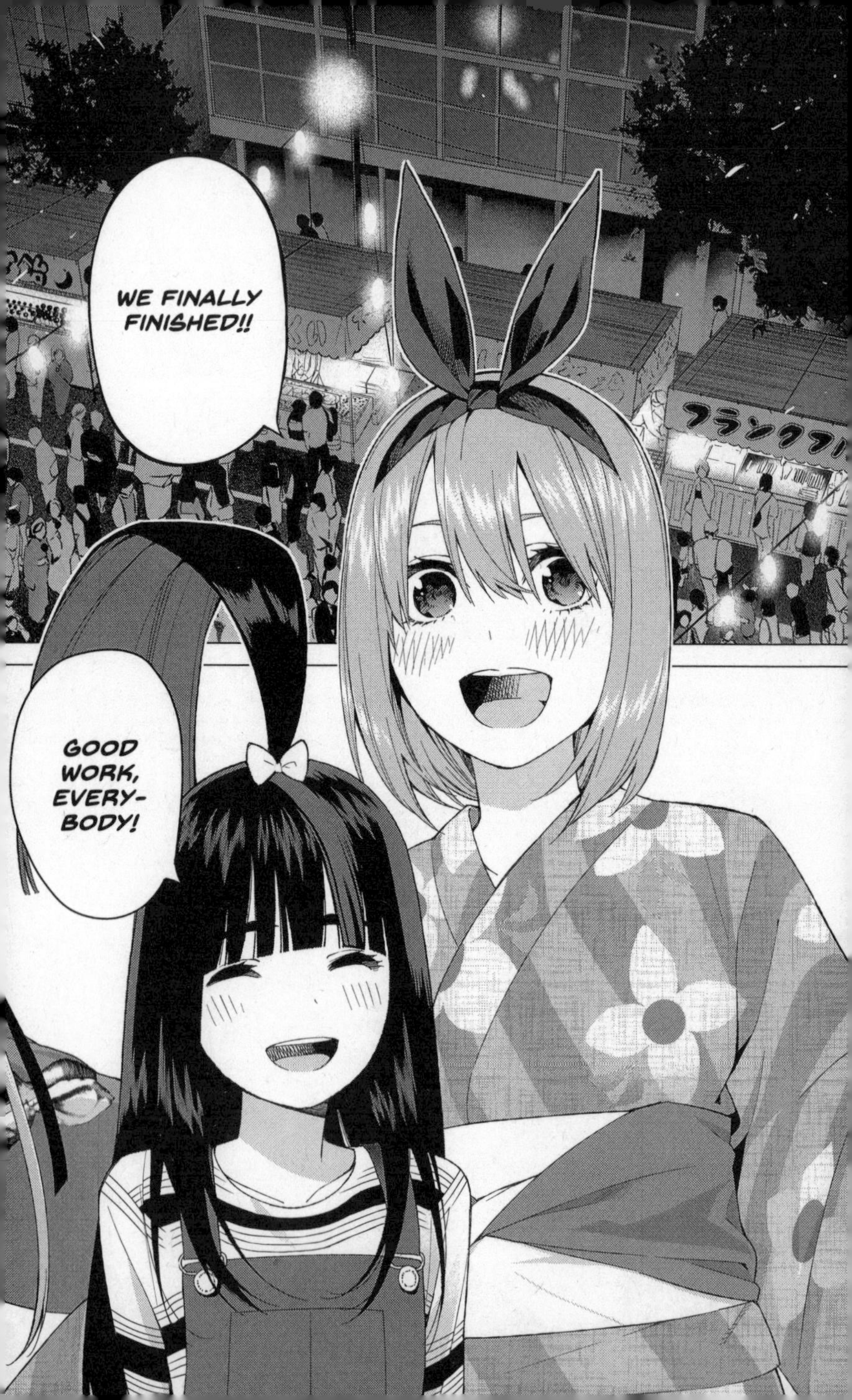
WE FINALLY FINISHED!!
フランクフル
GOOD WORK, EVERY-BODY!

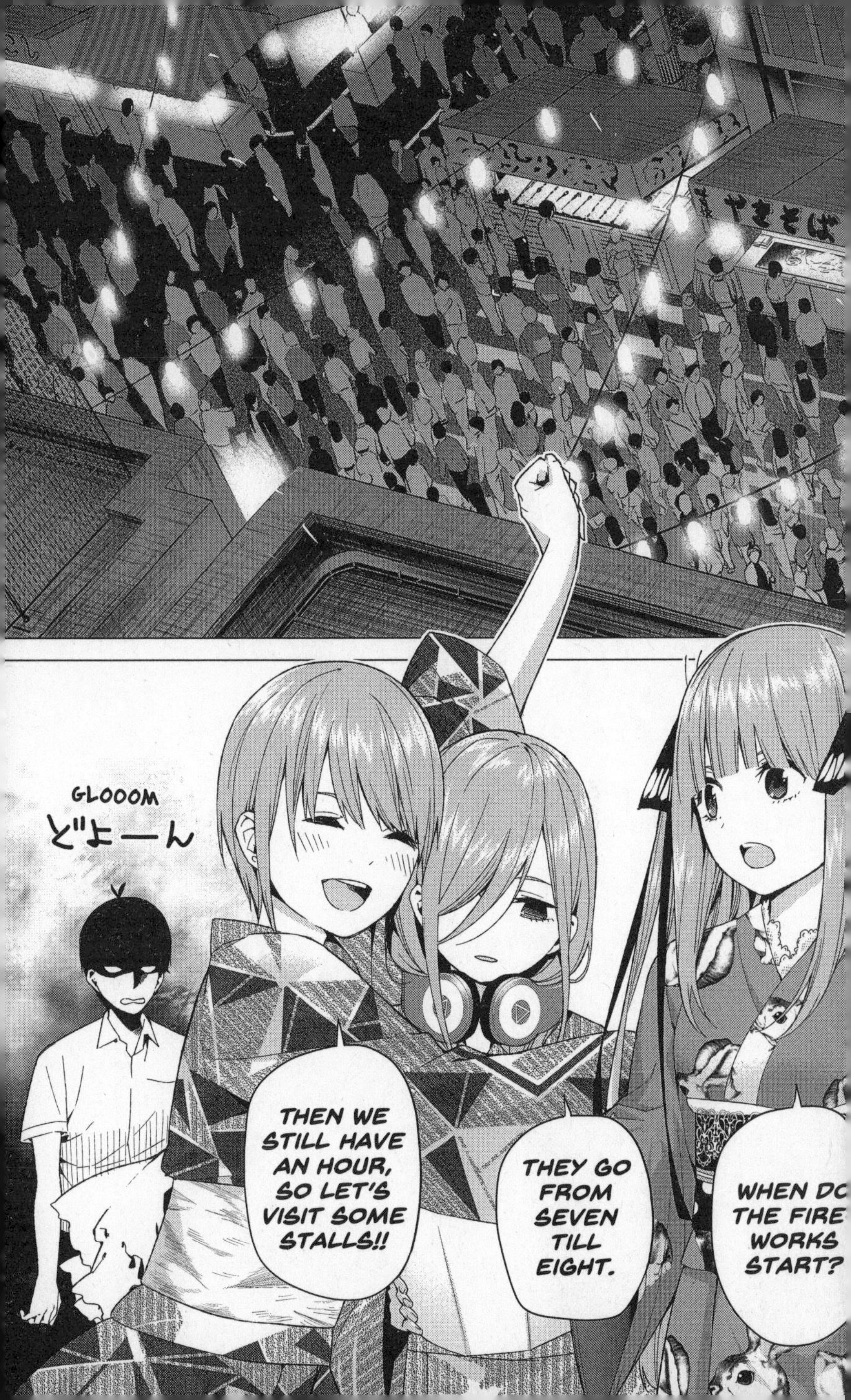
やきそば
WHEN DO THE FIREWORKS START?
THEY GO FROM SEVEN TILL EIGHT.
THEN WE STILL HAVE AN HOUR, SO LET'S VISIT SOME STALLS!!
GLOOOM
どよーん

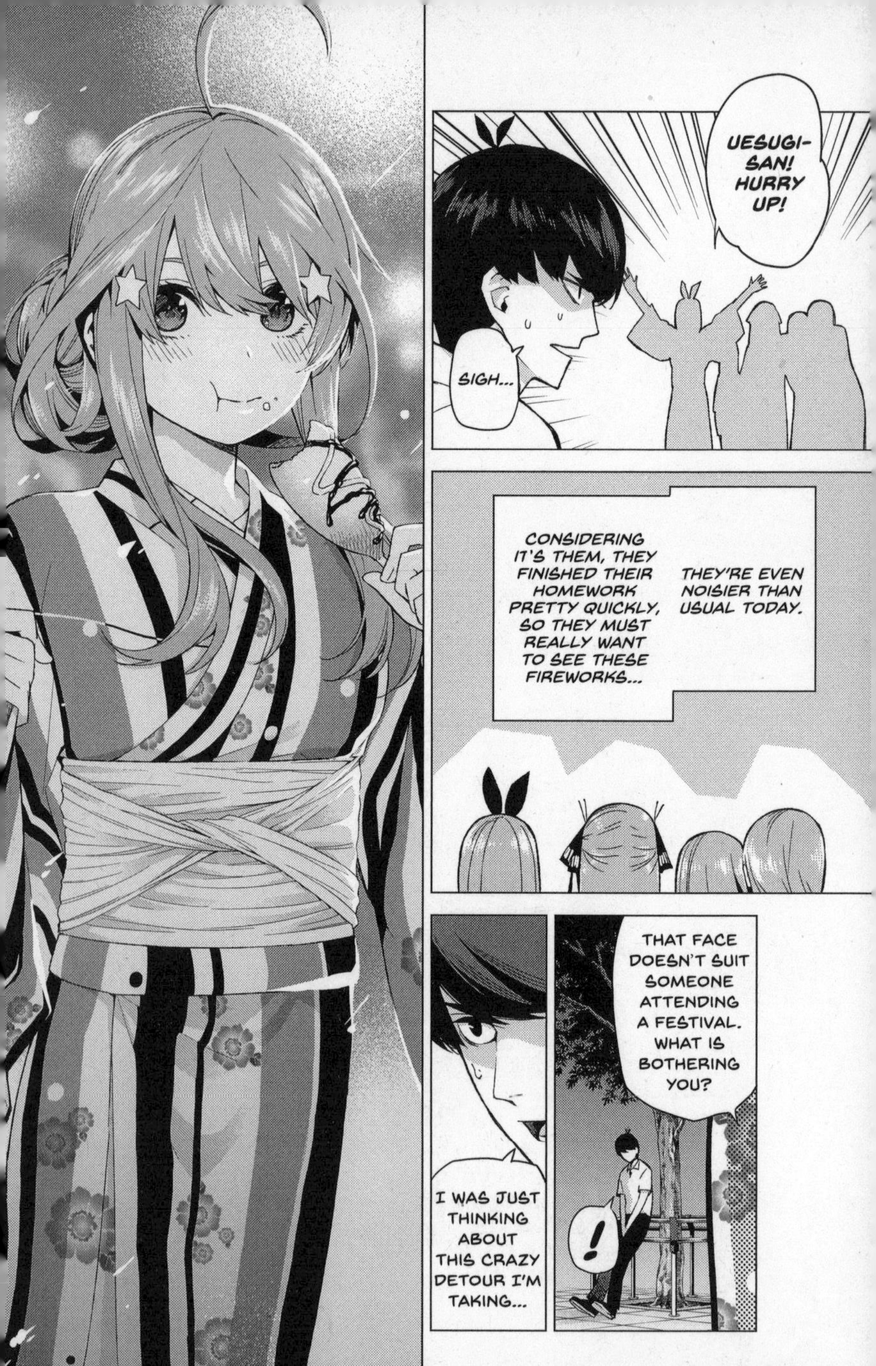
UESUGI-SAN! HURRY UP!
SIGH...
THEY'RE EVEN NOISIER THAN USUAL TODAY.
CONSIDERING IT'S THEM, THEY FINISHED THEIR HOMEWORK PRETTY QUICKLY, SO THEY MUST REALLY WANT TO SEE THESE FIREWORKS...
THAT FACE DOESN'T SUIT SOMEONE ATTENDING A FESTIVAL. WHAT IS BOTHERING YOU?
!
I WAS JUST THINKING ABOUT THIS CRAZY DETOUR I'M TAKING...

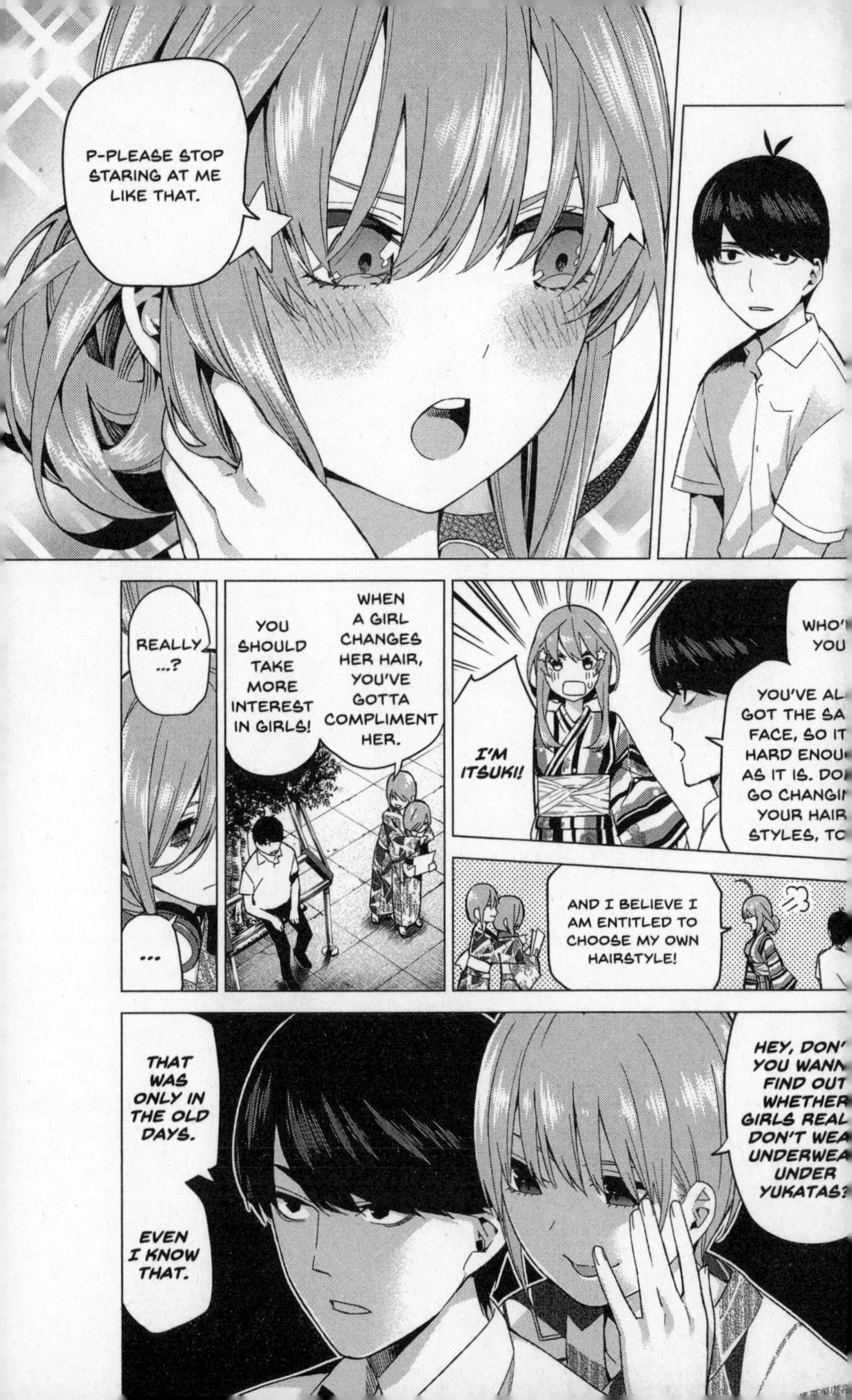
P-PLEASE STOP STARING AT ME LIKE THAT.
WHO' YOU
YOU'VE AL GOT THE SA FACE, SO IT HARD ENOU AS IT IS. DO GO CHANGI YOUR HAIR STYLES, TO
I'M ITSUKI!
AND I BELIEVE I AM ENTITLED TO CHOOSE MY OWN HAIRSTYLE!
WHEN A GIRL CHANGES HER HAIR, YOU'VE GOTTA COMPLIMENT HER.
YOU SHOULD TAKE MORE INTEREST IN GIRLS!
REALLY ...?
...
HEY, DON' YOU WANN FIND OUT WHETHER GIRLS REAL DON'T WEA UNDERWEA UNDER YUKATAS?
THAT WAS ONLY IN THE OLD DAYS.
EVEN I KNOW THAT.

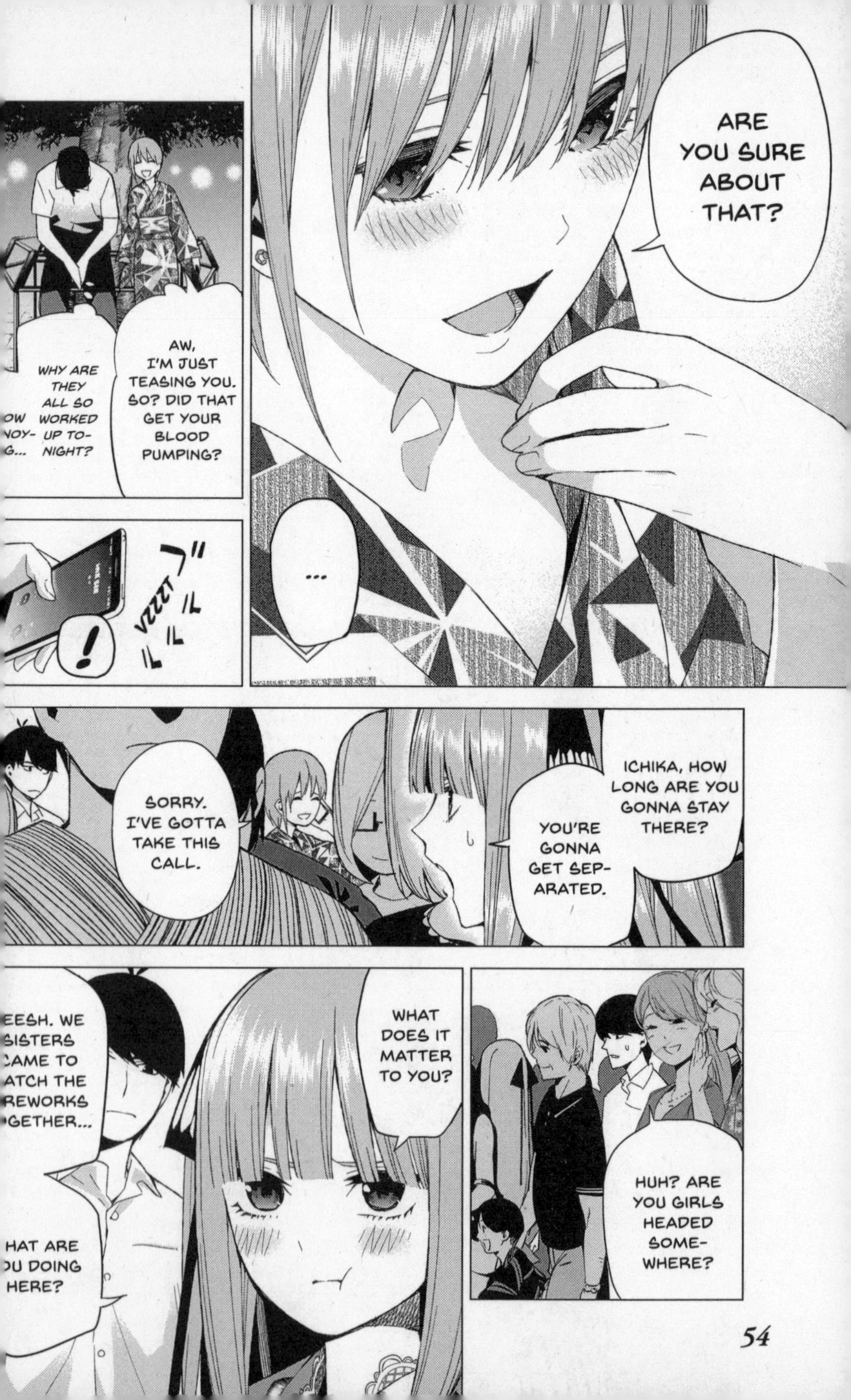
ARE YOU SURE ABOUT THAT?
...
AW, I'M JUST TEASING YOU. SO? DID THAT GET YOUR BLOOD PUMPING?
WHY ARE THEY ALL SO WORKED UP TO-NIGHT?
OW NOY- G...
VZZZT
!
ICHIKA, HOW LONG ARE YOU GONNA STAY THERE?
YOU'RE GONNA GET SEP-ARATED.
SORRY. I'VE GOTTA TAKE THIS CALL.
HUH? ARE YOU GIRLS HEADED SOME-WHERE?
WHAT DOES IT MATTER TO YOU?
EESH. WE SISTERS CAME TO ATCH THE REWORKS GETHER...
HAT ARE OU DOING HERE?

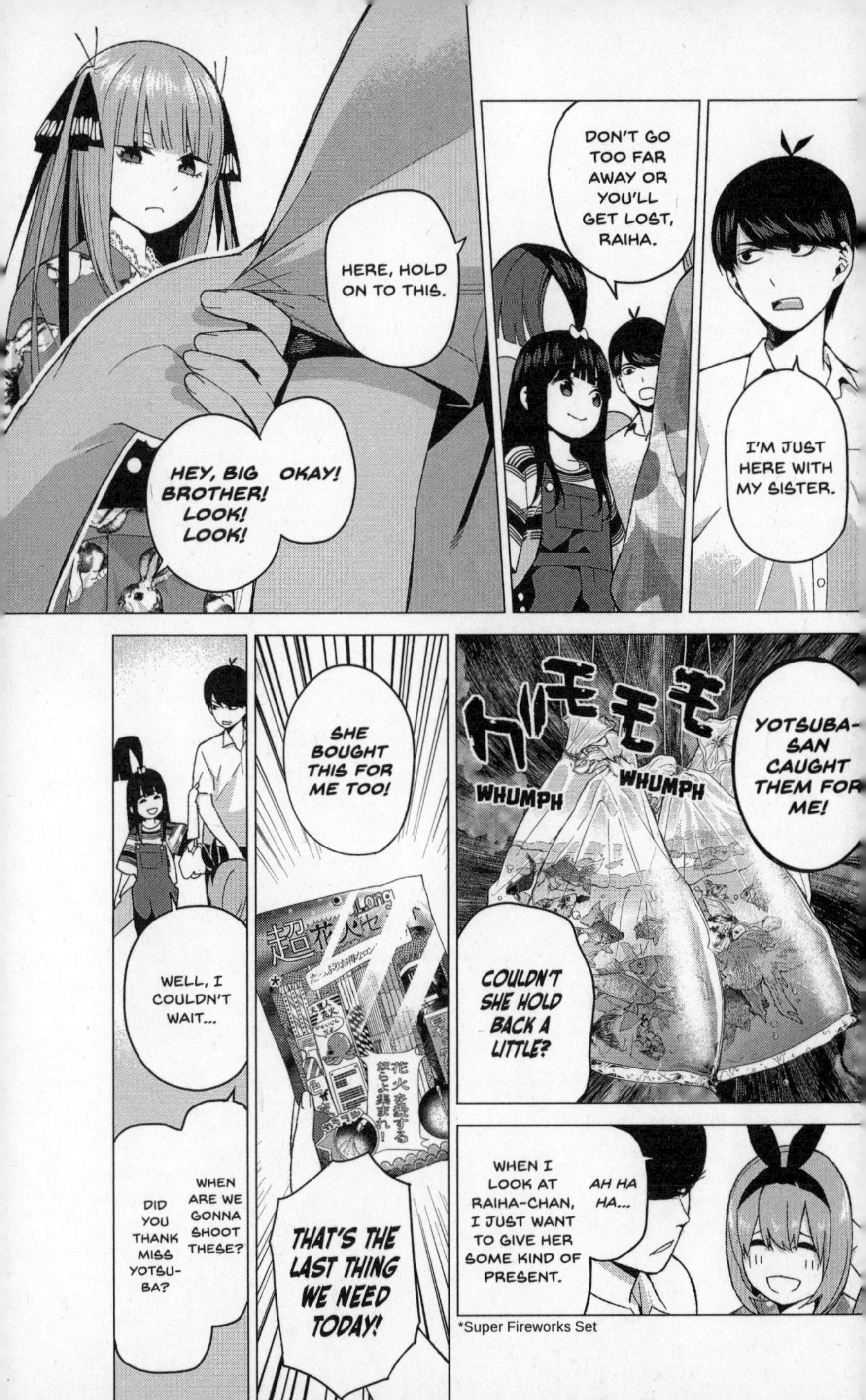
I'M JUST HERE WITH MY SISTER.
DON'T GO TOO FAR AWAY OR YOU'LL GET LOST, RAIHA.
OKAY!
HERE, HOLD ON TO THIS.
HEY, BIG BROTHER! LOOK! LOOK!
YOTSUBA-SAN CAUGHT THEM FOR ME!
WHUMPH
WHUMPH
COULDN'T SHE HOLD BACK A LITTLE?
AH HA HA...
WHEN I LOOK AT RAIHA-CHAN, I JUST WANT TO GIVE HER SOME KIND OF PRESENT.
SHE BOUGHT THIS FOR ME TOO!
THAT'S THE LAST THING WE NEED TODAY!
WELL, I COULDN'T WAIT...
WHEN ARE WE GONNA SHOOT THESE?
DID YOU THANK MISS YOTSUBA?

*Super Fireworks Set

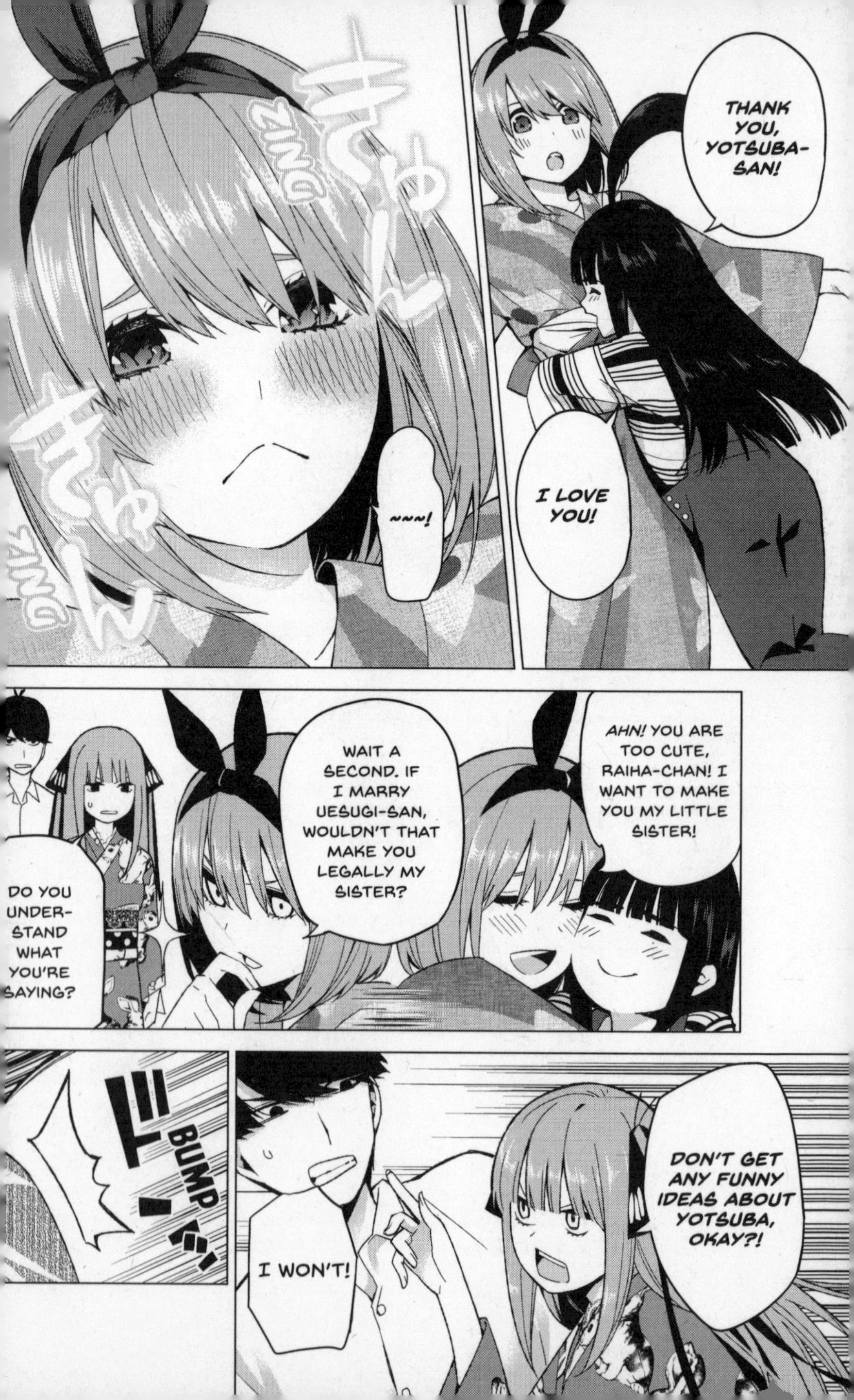
THANK YOU, YOTSUBA-SAN!
I LOVE YOU!
ZING
~~~!
ZING
AHN! YOU ARE TOO CUTE, RAIHA-CHAN! I WANT TO MAKE YOU MY LITTLE SISTER!
WAIT A SECOND. IF I MARRY UESUGI-SAN, WOULDN'T THAT MAKE YOU LEGALLY MY SISTER?
DO YOU UNDER-STAND WHAT YOU'RE SAYING?
DON'T GET ANY FUNNY IDEAS ABOUT YOTSUBA, OKAY?!
I WON'T!
BUMP
~~~

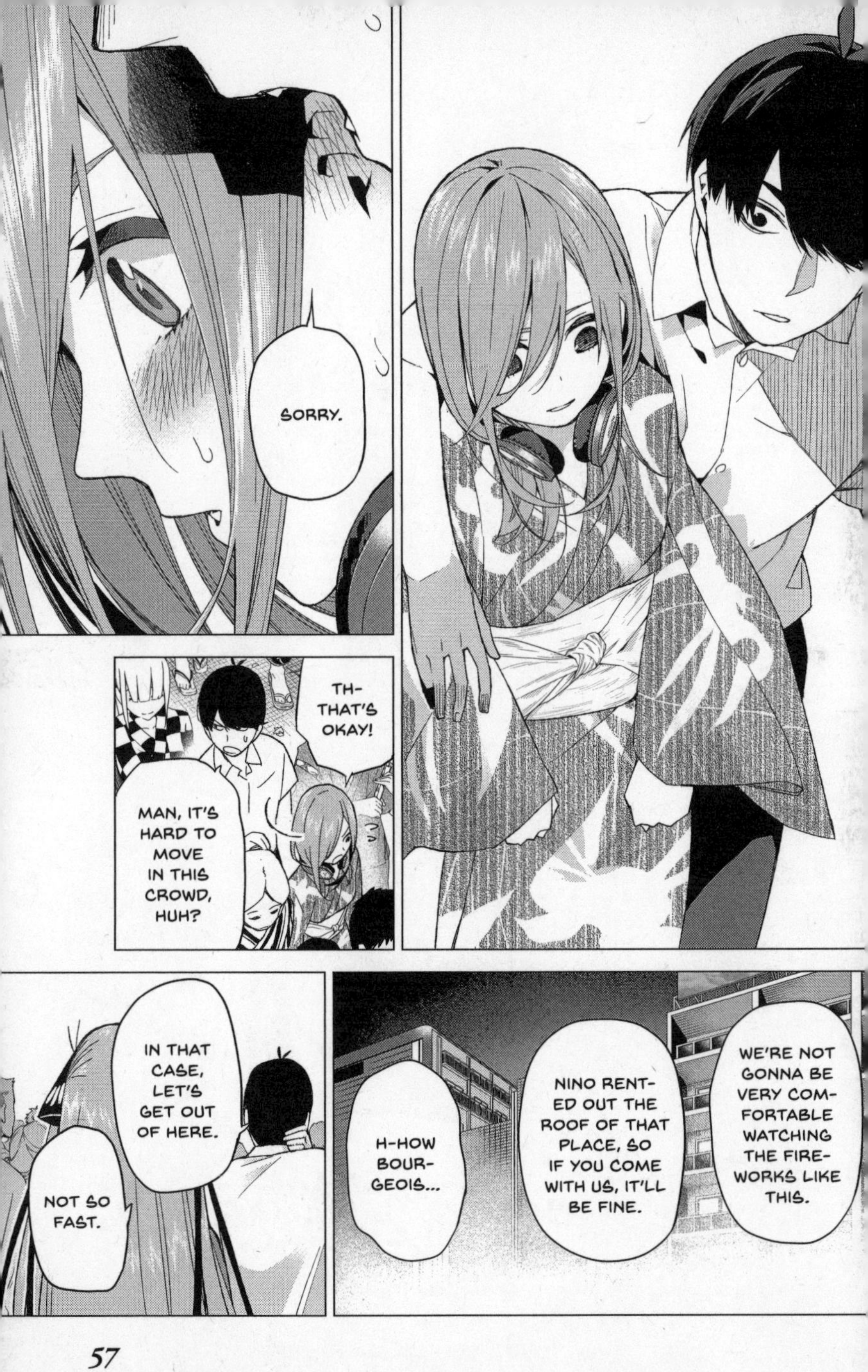
SORRY.
TH- THAT'S OKAY!
MAN, IT'S HARD TO MOVE IN THIS CROWD, HUH?
WE'RE NOT GONNA BE VERY COM- FORTABLE WATCHING THE FIRE- WORKS LIKE THIS.
NINO RENT- ED OUT THE ROOF OF THAT PLACE, SO IF YOU COME WITH US, IT'LL BE FINE.
H-HOW BOUR- GEOIS...
IN THAT CASE, LET'S GET OUT OF HERE.
NOT SO FAST.

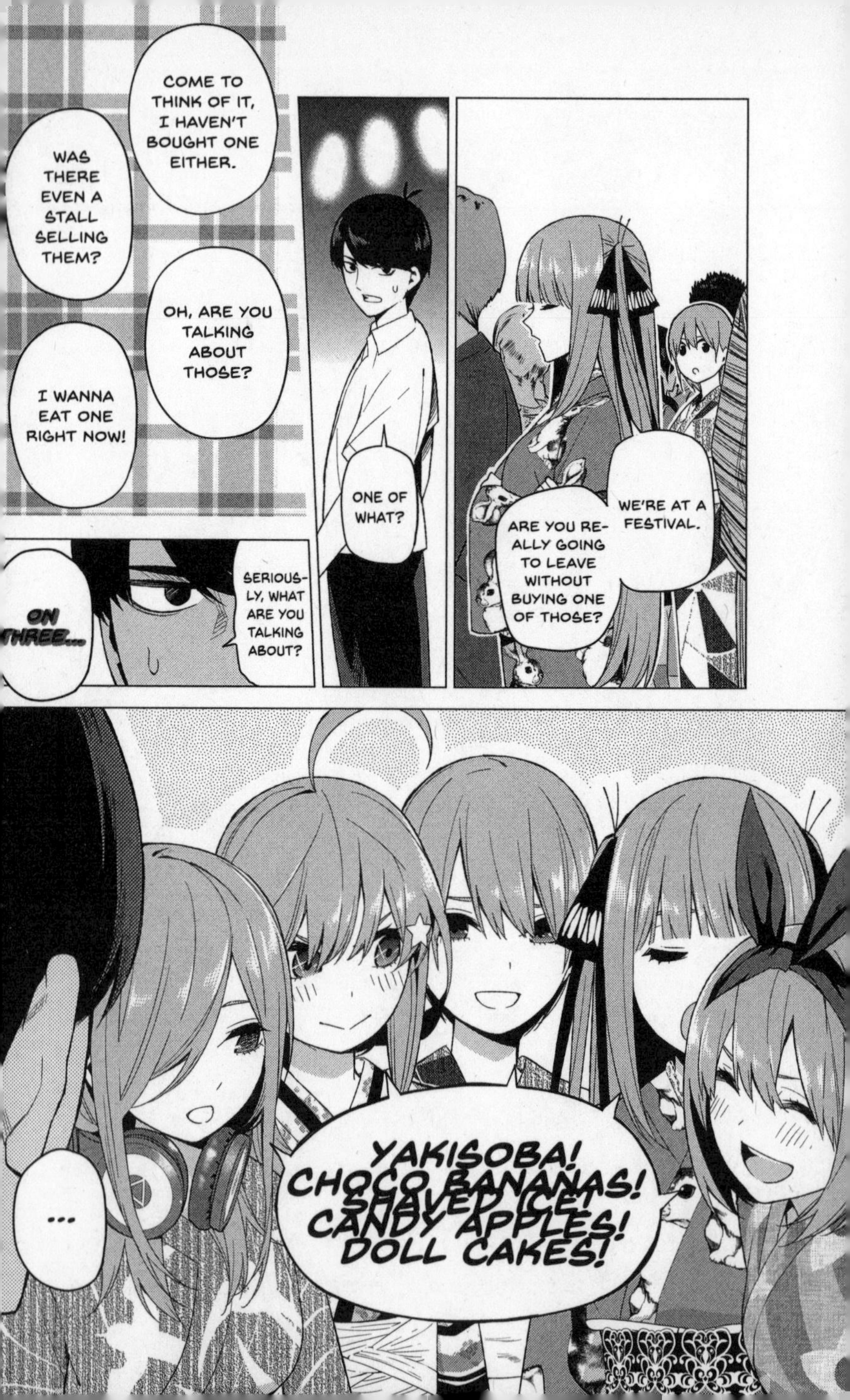
WE'RE AT A FESTIVAL.
ARE YOU REALLY GOING TO LEAVE WITHOUT BUYING ONE OF THOSE?
ONE OF WHAT?
COME TO THINK OF IT, I HAVEN'T BOUGHT ONE EITHER.
WAS THERE EVEN A STALL SELLING THEM?
OH, ARE YOU TALKING ABOUT THOSE?
I WANNA EAT ONE RIGHT NOW!
SERIOUSLY, WHAT ARE YOU TALKING ABOUT?
ON THREE...
YAKISOBA! CHOCO BANANAS! SHAVED ICE! CANDY APPLES! DOLL CAKES!
...

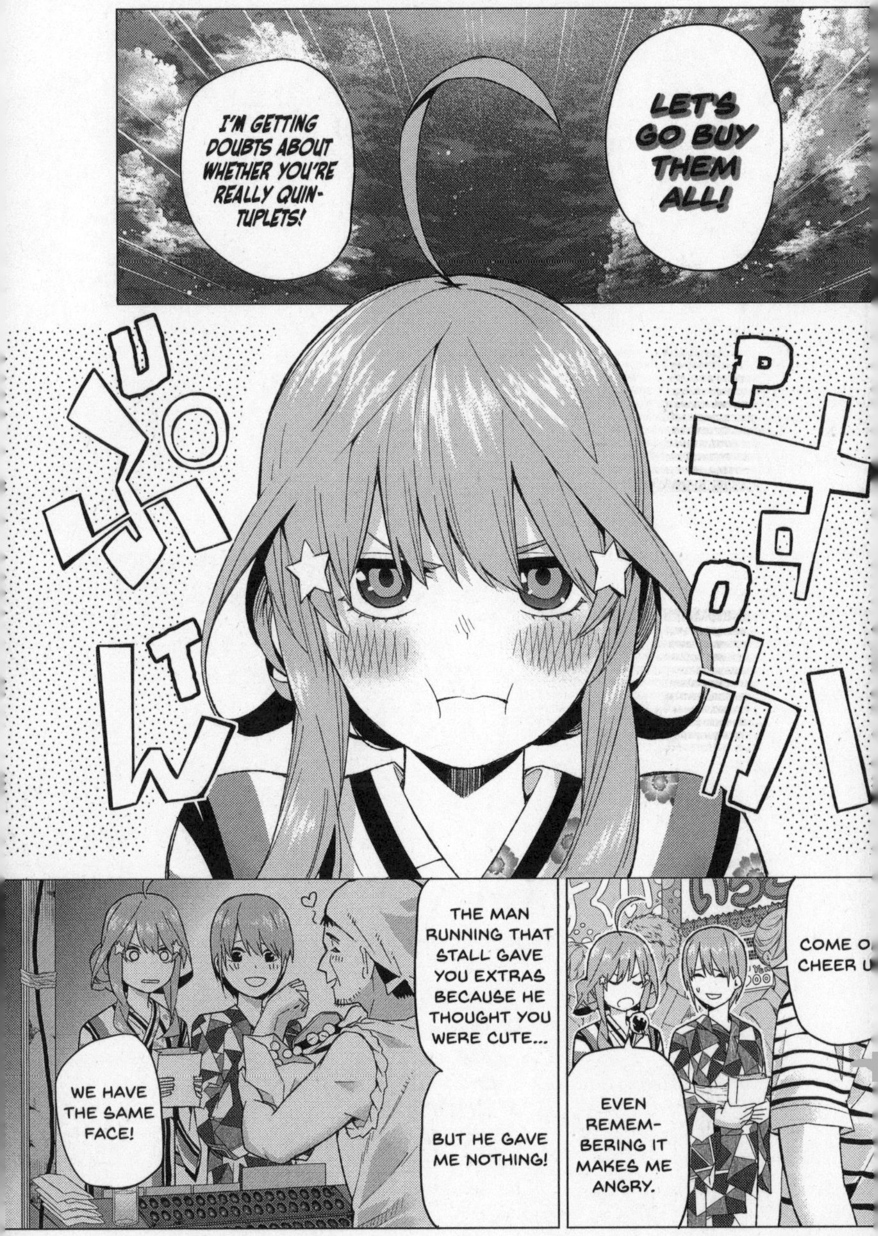
LET'S GO BUY THEM ALL!
I'M GETTING DOUBTS ABOUT WHETHER YOU'RE REALLY QUIN-TUPLETS!
COME O
CHEER U
EVEN REMEM-BERING IT MAKES ME ANGRY.
THE MAN RUNNING THAT STALL GAVE YOU EXTRAS BECAUSE HE THOUGHT YOU WERE CUTE...
BUT HE GAVE ME NOTHING!
WE HAVE THE SAME FACE!

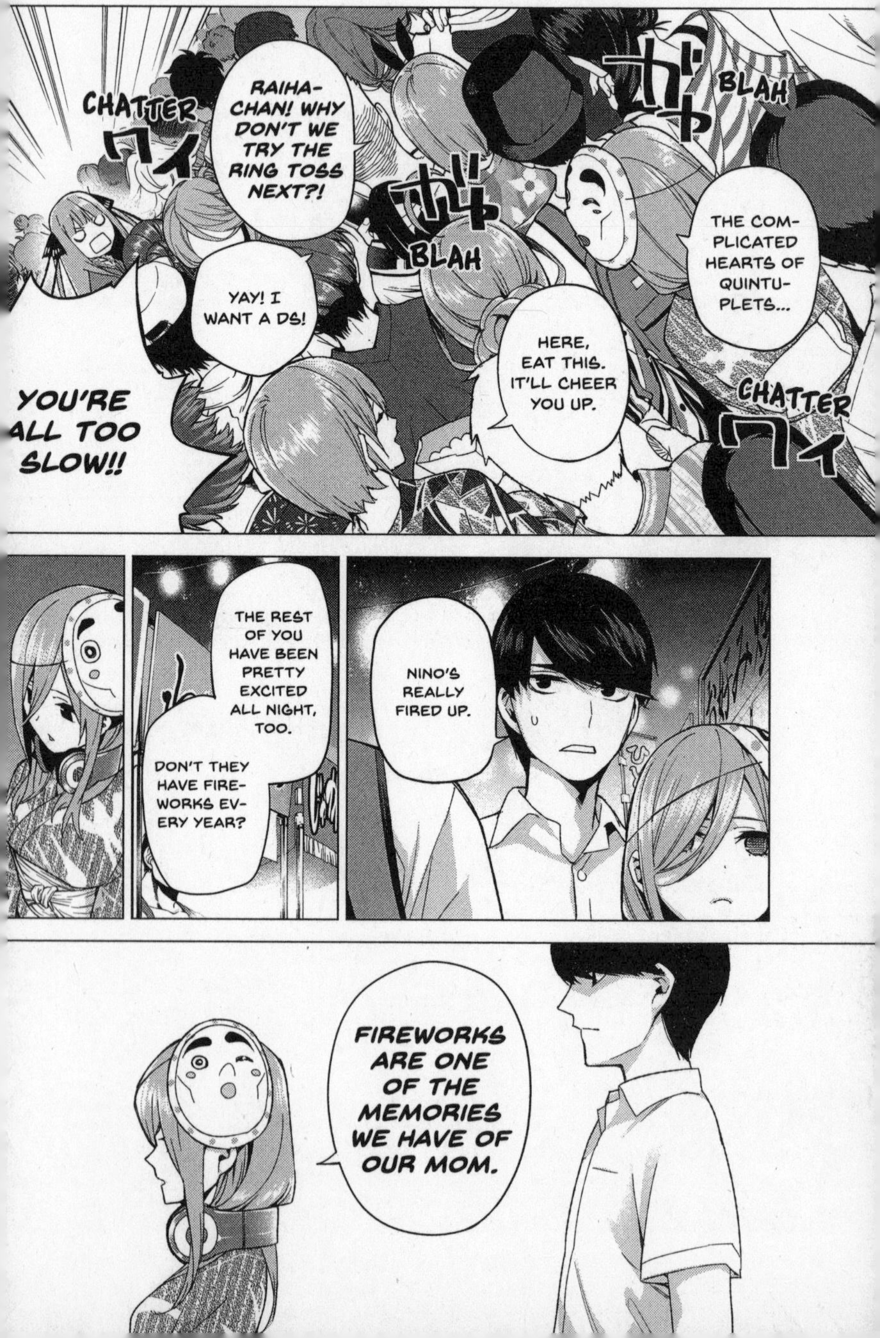
ガヤ
BLAH
THE COMPLICATED HEARTS OF QUINTUPLETS...
RAIHA-CHAN! WHY DON'T WE TRY THE RING TOSS NEXT?!
ガヤ
BLAH
CHATTER
ワイ
HERE, EAT THIS. IT'LL CHEER YOU UP.
YAY! I WANT A DS!
CHATTER
ワイ
YOU'RE ALL TOO SLOW!!
NINO'S REALLY FIRED UP.
THE REST OF YOU HAVE BEEN PRETTY EXCITED ALL NIGHT, TOO.
DON'T THEY HAVE FIREWORKS EVERY YEAR?
FIREWORKS ARE ONE OF THE MEMORIES WE HAVE OF OUR MOM.

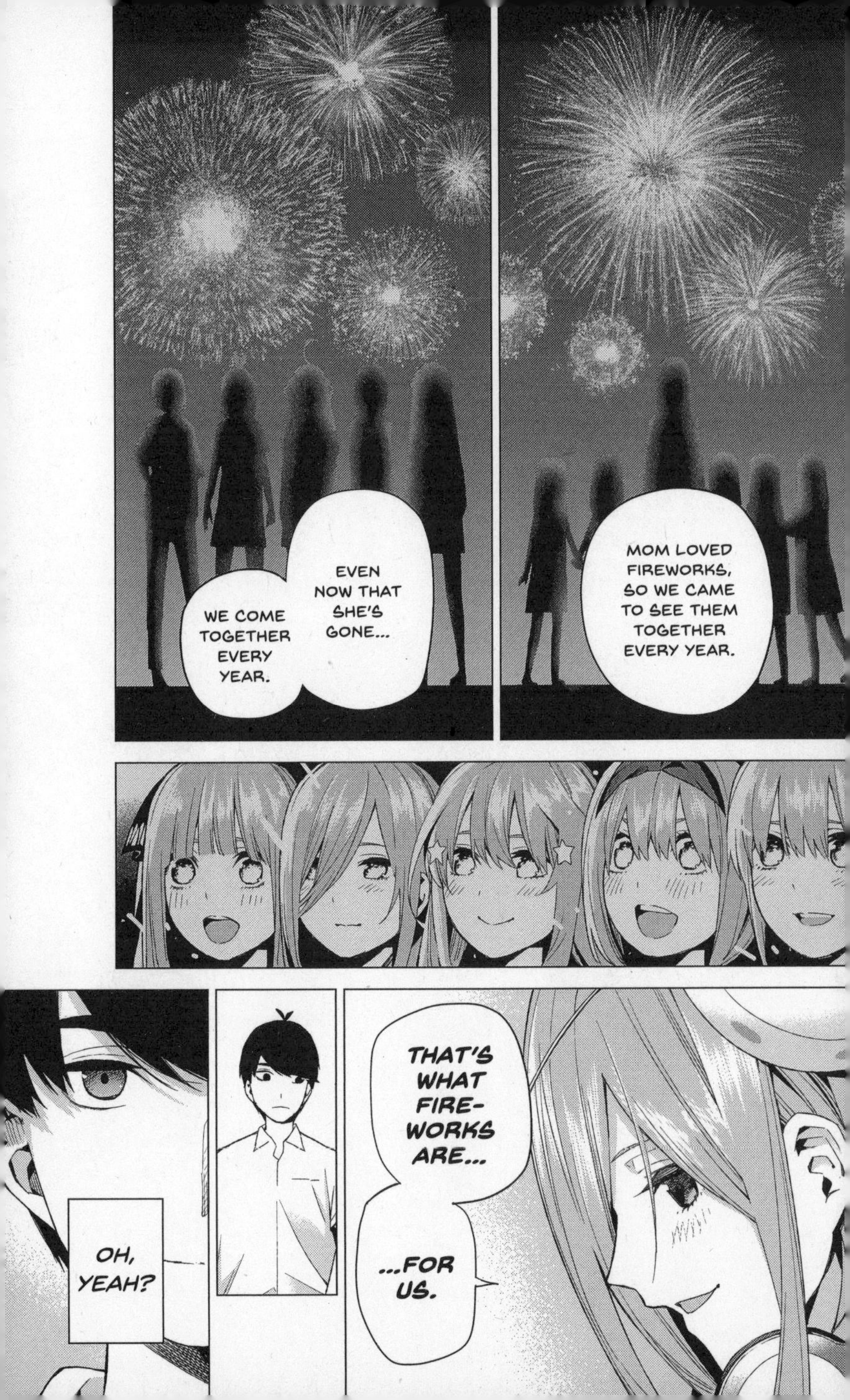

MOM LOVED FIREWORKS, SO WE CAME TO SEE THEM TOGETHER EVERY YEAR.
EVEN NOW THAT SHE'S GONE...
WE COME TOGETHER EVERY YEAR.
THAT'S WHAT FIRE-WORKS ARE...
...FOR US.
OH, YEAH?

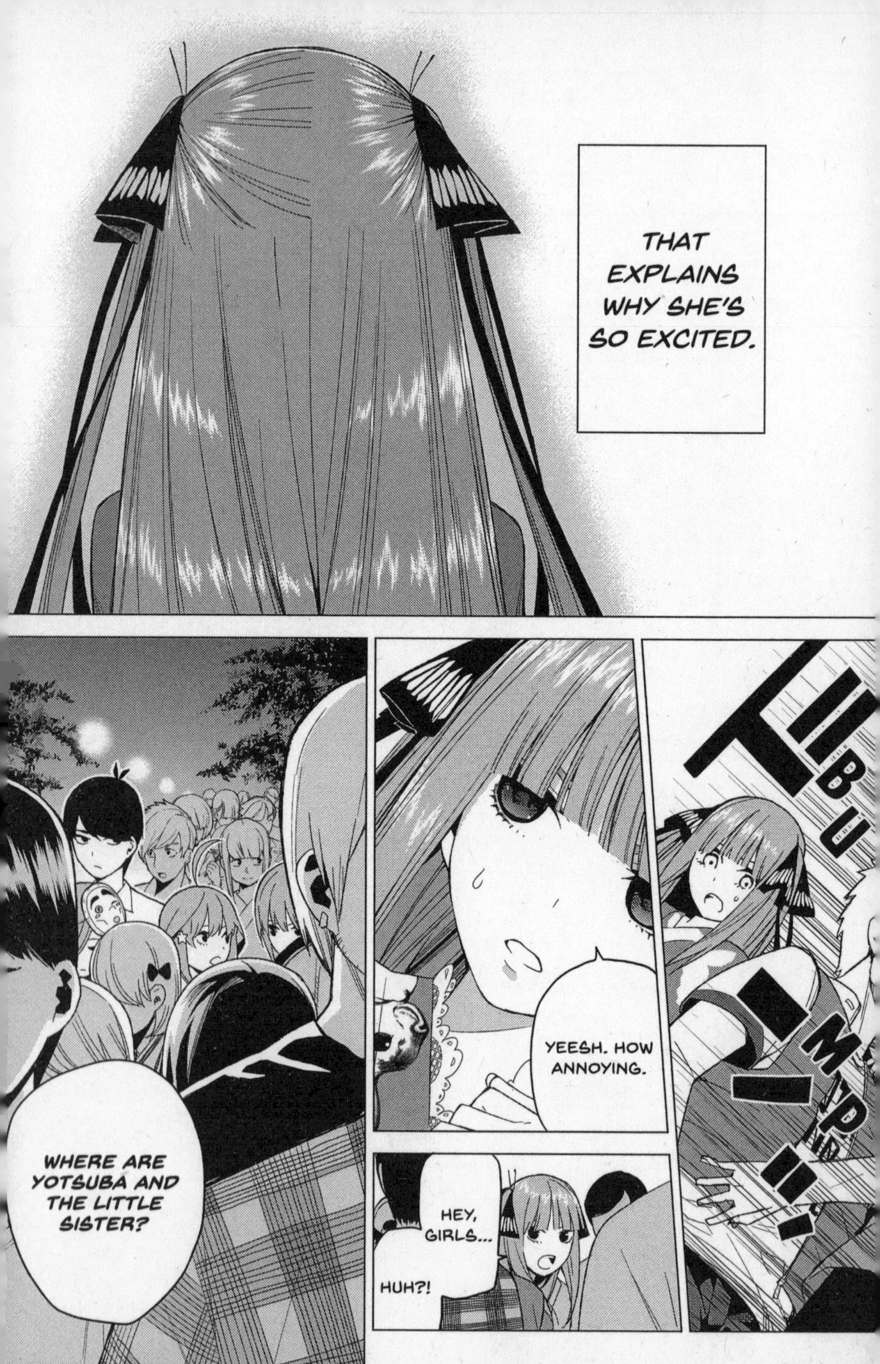
THAT EXPLAINS WHY SHE'S SO EXCITED.
BUMP!!
YEESH. HOW ANNOYING.
HEY, GIRLS...
HUH?!
WHERE ARE YOTSUBA AND THE LITTLE SISTER?

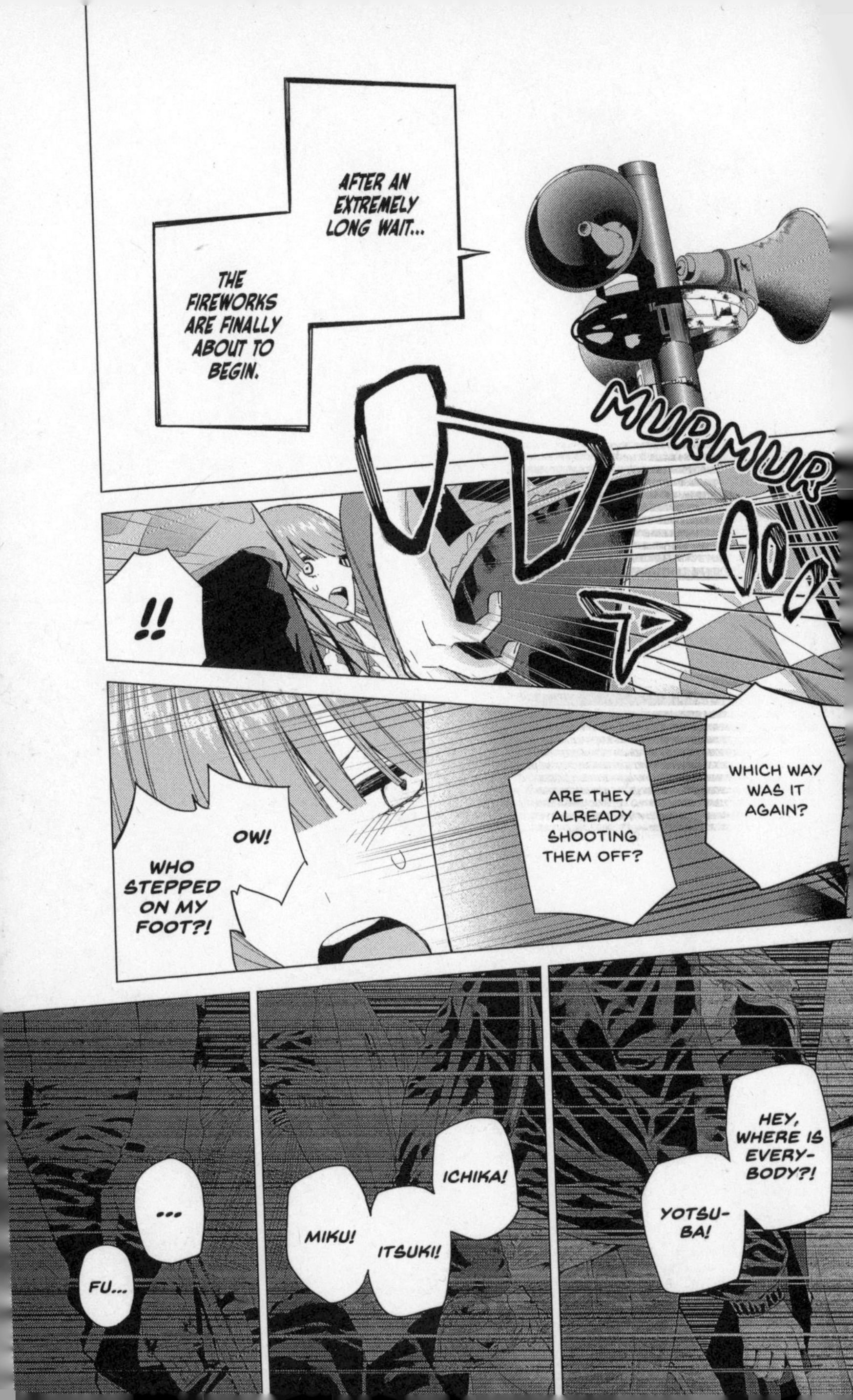
AFTER AN EXTREMELY LONG WAIT...
THE FIREWORKS ARE FINALLY ABOUT TO BEGIN.
MURMUR
!!
WHICH WAY WAS IT AGAIN?
ARE THEY ALREADY SHOOTING THEM OFF?
OW!
WHO STEPPED ON MY FOOT?!
HEY, WHERE IS EVERY-BODY?!
YOTSU-BA!
ICHIKA!
ITSUKI!
MIKU!
...
FU...

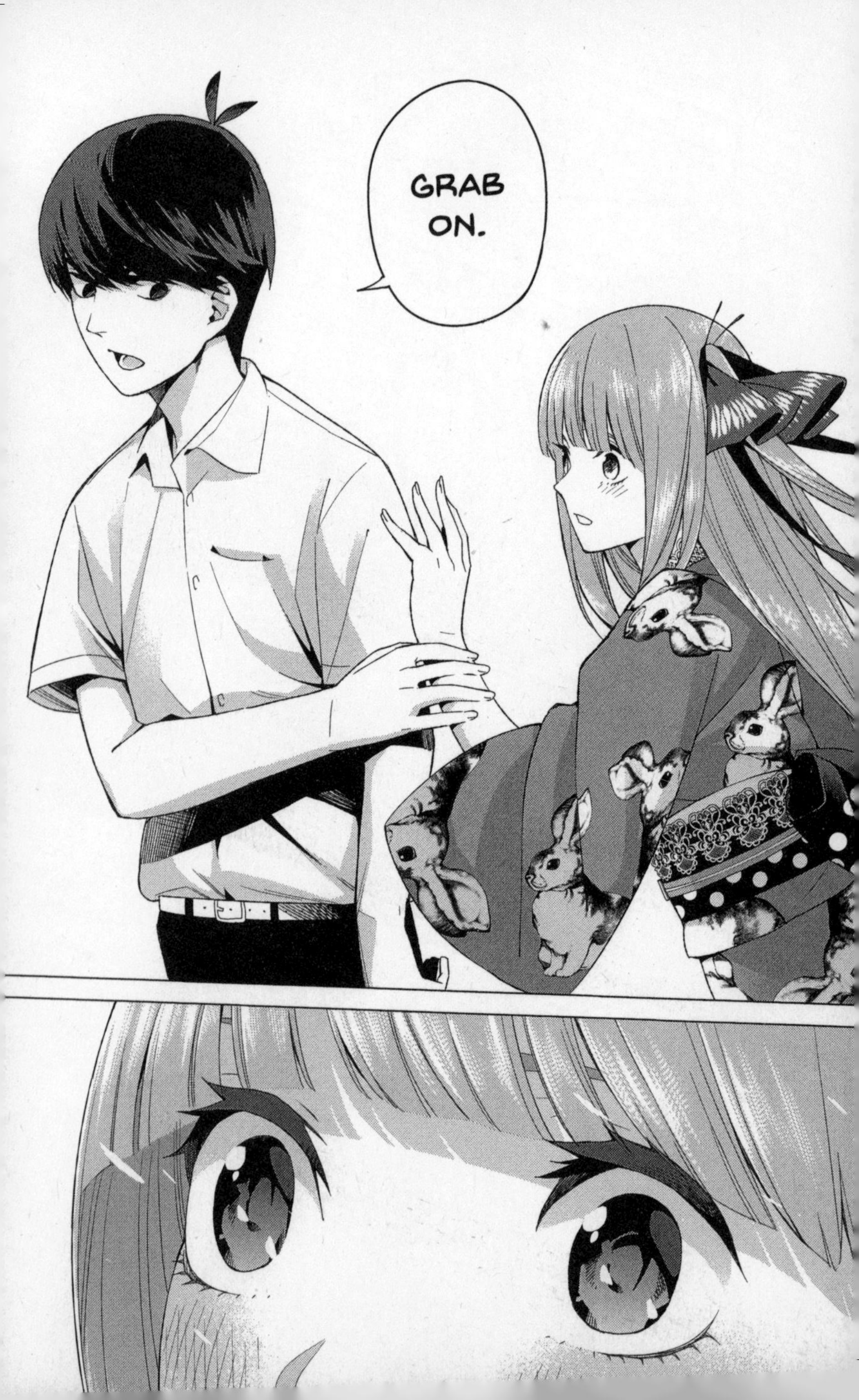
GRAB ON.

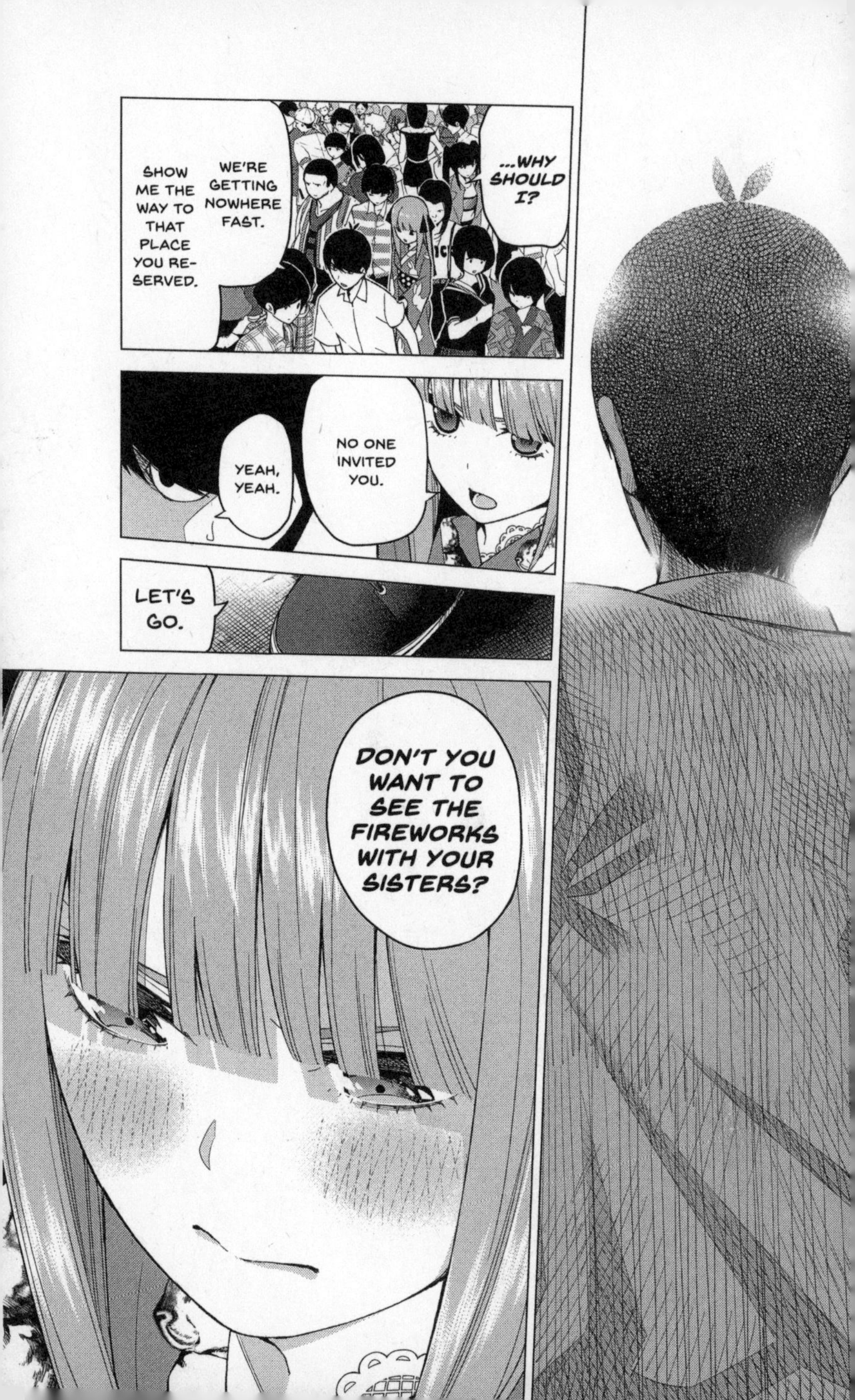
...WHY SHOULD I?
WE'RE GETTING NOWHERE FAST.
SHOW ME THE WAY TO THAT PLACE YOU RE-SERVED.
NO ONE INVITED YOU.
YEAH, YEAH.
LET'S GO.
DON'T YOU WANT TO SEE THE FIREWORKS WITH YOUR SISTERS?

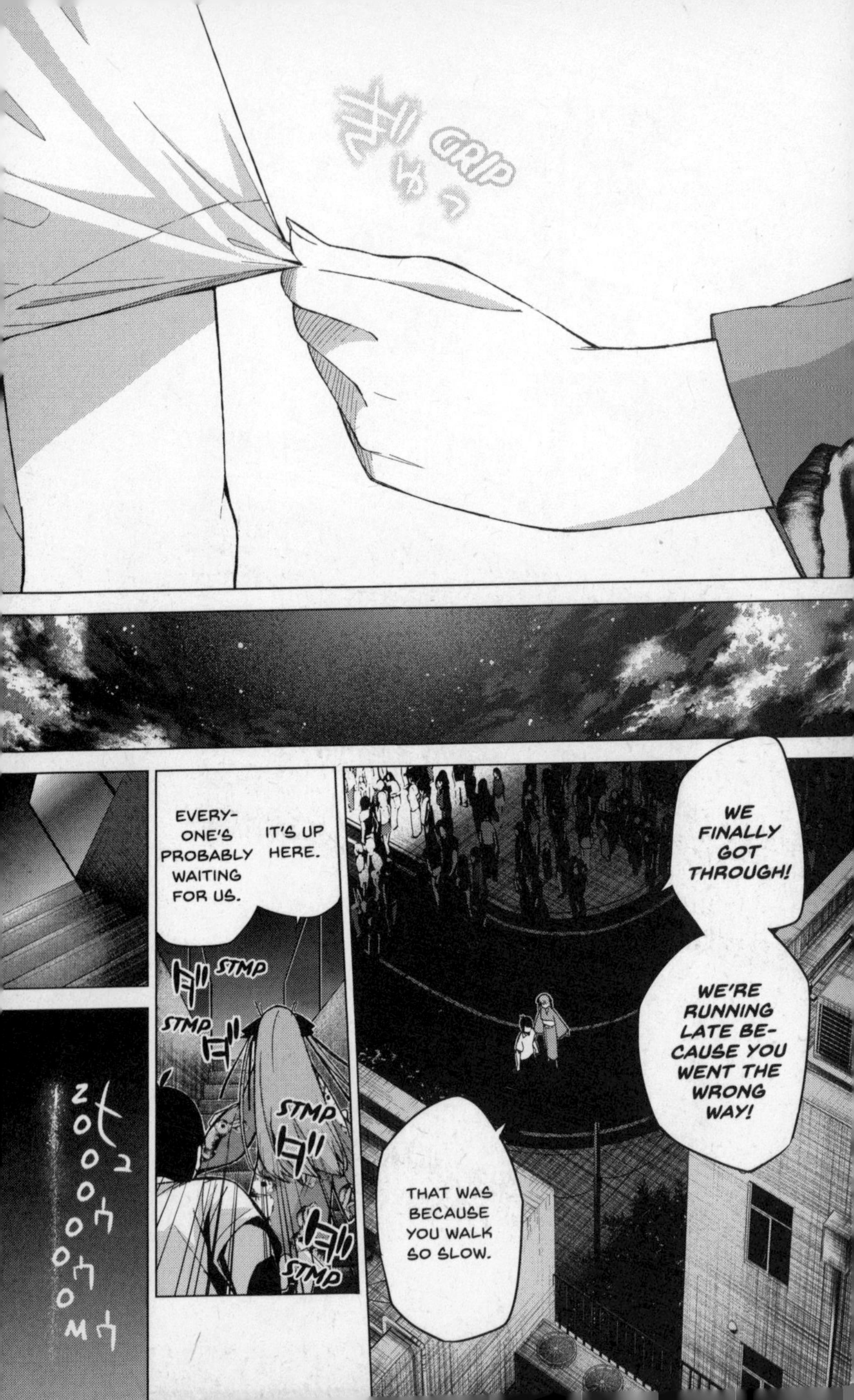
GRIP
WE FINALLY GOT THROUGH!
WE'RE RUNNING LATE BECAUSE YOU WENT THE WRONG WAY!
THAT WAS BECAUSE YOU WALK SO SLOW.
IT'S UP HERE.
EVERYONE'S PROBABLY WAITING FOR US.
STMP
STMP
STMP
STMP

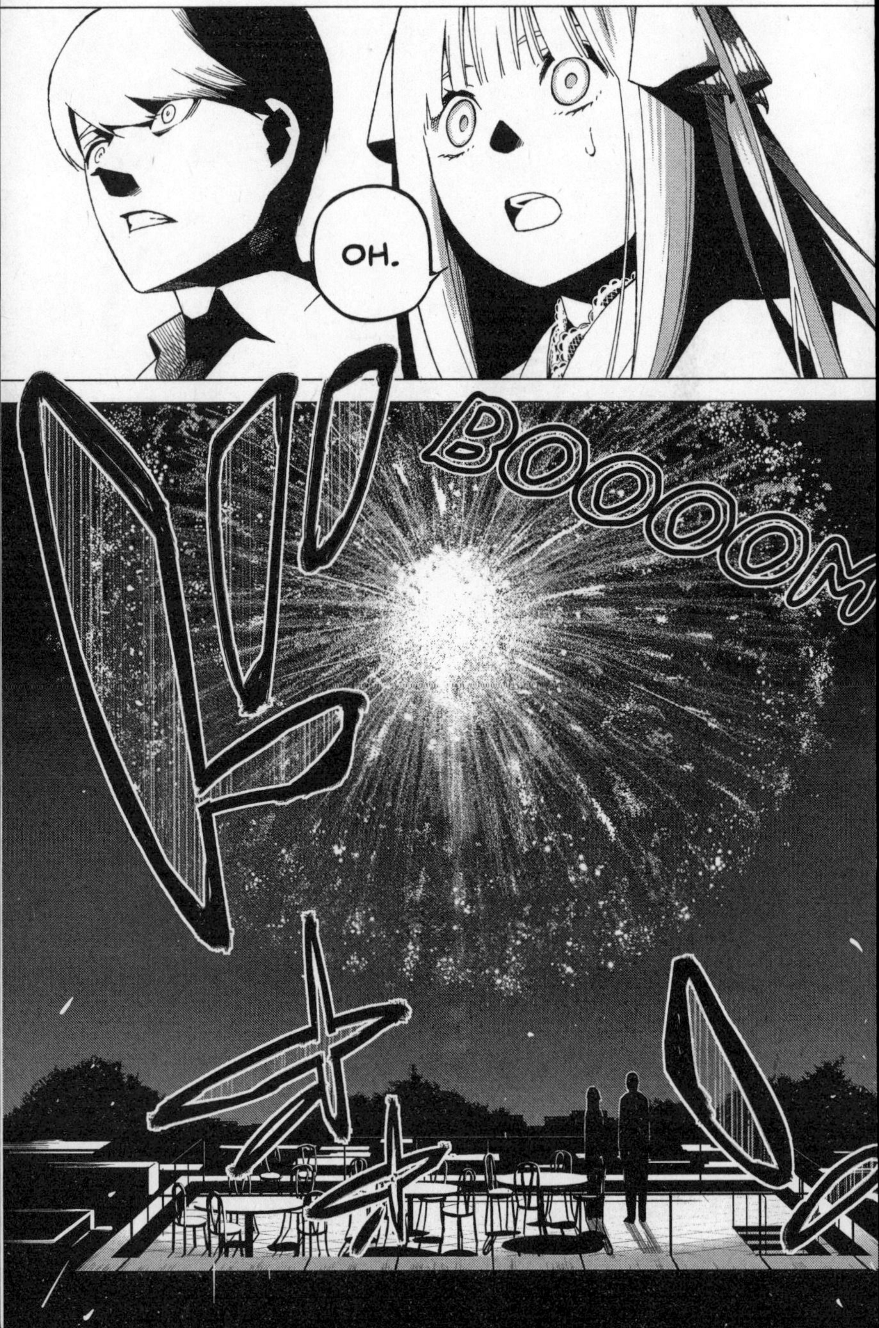
OH.
BOOOOOM

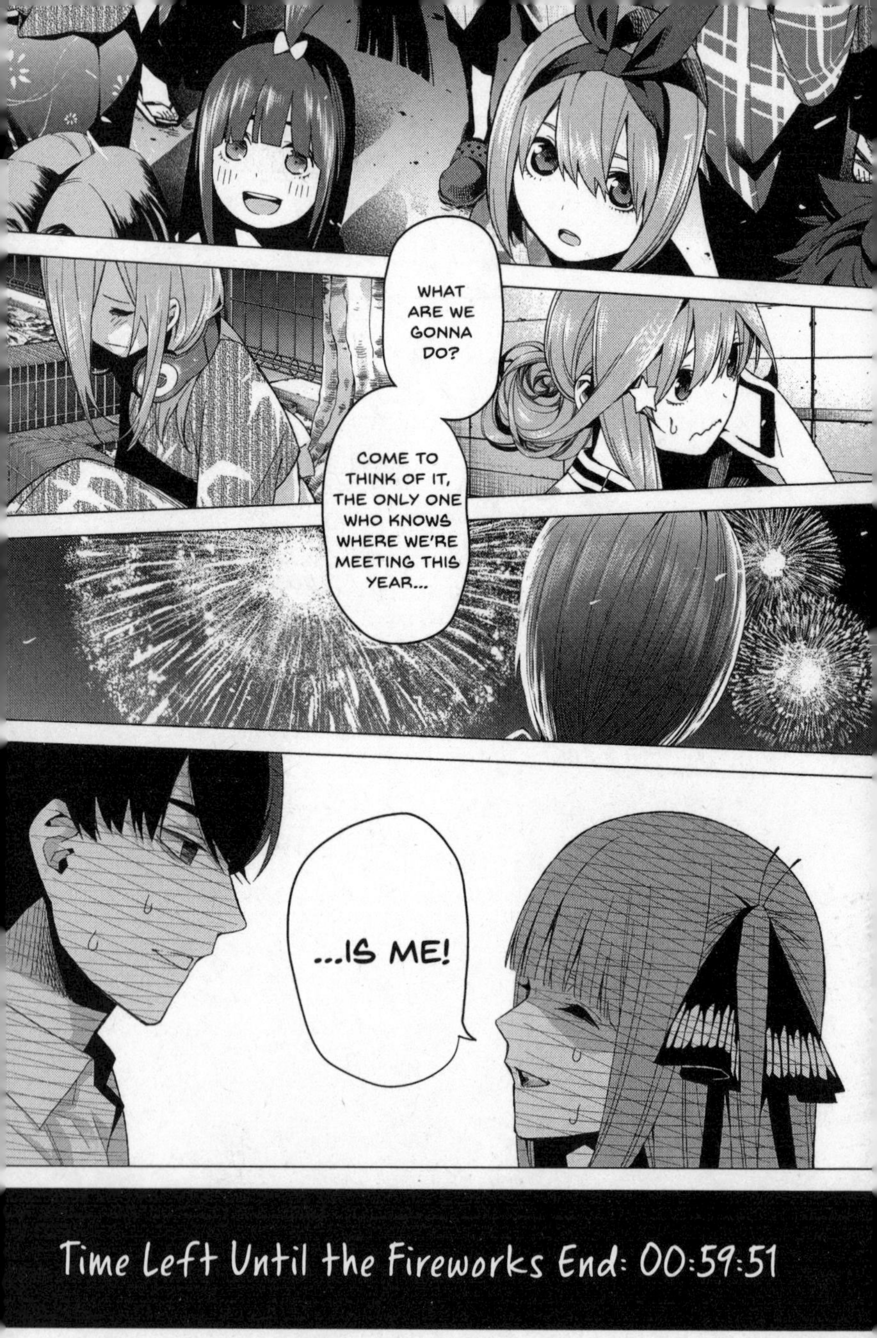
WHAT ARE WE GONNA DO?
COME TO THINK OF IT, THE ONLY ONE WHO KNOWS WHERE WE'RE MEETING THIS YEAR...
...IS ME!
Time Left Until the Fireworks End: 00:59:51

CHAPTER 9 OUR DAY OFF ③

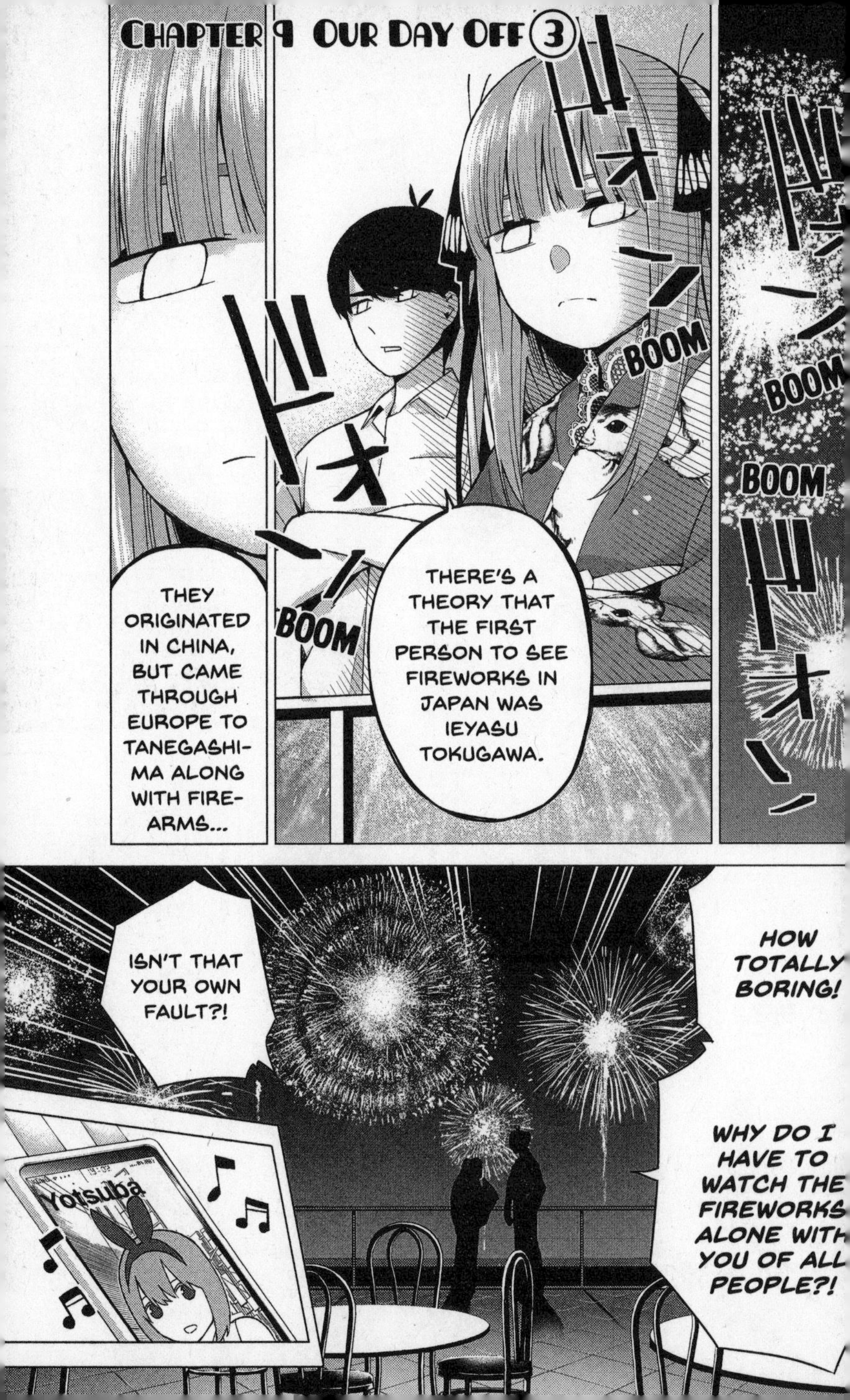
BOOM
BOOM
BOOM
THERE'S A THEORY THAT THE FIRST PERSON TO SEE FIREWORKS IN JAPAN WAS IEYASU TOKUGAWA.
BOOM
THEY ORIGINATED IN CHINA, BUT CAME THROUGH EUROPE TO TANEGASHIMA ALONG WITH FIREARMS...
HOW TOTALLY BORING!
WHY DO I HAVE TO WATCH THE FIREWORKS ALONE WITH YOU OF ALL PEOPLE?!
ISN'T THAT YOUR OWN FAULT?!
Yotsuba

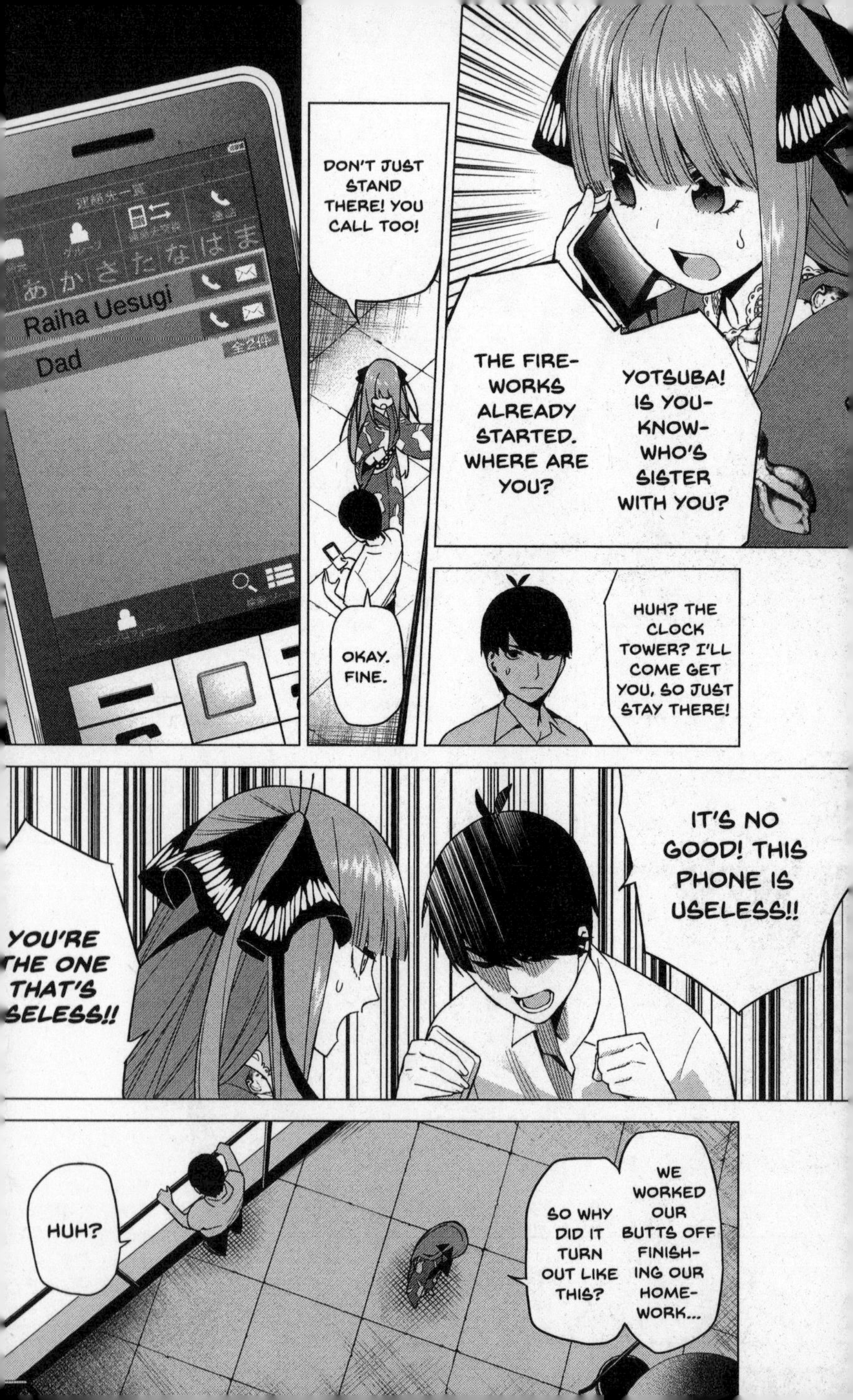
YOTSUBA! IS YOU-KNOW-WHO'S SISTER WITH YOU?
THE FIRE-WORKS ALREADY STARTED. WHERE ARE YOU?
HUH? THE CLOCK TOWER? I'LL COME GET YOU, SO JUST STAY THERE!
DON'T JUST STAND THERE! YOU CALL TOO!
OKAY. FINE.
あかさたなはま
Raiha Uesugi
Dad
IT'S NO GOOD! THIS PHONE IS USELESS!!
YOU'RE THE ONE THAT'S SELESS!!
WE WORKED OUR BUTTS OFF FINISH-ING OUR HOME-WORK...
SO WHY DID IT TURN OUT LIKE THIS?
HUH?

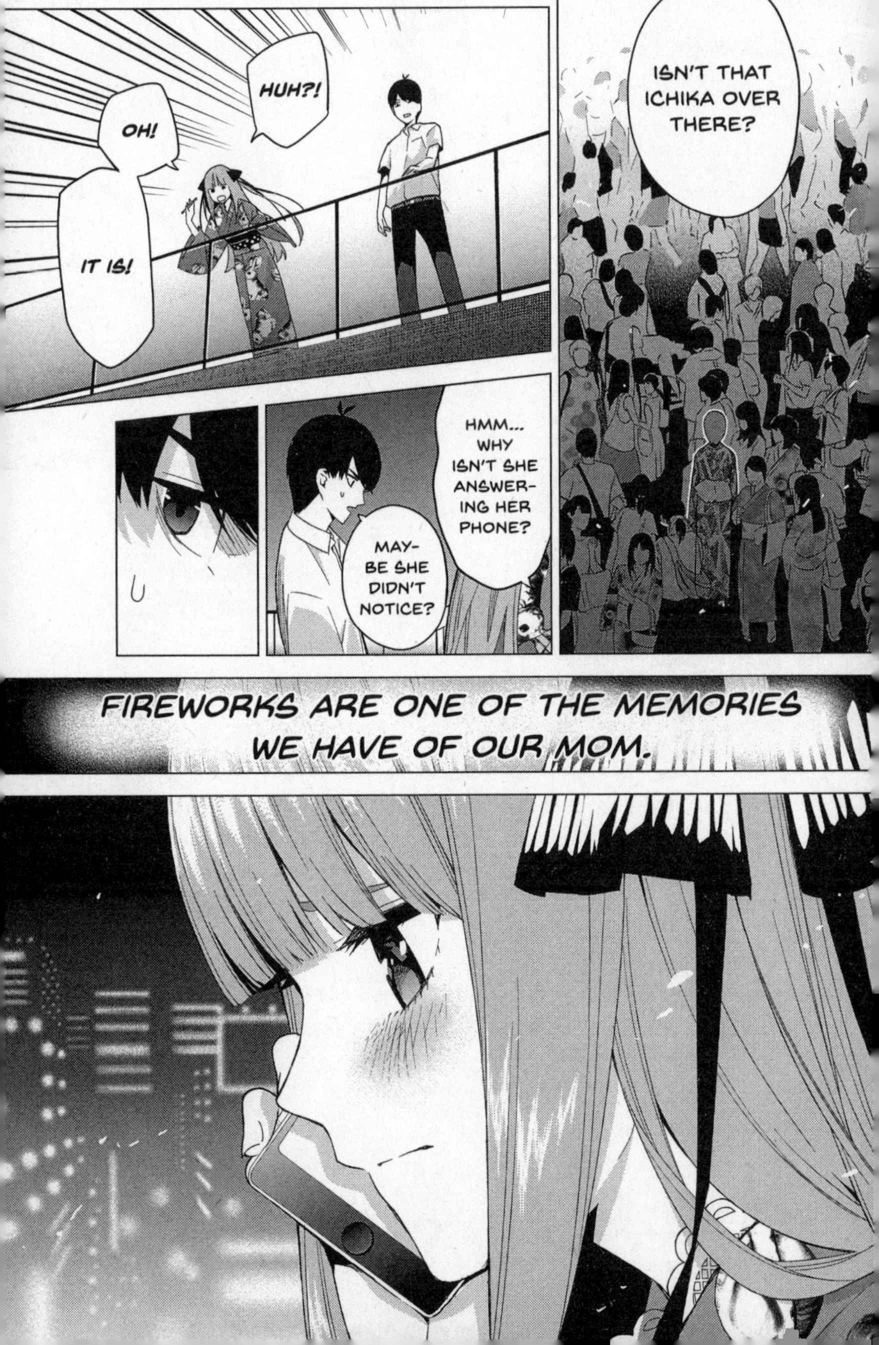
ISN'T THAT ICHIKA OVER THERE?
HUH?!
OH!
IT IS!
HMM... WHY ISN'T SHE ANSWERING HER PHONE?
MAY-BE SHE DIDN'T NOTICE?
FIREWORKS ARE ONE OF THE MEMORIES WE HAVE OF OUR MOM.

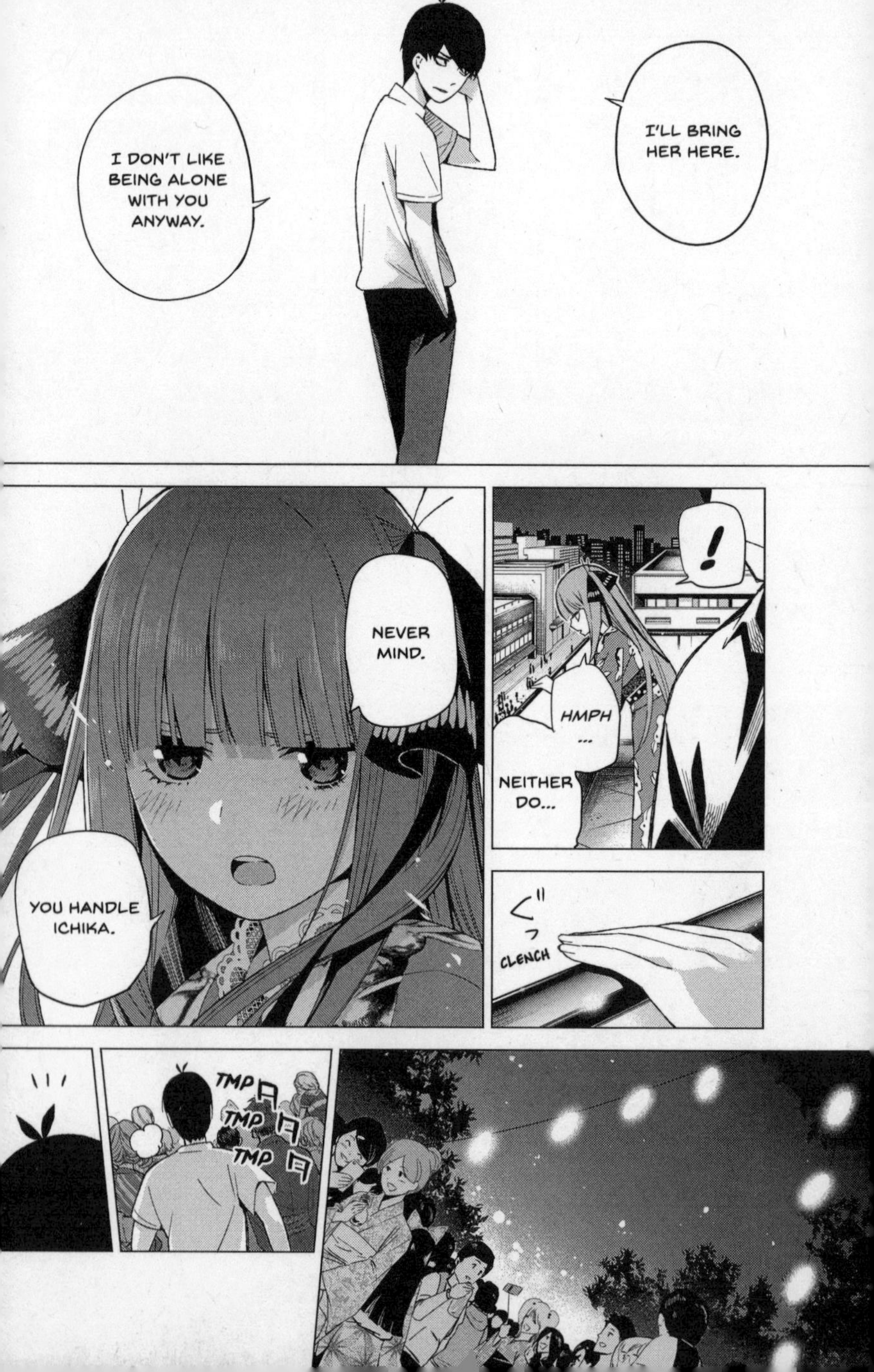
I'LL BRING HER HERE.
I DON'T LIKE BEING ALONE WITH YOU ANYWAY.
!
HMPH...
NEITHER DO...
CLENCH
NEVER MIND.
YOU HANDLE ICHIKA.
TMP
TMP
TMP

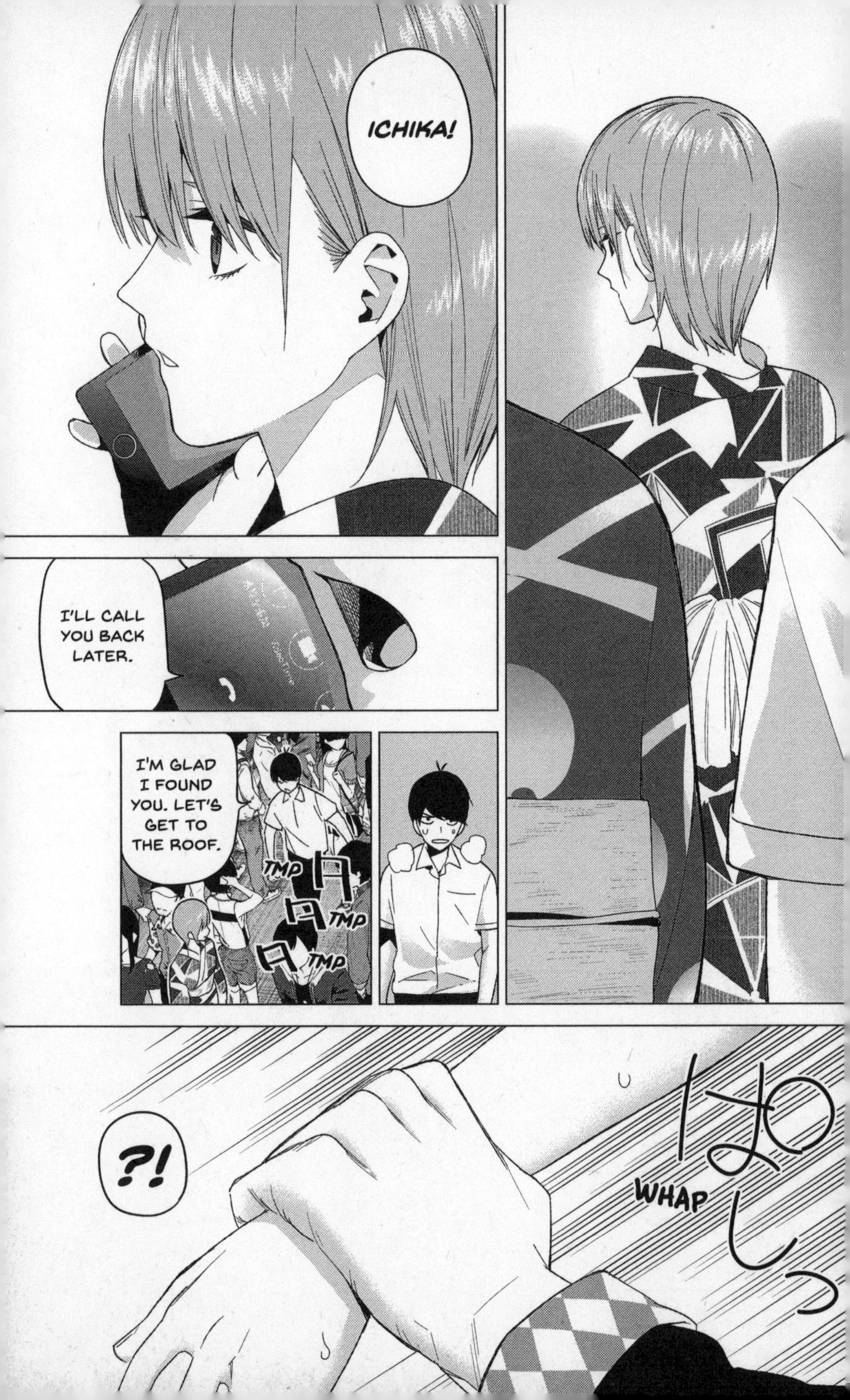
ICHIKA!
I'LL CALL YOU BACK LATER.
I'M GLAD I FOUND YOU. LET'S GET TO THE ROOF.
TMP
TMP
TMP
はしっ
WHAP
?!

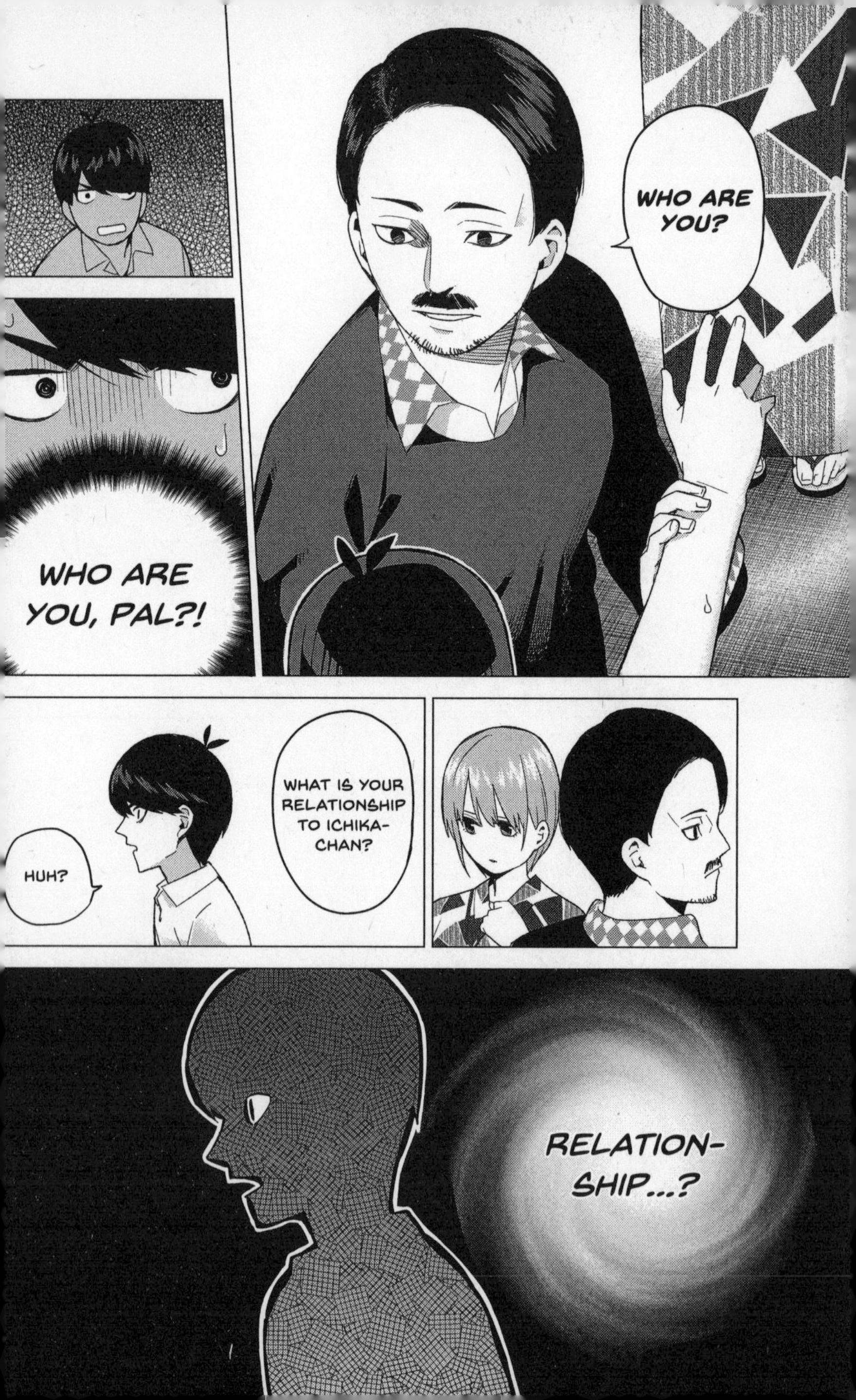
WHO ARE YOU?
WHO ARE YOU, PAL?!
WHAT IS YOUR RELATIONSHIP TO ICHIKA-CHAN?
HUH?
RELATION-SHIP...?

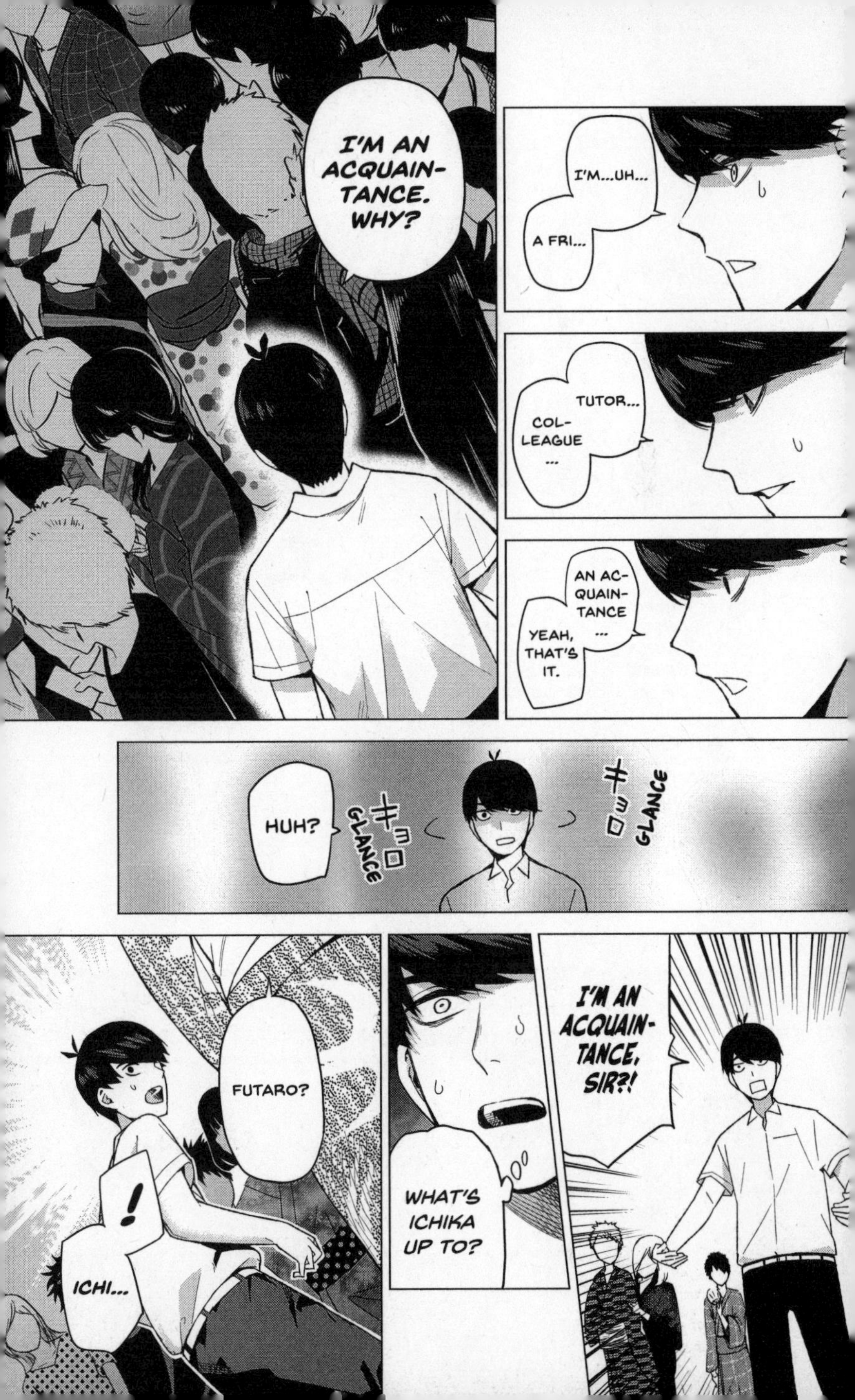
I'M...UH...
A FRI...
TUTOR...
COLLEAGUE...
AN ACQUAINTANCE...
YEAH, THAT'S IT.
I'M AN ACQUAINTANCE. WHY?
キョロ GLANCE
キョロ GLANCE
HUH?
I'M AN ACQUAINTANCE, SIR?!
WHAT'S ICHIKA UP TO?
FUTARO?
!
ICHI...

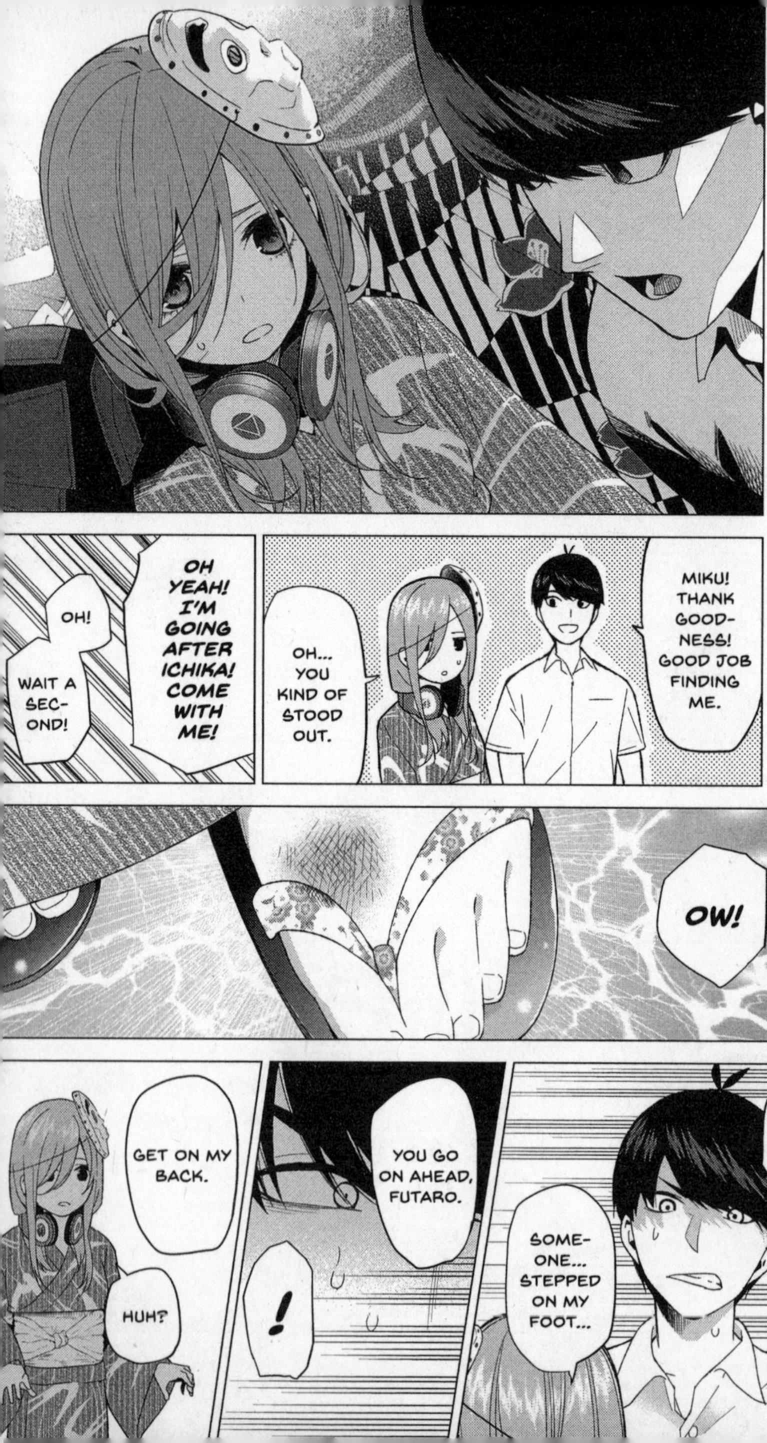
MIKU! THANK GOODNESS! GOOD JOB FINDING ME.
OH... YOU KIND OF STOOD OUT.
OH YEAH! I'M GOING AFTER ICHIKA! COME WITH ME!
OH!
WAIT A SEC-OND!
OW!
!
SOME-ONE... STEPPED ON MY FOOT...
YOU GO ON AHEAD, FUTARO.
!
GET ON MY BACK.
HUH?

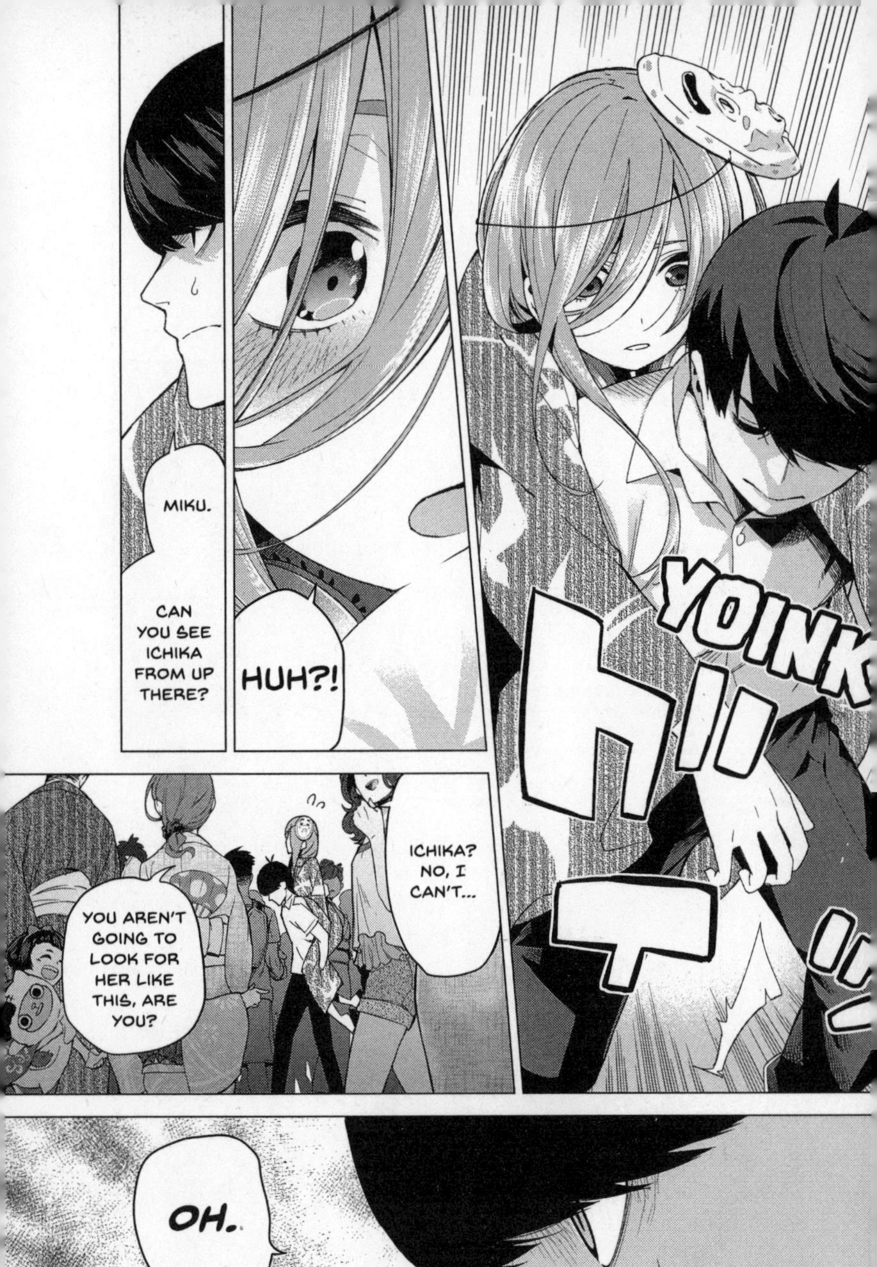
YOINK
HUH?!
MIKU.
CAN YOU SEE ICHIKA FROM UP THERE?
ICHIKA? NO, I CAN'T...
YOU AREN'T GOING TO LOOK FOR HER LIKE THIS, ARE YOU?
OH.

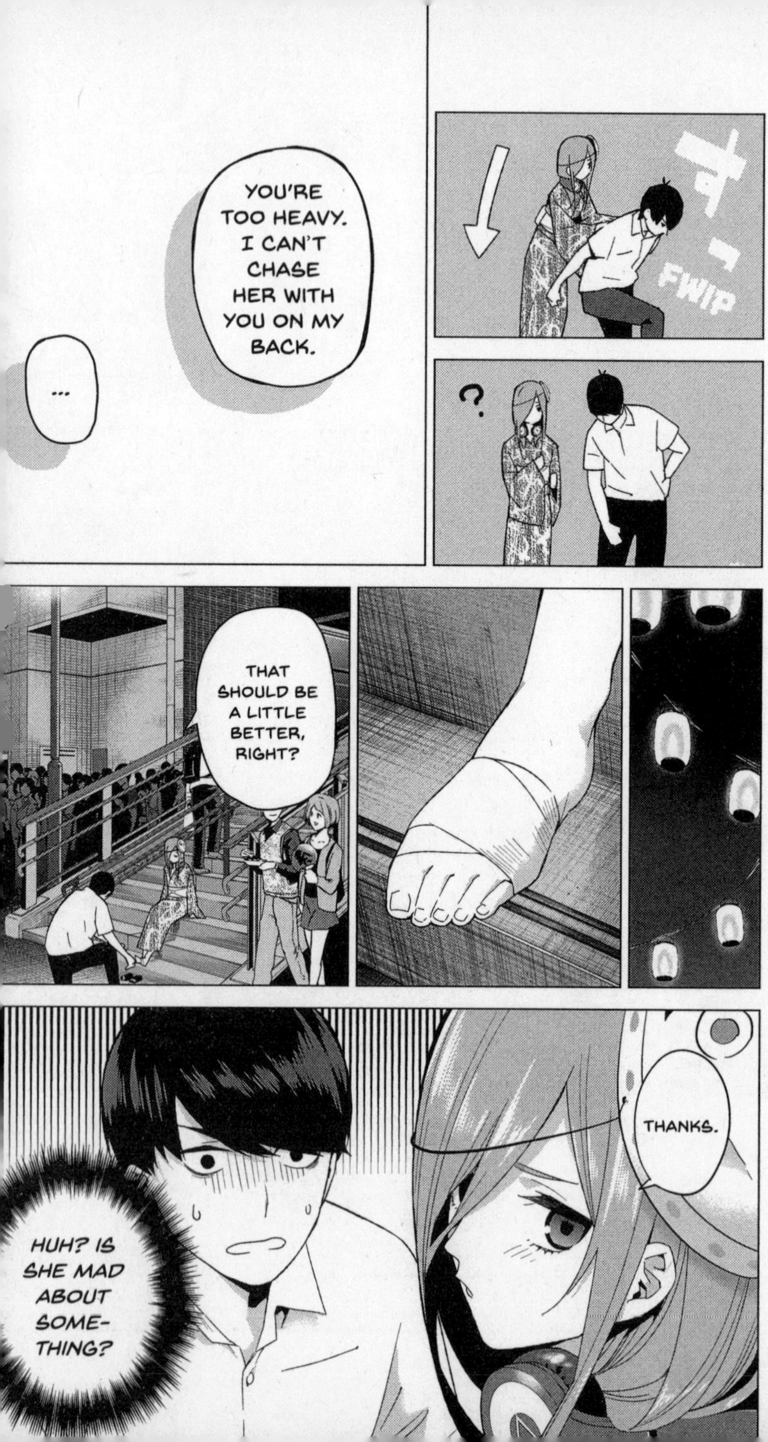
FWIP
?
YOU'RE TOO HEAVY. I CAN'T CHASE HER WITH YOU ON MY BACK.
...
THAT SHOULD BE A LITTLE BETTER, RIGHT?
THANKS.
HUH? IS SHE MAD ABOUT SOME-THING?

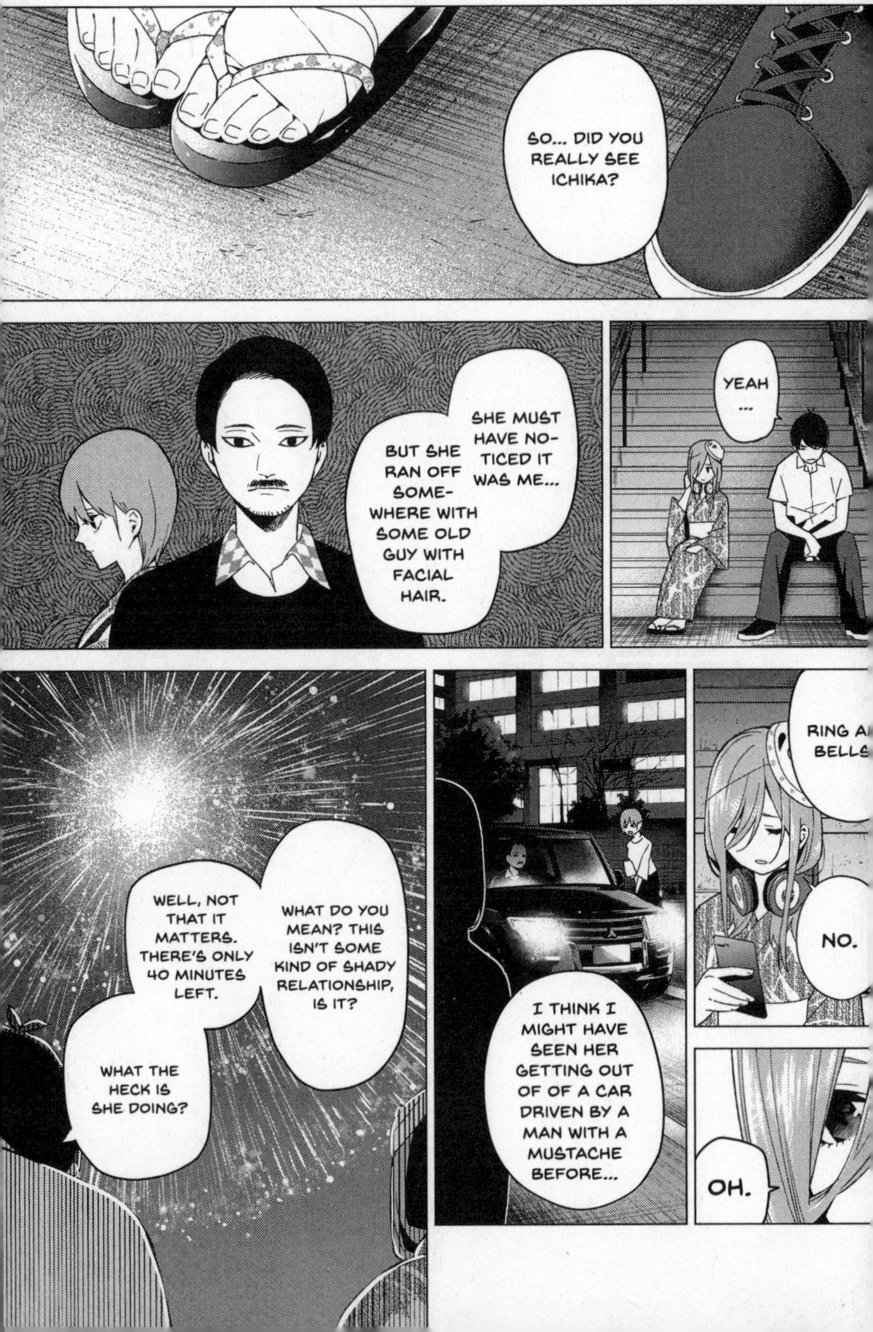
SO... DID YOU REALLY SEE ICHIKA?
YEAH ...
SHE MUST HAVE NO-TICED IT WAS ME...
BUT SHE RAN OFF SOME-WHERE WITH SOME OLD GUY WITH FACIAL HAIR.
RING A BELLS
NO.
OH.
I THINK I MIGHT HAVE SEEN HER GETTING OUT OF OF A CAR DRIVEN BY A MAN WITH A MUSTACHE BEFORE...
WHAT DO YOU MEAN? THIS ISN'T SOME KIND OF SHADY RELATIONSHIP, IS IT?
WELL, NOT THAT IT MATTERS. THERE'S ONLY 40 MINUTES LEFT.
WHAT THE HECK IS SHE DOING?

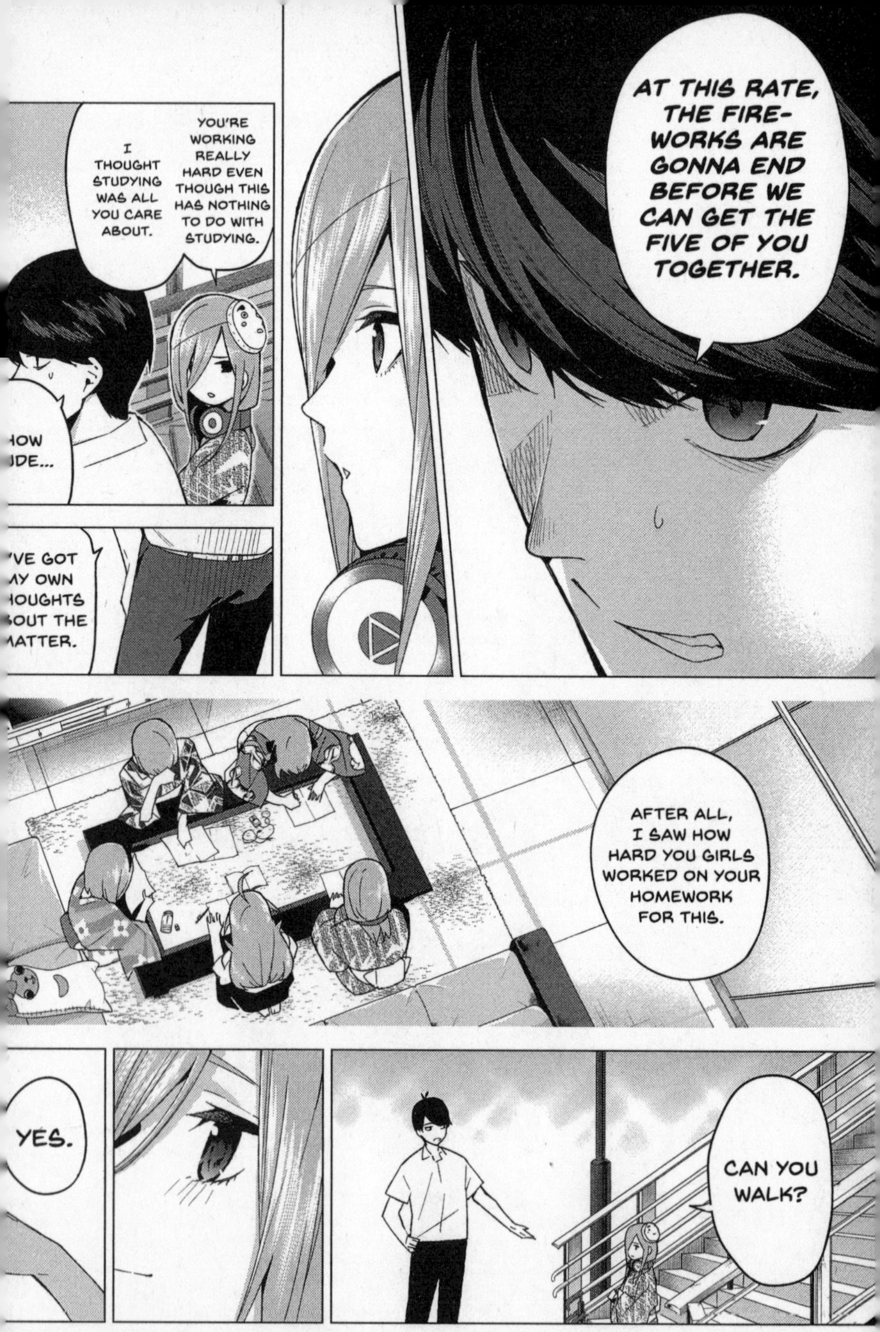
AT THIS RATE, THE FIRE-WORKS ARE GONNA END BEFORE WE CAN GET THE FIVE OF YOU TOGETHER.
YOU'RE WORKING REALLY HARD EVEN THOUGH THIS HAS NOTHING TO DO WITH STUDYING.
I THOUGHT STUDYING WAS ALL YOU CARE ABOUT.
HOW UDE...
'VE GOT MY OWN HOUGHTS BOUT THE MATTER.
AFTER ALL, I SAW HOW HARD YOU GIRLS WORKED ON YOUR HOMEWORK FOR THIS.
CAN YOU WALK?
YES.

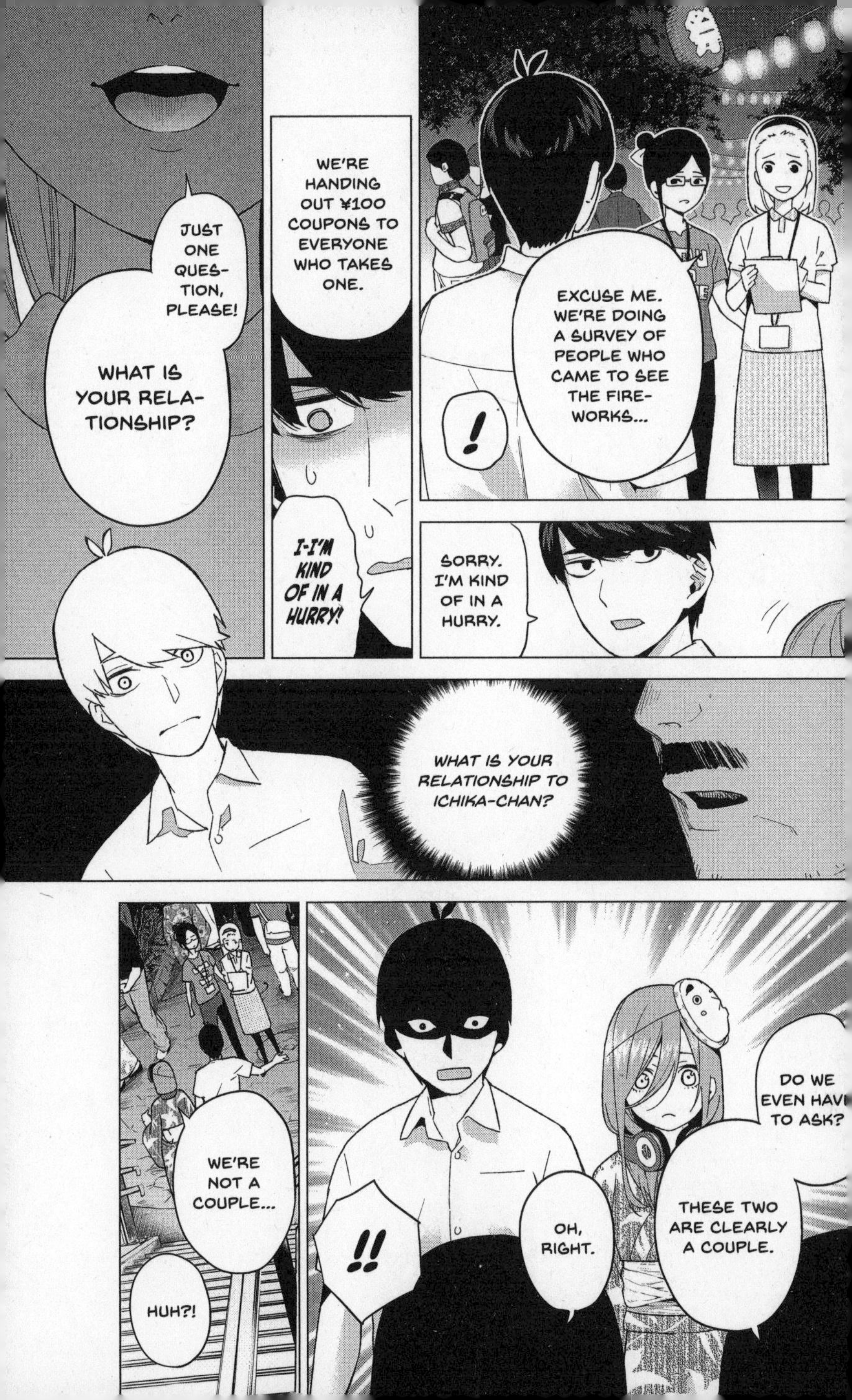
EXCUSE ME. WE'RE DOING A SURVEY OF PEOPLE WHO CAME TO SEE THE FIRE-WORKS...
!
SORRY. I'M KIND OF IN A HURRY.
WE'RE HANDING OUT ¥100 COUPONS TO EVERYONE WHO TAKES ONE.
I-I'M KIND OF IN A HURRY!
JUST ONE QUES-TION, PLEASE!
WHAT IS YOUR RELA-TIONSHIP?
WHAT IS YOUR RELATIONSHIP TO ICHIKA-CHAN?
DO WE EVEN HAVE TO ASK?
THESE TWO ARE CLEARLY A COUPLE.
OH, RIGHT.
!!
WE'RE NOT A COUPLE...
HUH?!

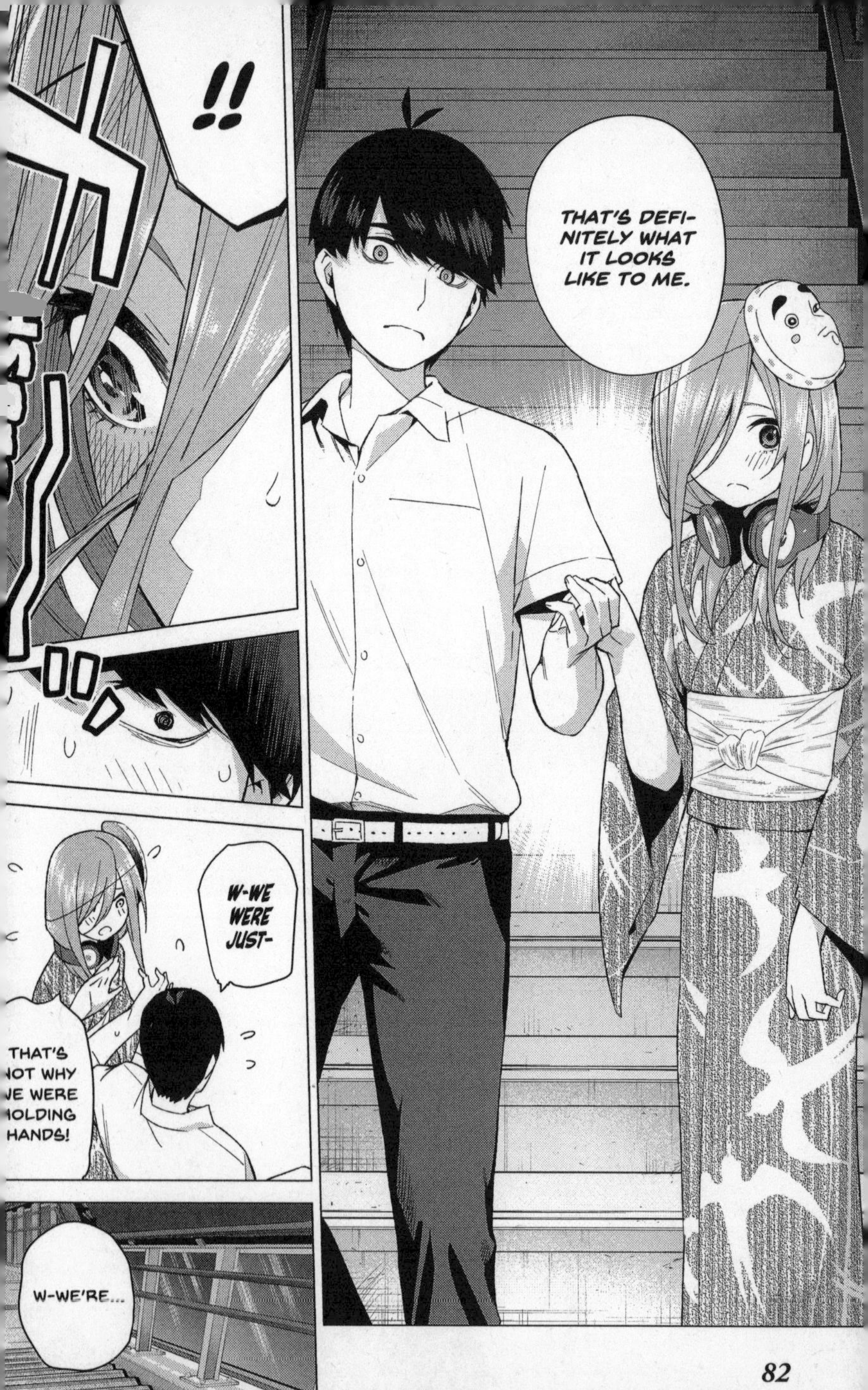
THAT'S DEFINITELY WHAT IT LOOKS LIKE TO ME.
!!
W-WE WERE JUST-
THAT'S NOT WHY WE WERE HOLDING HANDS!
W-WE'RE...

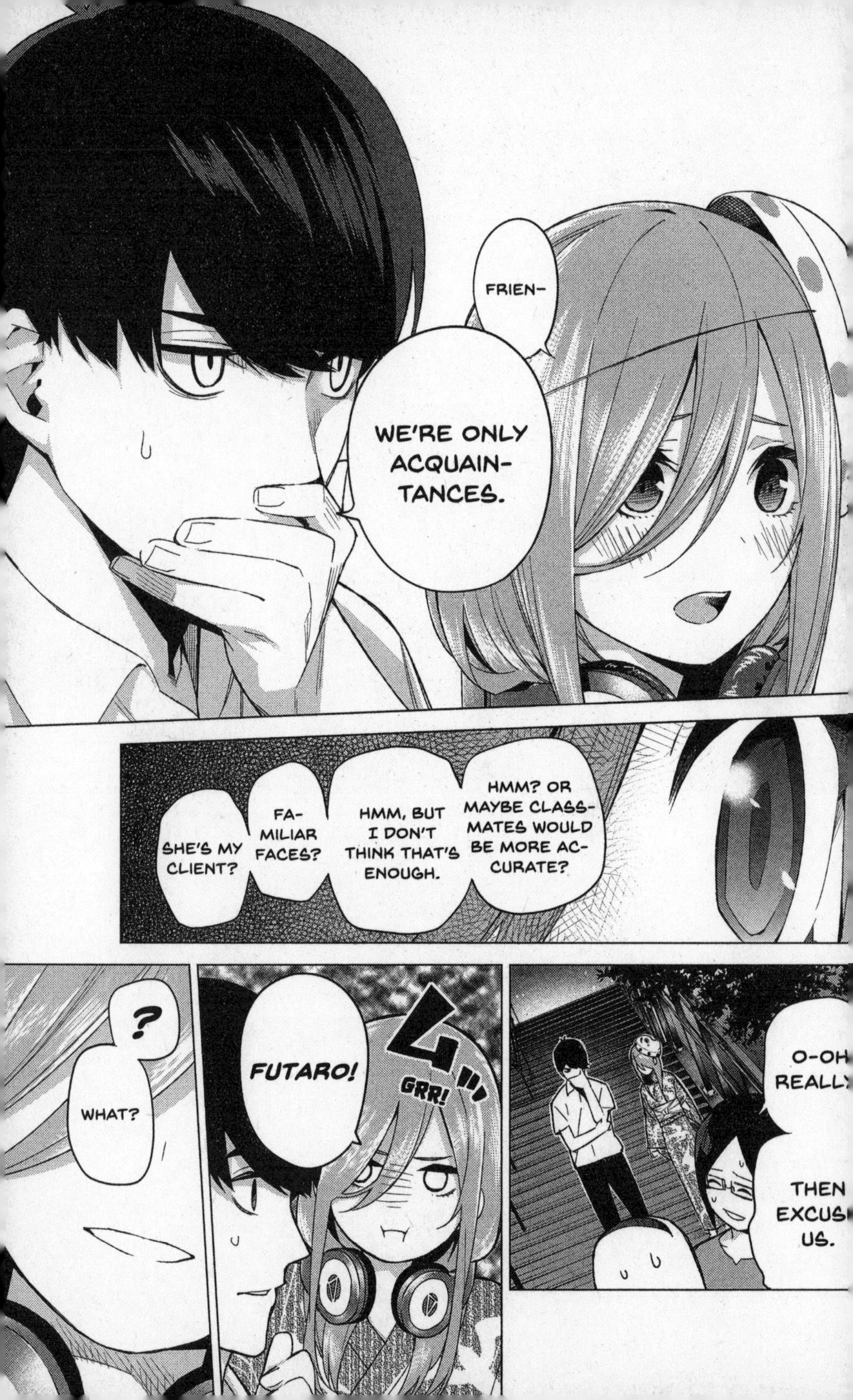
FRIEN-
WE'RE ONLY ACQUAINTANCES.
HMM? OR MAYBE CLASSMATES WOULD BE MORE ACCURATE?
HMM, BUT I DON'T THINK THAT'S ENOUGH.
FAMILIAR FACES?
SHE'S MY CLIENT?
O-OH REALLY
THEN EXCUS US.
FUTARO!
GRR!
?
WHAT?

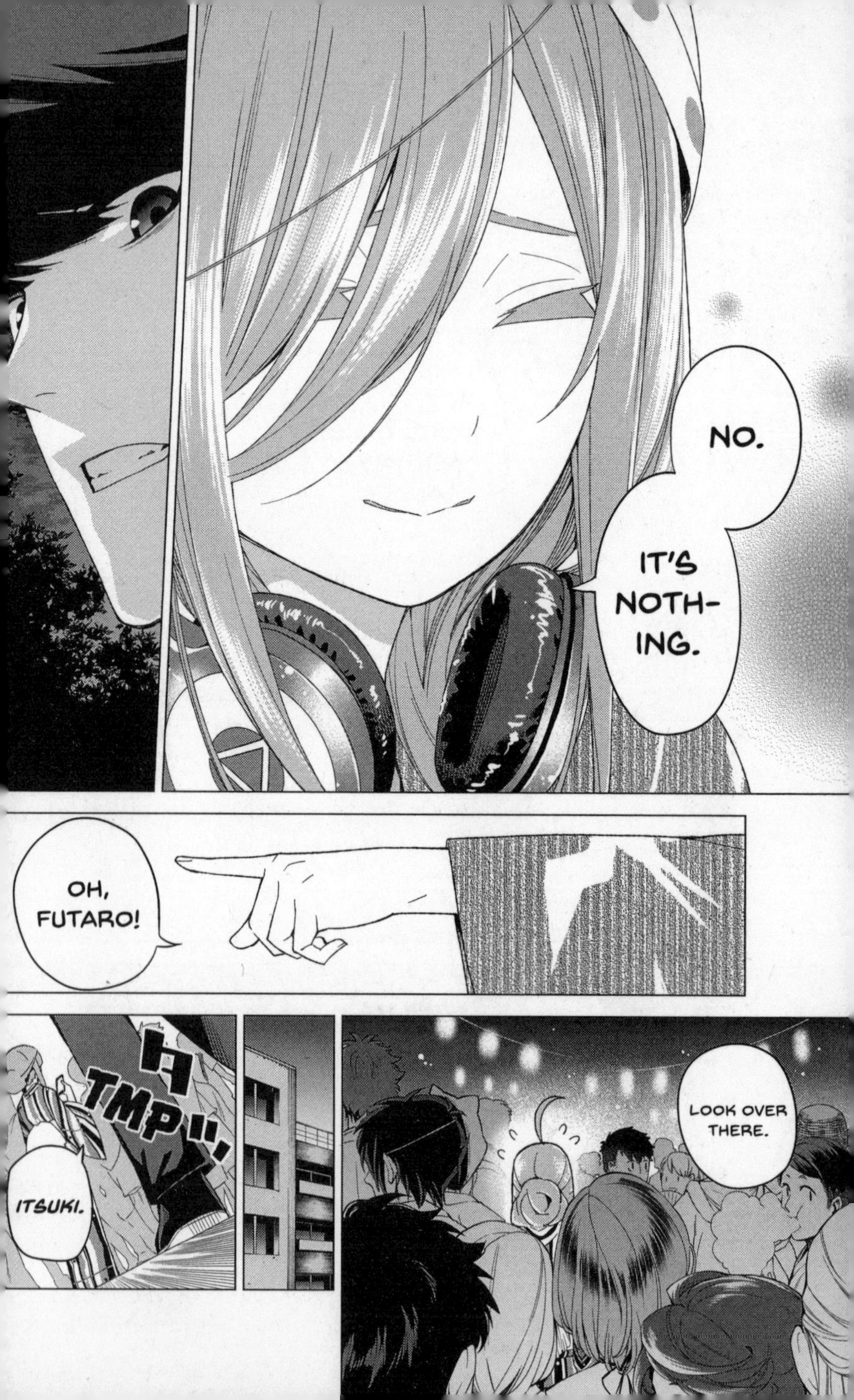
NO.
IT'S NOTHING.
OH, FUTARO!
LOOK OVER THERE.
TMP!!
ITSUKI.

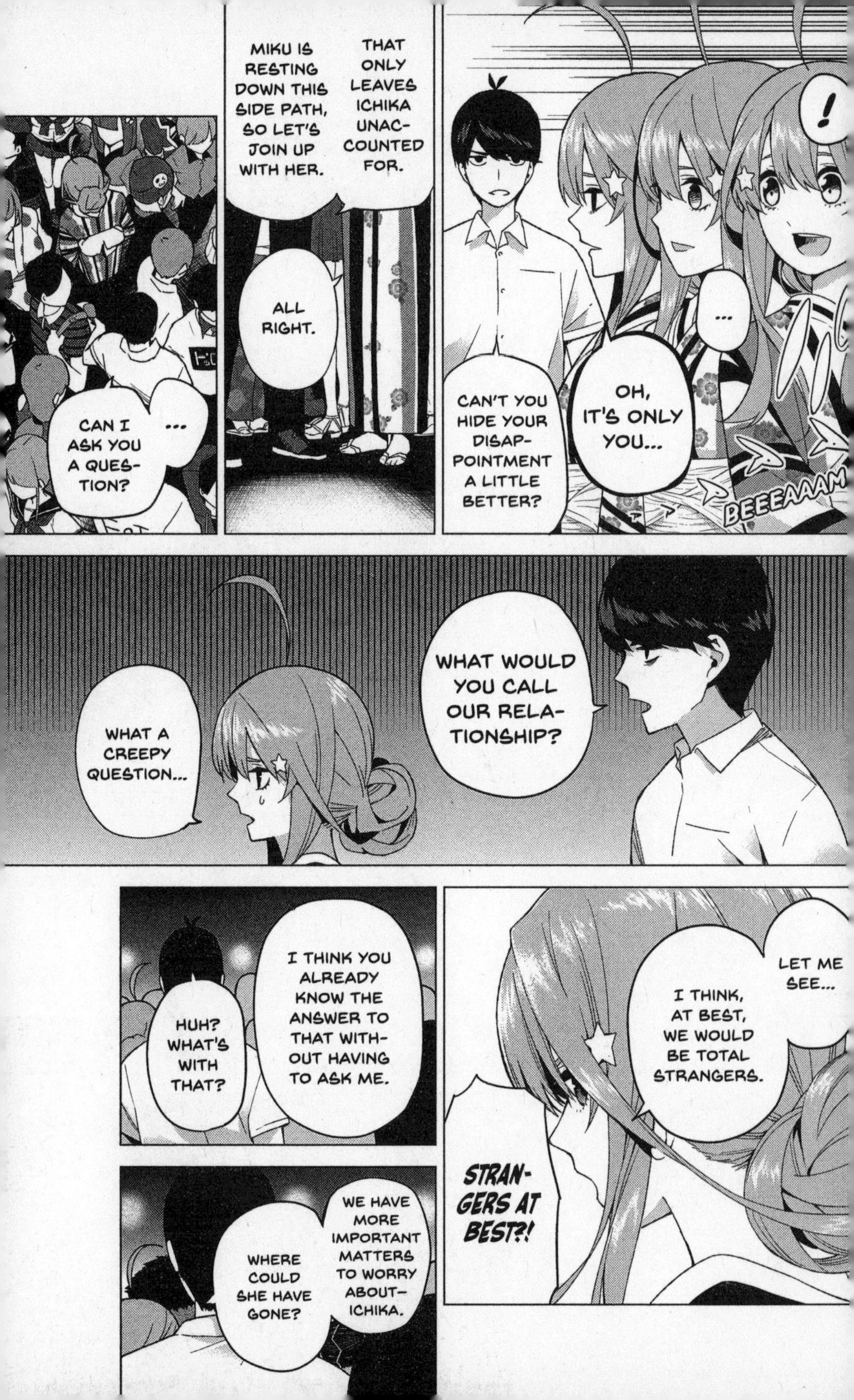
!
...
OH, IT'S ONLY YOU...
CAN'T YOU HIDE YOUR DISAPPOINTMENT A LITTLE BETTER?
BEEEAAAM
THAT ONLY LEAVES ICHIKA UNACCOUNTED FOR.
MIKU IS RESTING DOWN THIS SIDE PATH, SO LET'S JOIN UP WITH HER.
ALL RIGHT.
...
CAN I ASK YOU A QUESTION?
WHAT WOULD YOU CALL OUR RELATIONSHIP?
WHAT A CREEPY QUESTION...
LET ME SEE...
I THINK, AT BEST, WE WOULD BE TOTAL STRANGERS.
STRANGERS AT BEST?!
I THINK YOU ALREADY KNOW THE ANSWER TO THAT WITHOUT HAVING TO ASK ME.
HUH? WHAT'S WITH THAT?
WE HAVE MORE IMPORTANT MATTERS TO WORRY ABOUT—ICHIKA.
WHERE COULD SHE HAVE GONE?

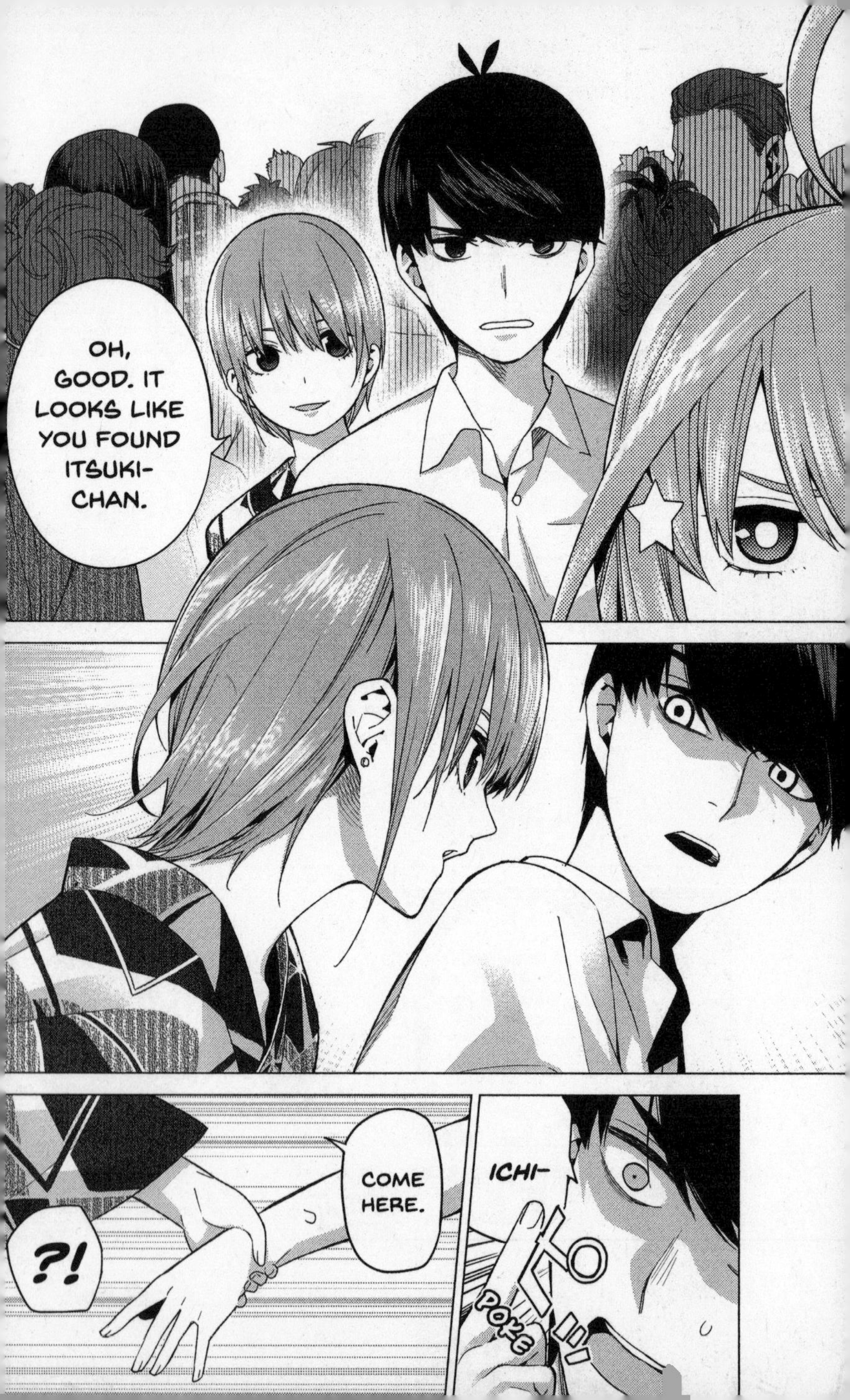
OH, GOOD. IT LOOKS LIKE YOU FOUND ITSUKI-CHAN.
ICHI-
POKE
COME HERE.
?!

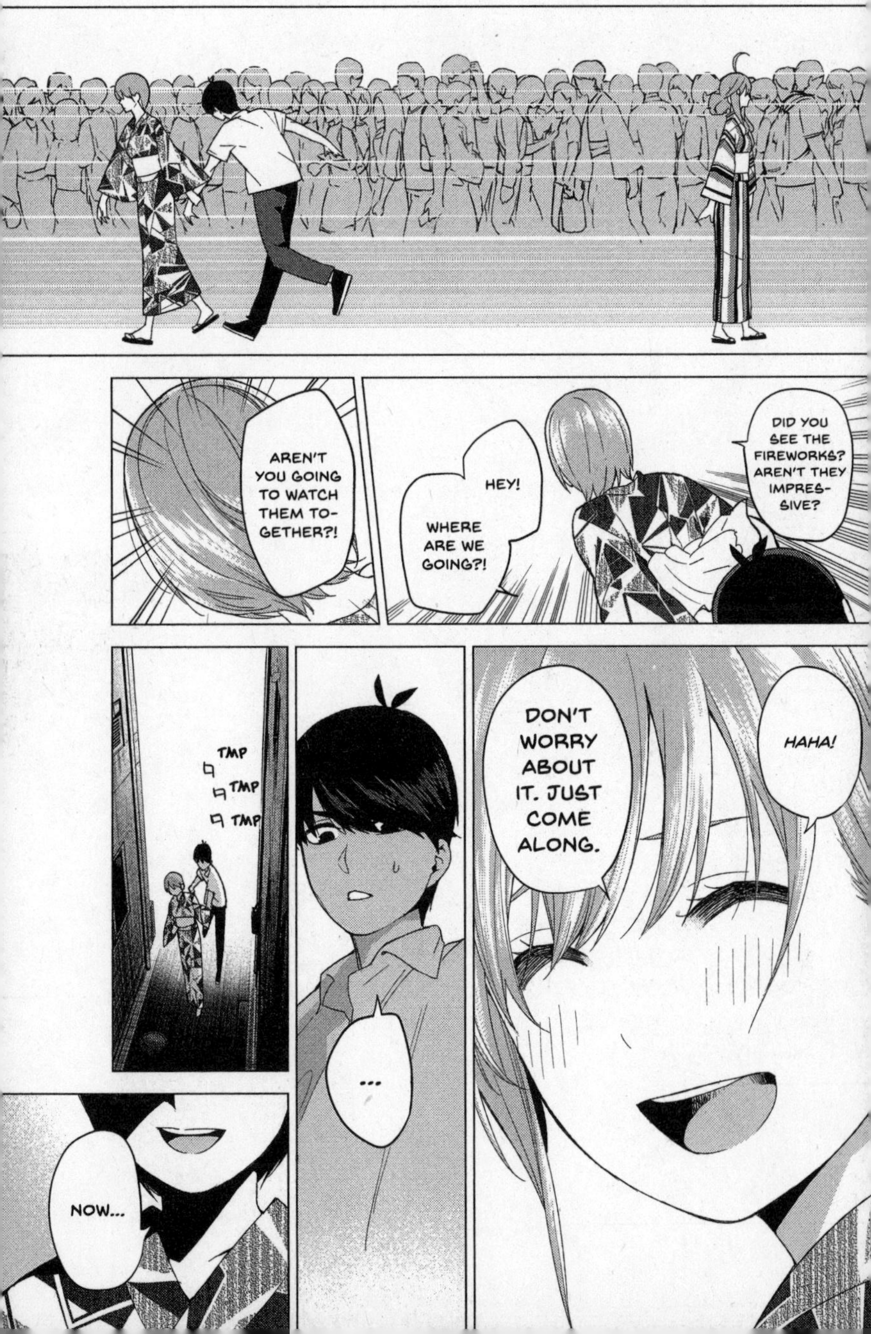
DID YOU SEE THE FIREWORKS? AREN'T THEY IMPRES-SIVE?
HEY!
WHERE ARE WE GOING?!
AREN'T YOU GOING TO WATCH THEM TO-GETHER?!
HAHA!
DON'T WORRY ABOUT IT. JUST COME ALONG.
...
TMP TMP TMP
NOW...

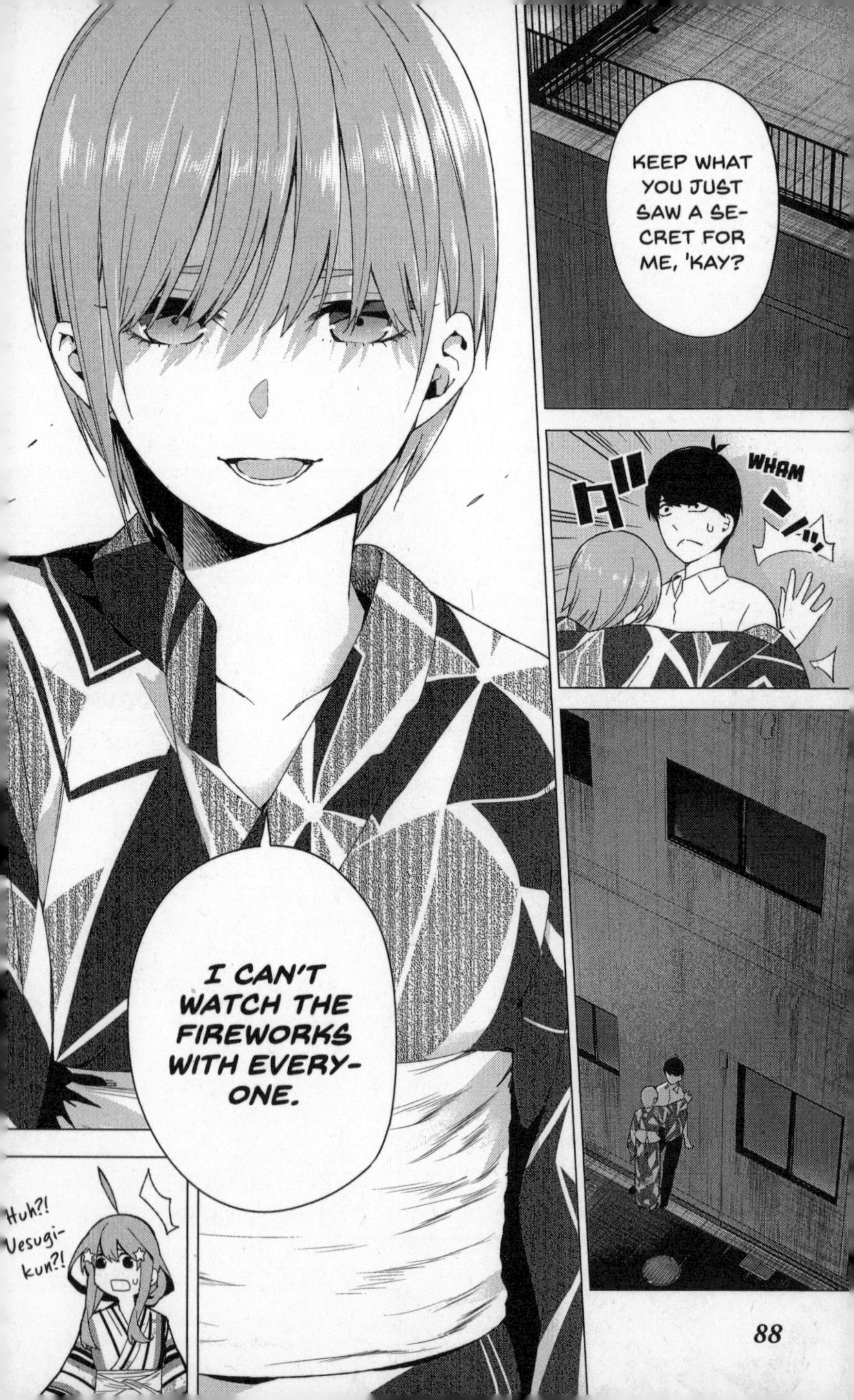
KEEP WHAT YOU JUST SAW A SE-CRET FOR ME, 'KAY?
WHAM
I CAN'T WATCH THE FIREWORKS WITH EVERY-ONE.
Huh?! Uesugi-kun?!

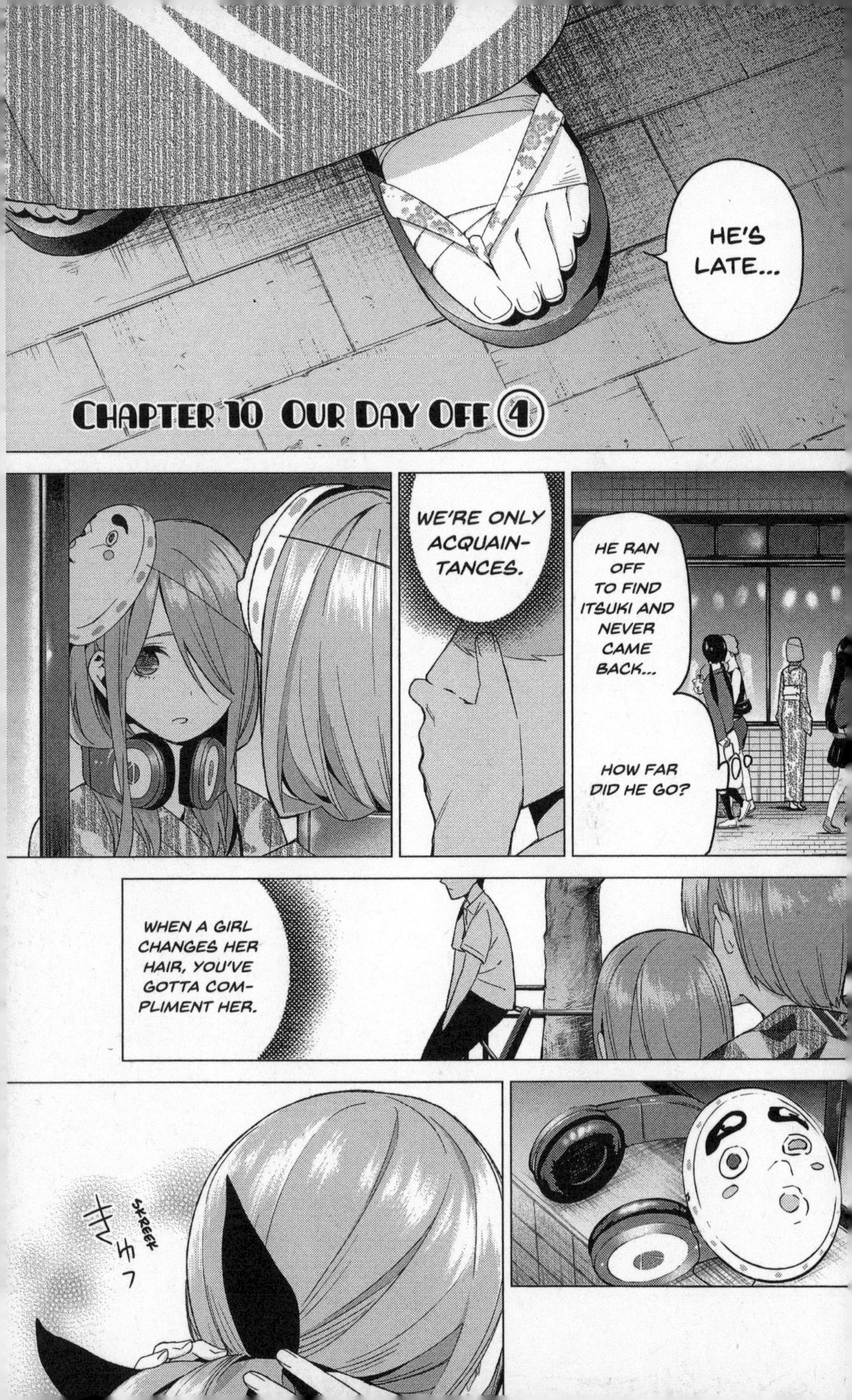
HE'S LATE...
CHAPTER 10 OUR DAY OFF ④
HE RAN OFF TO FIND ITSUKI AND NEVER CAME BACK...
HOW FAR DID HE GO?
WE'RE ONLY ACQUAIN-TANCES.
WHEN A GIRL CHANGES HER HAIR, YOU'VE GOTTA COM-PLIMENT HER.
きゅっ
SKREEK

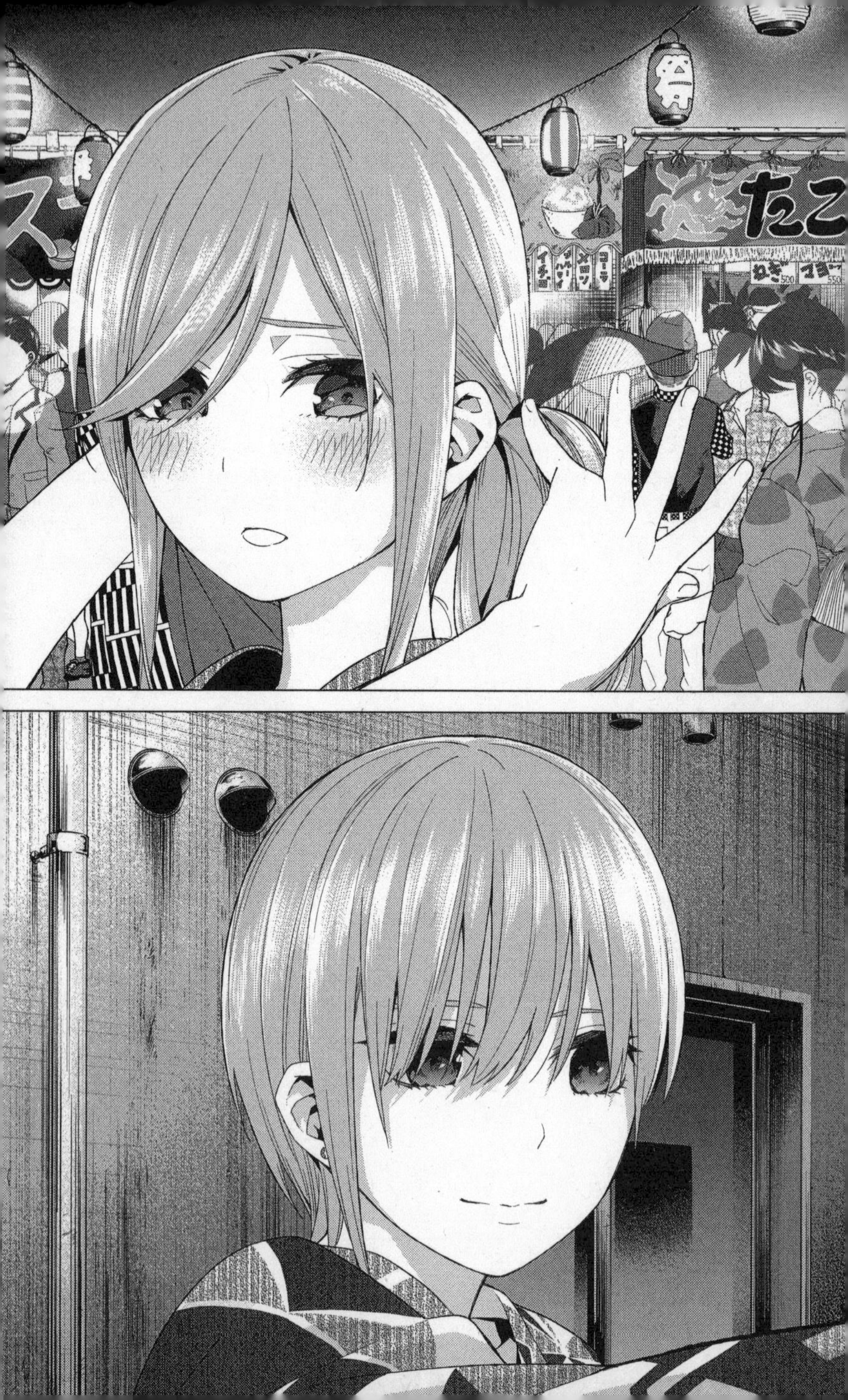
祭
たこ

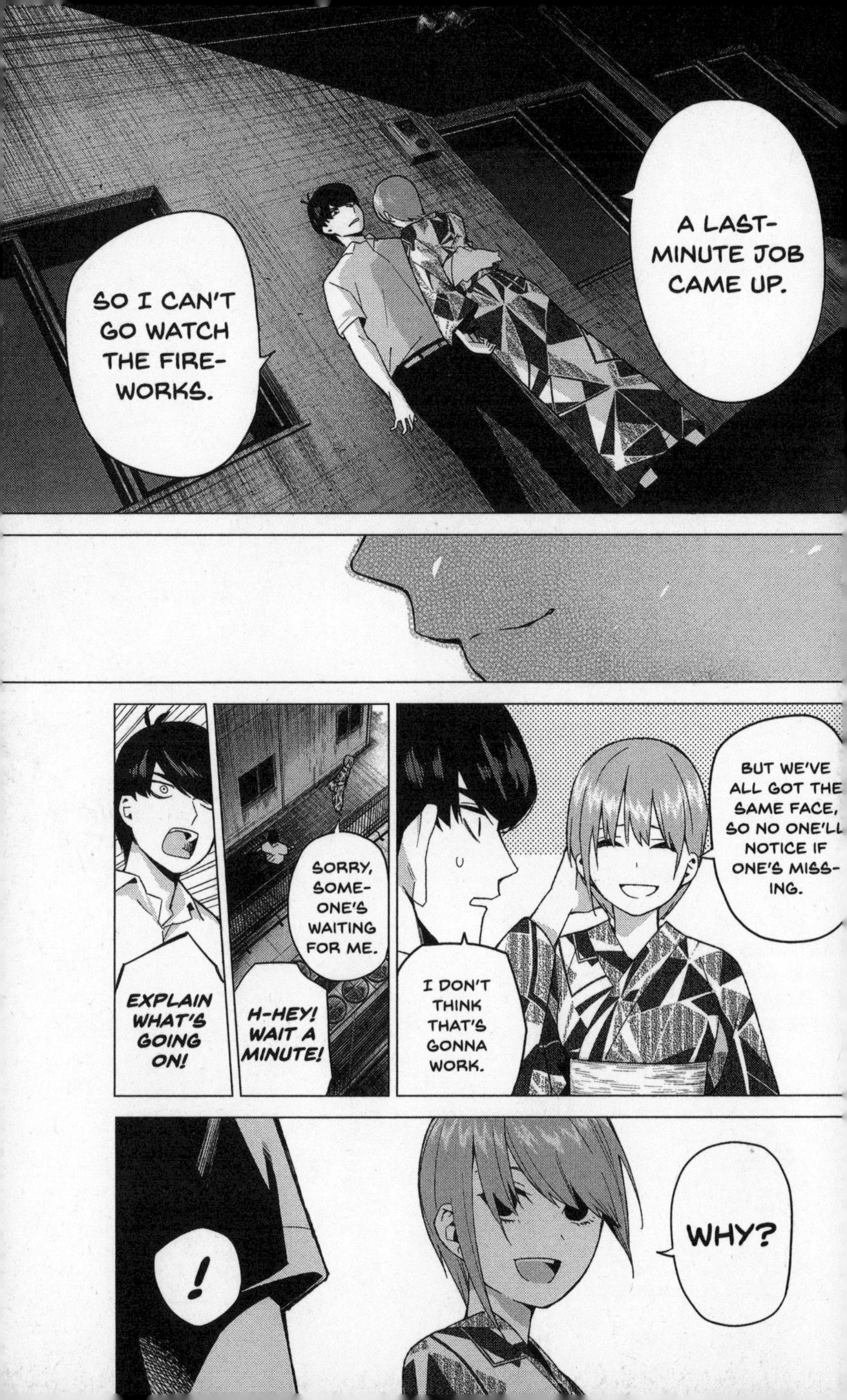
A LAST-MINUTE JOB CAME UP.
SO I CAN'T GO WATCH THE FIRE-WORKS.
BUT WE'VE ALL GOT THE SAME FACE, SO NO ONE'LL NOTICE IF ONE'S MISS-ING.
I DON'T THINK THAT'S GONNA WORK.
SORRY, SOME-ONE'S WAITING FOR ME.
H-HEY! WAIT A MINUTE!
EXPLAIN WHAT'S GOING ON!
WHY?
!

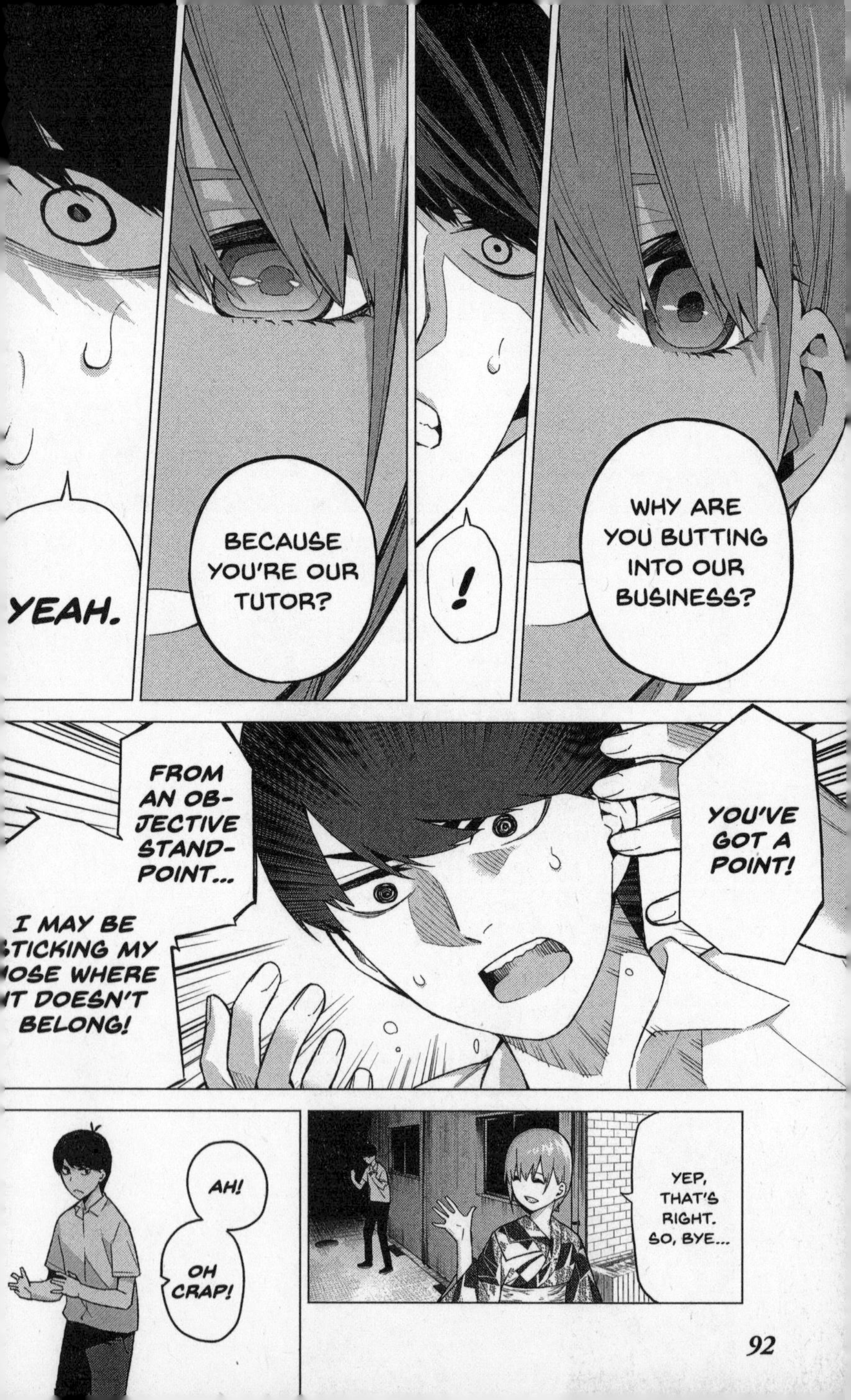
WHY ARE YOU BUTTING INTO OUR BUSINESS?
!
BECAUSE YOU'RE OUR TUTOR?
YEAH.
YOU'VE GOT A POINT!
FROM AN OBJECTIVE STANDPOINT...
I MAY BE TICKING MY OSE WHERE T DOESN'T BELONG!
YEP, THAT'S RIGHT. SO, BYE...
AH!
OH CRAP!

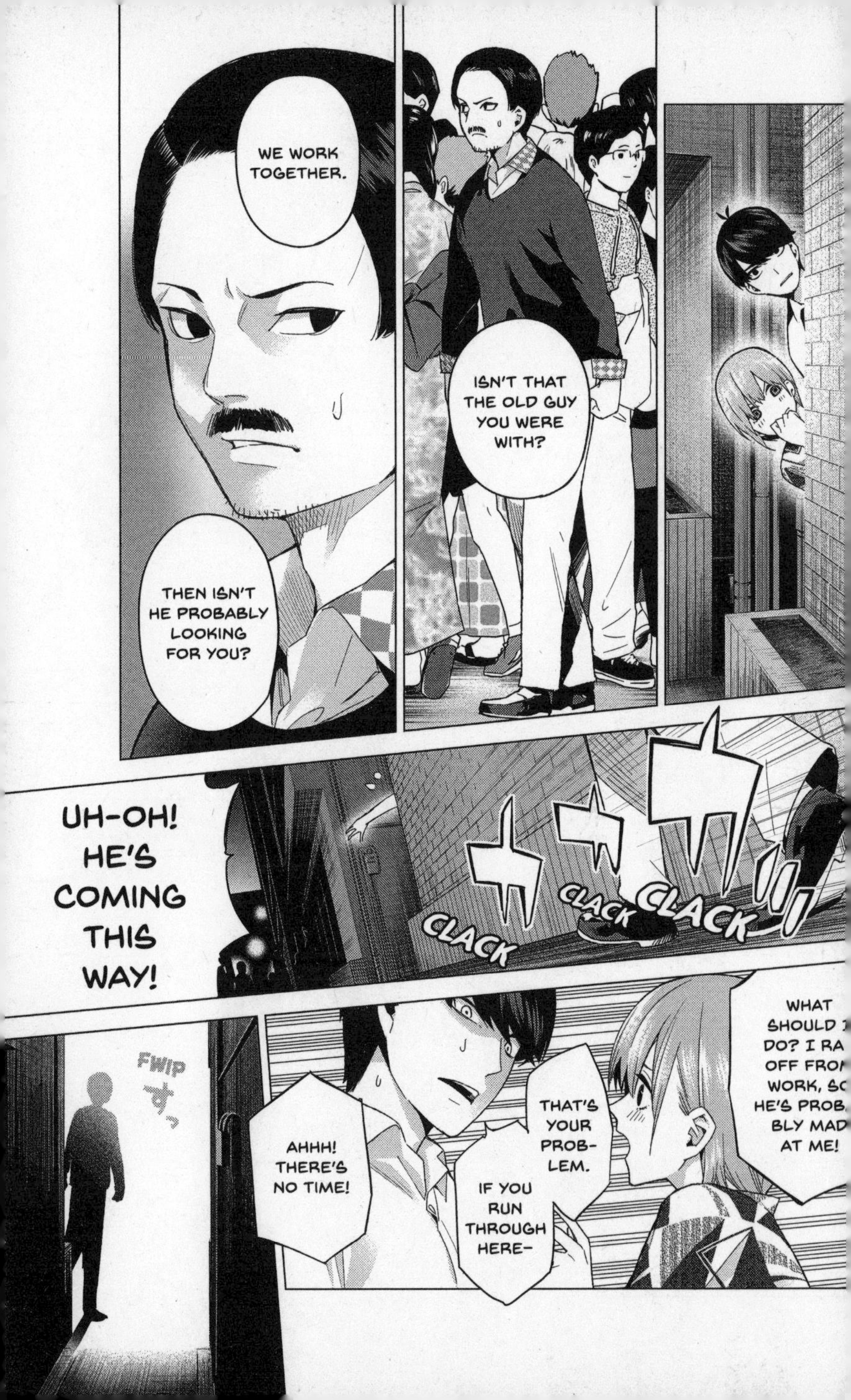
ISN'T THAT THE OLD GUY YOU WERE WITH?
WE WORK TOGETHER.
THEN ISN'T HE PROBABLY LOOKING FOR YOU?
CLACK
CLACK
CLACK
UH-OH! HE'S COMING THIS WAY!
WHAT SHOULD I DO? I RA OFF FROM WORK, SO HE'S PROBA- BLY MAD AT ME!
THAT'S YOUR PROB- LEM.
IF YOU RUN THROUGH HERE-
AHHH! THERE'S NO TIME!
FWIP
すっ

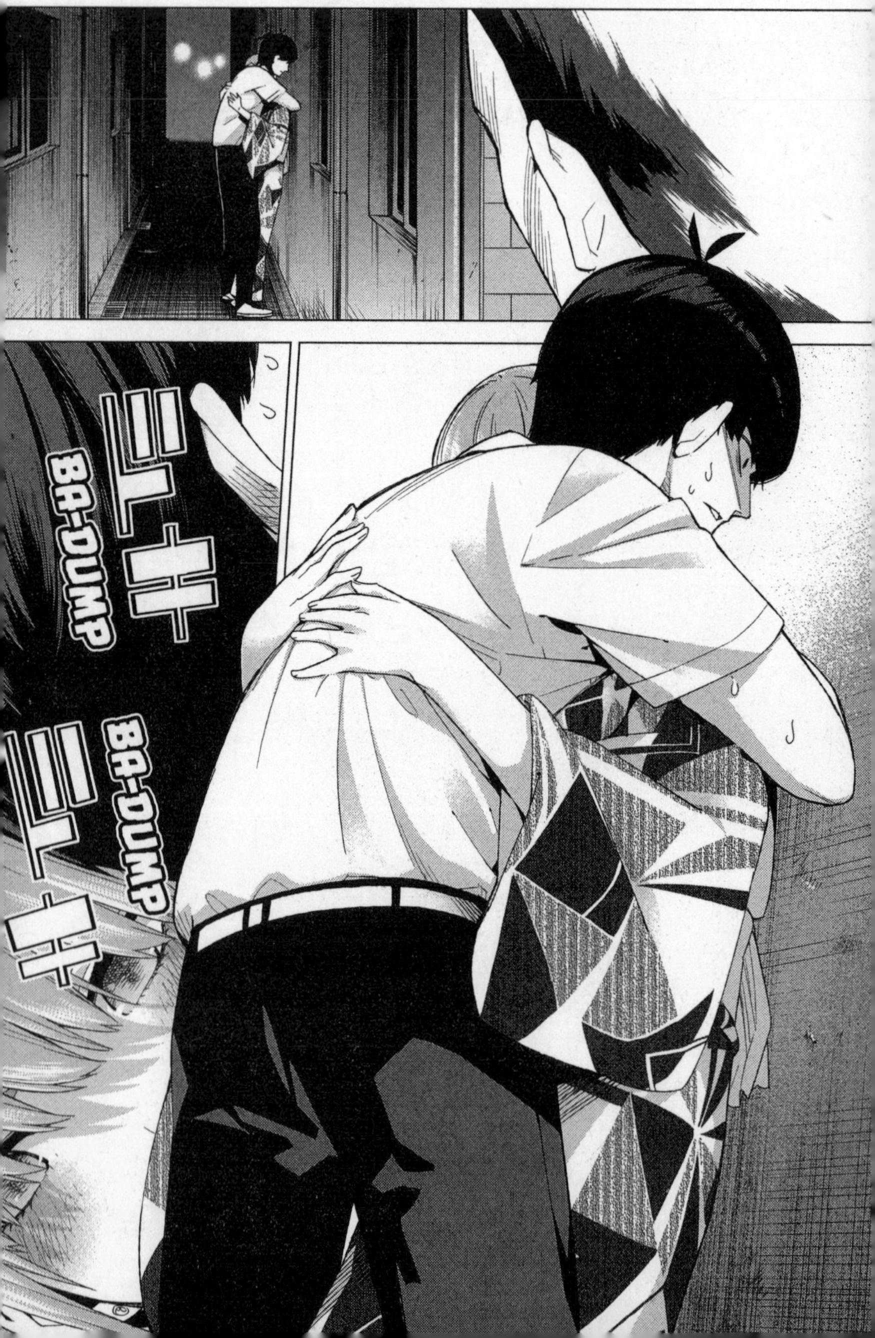
BA-DUMP
BA-DUMP

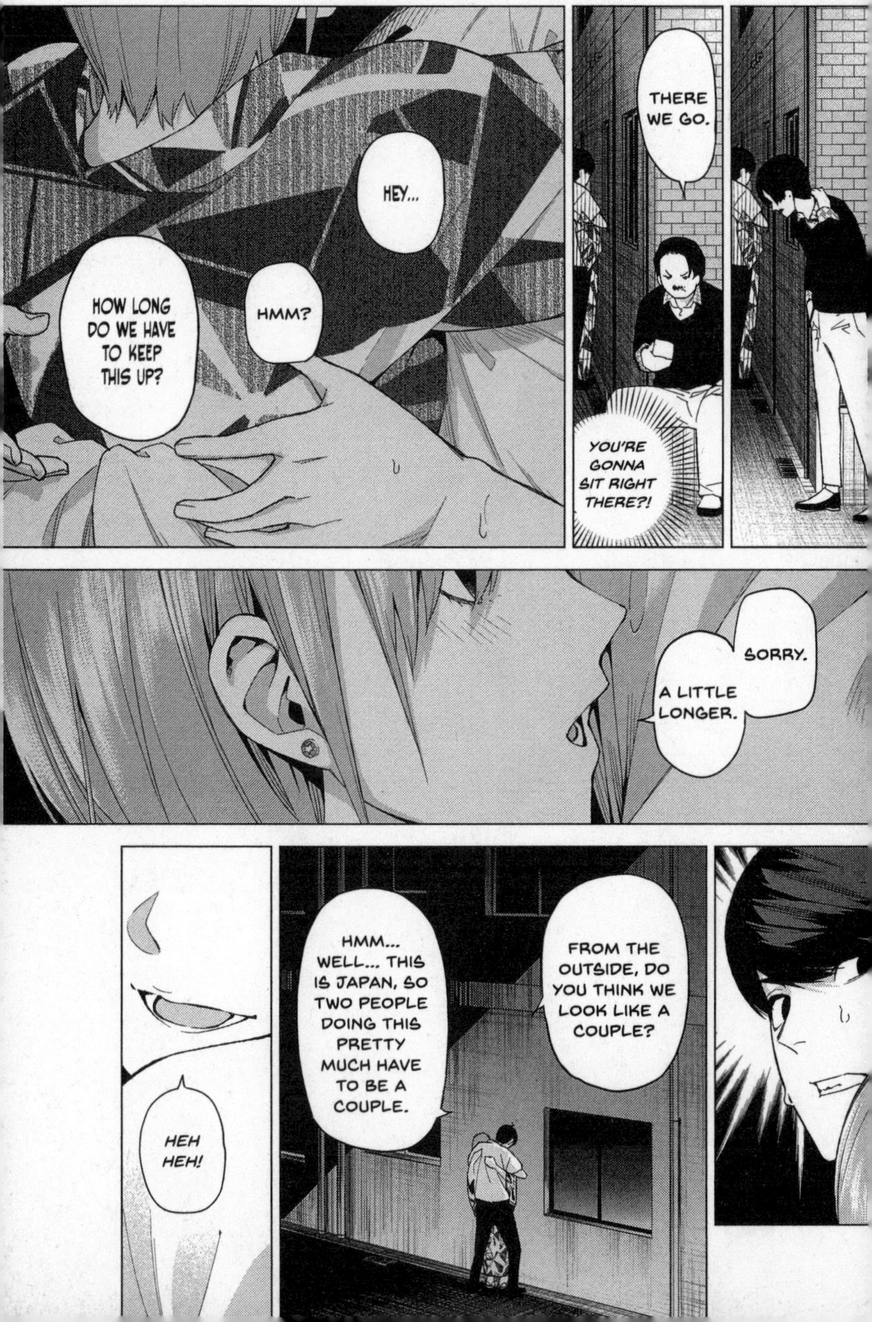
THERE WE GO.
YOU'RE GONNA SIT RIGHT THERE?!
HEY...
HMM?
HOW LONG DO WE HAVE TO KEEP THIS UP?
SORRY.
A LITTLE LONGER.
FROM THE OUTSIDE, DO YOU THINK WE LOOK LIKE A COUPLE?
HMM... WELL... THIS IS JAPAN, SO TWO PEOPLE DOING THIS PRETTY MUCH HAVE TO BE A COUPLE.
HEH HEH!

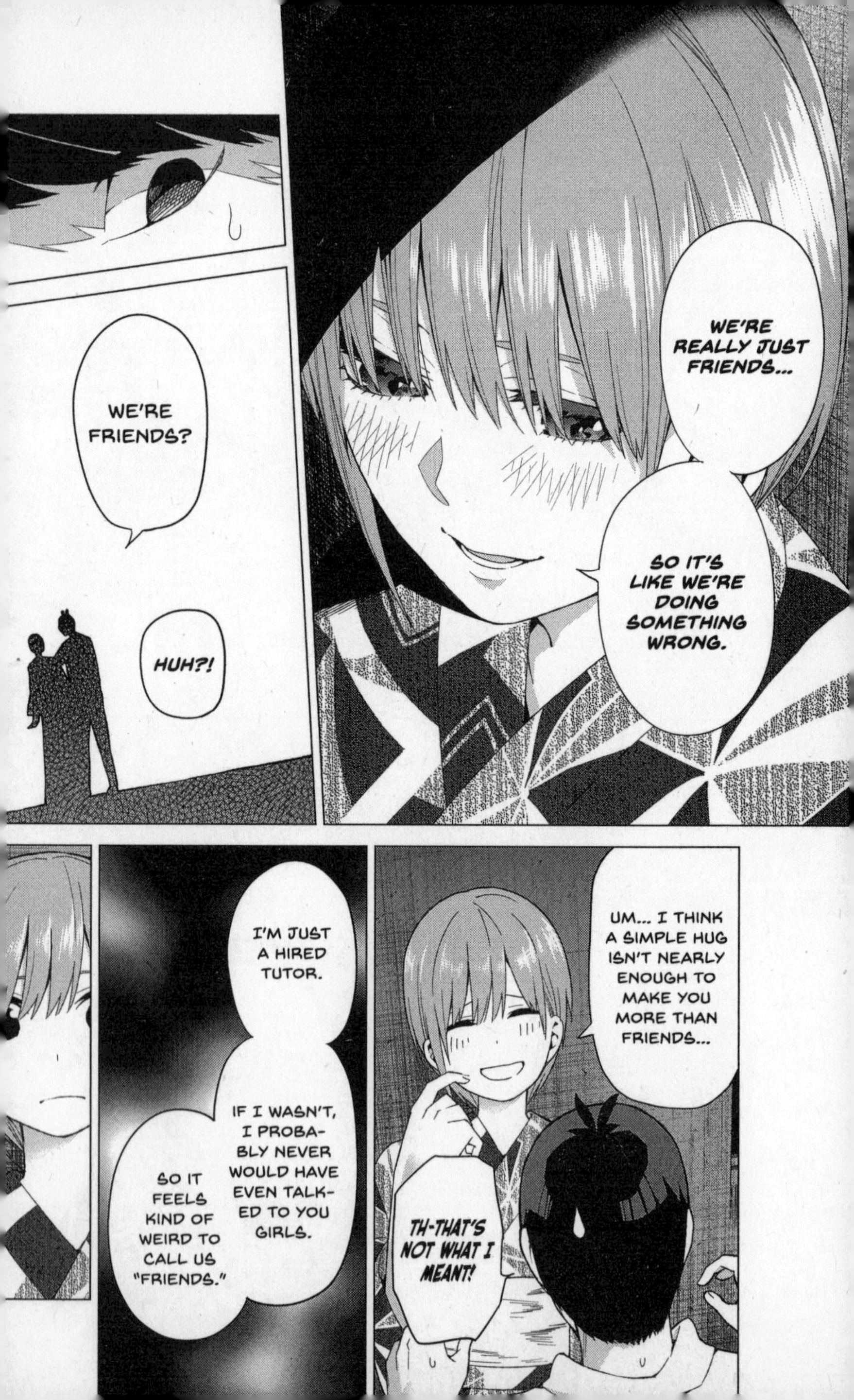
WE'RE REALLY JUST FRIENDS...
SO IT'S LIKE WE'RE DOING SOMETHING WRONG.
WE'RE FRIENDS?
HUH?!
UM... I THINK A SIMPLE HUG ISN'T NEARLY ENOUGH TO MAKE YOU MORE THAN FRIENDS...
TH-THAT'S NOT WHAT I MEANT!
I'M JUST A HIRED TUTOR.
IF I WASN'T, I PROBABLY NEVER WOULD HAVE EVEN TALKED TO YOU GIRLS.
SO IT FEELS KIND OF WEIRD TO CALL US "FRIENDS."

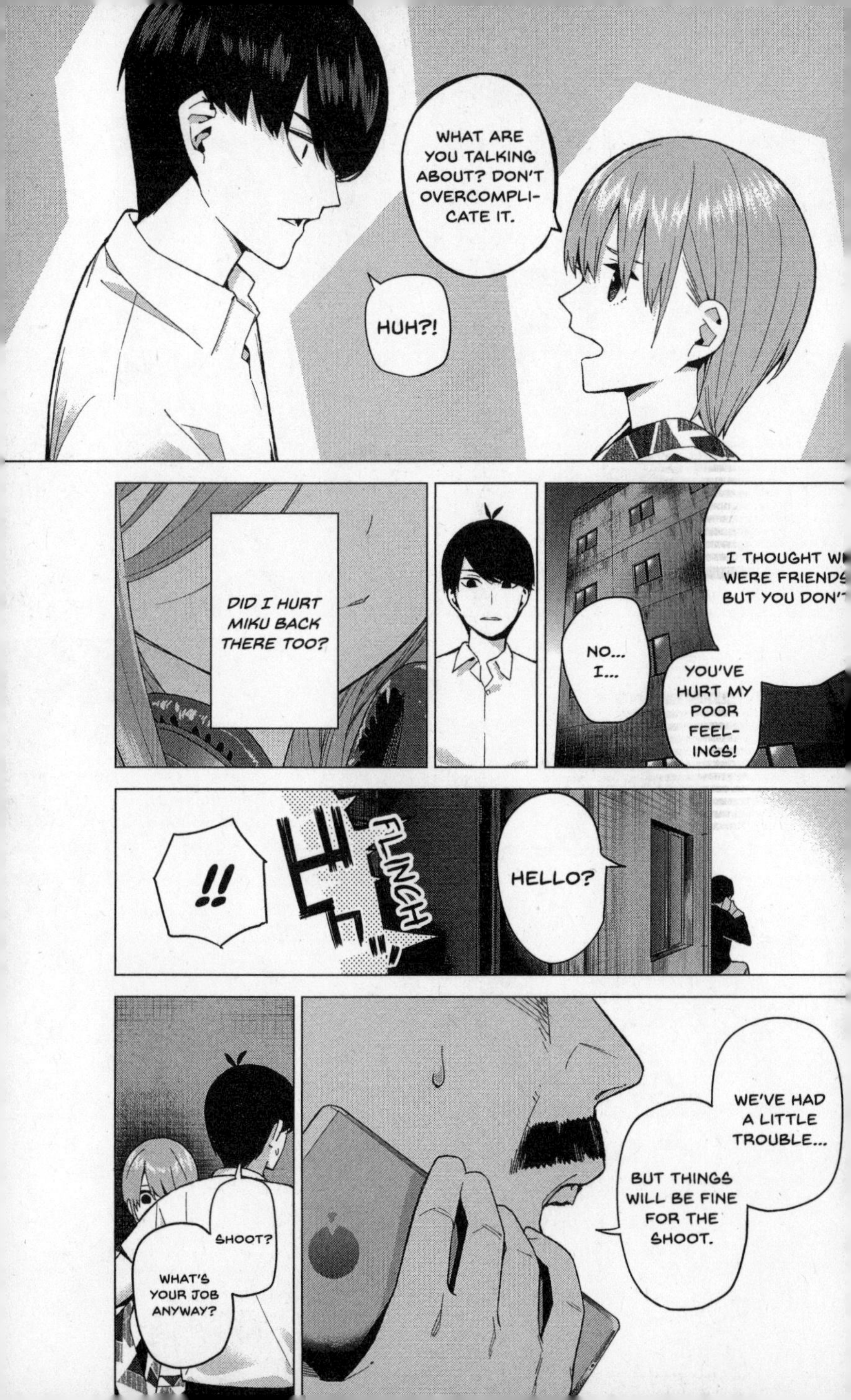
WHAT ARE YOU TALKING ABOUT? DON'T OVERCOMPLI-CATE IT.
HUH?!
I THOUGHT WE WERE FRIENDS BUT YOU DON'T
YOU'VE HURT MY POOR FEEL-INGS!
NO... I...
DID I HURT MIKU BACK THERE TOO?
HELLO?
FLINCH
!!
WE'VE HAD A LITTLE TROUBLE...
BUT THINGS WILL BE FINE FOR THE SHOOT.
SHOOT?
WHAT'S YOUR JOB ANYWAY?

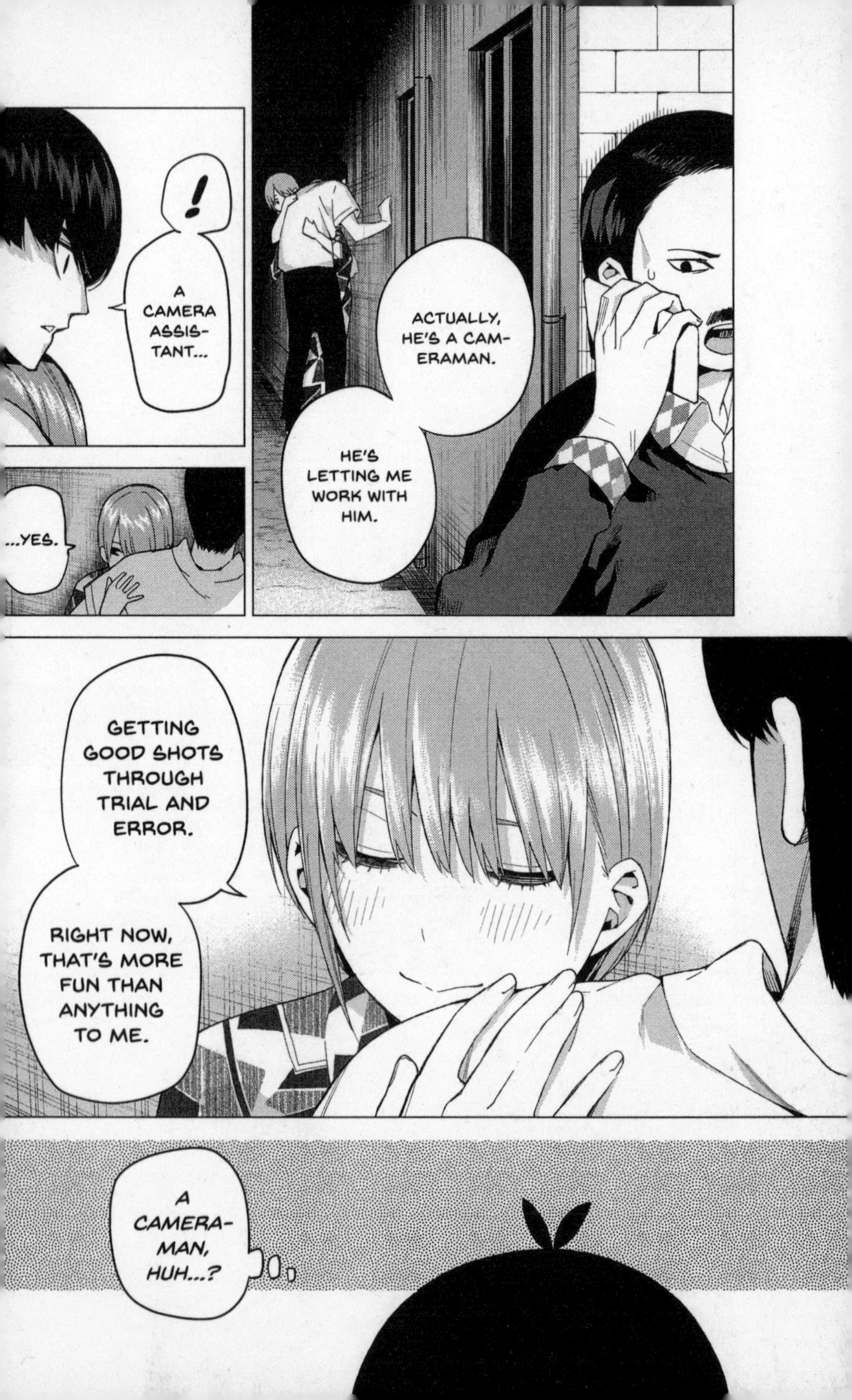
ACTUALLY, HE'S A CAMERAMAN.
HE'S LETTING ME WORK WITH HIM.
!
A CAMERA ASSISTANT...
...YES.
GETTING GOOD SHOTS THROUGH TRIAL AND ERROR.
RIGHT NOW, THAT'S MORE FUN THAN ANYTHING TO ME.
A CAMERAMAN, HUH...?

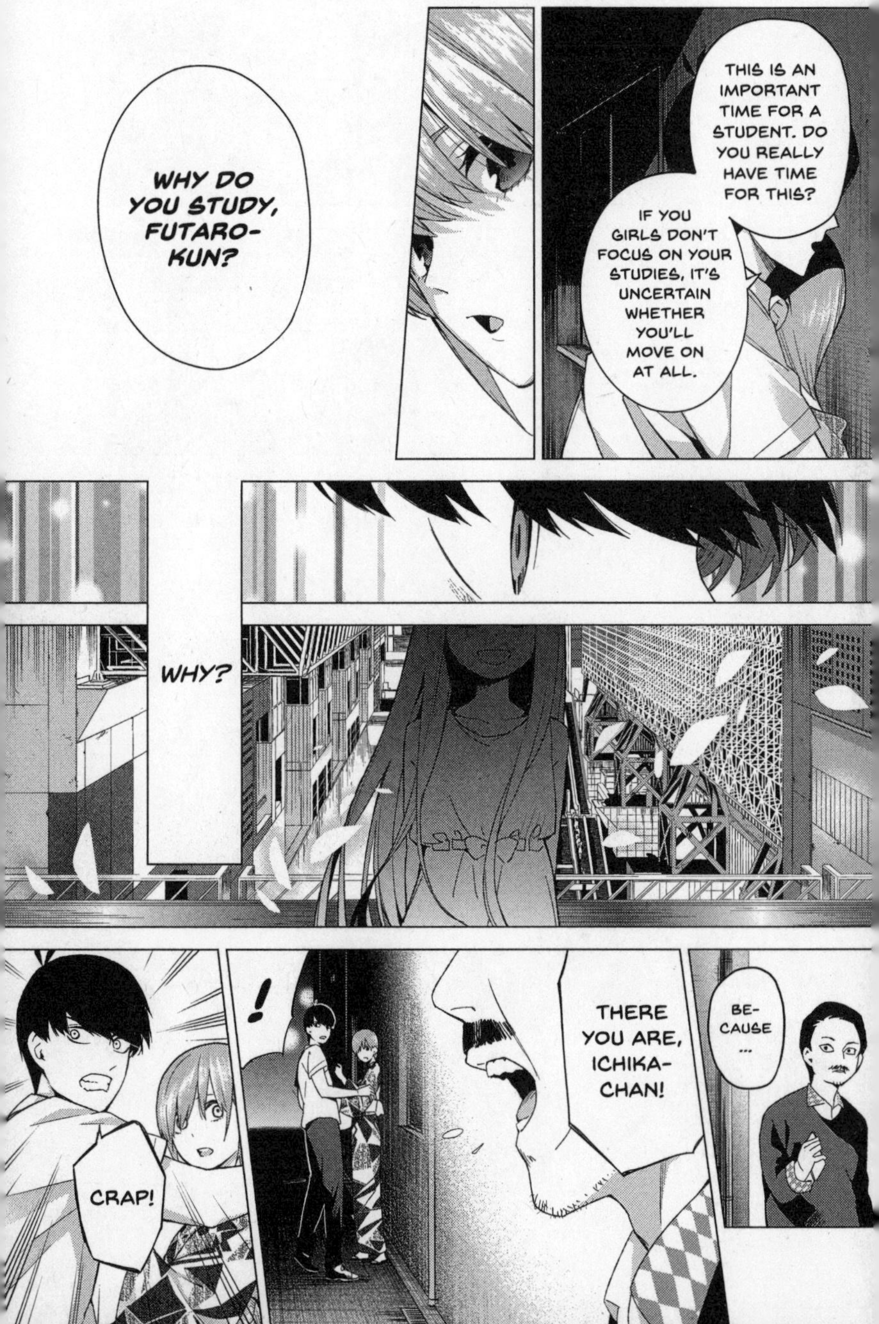
THIS IS AN IMPORTANT TIME FOR A STUDENT. DO YOU REALLY HAVE TIME FOR THIS?
IF YOU GIRLS DON'T FOCUS ON YOUR STUDIES, IT'S UNCERTAIN WHETHER YOU'LL MOVE ON AT ALL.
WHY DO YOU STUDY, FUTARO-KUN?
WHY?
BE-CAUSE ...
THERE YOU ARE, ICHIKA-CHAN!
!
CRAP!

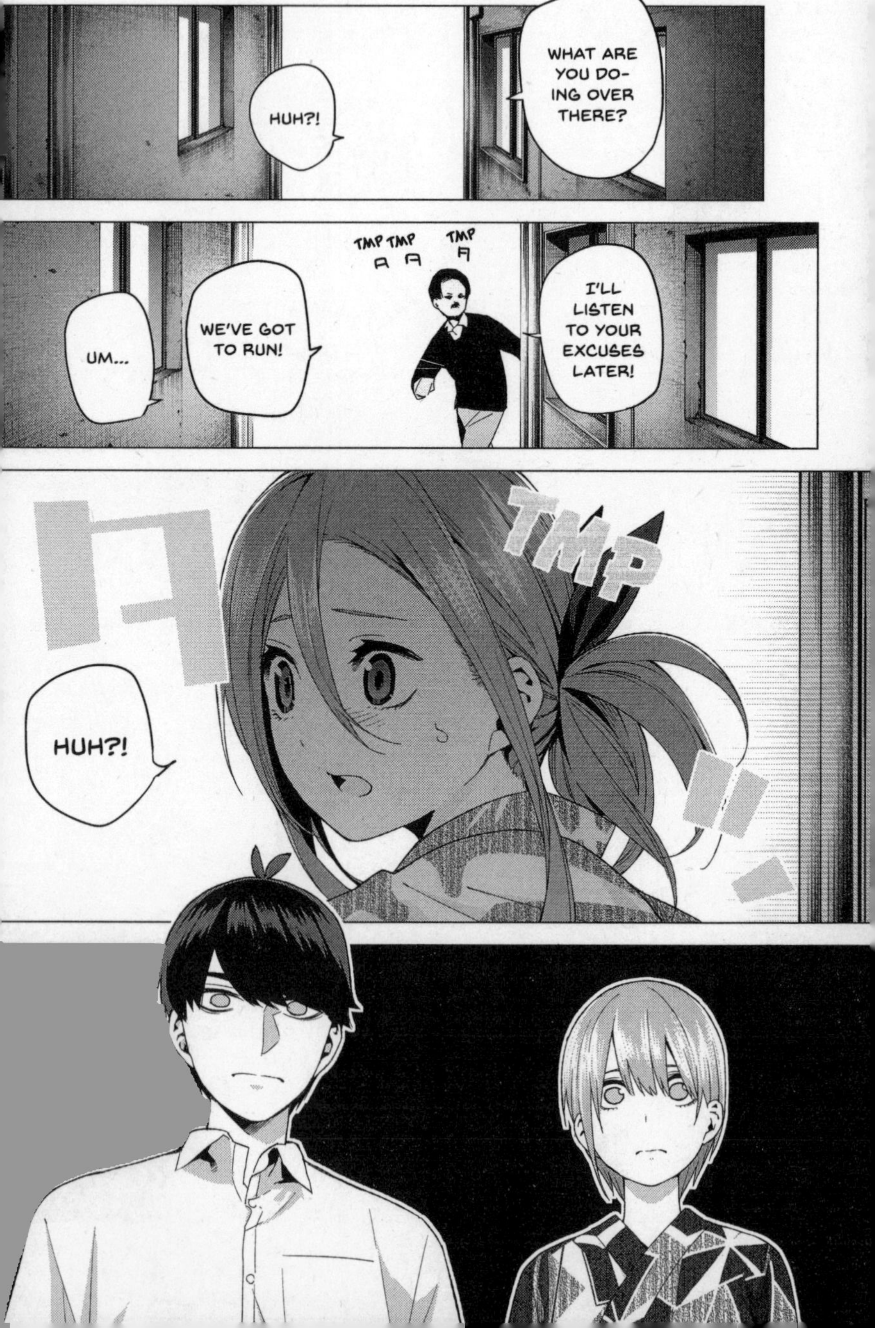
WHAT ARE YOU DO-ING OVER THERE?
HUH?!
I'LL LISTEN TO YOUR EXCUSES LATER!
TMP TMP TMP
WE'VE GOT TO RUN!
UM...
TMP
HUH?!

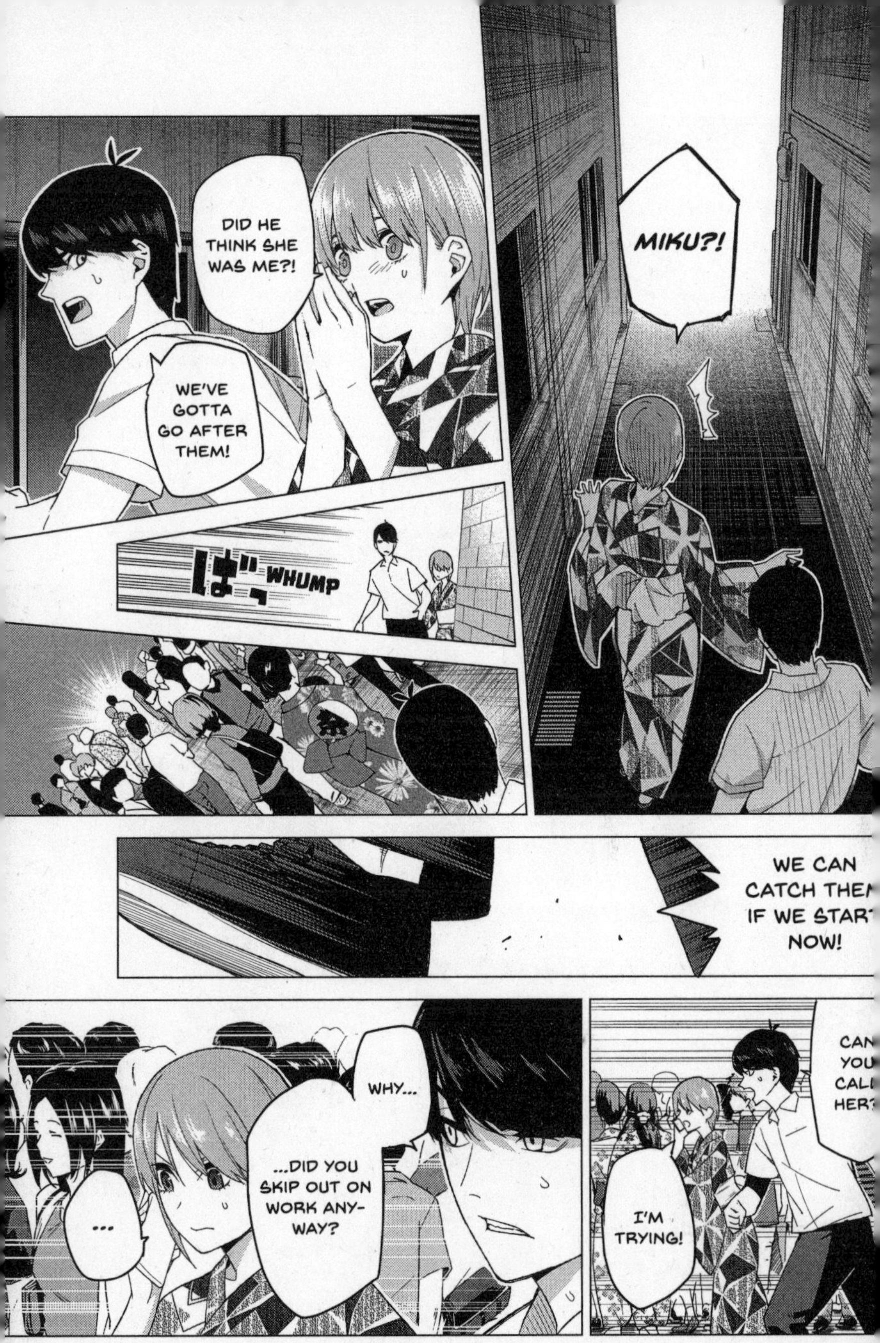
MIKU?!
DID HE THINK SHE WAS ME?!
WE'VE GOTTA GO AFTER THEM!
はっ
WHUMP
WE CAN CATCH THEM IF WE START NOW!
CAN YOU CALL HER?
I'M TRYING!
WHY...
...DID YOU SKIP OUT ON WORK ANY-WAY?
...

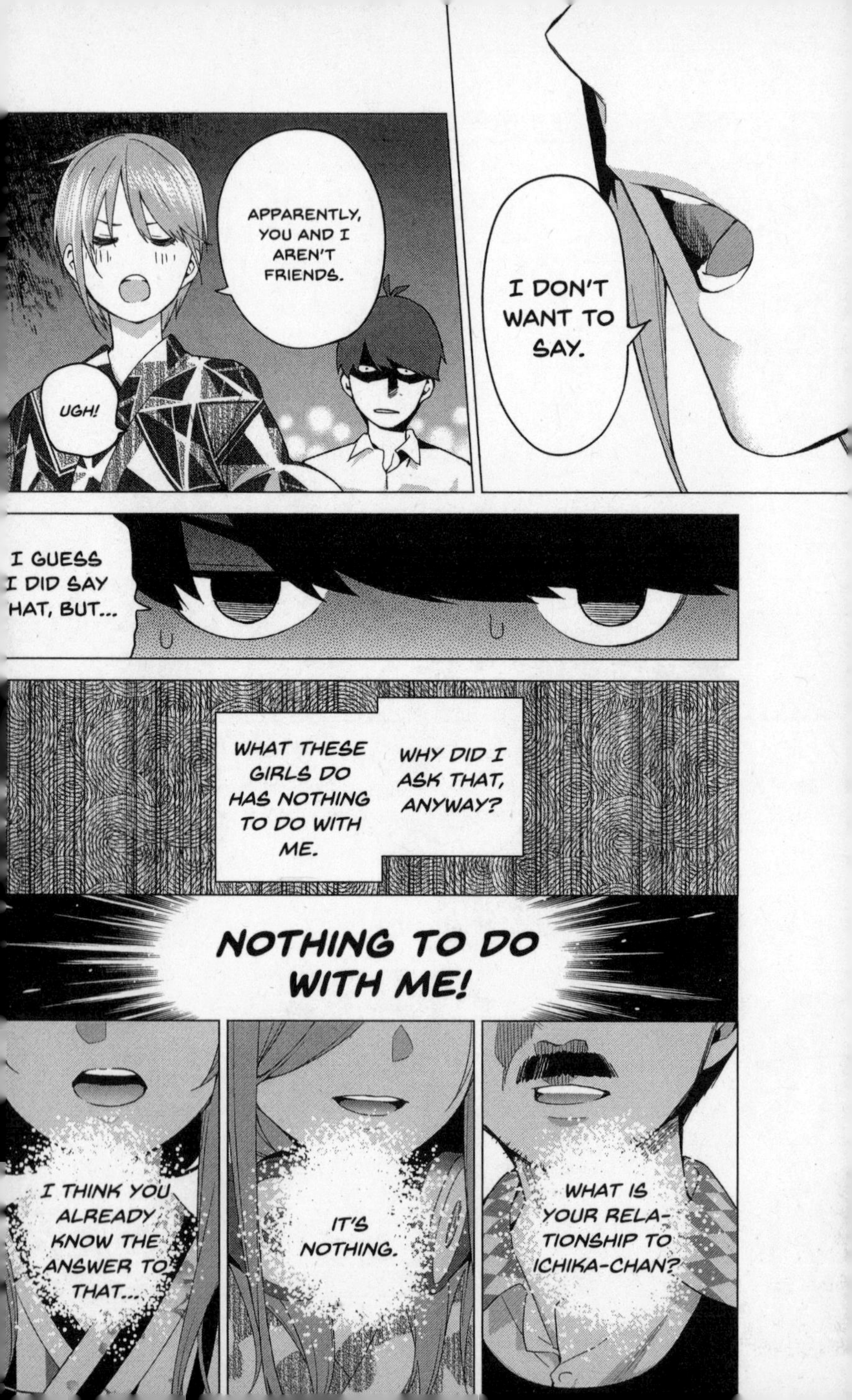
I DON'T WANT TO SAY.
APPARENTLY, YOU AND I AREN'T FRIENDS.
UGH!
I GUESS I DID SAY HAT, BUT...
WHY DID I ASK THAT, ANYWAY?
WHAT THESE GIRLS DO HAS NOTHING TO DO WITH ME.
NOTHING TO DO WITH ME!
WHAT IS YOUR RELA-TIONSHIP TO ICHIKA-CHAN?
IT'S NOTHING.
I THINK YOU ALREADY KNOW THE ANSWER TO THAT...

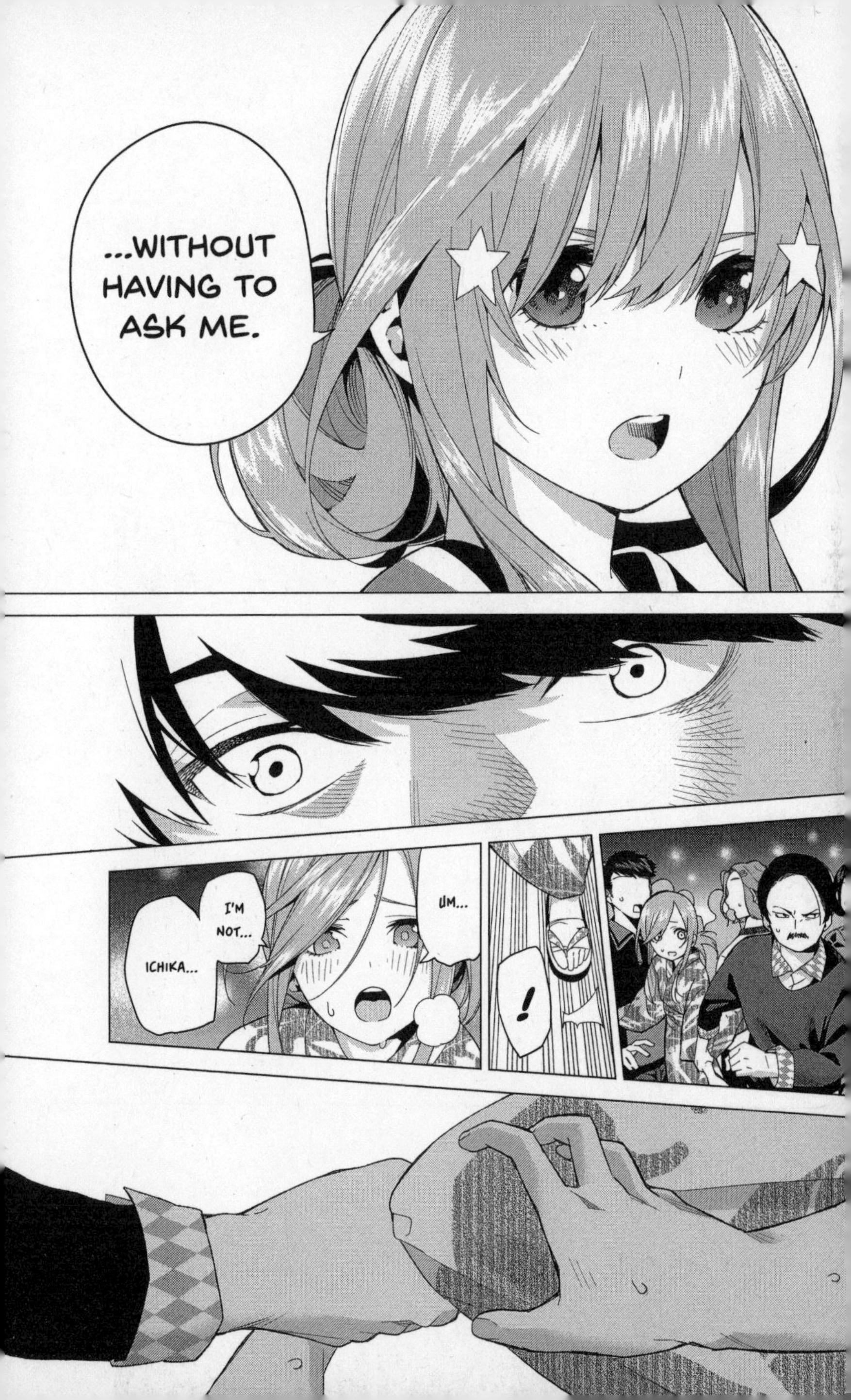
...WITHOUT HAVING TO ASK ME.
UM...
!
I'M NOT...
ICHIKA...

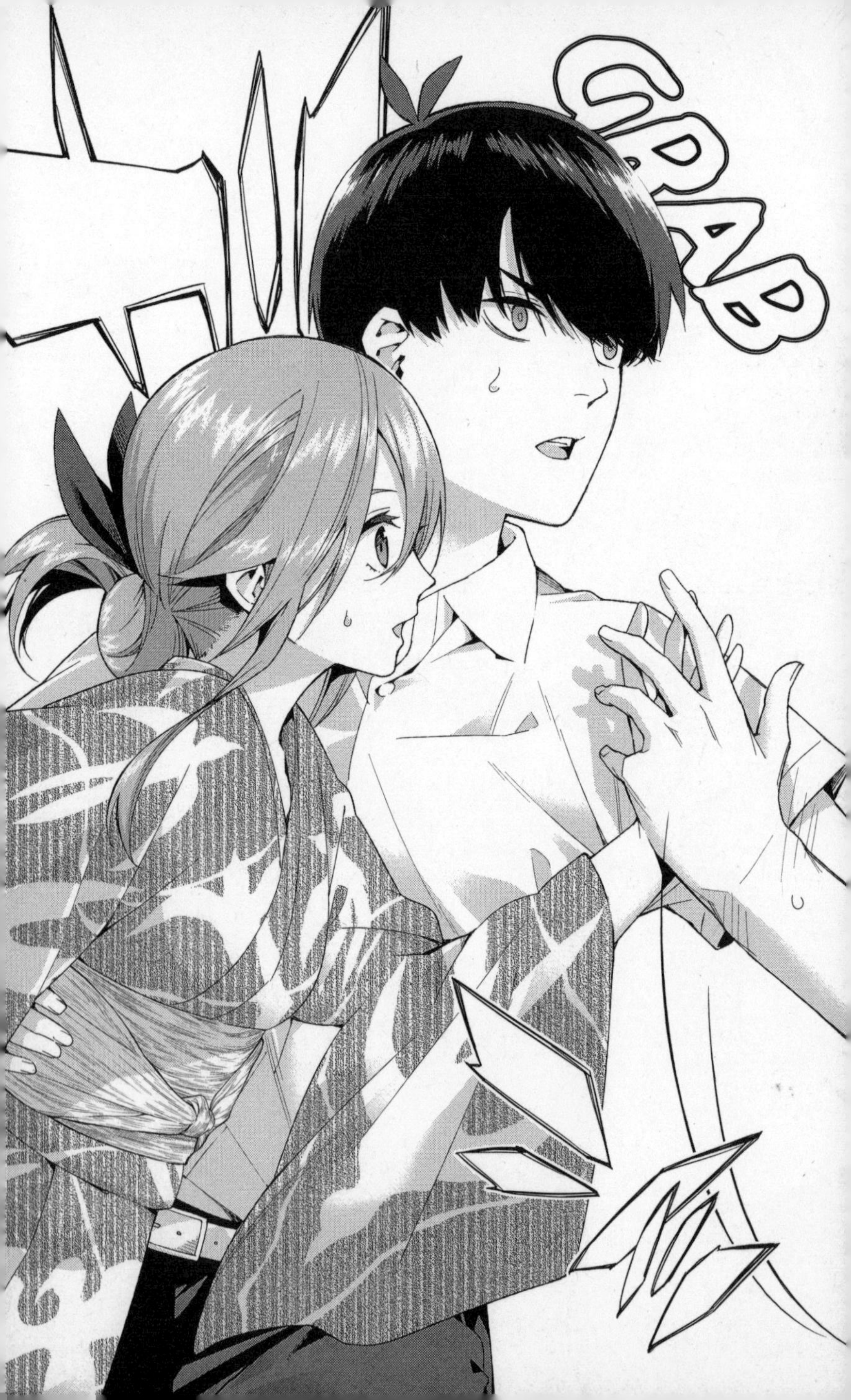
GRAB

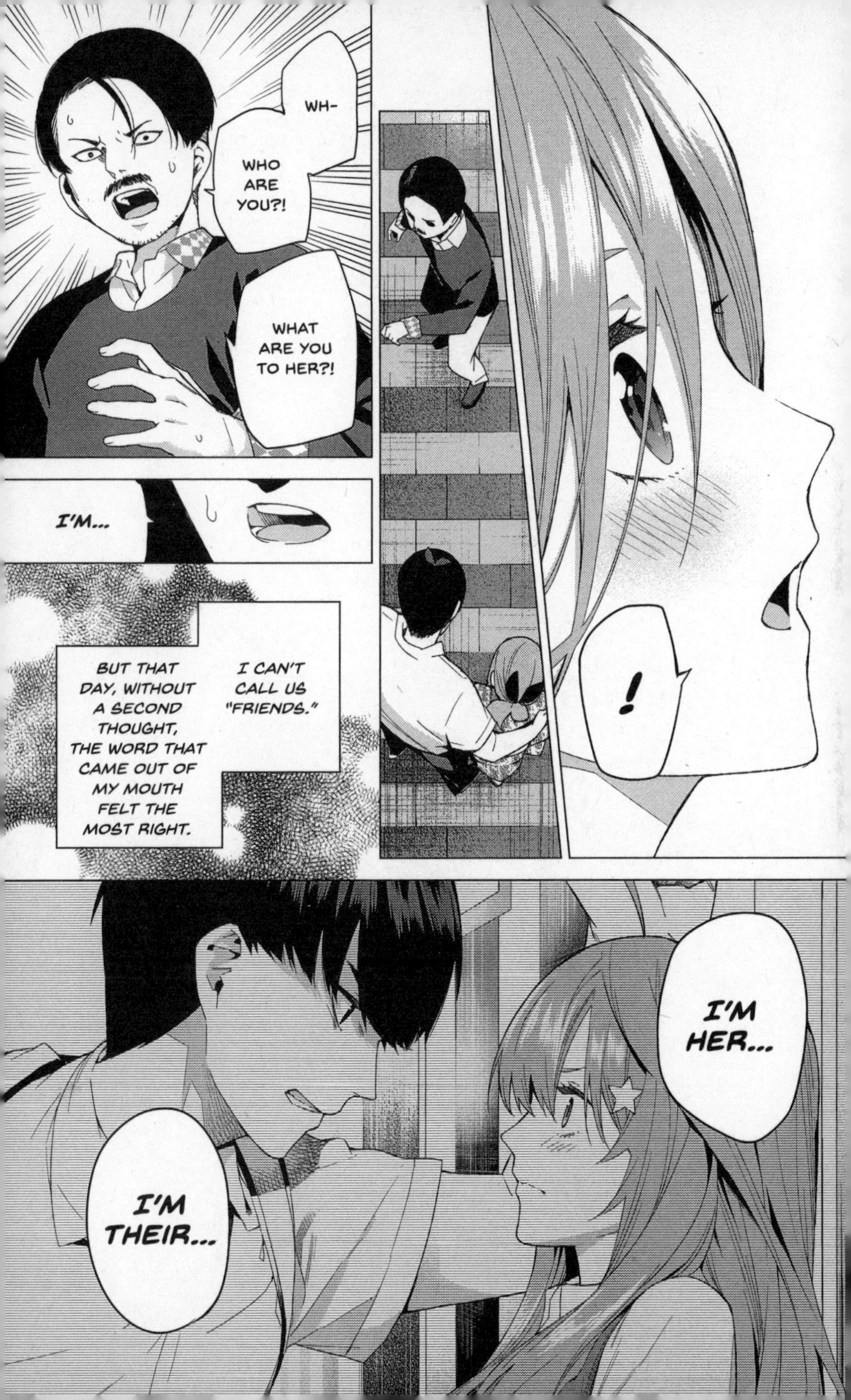
!
WH-
WHO ARE YOU?!
WHAT ARE YOU TO HER?!
I'M...
I CAN'T CALL US "FRIENDS."
BUT THAT DAY, WITHOUT A SECOND THOUGHT, THE WORD THAT CAME OUT OF MY MOUTH FELT THE MOST RIGHT.
I'M HER...
I'M THEIR...

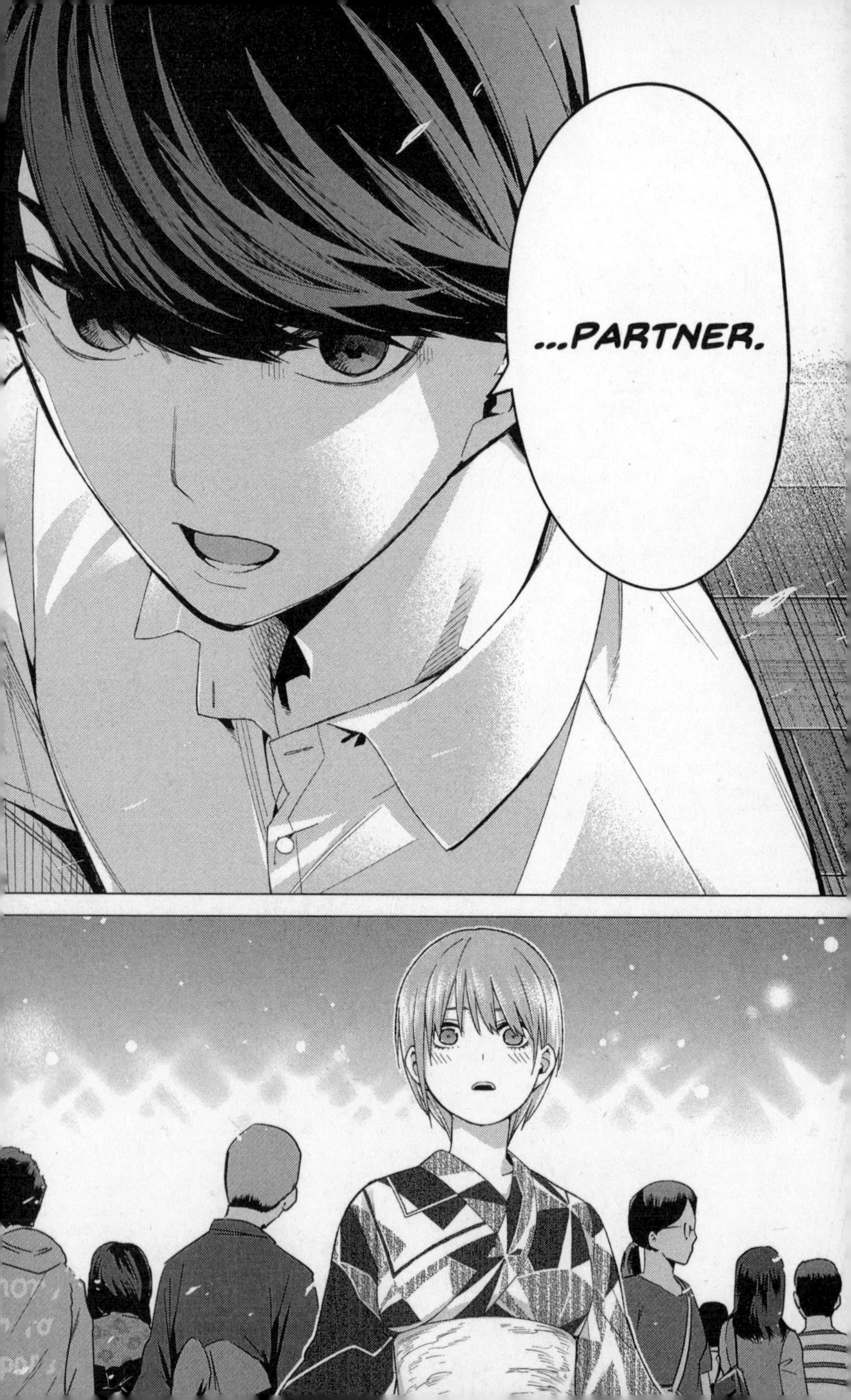
...PARTNER.

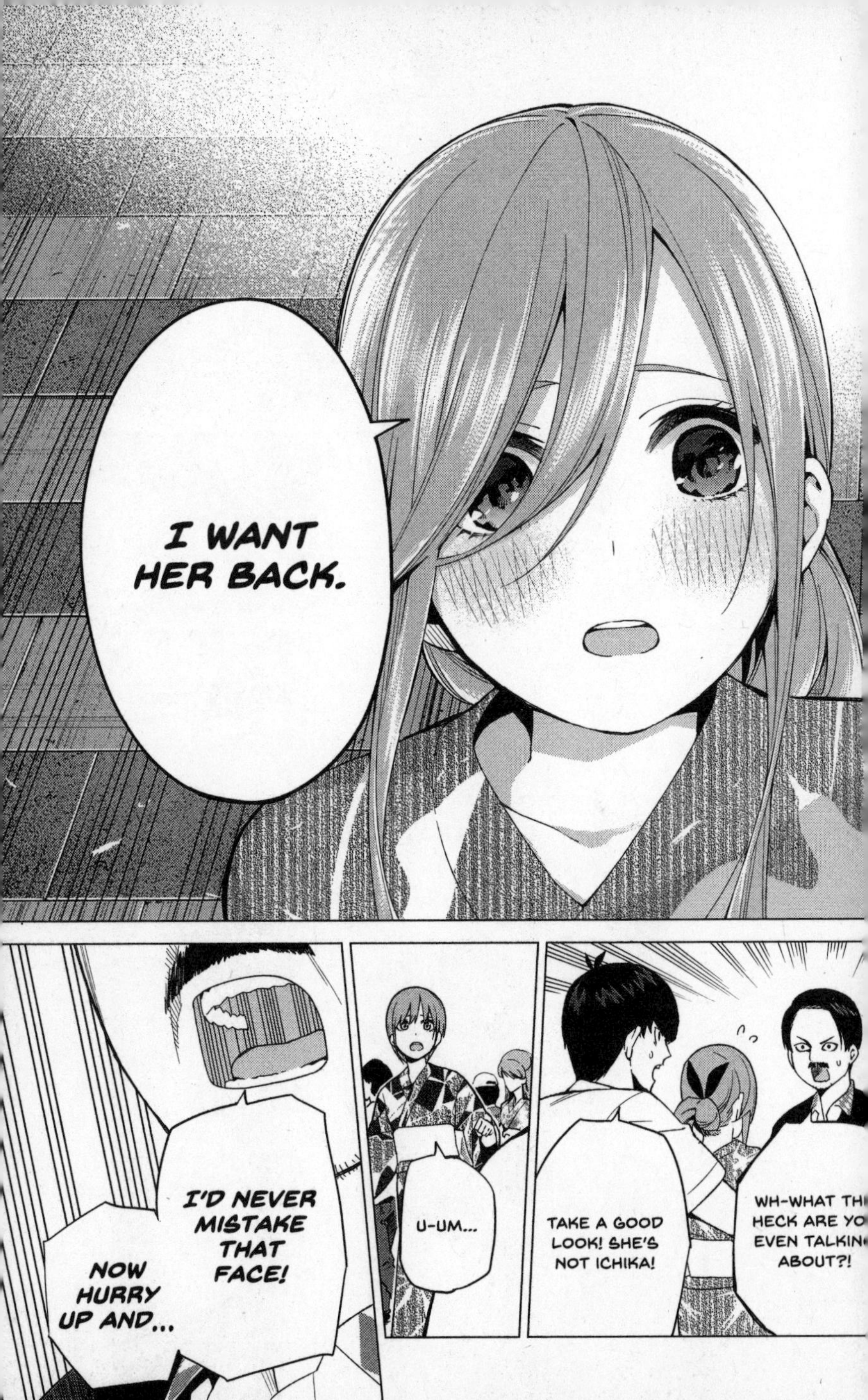
I WANT HER BACK.
WH-WHAT TH HECK ARE YO EVEN TALKIN ABOUT?!
TAKE A GOOD LOOK! SHE'S NOT ICHIKA!
U-UM...
I'D NEVER MISTAKE THAT FACE!
NOW HURRY UP AND...

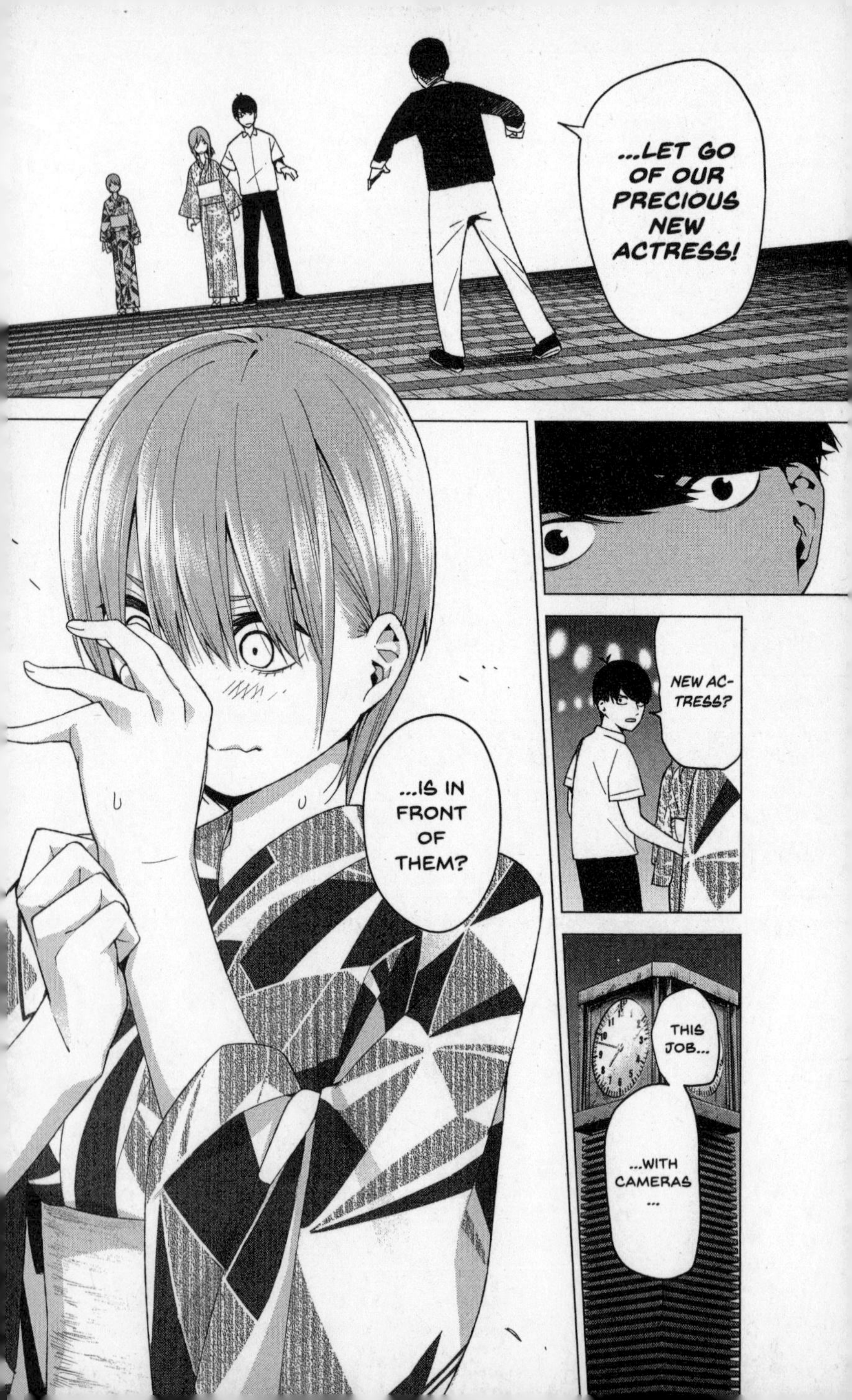
...LET GO OF OUR PRECIOUS NEW ACTRESS!
NEW ACTRESS?
THIS JOB...
...WITH CAMERAS ...
...IS IN FRONT OF THEM?

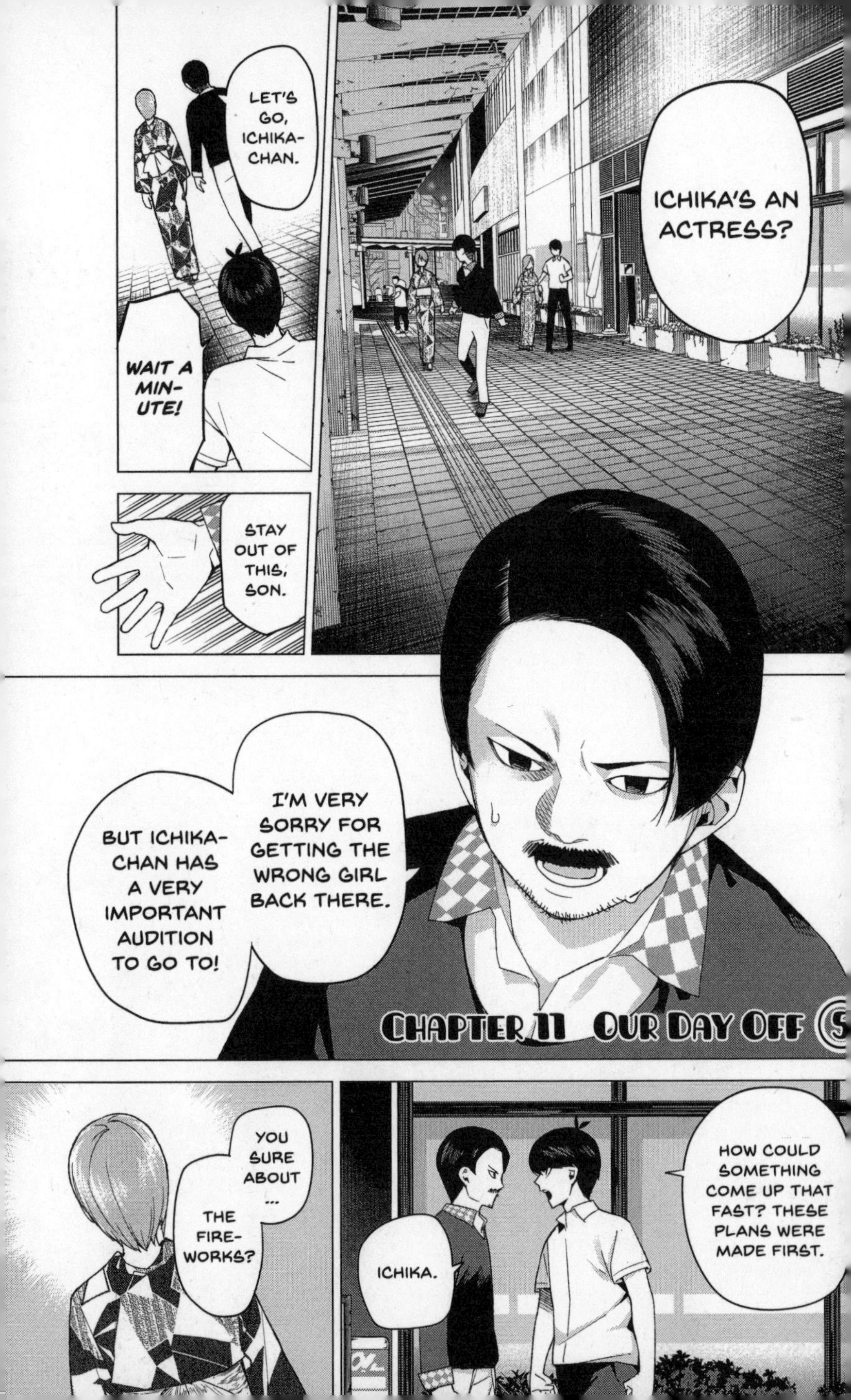
ICHIKA'S AN ACTRESS?
LET'S GO, ICHIKA-CHAN.
WAIT A MIN-UTE!
STAY OUT OF THIS, SON.
I'M VERY SORRY FOR GETTING THE WRONG GIRL BACK THERE.
BUT ICHIKA-CHAN HAS A VERY IMPORTANT AUDITION TO GO TO!
CHAPTER 11 OUR DAY OFF 5
HOW COULD SOMETHING COME UP THAT FAST? THESE PLANS WERE MADE FIRST.
ICHIKA.
YOU SURE ABOUT ...
THE FIRE-WORKS?

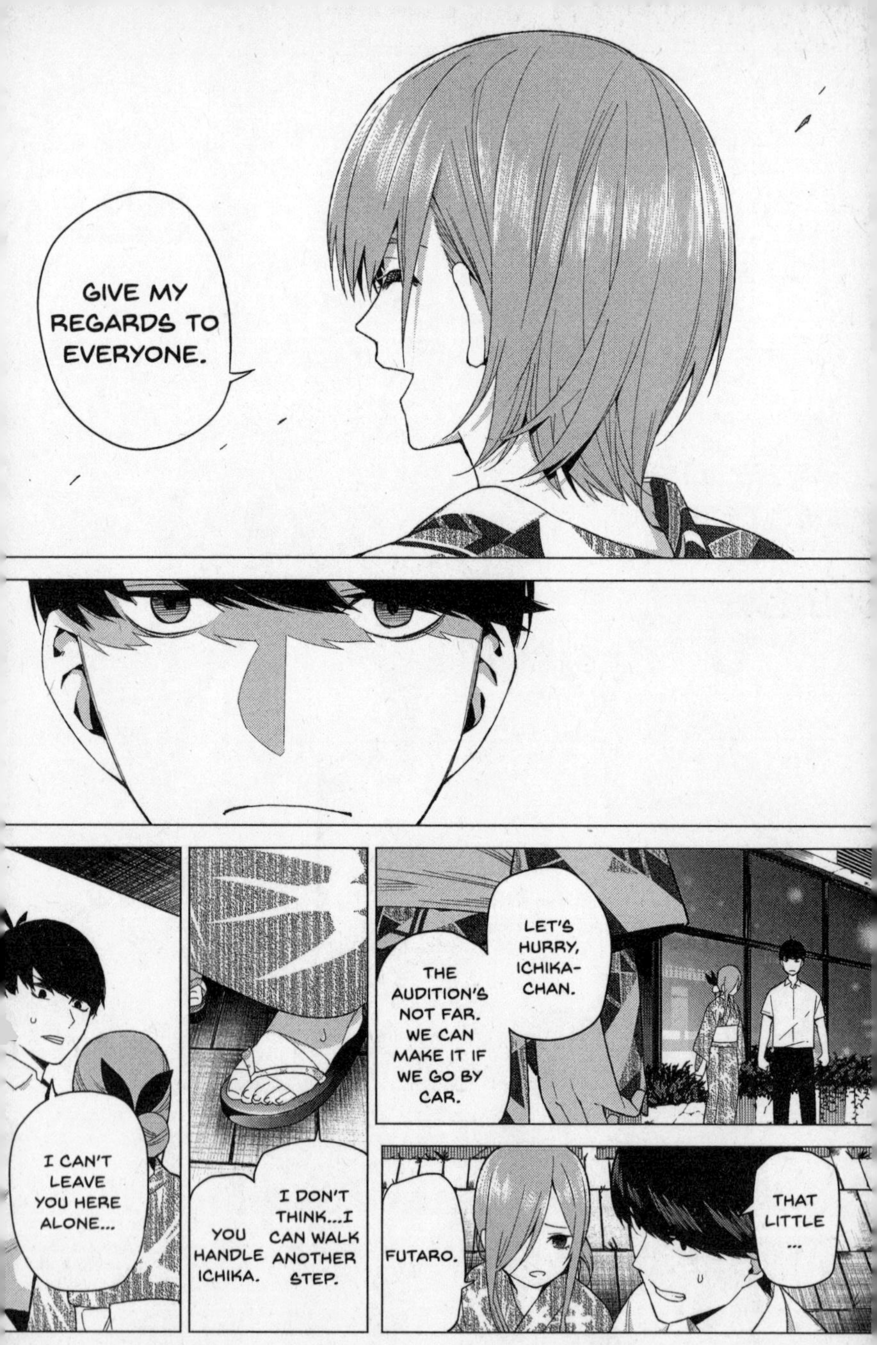
GIVE MY REGARDS TO EVERYONE.
LET'S HURRY, ICHIKA-CHAN.
THE AUDITION'S NOT FAR. WE CAN MAKE IT IF WE GO BY CAR.
THAT LITTLE ...
FUTARO.
I DON'T THINK...I CAN WALK ANOTHER STEP.
YOU HANDLE ICHIKA.
I CAN'T LEAVE YOU HERE ALONE...

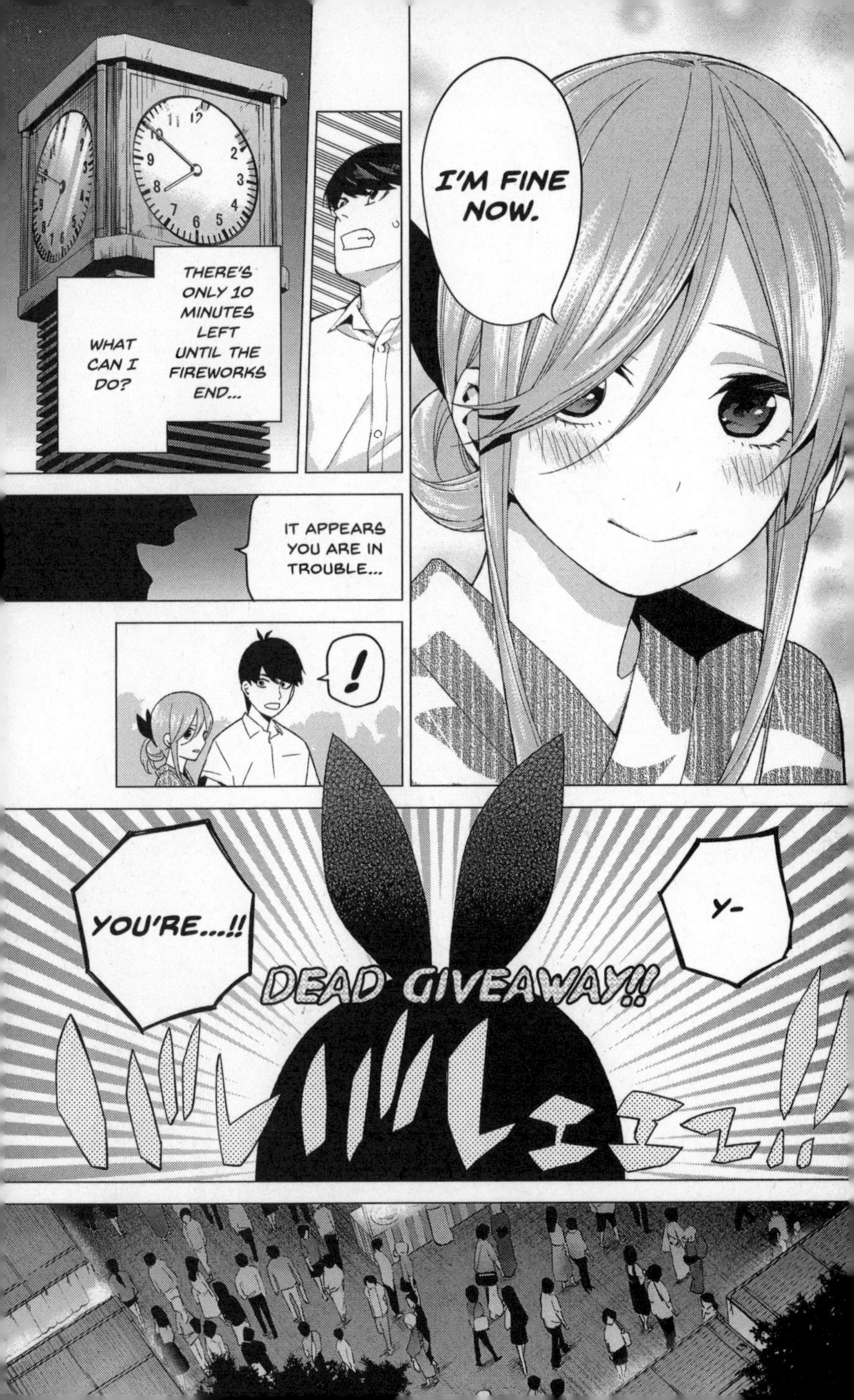
I'M FINE NOW.
THERE'S ONLY 10 MINUTES LEFT UNTIL THE FIREWORKS END...
WHAT CAN I DO?
IT APPEARS YOU ARE IN TROUBLE...
!
Y-
YOU'RE...!!
DEAD GIVEAWAY!!

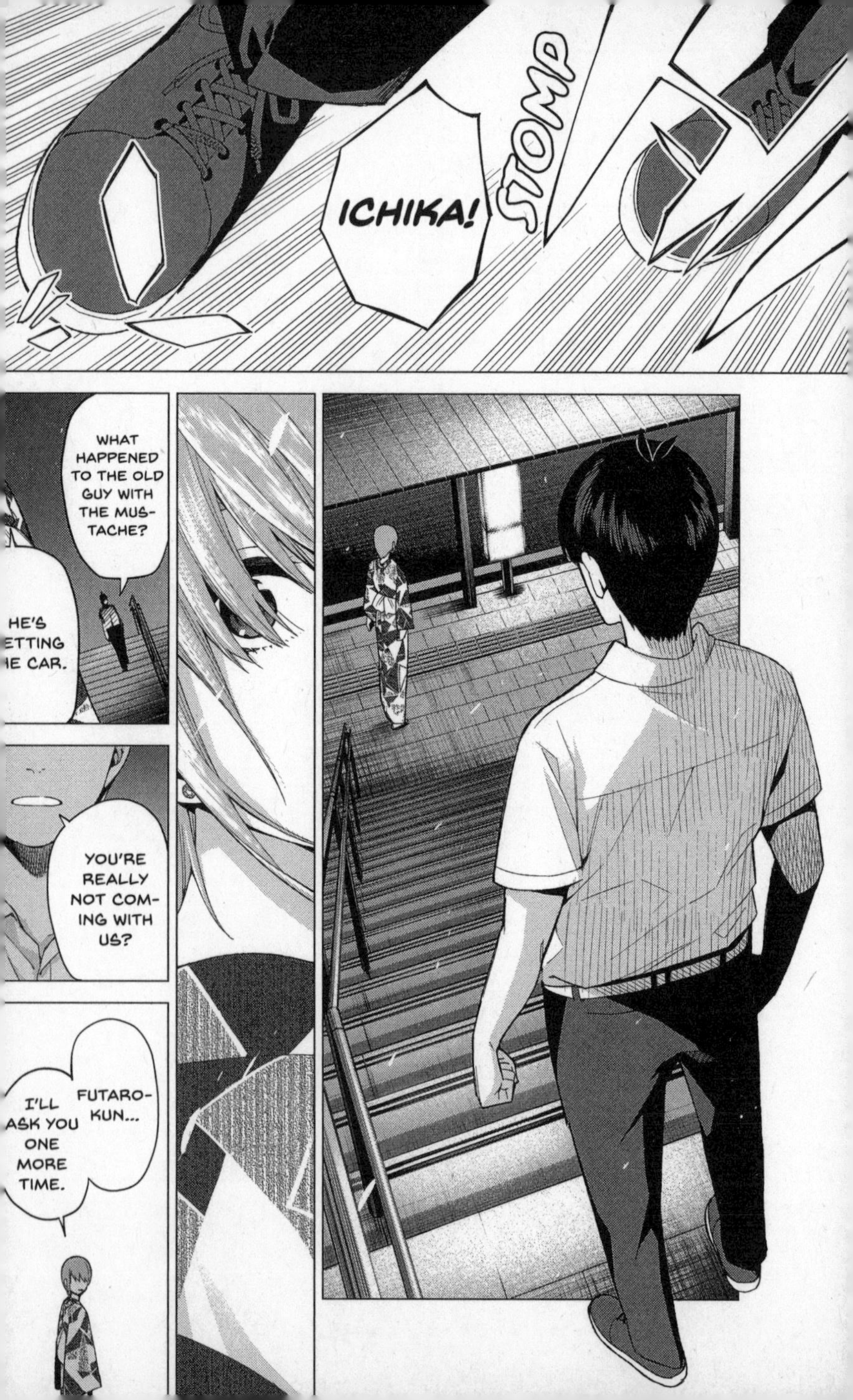
STOMP
ICHIKA!
WHAT HAPPENED TO THE OLD GUY WITH THE MUS-TACHE?
HE'S ETTING HE CAR.
YOU'RE REALLY NOT COM-ING WITH US?
FUTARO-KUN...
I'LL ASK YOU ONE MORE TIME.

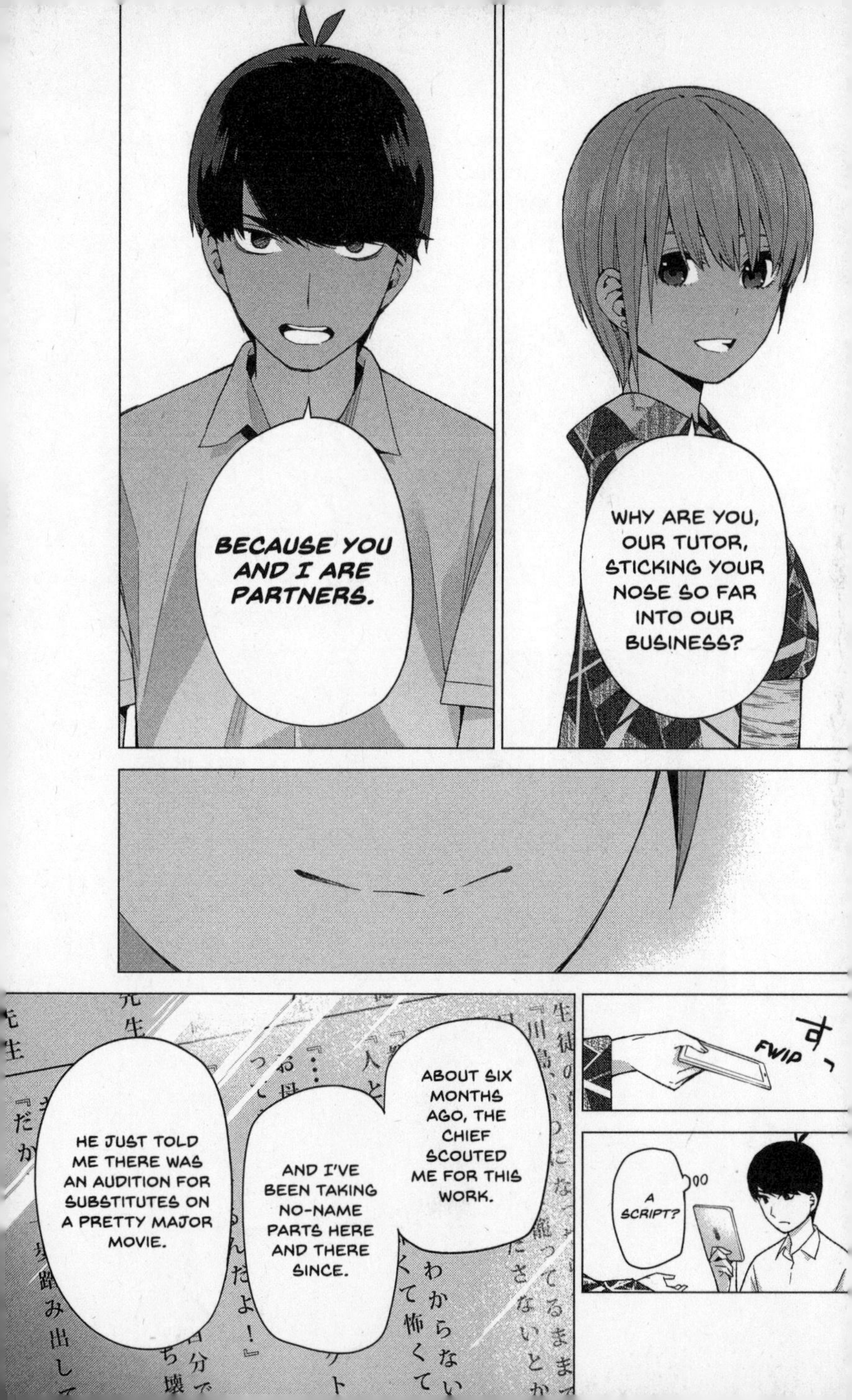
WHY ARE YOU, OUR TUTOR, STICKING YOUR NOSE SO FAR INTO OUR BUSINESS?
BECAUSE YOU AND I ARE PARTNERS.
す FWIP
A SCRIPT?
ABOUT SIX MONTHS AGO, THE CHIEF SCOUTED ME FOR THIS WORK.
AND I'VE BEEN TAKING NO-NAME PARTS HERE AND THERE SINCE.
HE JUST TOLD ME THERE WAS AN AUDITION FOR SUBSTITUTES ON A PRETTY MAJOR MOVIE.

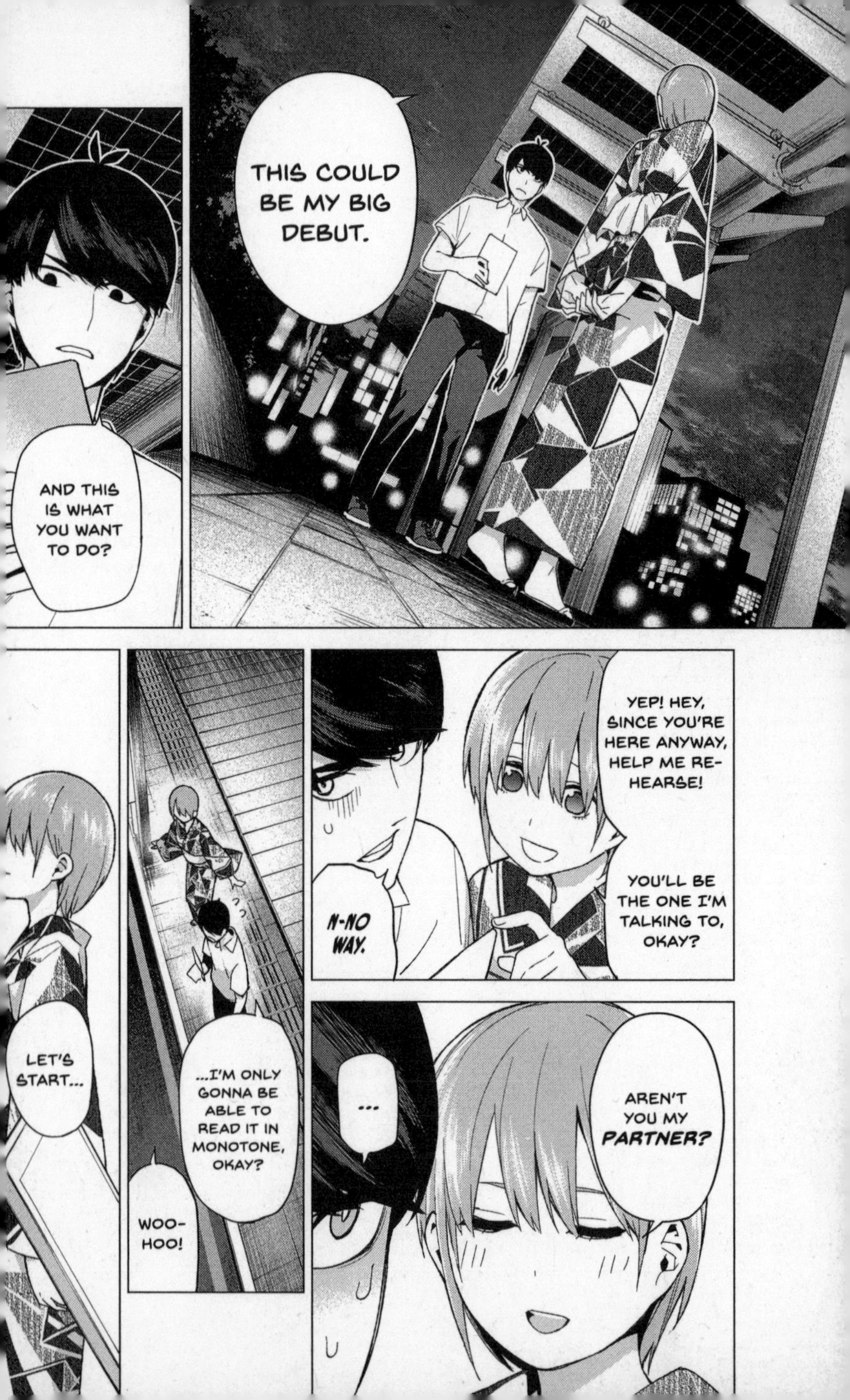
THIS COULD BE MY BIG DEBUT.
AND THIS IS WHAT YOU WANT TO DO?
YEP! HEY, SINCE YOU'RE HERE ANYWAY, HELP ME RE-HEARSE!
YOU'LL BE THE ONE I'M TALKING TO, OKAY?
N-NO WAY.
AREN'T YOU MY **PARTNER?**
...
...I'M ONLY GONNA BE ABLE TO READ IT IN MONOTONE, OKAY?
WOO-HOO!
LET'S START...

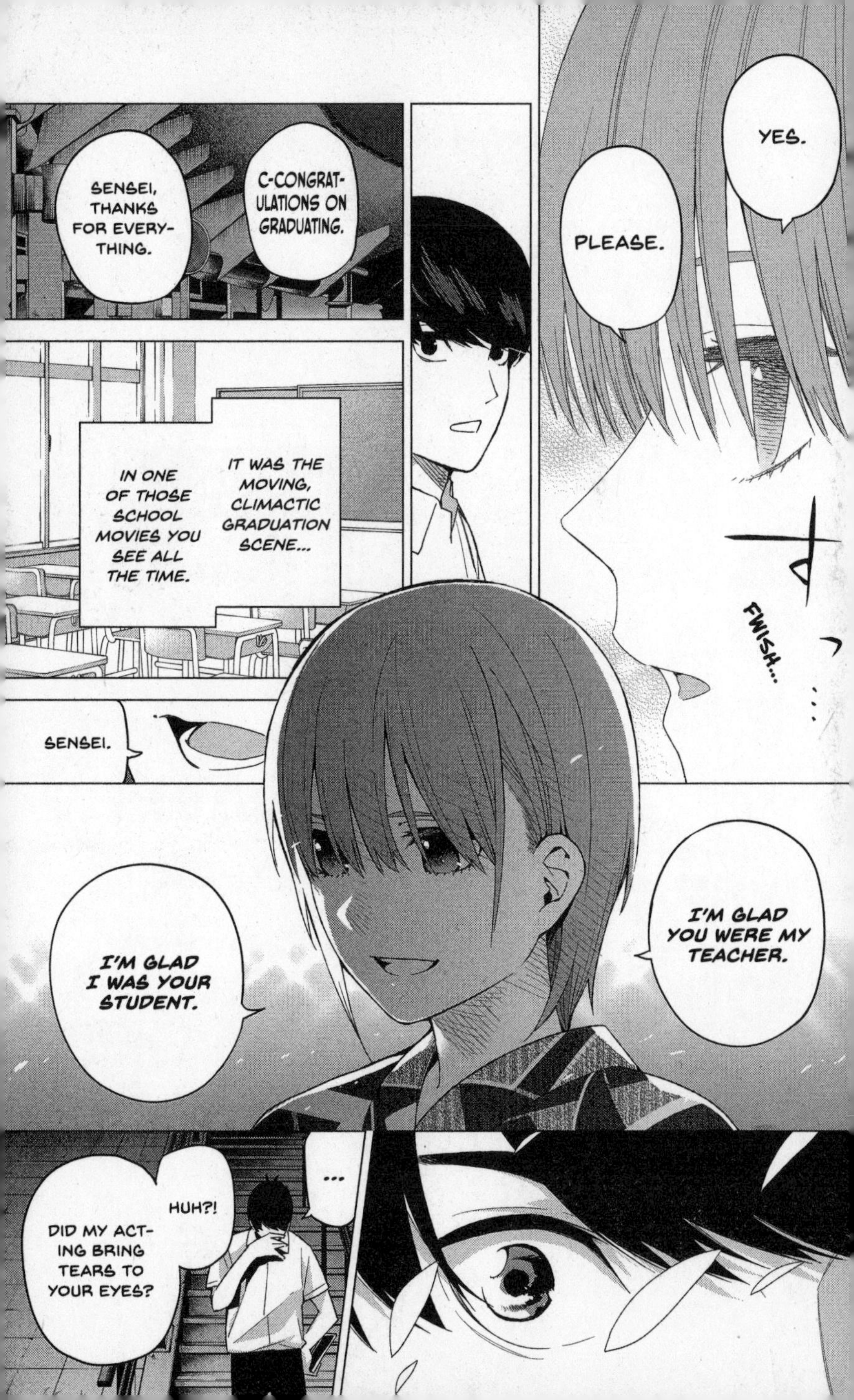
YES.
PLEASE.
FWISH...
C-CONGRATULATIONS ON GRADUATING.
SENSEI, THANKS FOR EVERYTHING.
IT WAS THE MOVING, CLIMACTIC GRADUATION SCENE...
IN ONE OF THOSE SCHOOL MOVIES YOU SEE ALL THE TIME.
SENSEI.
I'M GLAD YOU WERE MY TEACHER.
I'M GLAD I WAS YOUR STUDENT.
...
HUH?!
DID MY ACTING BRING TEARS TO YOUR EYES?

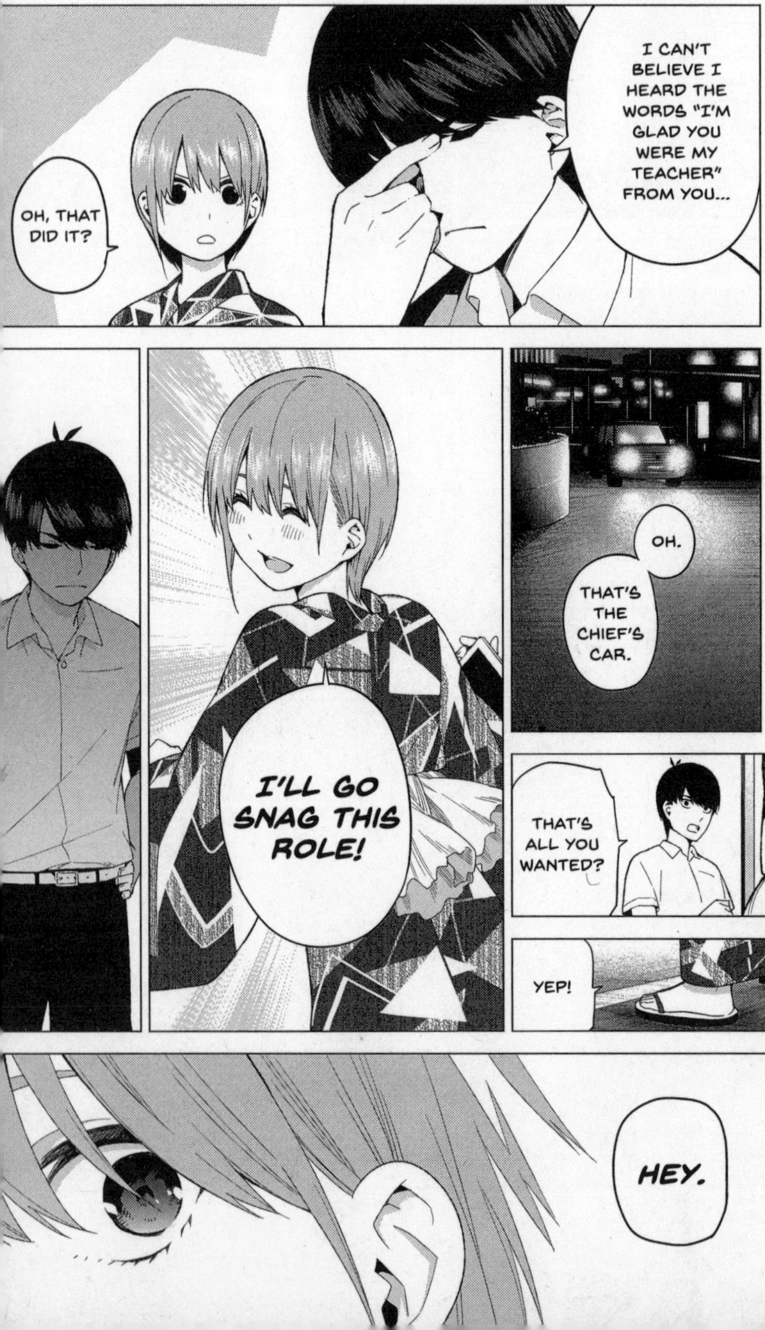
I CAN'T BELIEVE I HEARD THE WORDS "I'M GLAD YOU WERE MY TEACHER" FROM YOU...
OH, THAT DID IT?
OH.
THAT'S THE CHIEF'S CAR.
SEE YA.
THAT'S ALL YOU WANTED?
YEP!
I'LL GO SNAG THIS ROLE!
HEY.

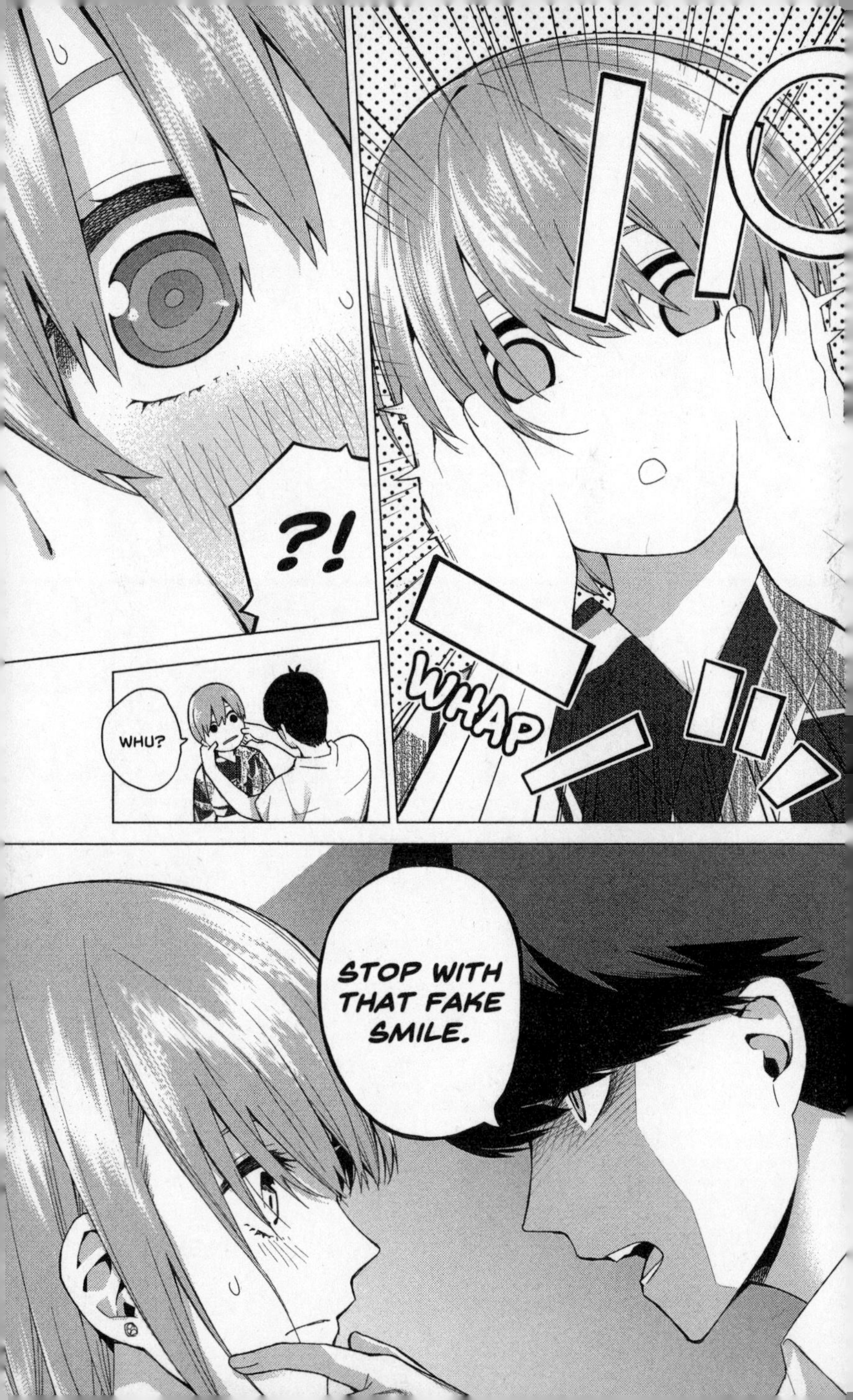
WHAP
?!
WHU?
STOP WITH THAT FAKE SMILE.

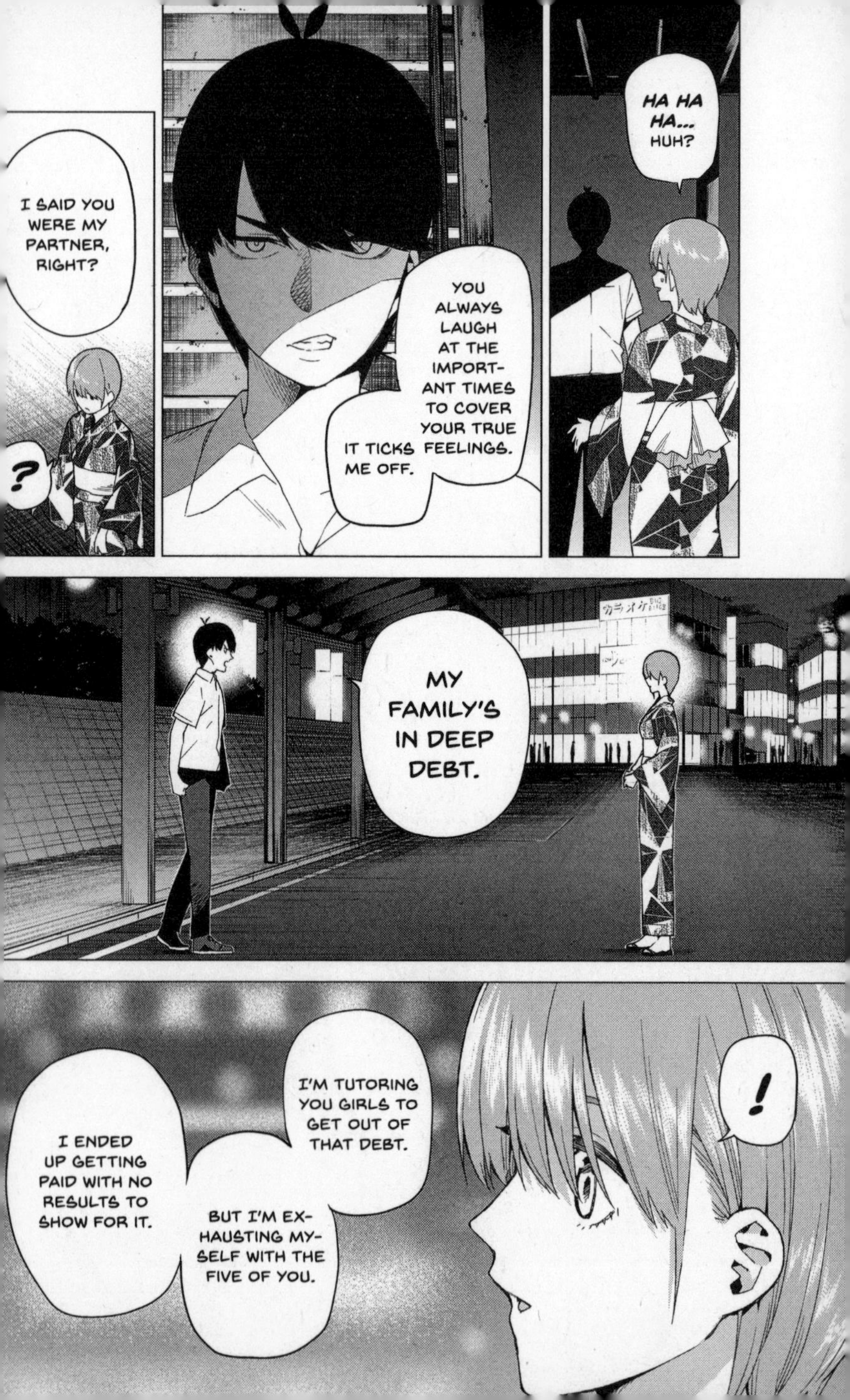
HA HA HA... HUH?
YOU ALWAYS LAUGH AT THE IMPORTANT TIMES TO COVER YOUR TRUE FEELINGS.
IT TICKS ME OFF.
I SAID YOU WERE MY PARTNER, RIGHT?
?
MY FAMILY'S IN DEEP DEBT.
!
I'M TUTORING YOU GIRLS TO GET OUT OF THAT DEBT.
BUT I'M EXHAUSTING MYSELF WITH THE FIVE OF YOU.
I ENDED UP GETTING PAID WITH NO RESULTS TO SHOW FOR IT.

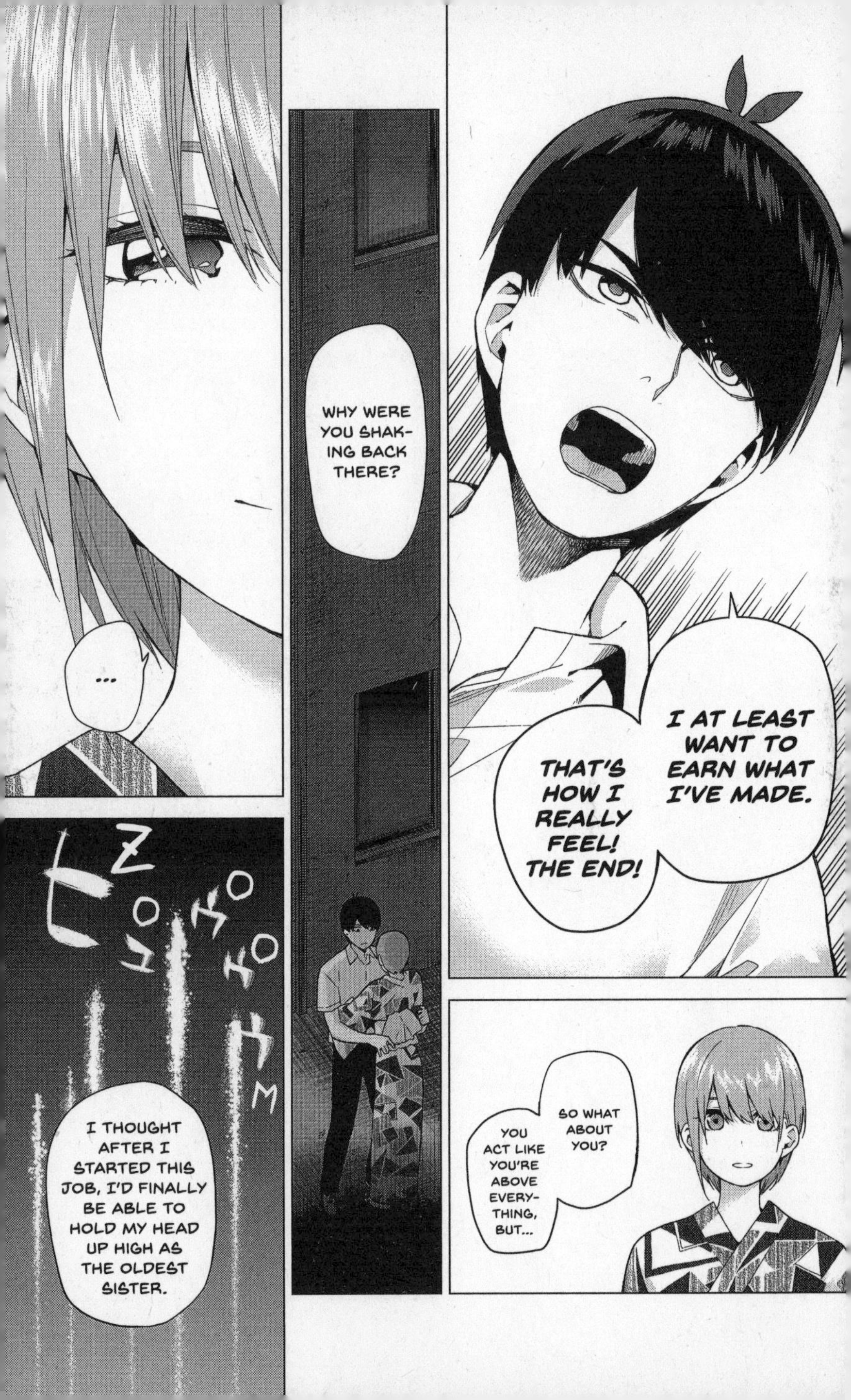
I AT LEAST WANT TO EARN WHAT I'VE MADE.
THAT'S HOW I REALLY FEEL! THE END!
SO WHAT ABOUT YOU?
YOU ACT LIKE YOU'RE ABOVE EVERY-THING, BUT...
WHY WERE YOU SHAK-ING BACK THERE?
...
I THOUGHT AFTER I STARTED THIS JOB, I'D FINALLY BE ABLE TO HOLD MY HEAD UP HIGH AS THE OLDEST SISTER.

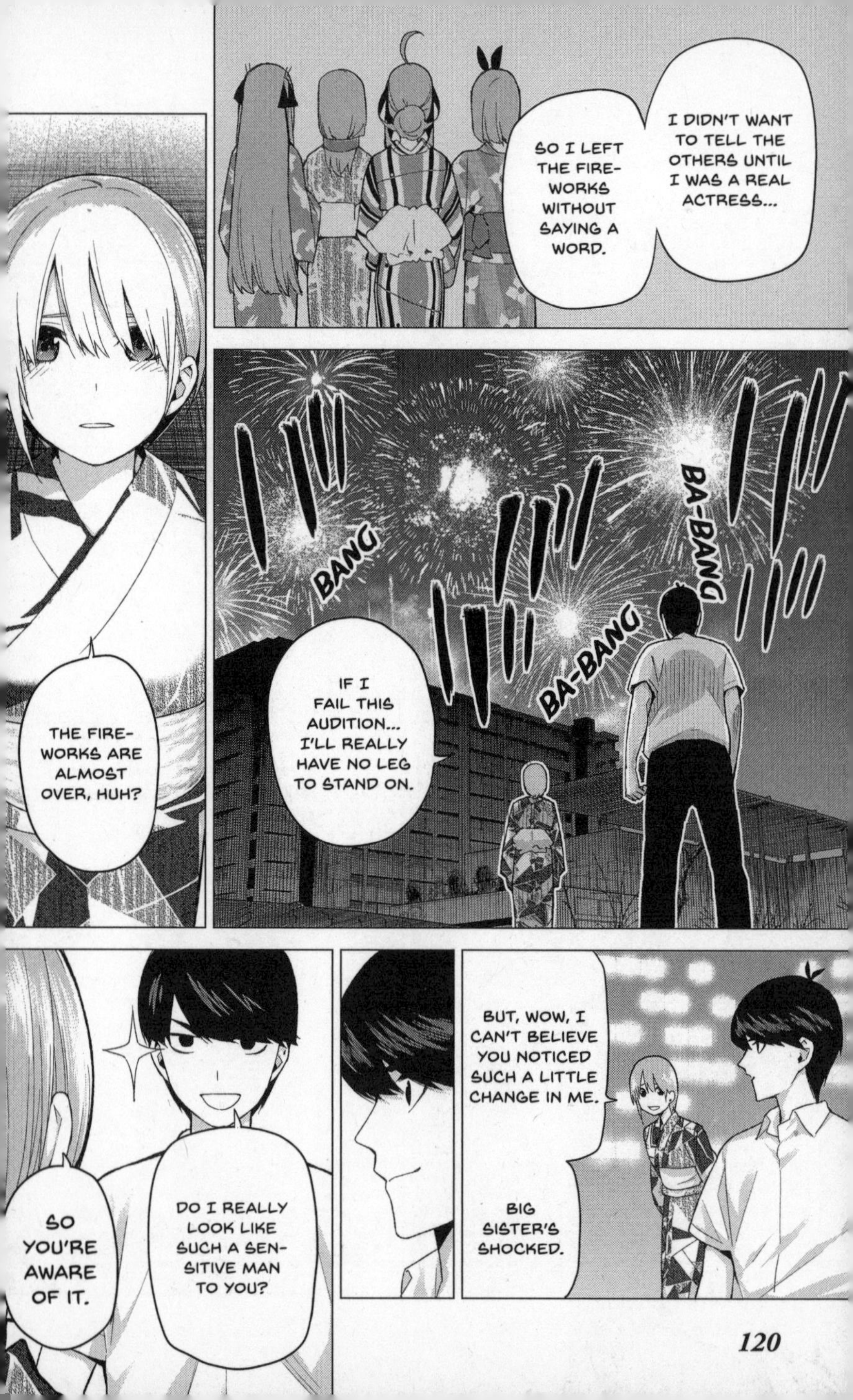
I DIDN'T WANT TO TELL THE OTHERS UNTIL I WAS A REAL ACTRESS...
SO I LEFT THE FIRE-WORKS WITHOUT SAYING A WORD.
BA-BANG
BA-BANG
BANG
IF I FAIL THIS AUDITION... I'LL REALLY HAVE NO LEG TO STAND ON.
THE FIRE-WORKS ARE ALMOST OVER, HUH?
BUT, WOW, I CAN'T BELIEVE YOU NOTICED SUCH A LITTLE CHANGE IN ME.
BIG SISTER'S SHOCKED.
DO I REALLY LOOK LIKE SUCH A SEN-SITIVE MAN TO YOU?
SO YOU'RE AWARE OF IT.

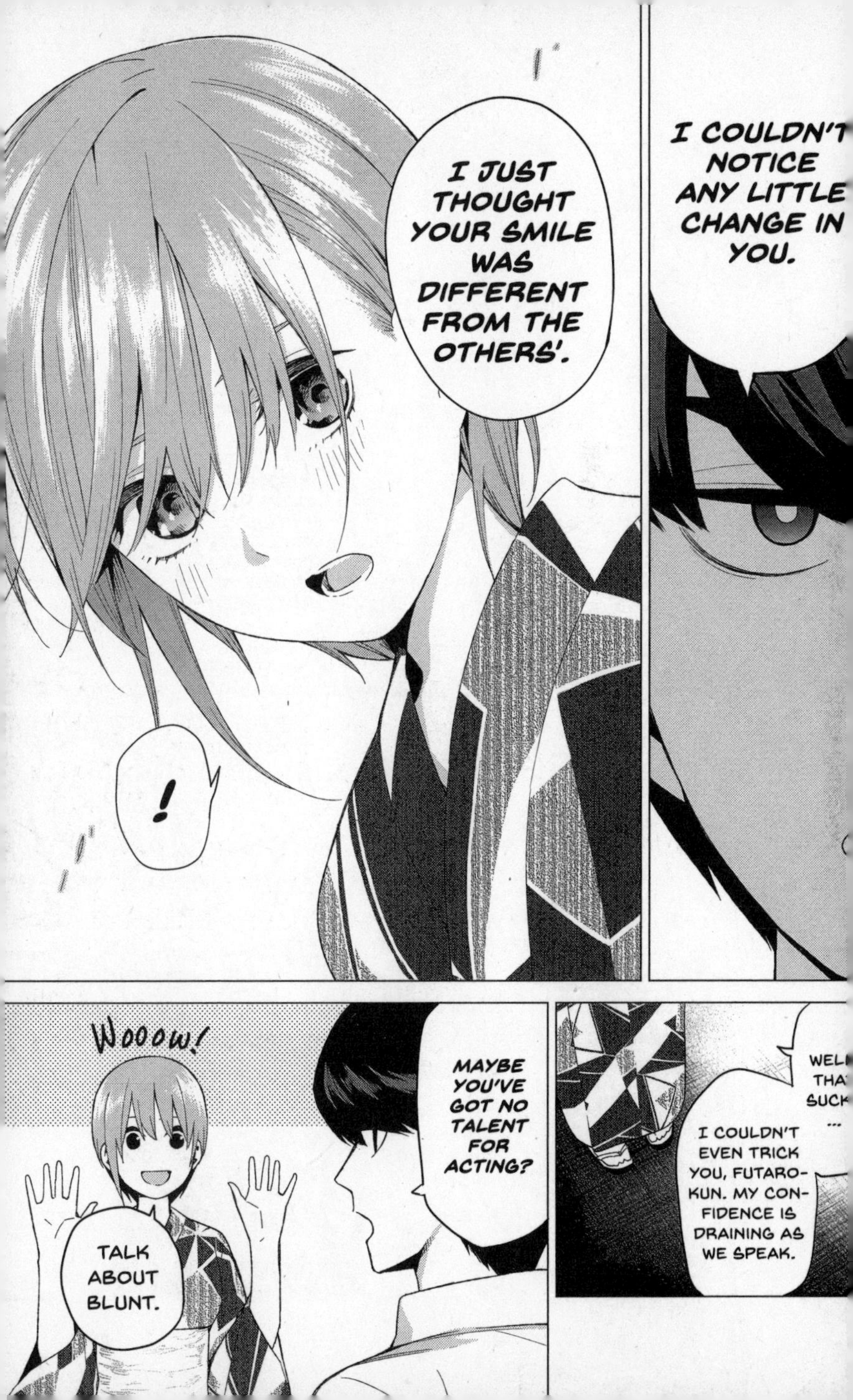
I COULDN'T NOTICE ANY LITTLE CHANGE IN YOU.
I JUST THOUGHT YOUR SMILE WAS DIFFERENT FROM THE OTHERS'.
!
WEL THA SUCK ...
I COULDN'T EVEN TRICK YOU, FUTARO-KUN. MY CONFIDENCE IS DRAINING AS WE SPEAK.
MAYBE YOU'VE GOT NO TALENT FOR ACTING?
WOOOW!
TALK ABOUT BLUNT.

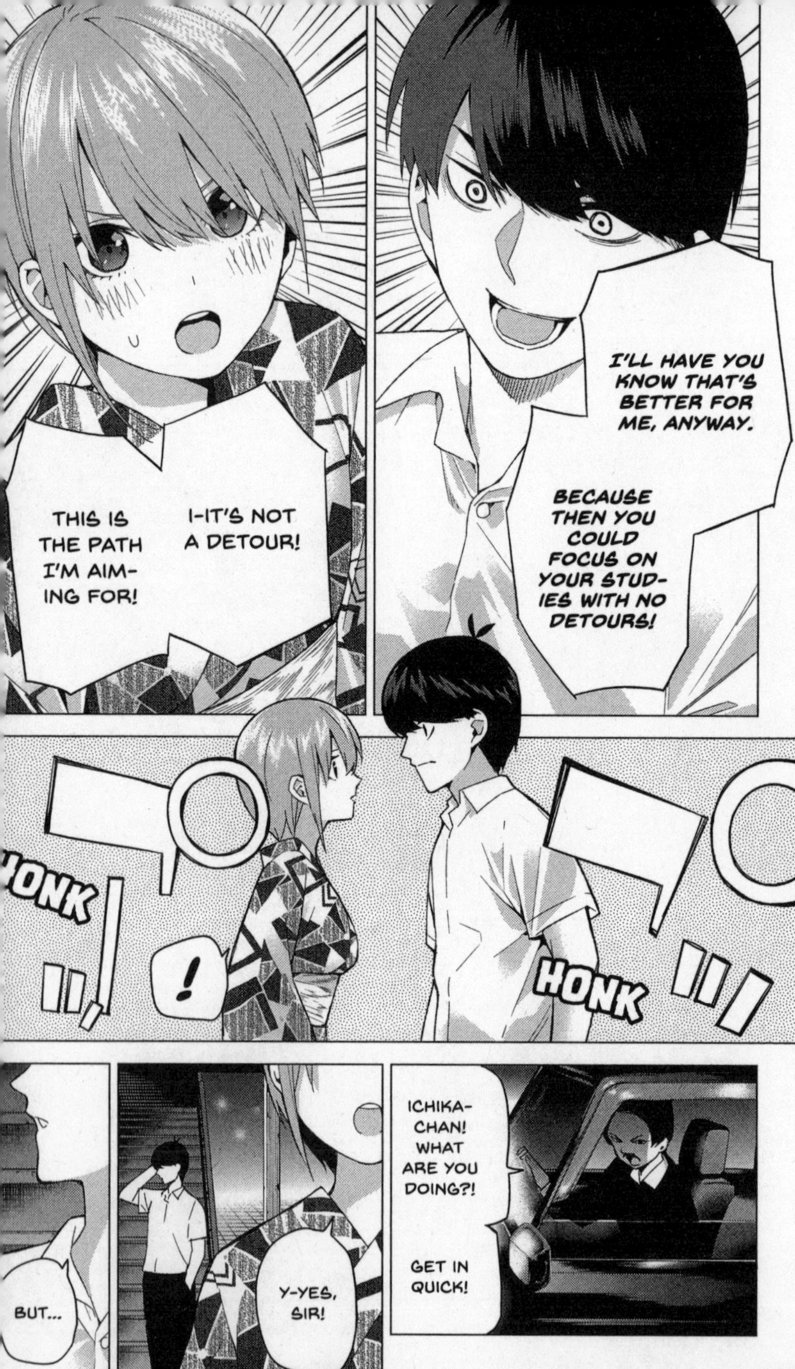
I'LL HAVE YOU KNOW THAT'S BETTER FOR ME, ANYWAY.
BECAUSE THEN YOU COULD FOCUS ON YOUR STUDIES WITH NO DETOURS!
I-IT'S NOT A DETOUR!
THIS IS THE PATH I'M AIMING FOR!
HONK
HONK
!
ICHIKA-CHAN! WHAT ARE YOU DOING?!
GET IN QUICK!
Y-YES, SIR!
BUT...

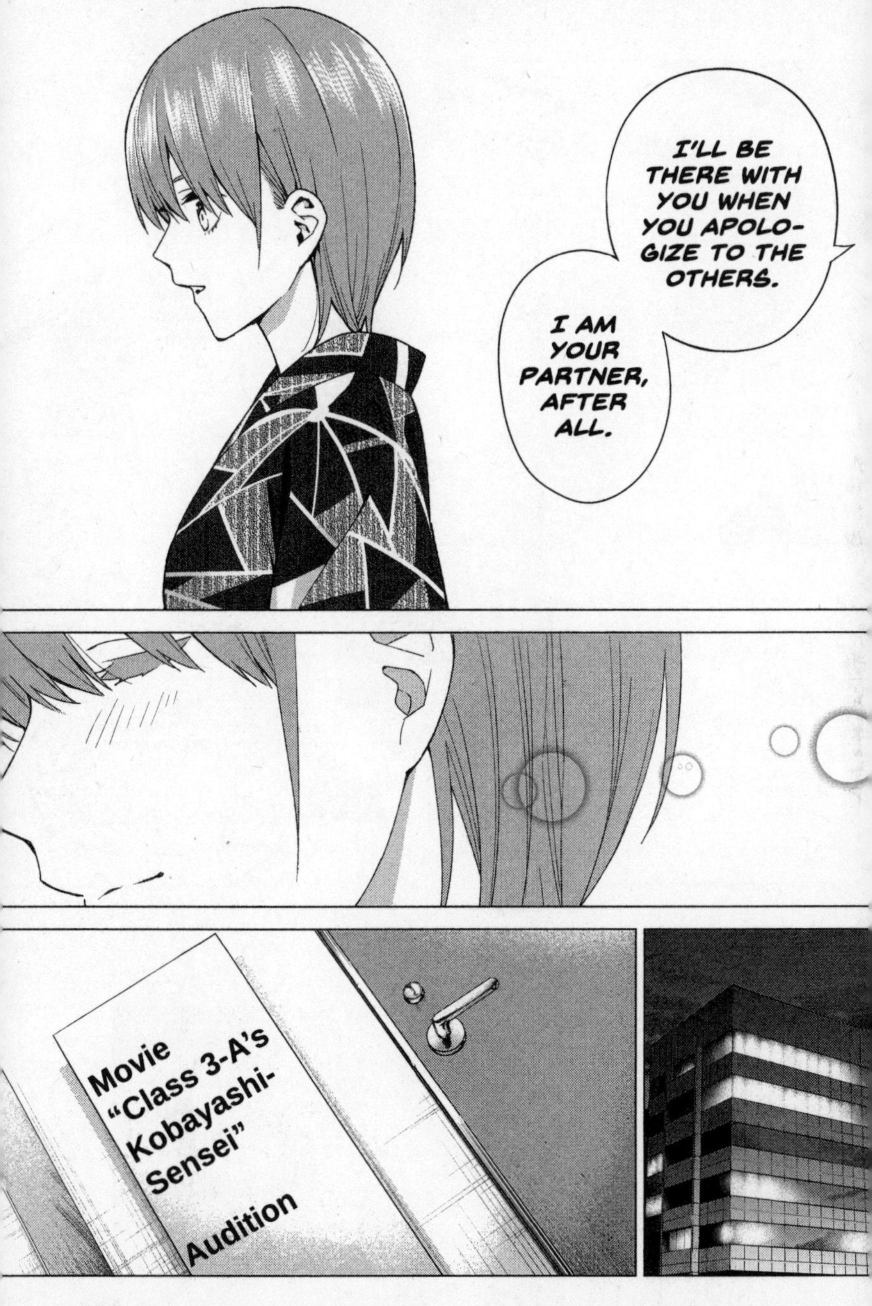
I'LL BE THERE WITH YOU WHEN YOU APOLOGIZE TO THE OTHERS.
I AM YOUR PARTNER, AFTER ALL.
Movie
"Class 3-A's Kobayashi-Sensei"
Audition

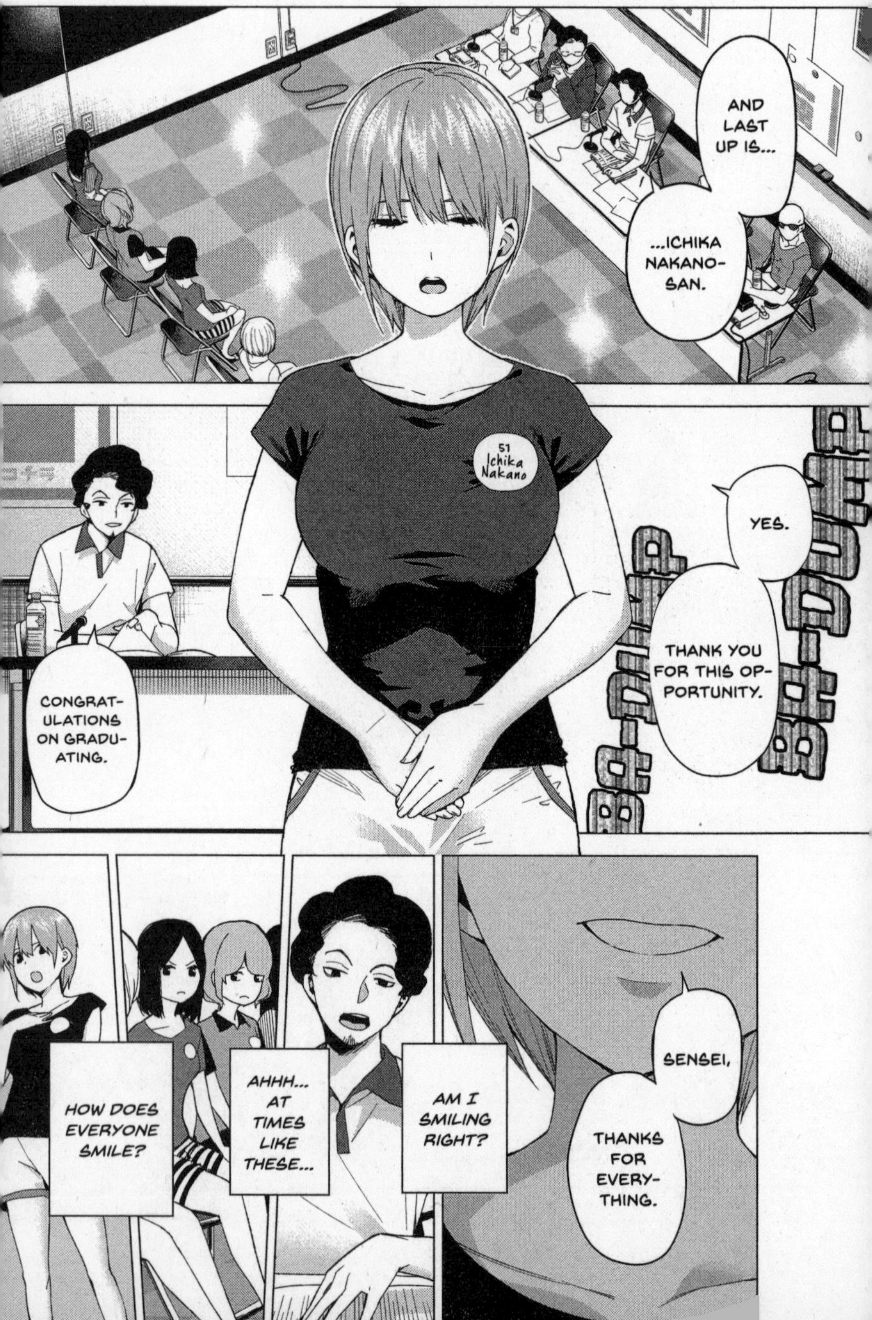
AND LAST UP IS...
...ICHIKA NAKANO-SAN.
YES.
THANK YOU FOR THIS OPPORTUNITY.
BA-DUMP
BA-DUMP
51 Ichika Nakano
CONGRATULATIONS ON GRADUATING.
SENSEI,
THANKS FOR EVERYTHING.
AM I SMILING RIGHT?
AHHH... AT TIMES LIKE THESE...
HOW DOES EVERYONE SMILE?

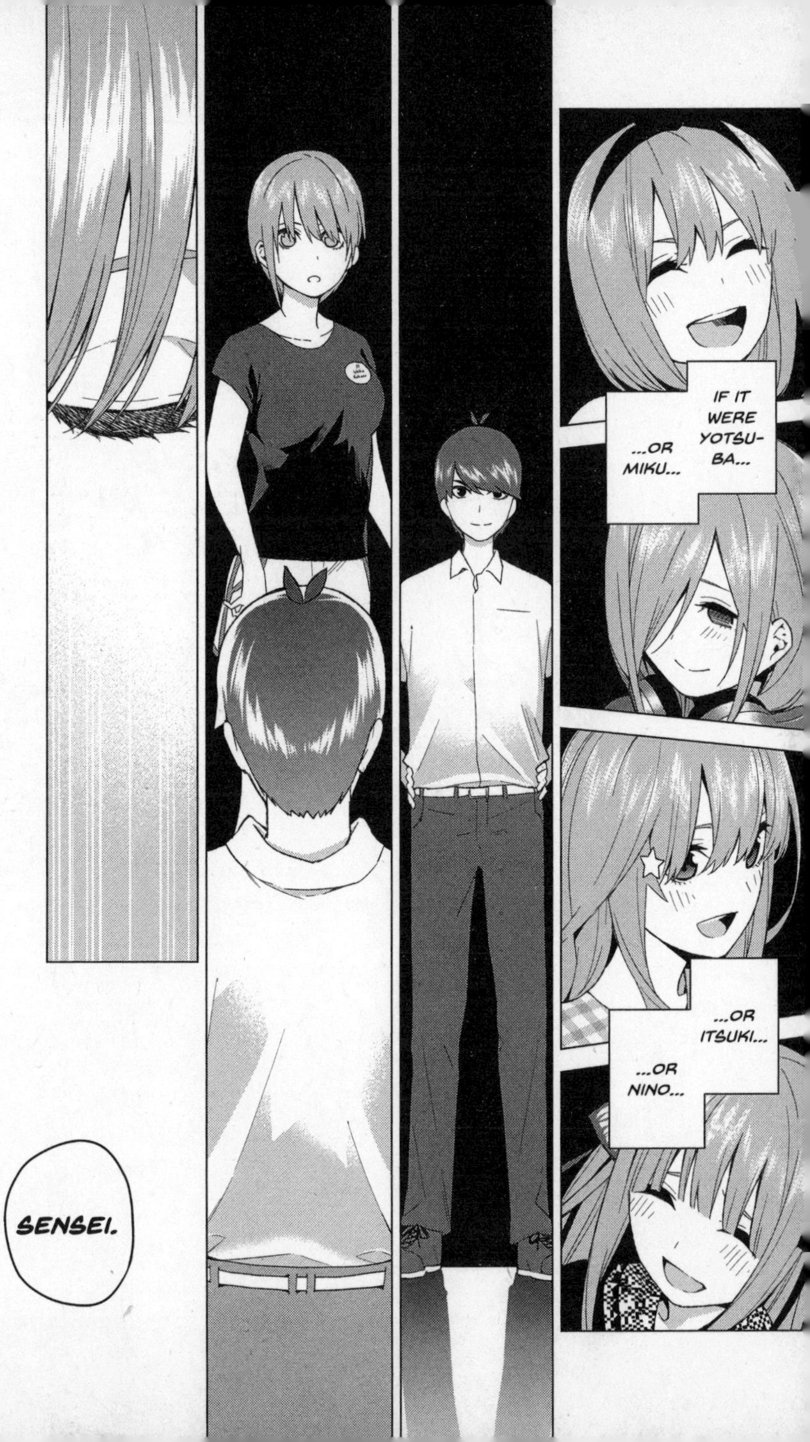
IF IT WERE YOTSUBA...
...OR MIKU...
...OR ITSUKI...
...OR NINO...
SENSEI.

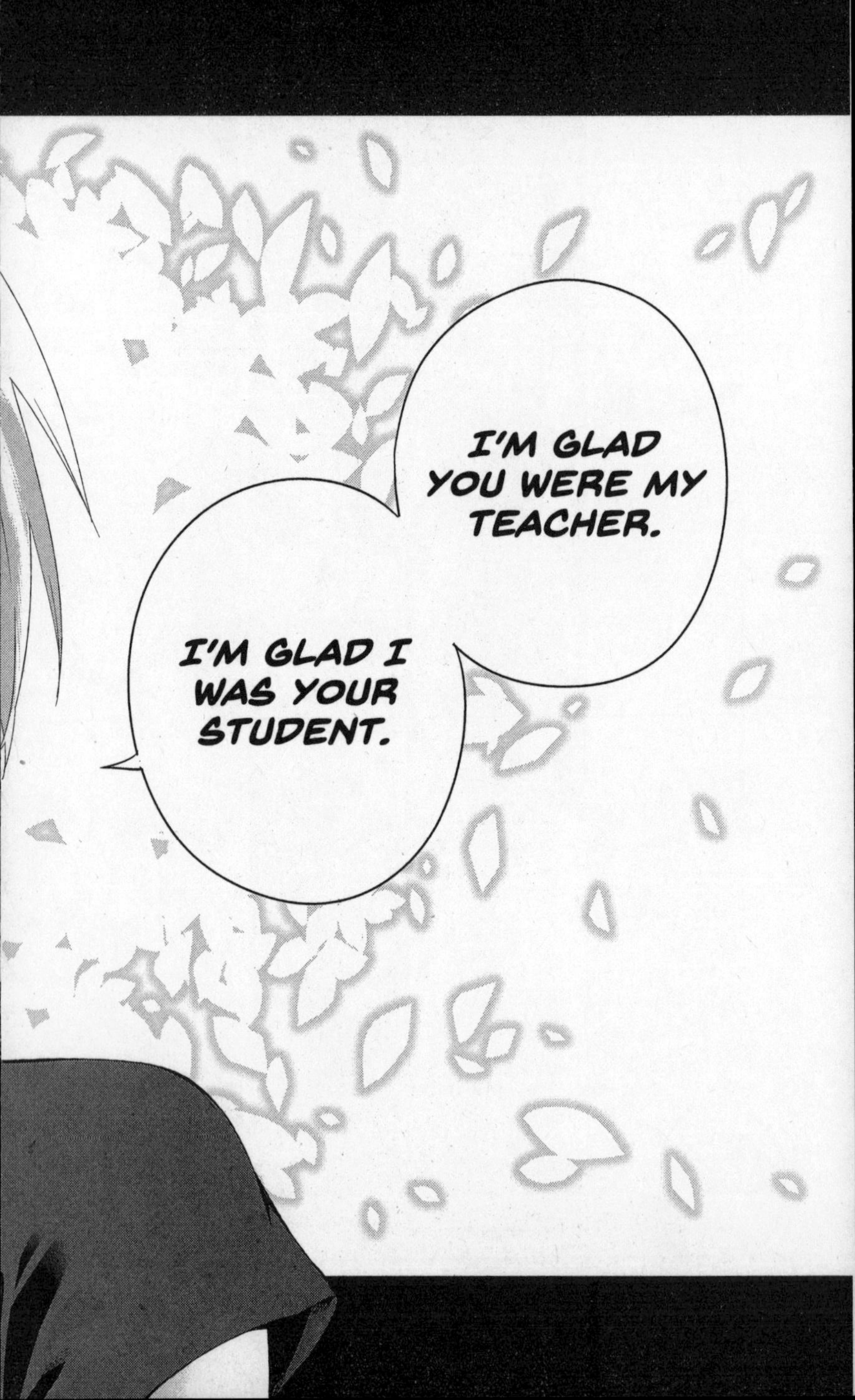
I'M GLAD YOU WERE MY TEACHER.
I'M GLAD I WAS YOUR STUDENT.

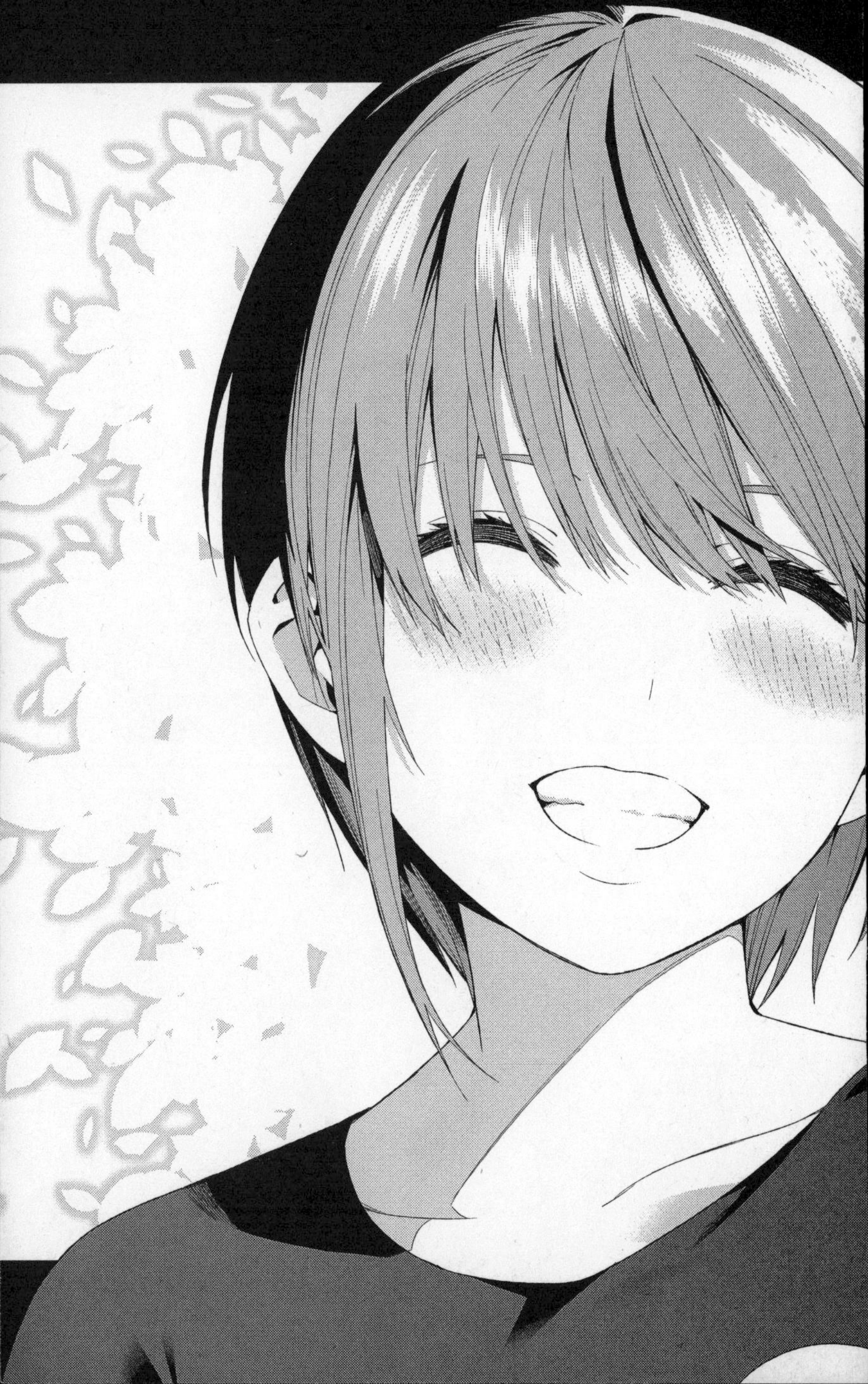

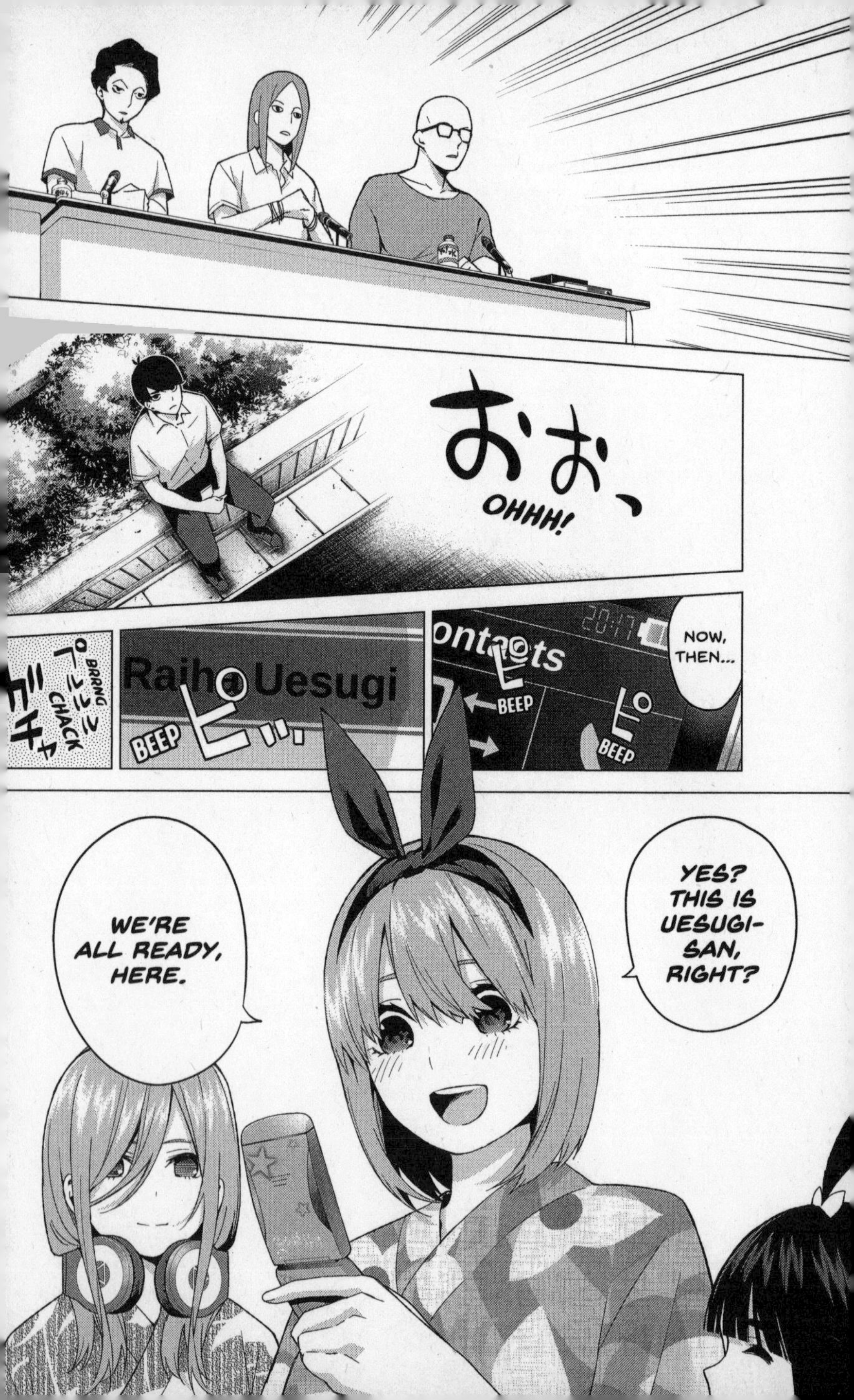
おお、
OHHH!
NOW, THEN...
Contacts
BEEP
BEEP
Raiha Uesugi
BEEP
BRRNG
CHACK
YES? THIS IS UESUGI-SAN, RIGHT?
WE'RE ALL READY, HERE.

CHAPTER 12 OUR DAY OFF ⑥

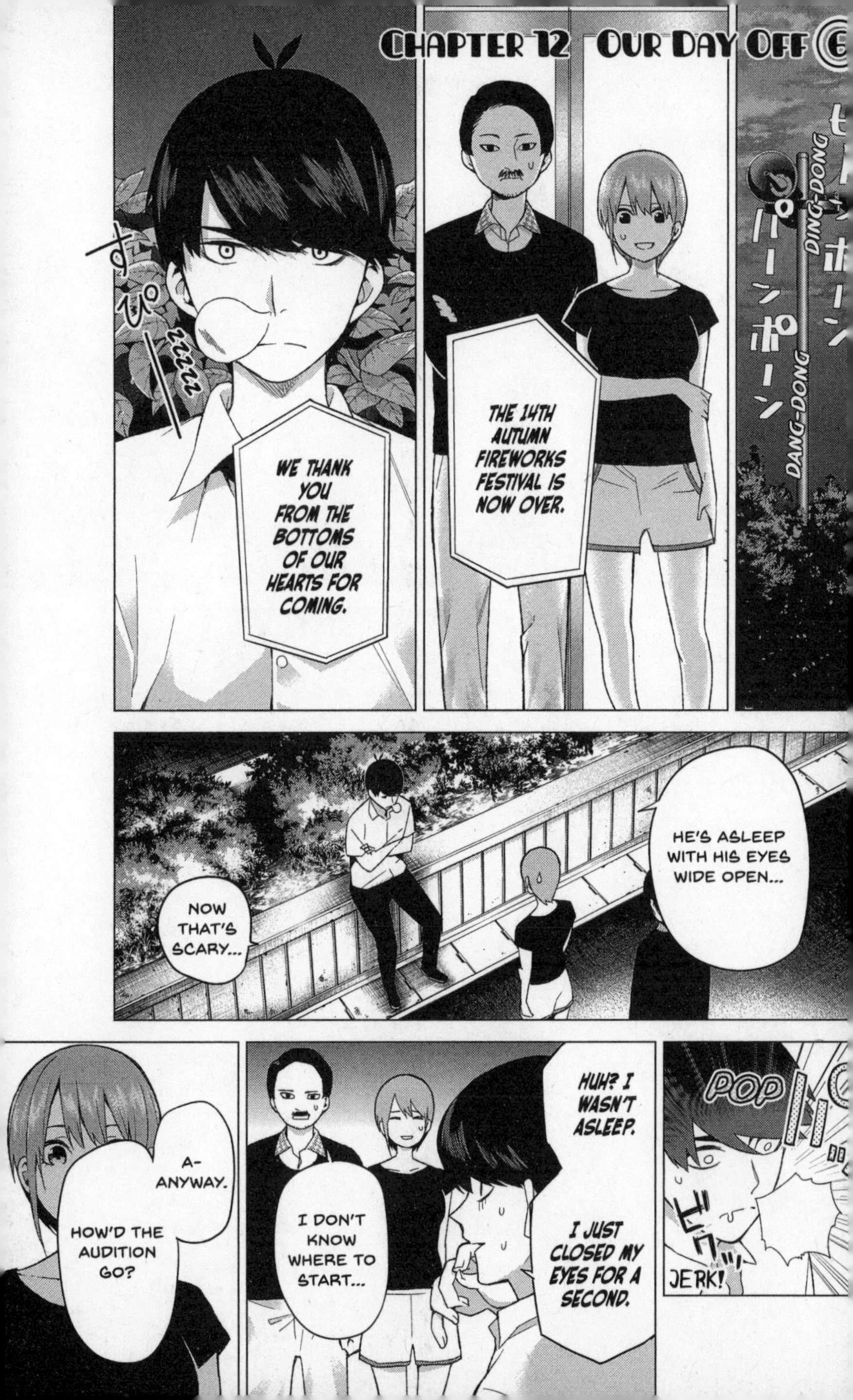
DING-DONG
DANG-DONG
THE 14TH AUTUMN FIREWORKS FESTIVAL IS NOW OVER.
WE THANK YOU FROM THE BOTTOMS OF OUR HEARTS FOR COMING.
すぴー
ZZZZZ
HE'S ASLEEP WITH HIS EYES WIDE OPEN...
NOW THAT'S SCARY...
POP
JERK!
HUH? I WASN'T ASLEEP.
I JUST CLOSED MY EYES FOR A SECOND.
I DON'T KNOW WHERE TO START...
A- ANYWAY.
HOW'D THE AUDITION GO?

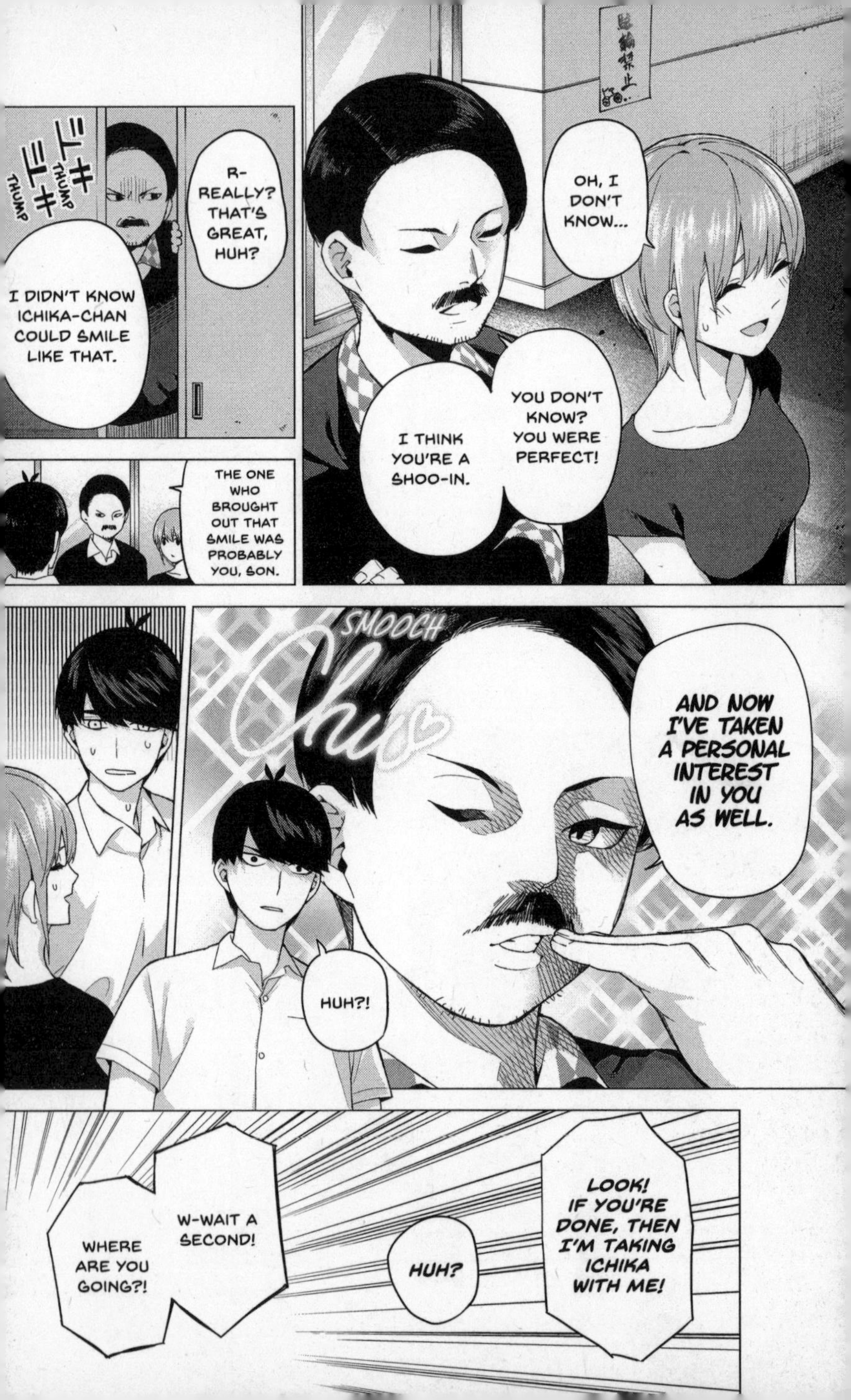
駐輪禁止
OH, I DON'T KNOW...
YOU DON'T KNOW? YOU WERE PERFECT!
I THINK YOU'RE A SHOO-IN.
ドキ ドキ
THUMP THUMP
R- REALLY? THAT'S GREAT, HUH?
I DIDN'T KNOW ICHIKA-CHAN COULD SMILE LIKE THAT.
THE ONE WHO BROUGHT OUT THAT SMILE WAS PROBABLY YOU, SON.
SMOOCH
Chu
AND NOW I'VE TAKEN A PERSONAL INTEREST IN YOU AS WELL.
HUH?!
LOOK! IF YOU'RE DONE, THEN I'M TAKING ICHIKA WITH ME!
HUH?
W-WAIT A SECOND!
WHERE ARE YOU GOING?!

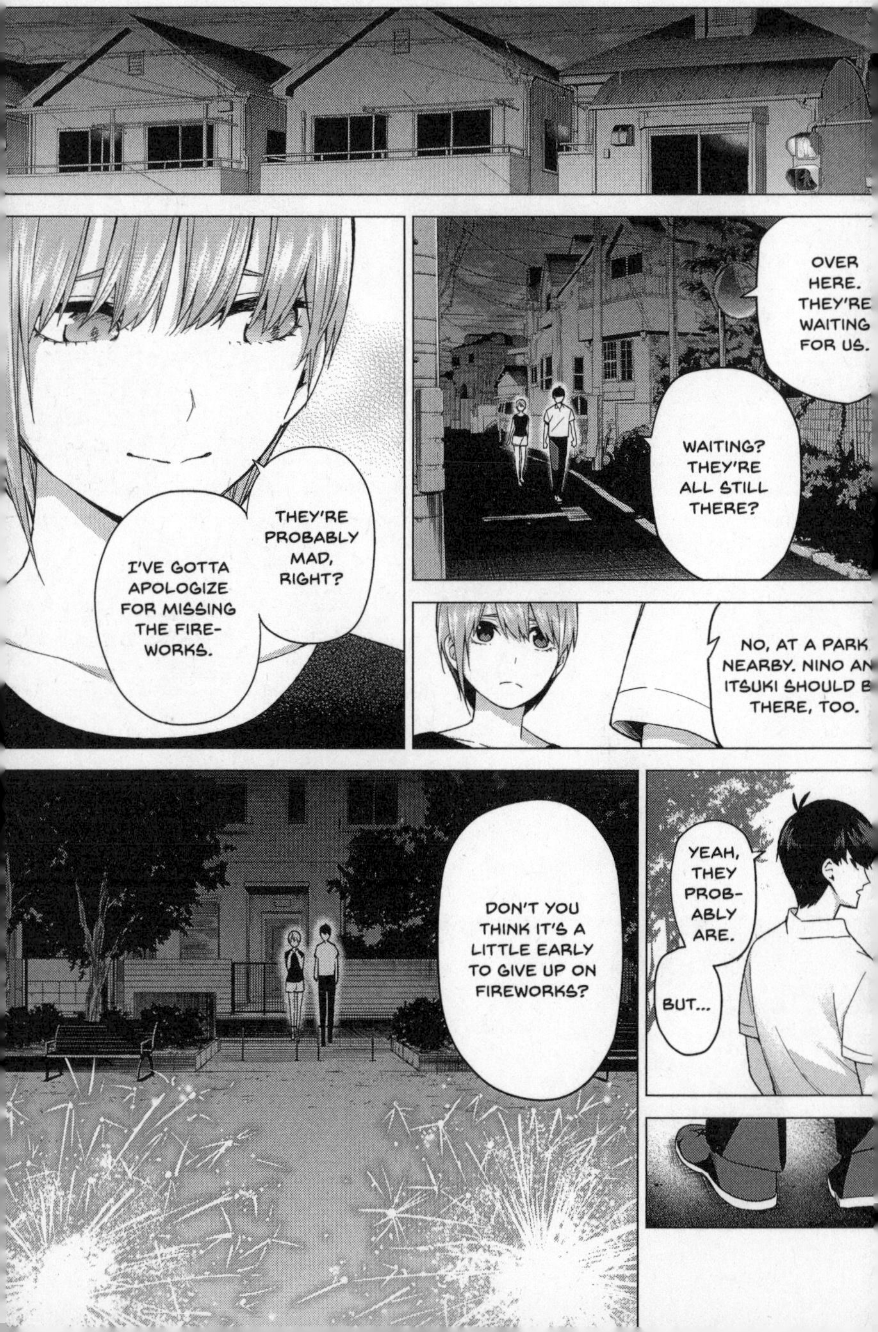
OVER HERE. THEY'RE WAITING FOR US.
WAITING? THEY'RE ALL STILL THERE?
NO, AT A PARK NEARBY. NINO AN ITSUKI SHOULD B THERE, TOO.
THEY'RE PROBABLY MAD, RIGHT?
I'VE GOTTA APOLOGIZE FOR MISSING THE FIRE-WORKS.
YEAH, THEY PROB-ABLY ARE.
BUT...
DON'T YOU THINK IT'S A LITTLE EARLY TO GIVE UP ON FIREWORKS?

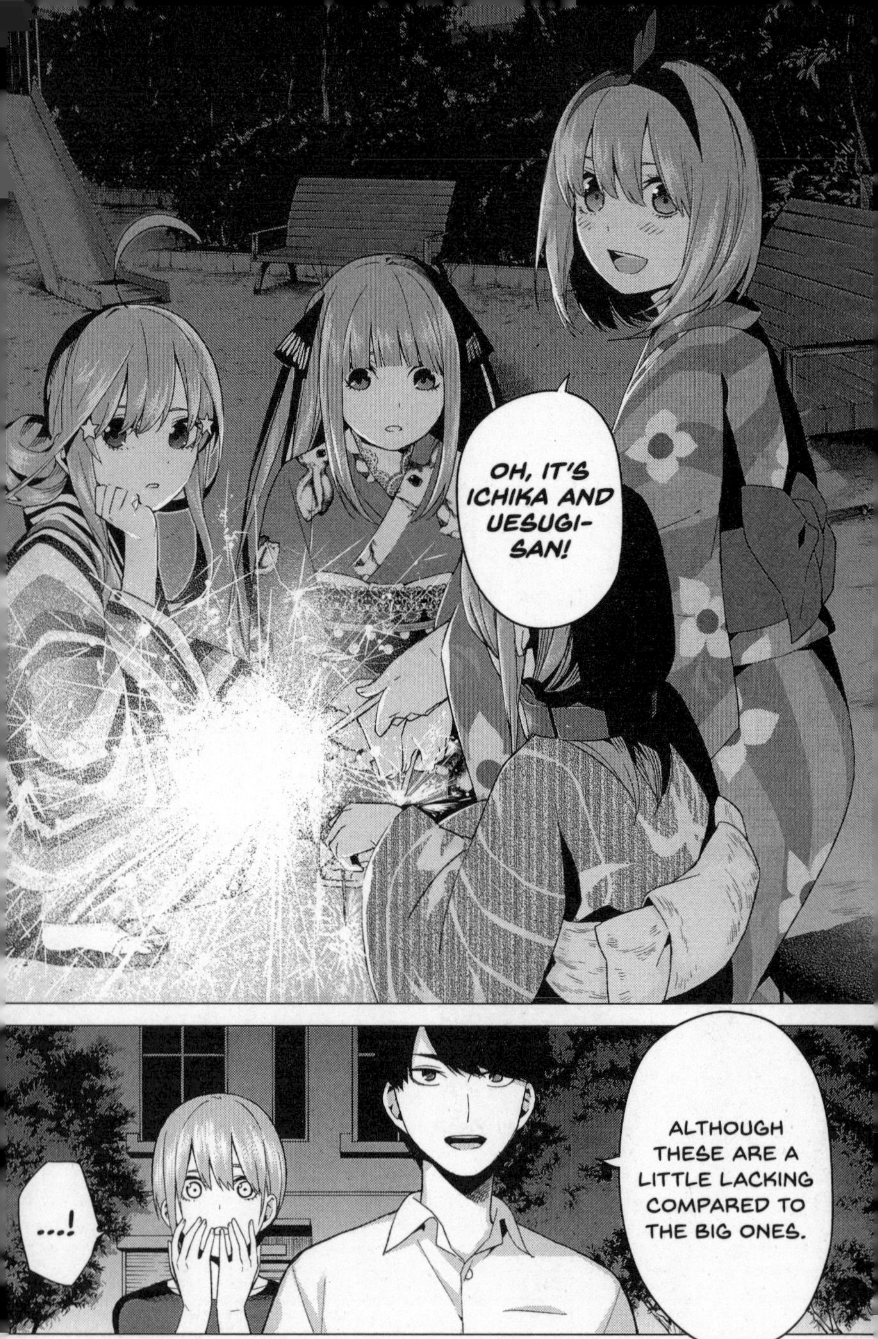
OH, IT'S ICHIKA AND UESUGI-SAN!
ALTHOUGH THESE ARE A LITTLE LACKING COMPARED TO THE BIG ONES.
...!

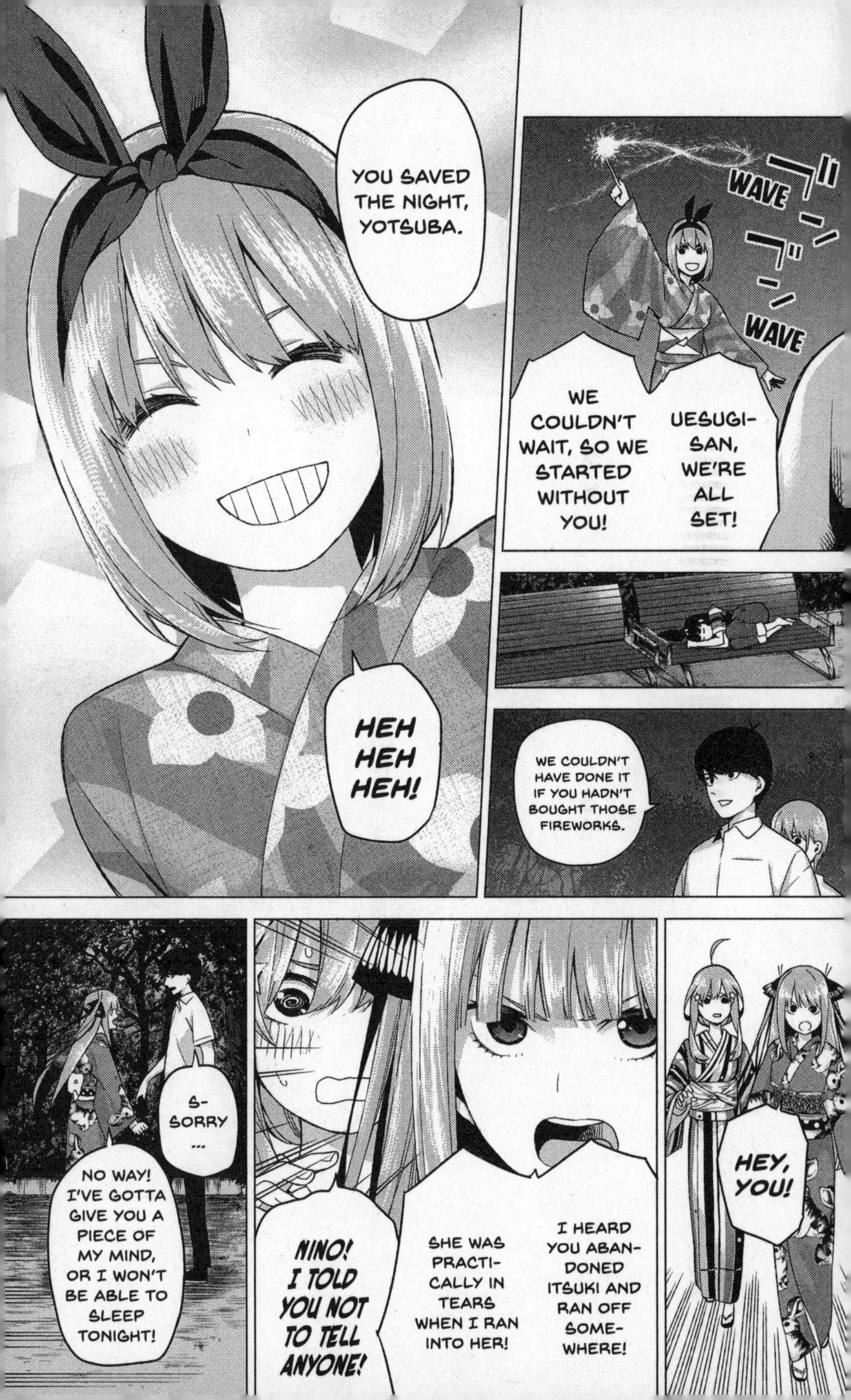
WAVE
WAVE
UESUGI-SAN, WE'RE ALL SET!
WE COULDN'T WAIT, SO WE STARTED WITHOUT YOU!
WE COULDN'T HAVE DONE IT IF YOU HADN'T BOUGHT THOSE FIREWORKS.
YOU SAVED THE NIGHT, YOTSUBA.
HEH HEH HEH!
HEY, YOU!
I HEARD YOU ABANDONED ITSUKI AND RAN OFF SOMEWHERE!
SHE WAS PRACTICALLY IN TEARS WHEN I RAN INTO HER!
NINO! I TOLD YOU NOT TO TELL ANYONE!
S-SORRY...
NO WAY! I'VE GOTTA GIVE YOU A PIECE OF MY MIND, OR I WON'T BE ABLE TO SLEEP TONIGHT!

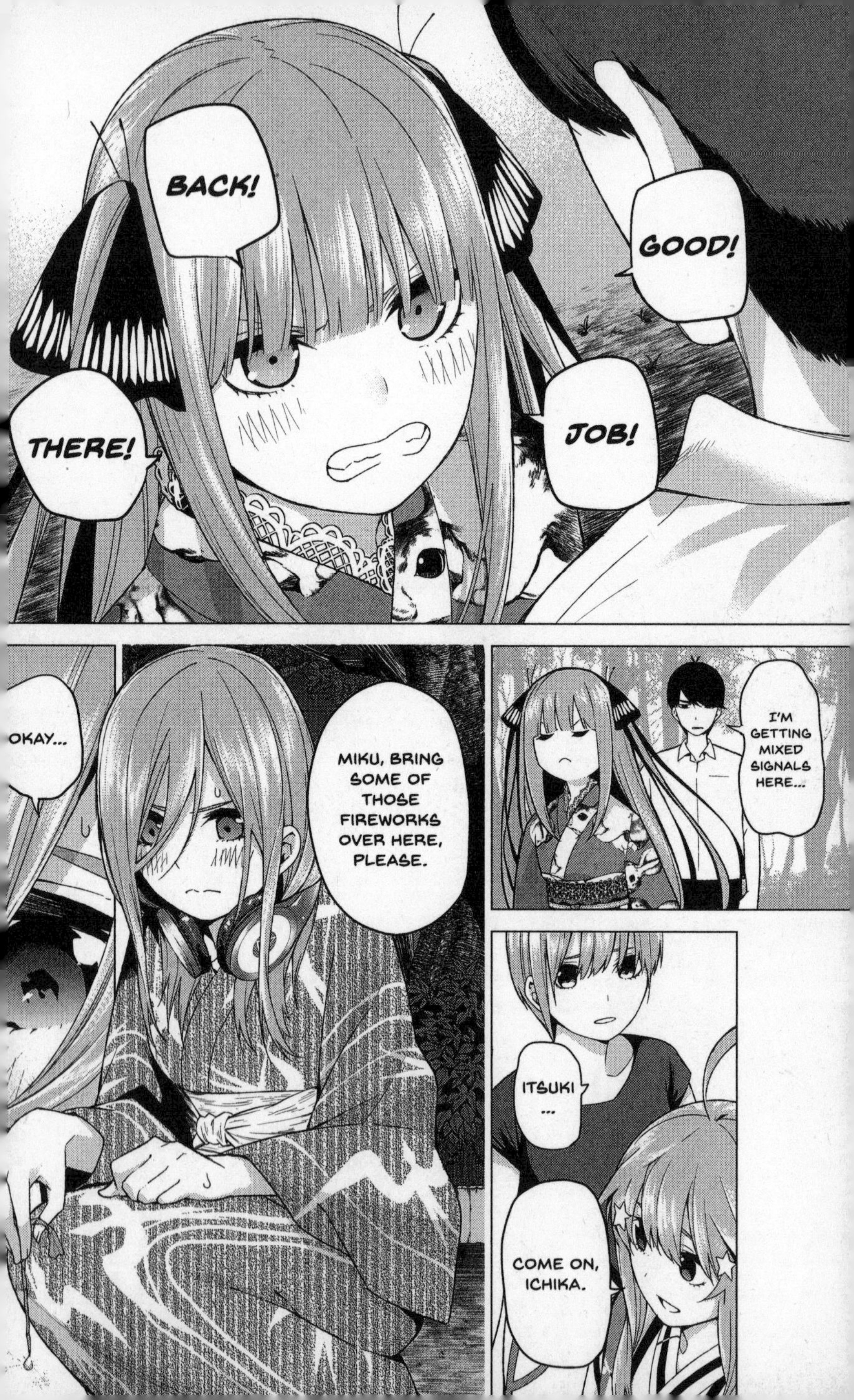
GOOD!
JOB!
BACK!
THERE!
I'M GETTING MIXED SIGNALS HERE...
ITSUKI ...
COME ON, ICHIKA.
MIKU, BRING SOME OF THOSE FIREWORKS OVER HERE, PLEASE.
OKAY...

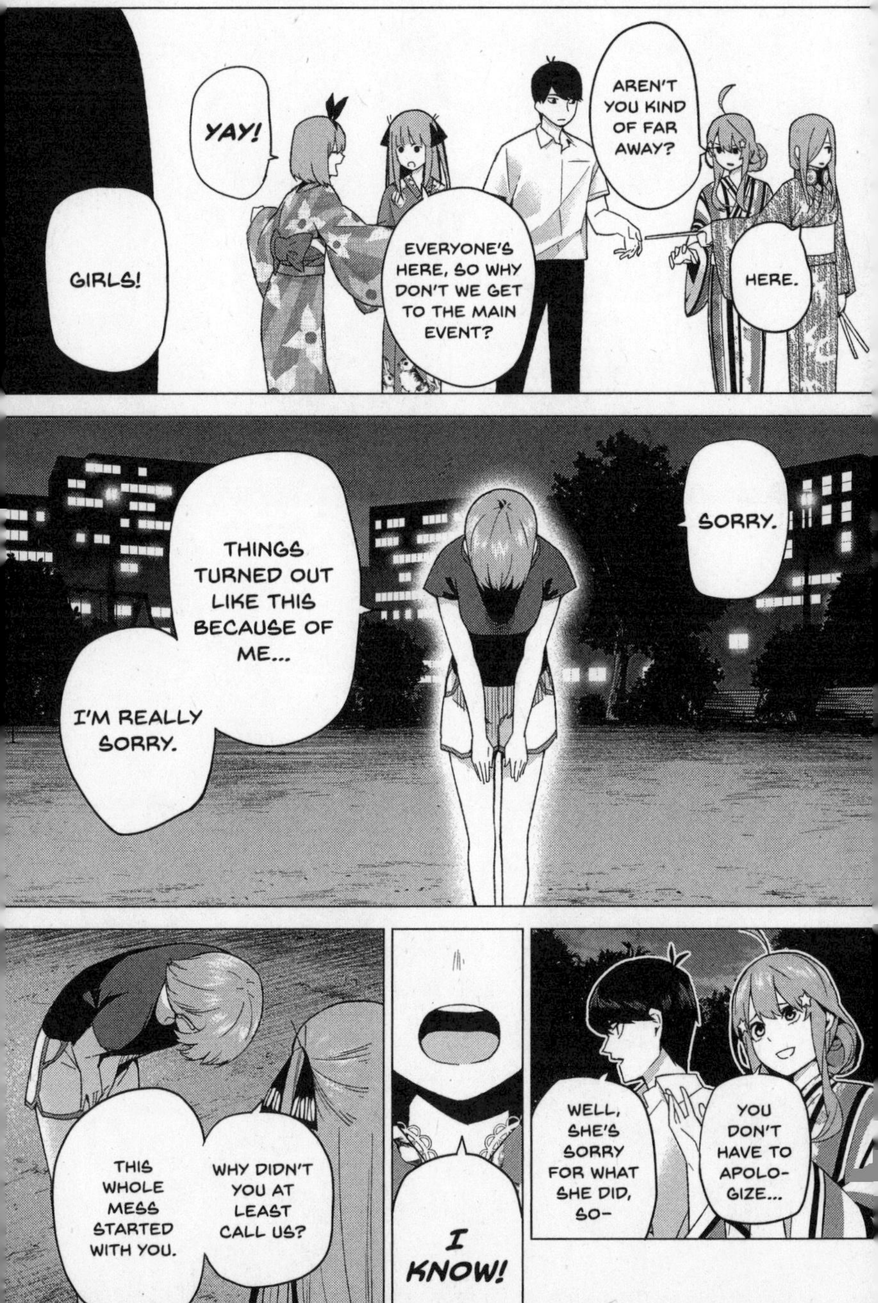
AREN'T YOU KIND OF FAR AWAY?
HERE.
EVERYONE'S HERE, SO WHY DON'T WE GET TO THE MAIN EVENT?
YAY!
GIRLS!
SORRY.
THINGS TURNED OUT LIKE THIS BECAUSE OF ME...
I'M REALLY SORRY.
YOU DON'T HAVE TO APOLO-GIZE...
WELL, SHE'S SORRY FOR WHAT SHE DID, SO-
I KNOW!
WHY DIDN'T YOU AT LEAST CALL US?
THIS WHOLE MESS STARTED WITH YOU.

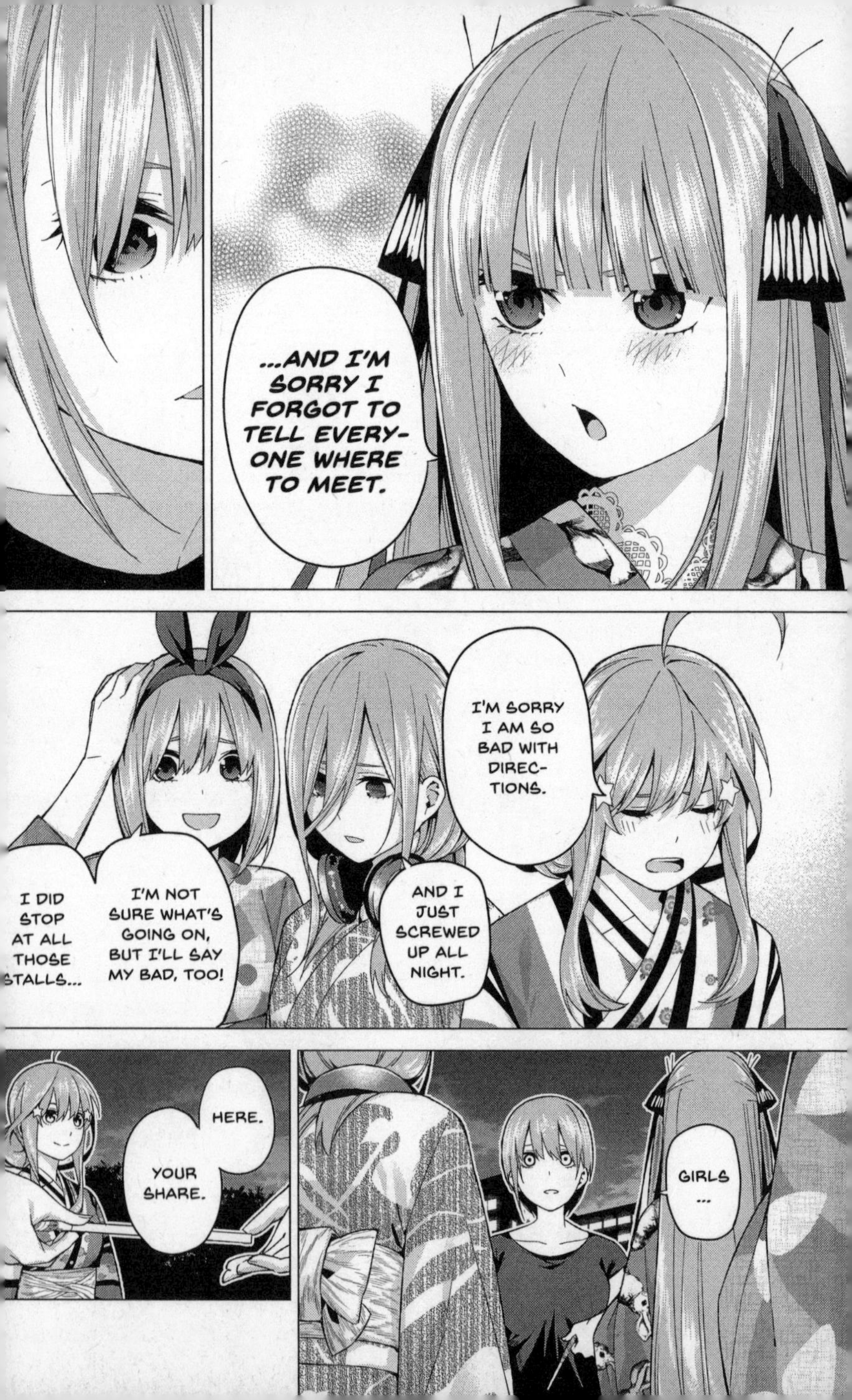
...AND I'M SORRY I FORGOT TO TELL EVERYONE WHERE TO MEET.
I'M SORRY I AM SO BAD WITH DIRECTIONS.
AND I JUST SCREWED UP ALL NIGHT.
I'M NOT SURE WHAT'S GOING ON, BUT I'LL SAY MY BAD, TOO!
I DID STOP AT ALL THOSE STALLS...
GIRLS...
HERE.
YOUR SHARE.

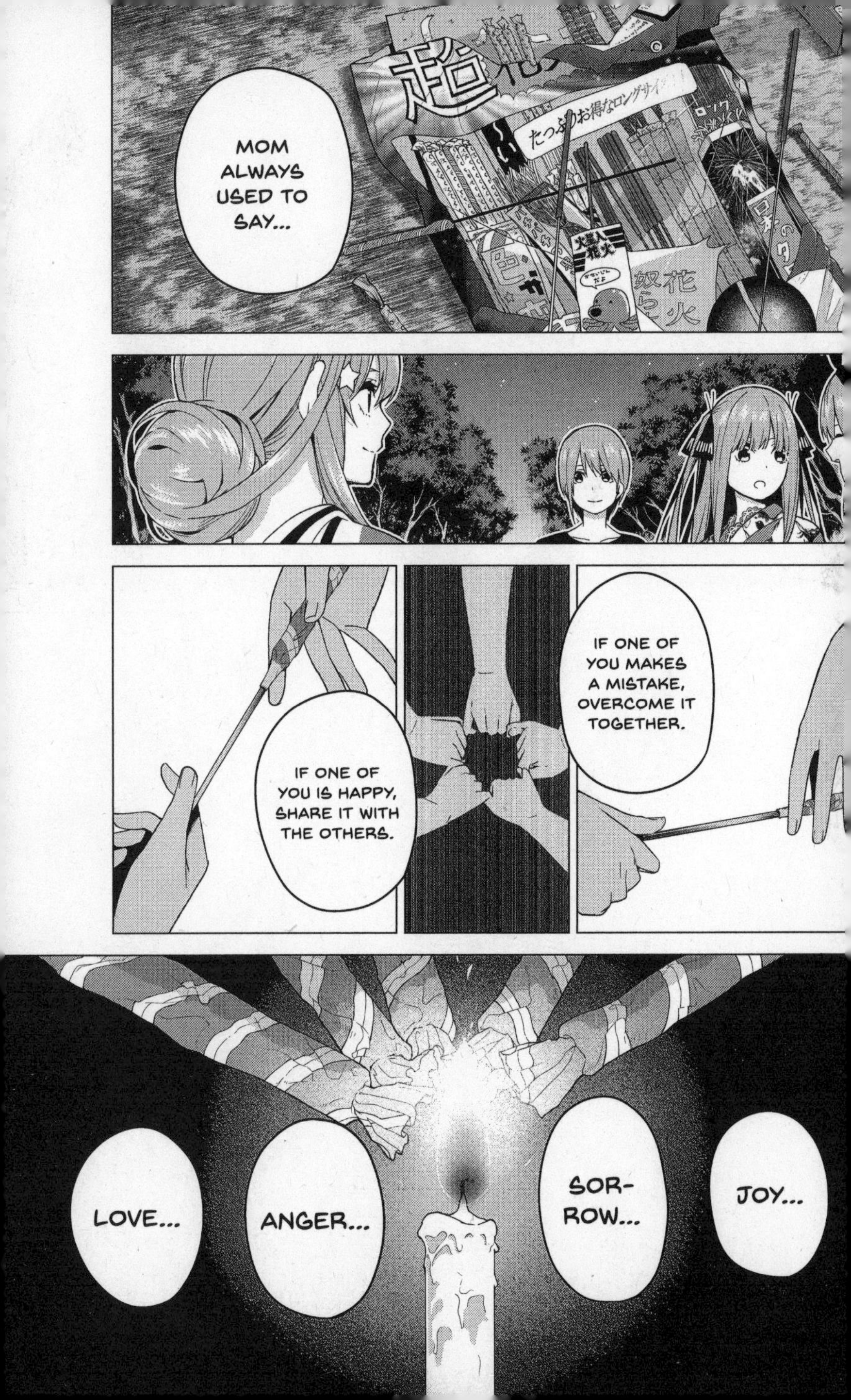
MOM ALWAYS USED TO SAY...
IF ONE OF YOU MAKES A MISTAKE, OVERCOME IT TOGETHER.
IF ONE OF YOU IS HAPPY, SHARE IT WITH THE OTHERS.
JOY...
SOR-ROW...
ANGER...
LOVE...

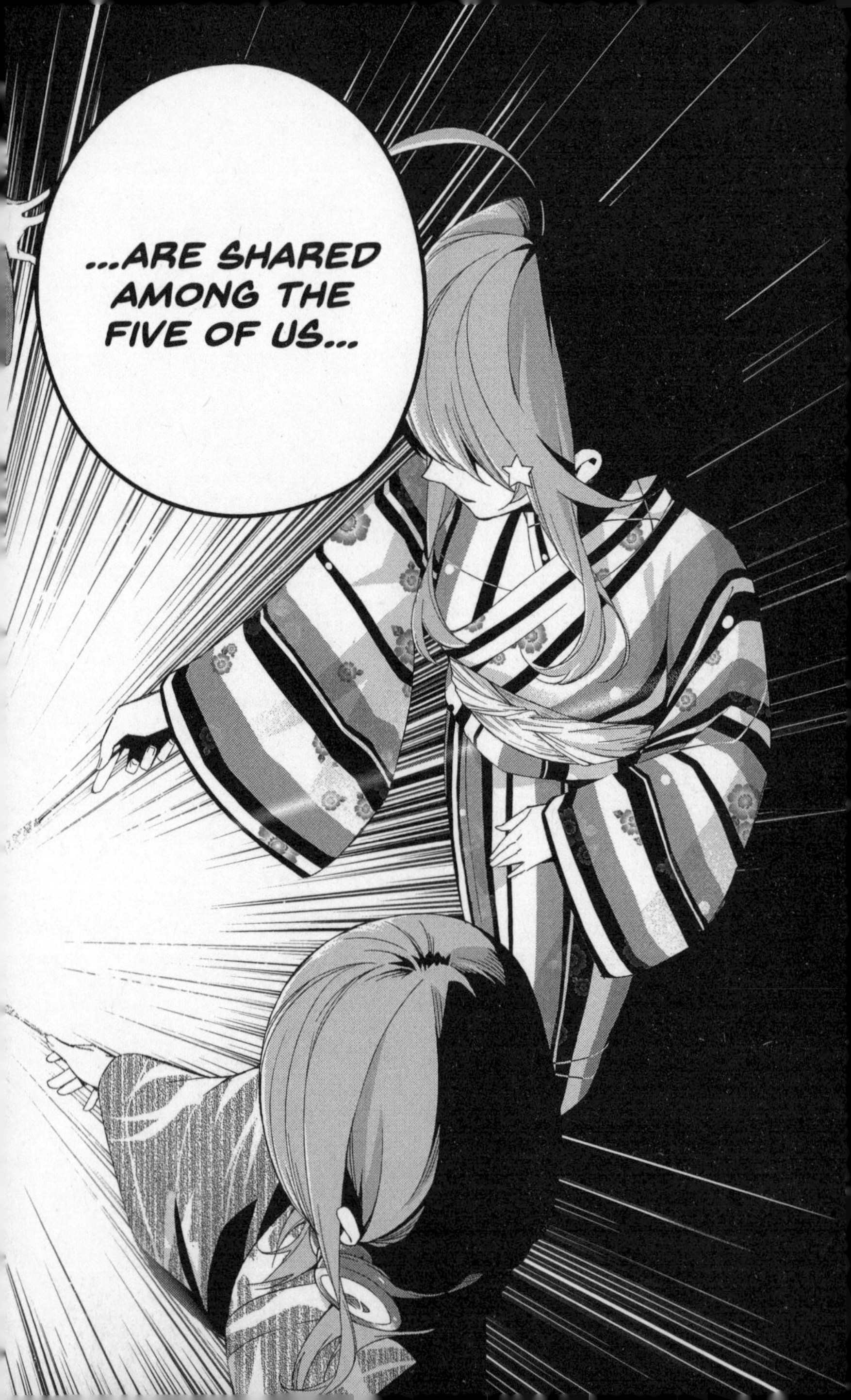
...ARE SHARED AMONG THE FIVE OF US...

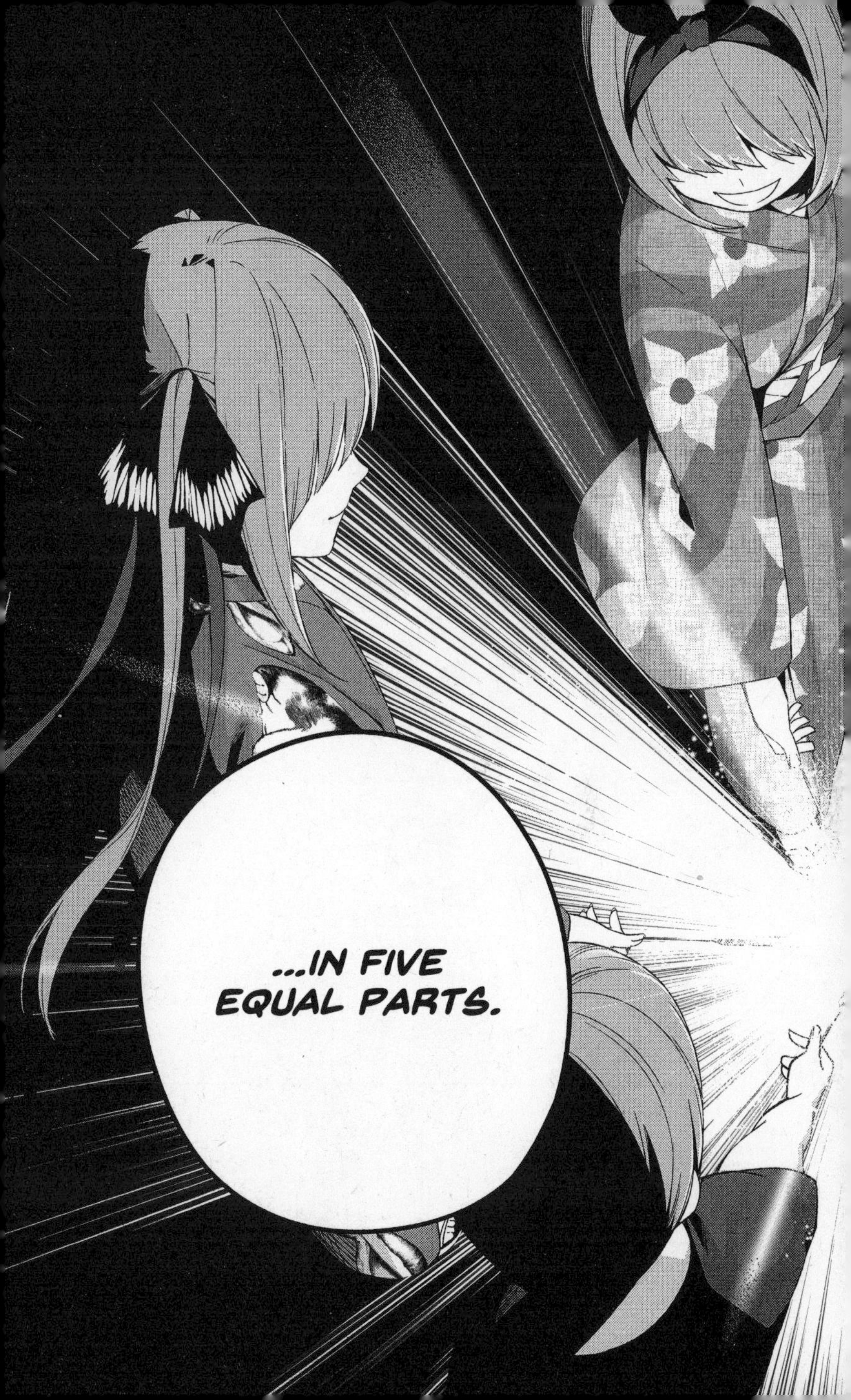
...IN FIVE EQUAL PARTS.

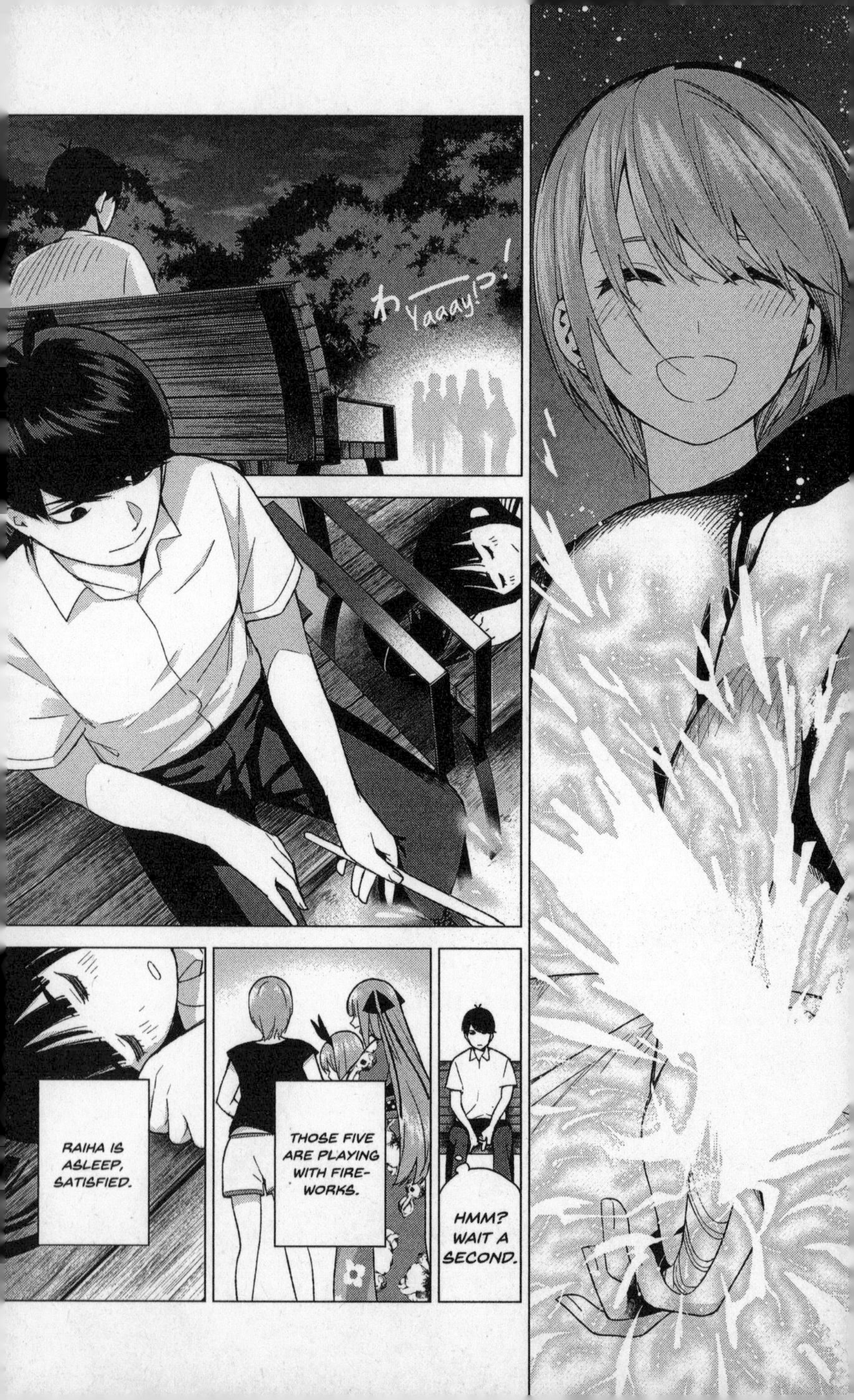
Yaaay!!
HMM? WAIT A SECOND.
THOSE FIVE ARE PLAYING WITH FIRE-WORKS.
RAIHA IS ASLEEP, SATISFIED.

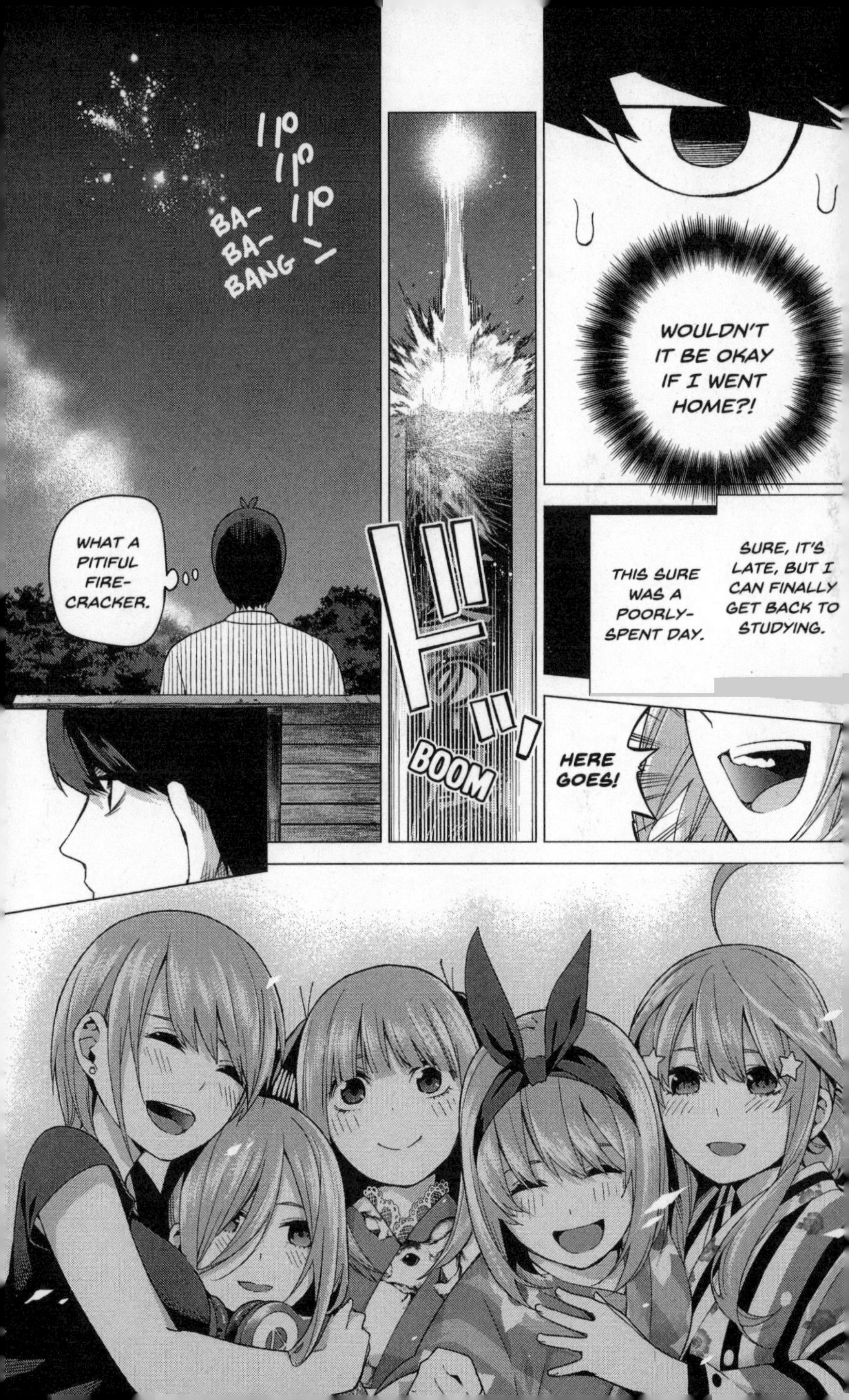
WOULDN'T IT BE OKAY IF I WENT HOME?!
SURE, IT'S LATE, BUT I CAN FINALLY GET BACK TO STUDYING.
THIS SURE WAS A POORLY-SPENT DAY.
HERE GOES!
BOOM
BA- BA- BANG
WHAT A PITIFUL FIRE-CRACKER.

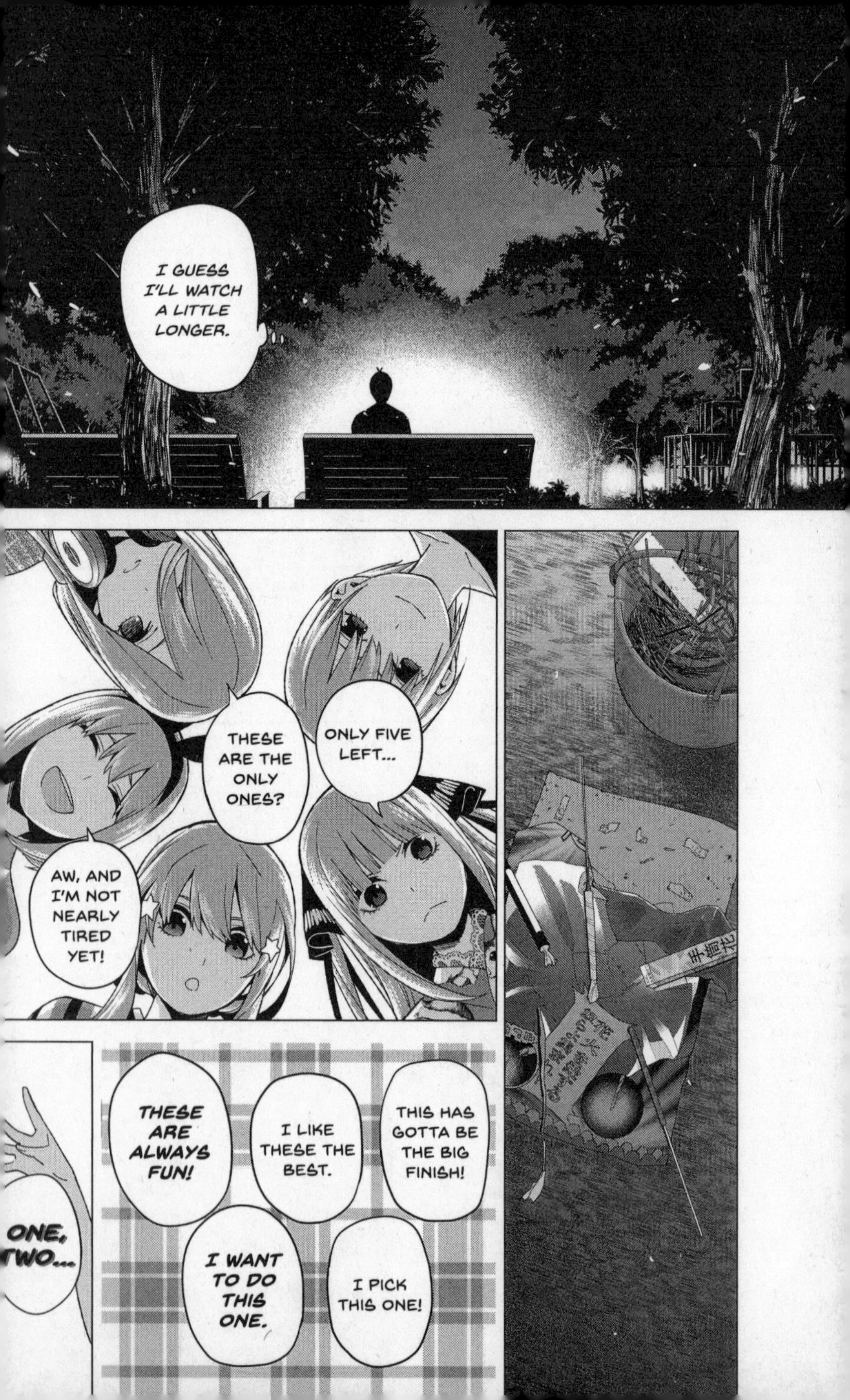
I GUESS I'LL WATCH A LITTLE LONGER.
ONLY FIVE LEFT...
THESE ARE THE ONLY ONES?
AW, AND I'M NOT NEARLY TIRED YET!
THIS HAS GOTTA BE THE BIG FINISH!
I LIKE THESE THE BEST.
THESE ARE ALWAYS FUN!
I PICK THIS ONE!
I WANT TO DO THIS ONE.
ONE, TWO...

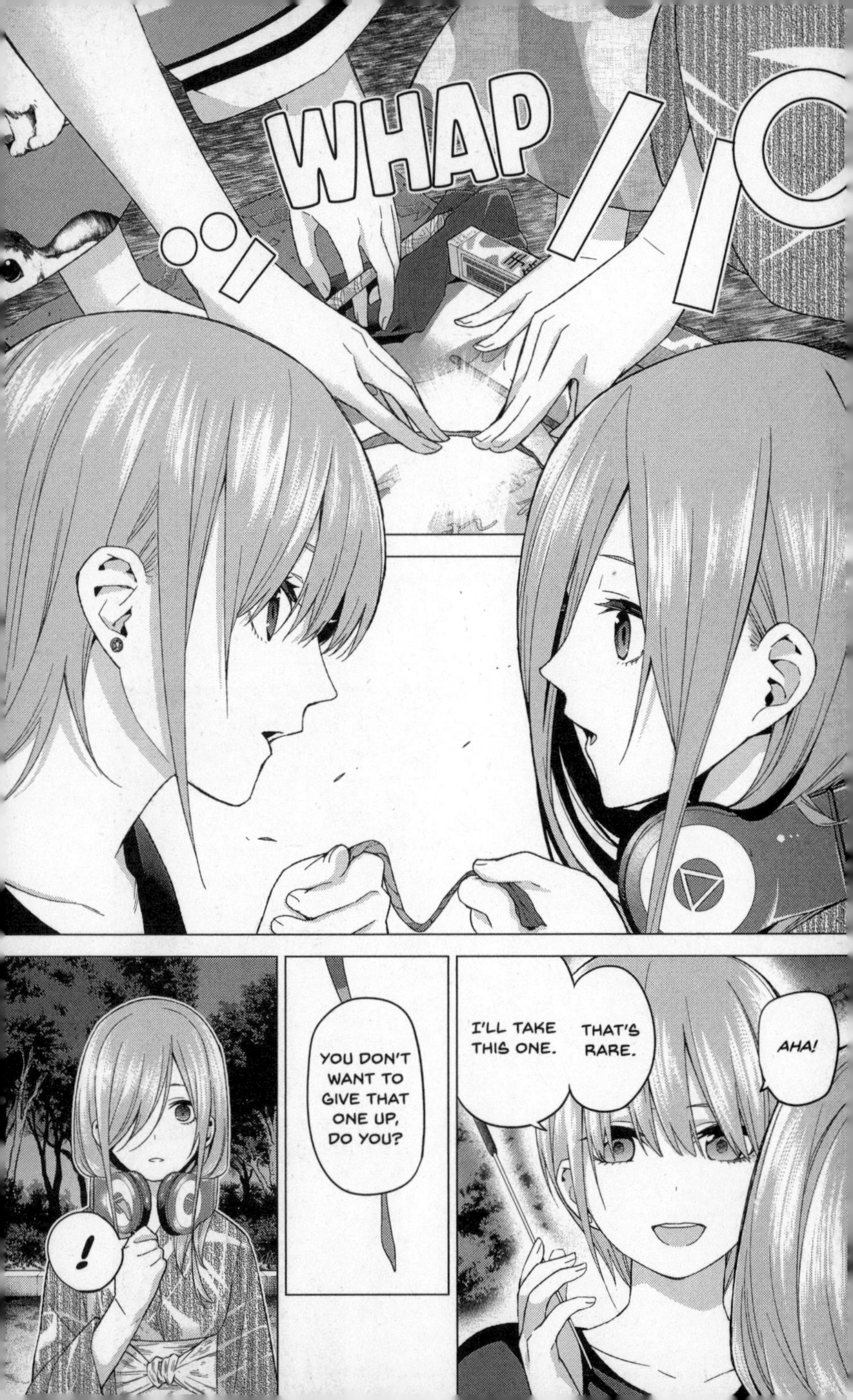
WHAP
AHA!
THAT'S RARE.
I'LL TAKE THIS ONE.
YOU DON'T WANT TO GIVE THAT ONE UP, DO YOU?
!

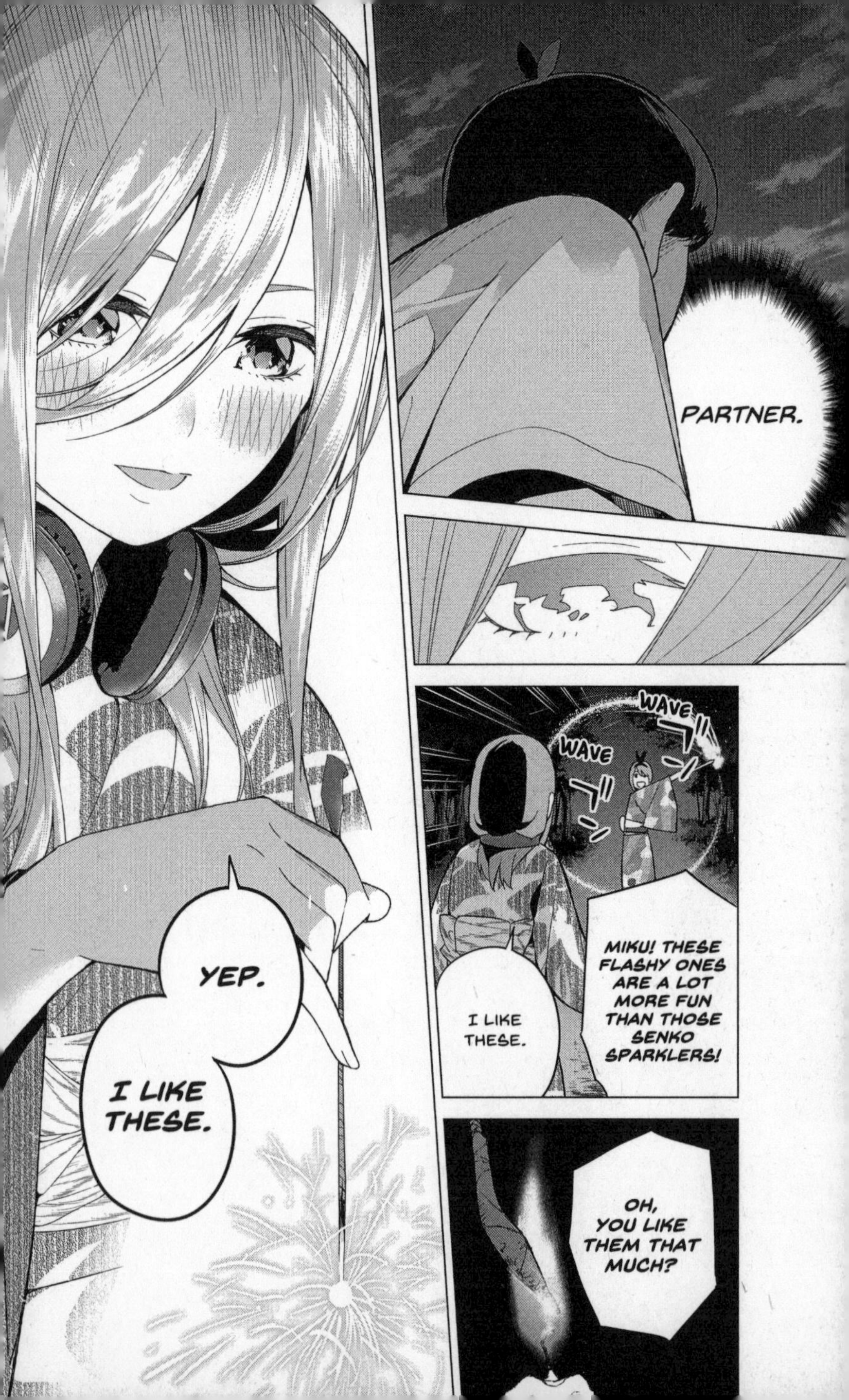
PARTNER.
WAVE
WAVE
MIKU! THESE FLASHY ONES ARE A LOT MORE FUN THAN THOSE SENKO SPARKLERS!
I LIKE THESE.
OH, YOU LIKE THEM THAT MUCH?
YEP.
I LIKE THESE.

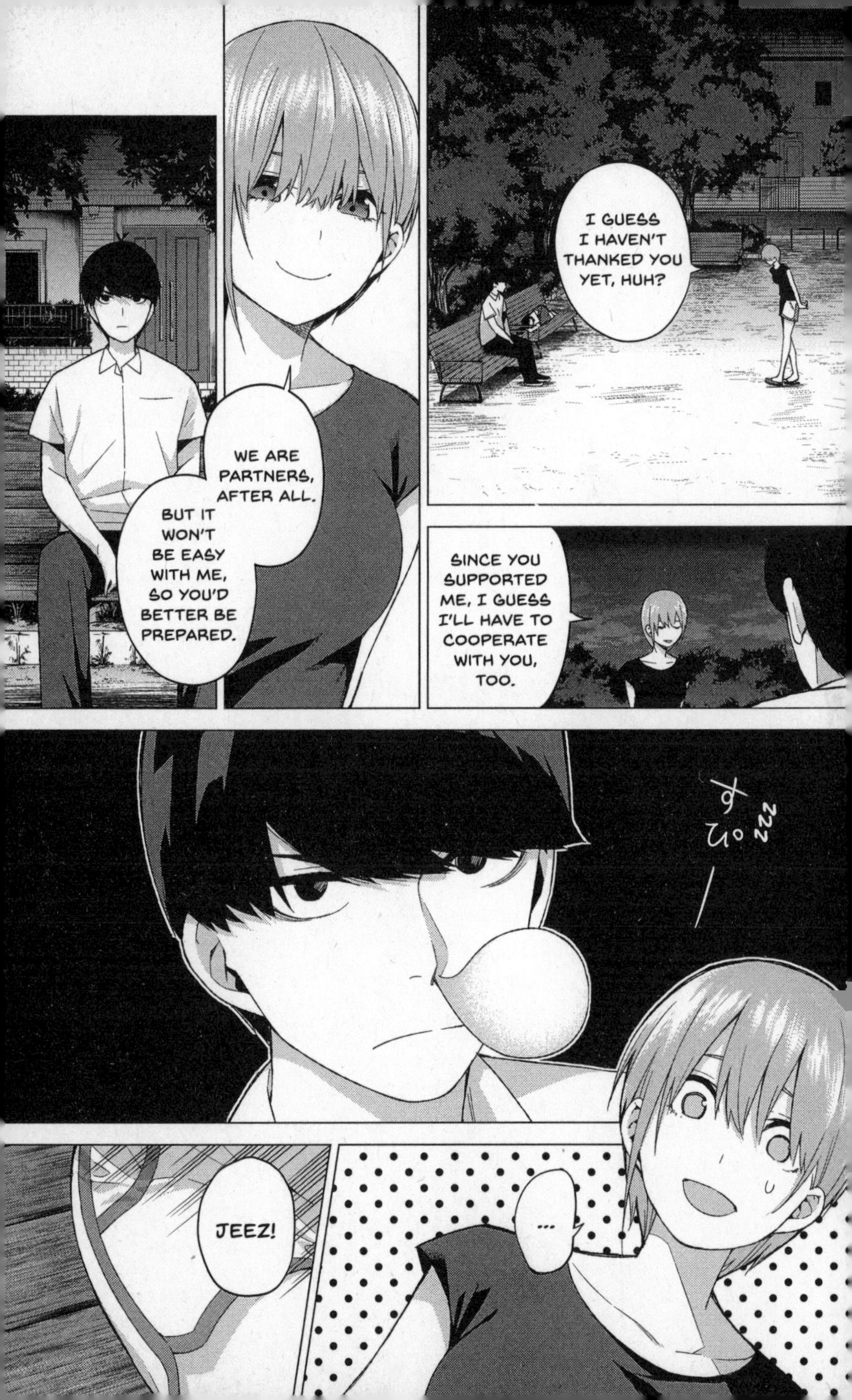
I GUESS I HAVEN'T THANKED YOU YET, HUH?
SINCE YOU SUPPORTED ME, I GUESS I'LL HAVE TO COOPERATE WITH YOU, TOO.
WE ARE PARTNERS, AFTER ALL.
BUT IT WON'T BE EASY WITH ME, SO YOU'D BETTER BE PREPARED.
すぴー zzz
...
JEEZ!

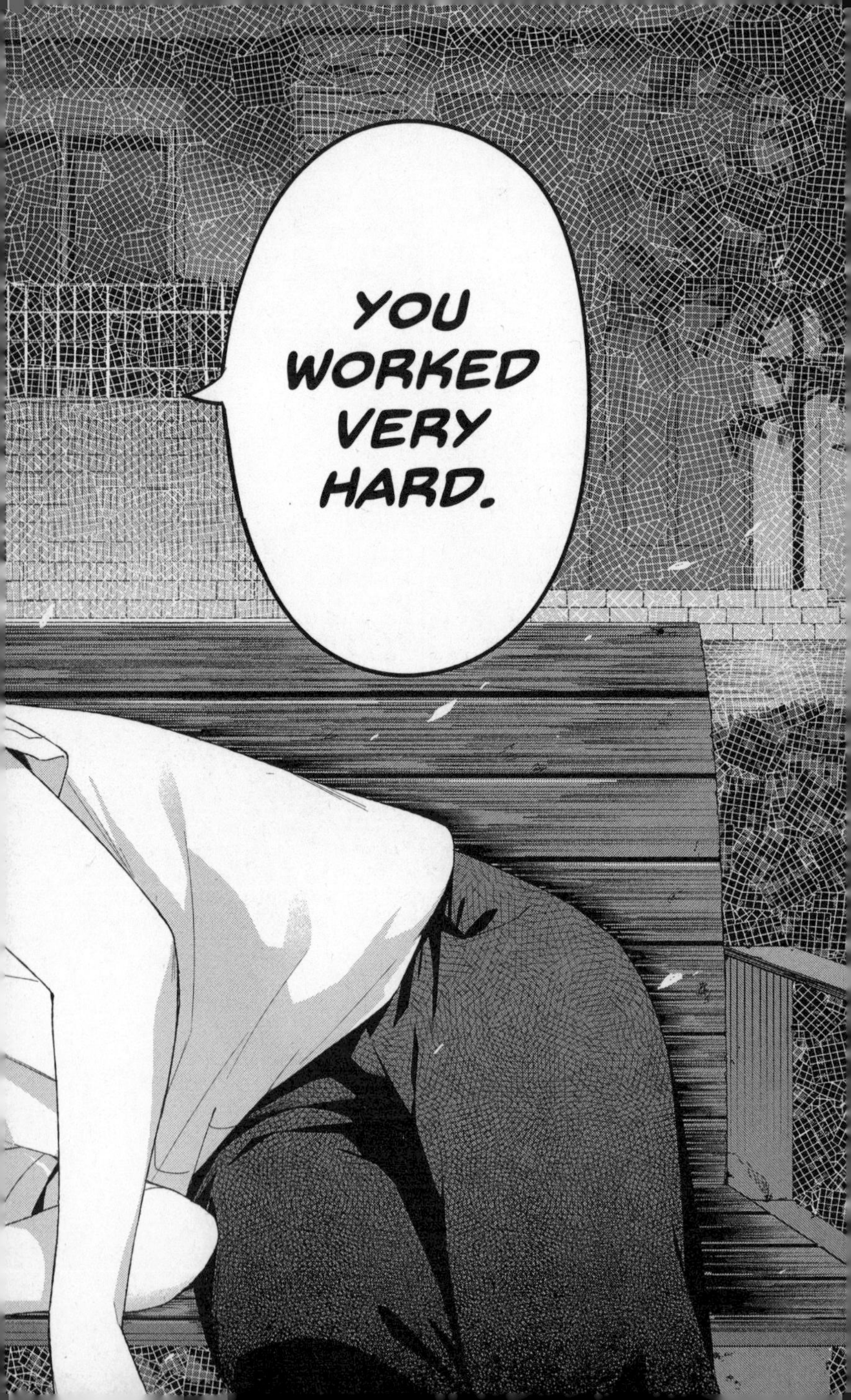
YOU WORKED VERY HARD.

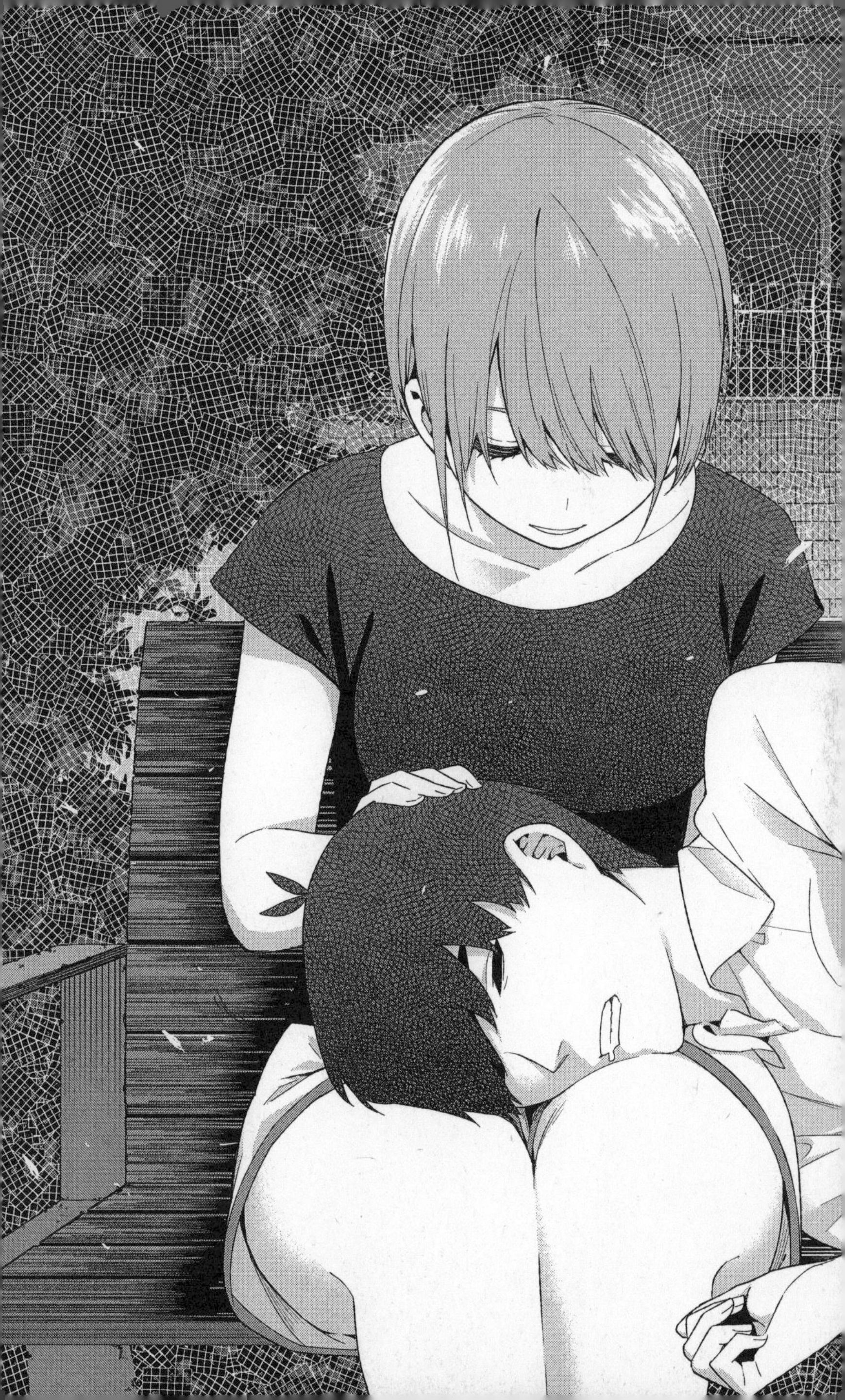

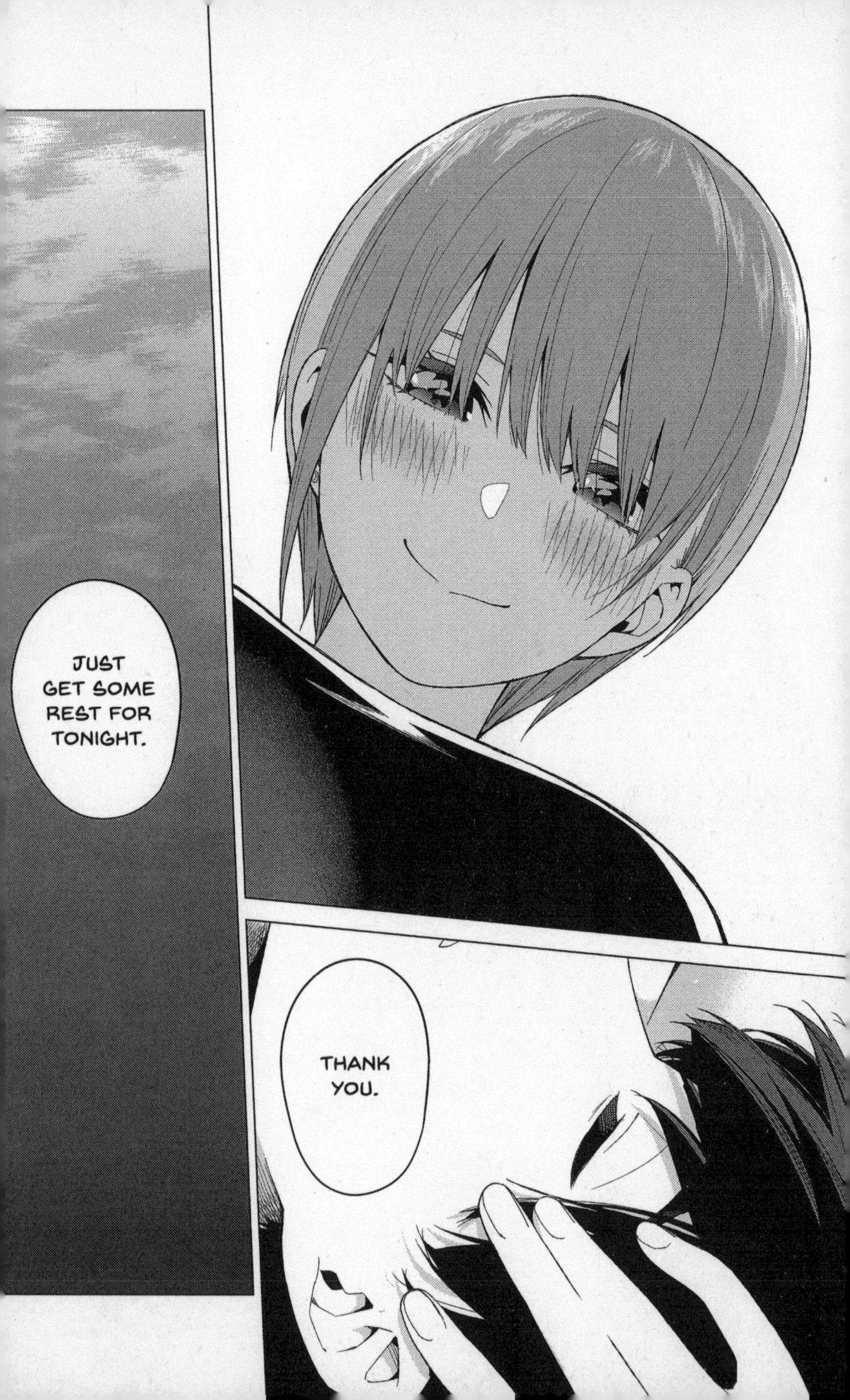
THANK YOU.
JUST GET SOME REST FOR TONIGHT.

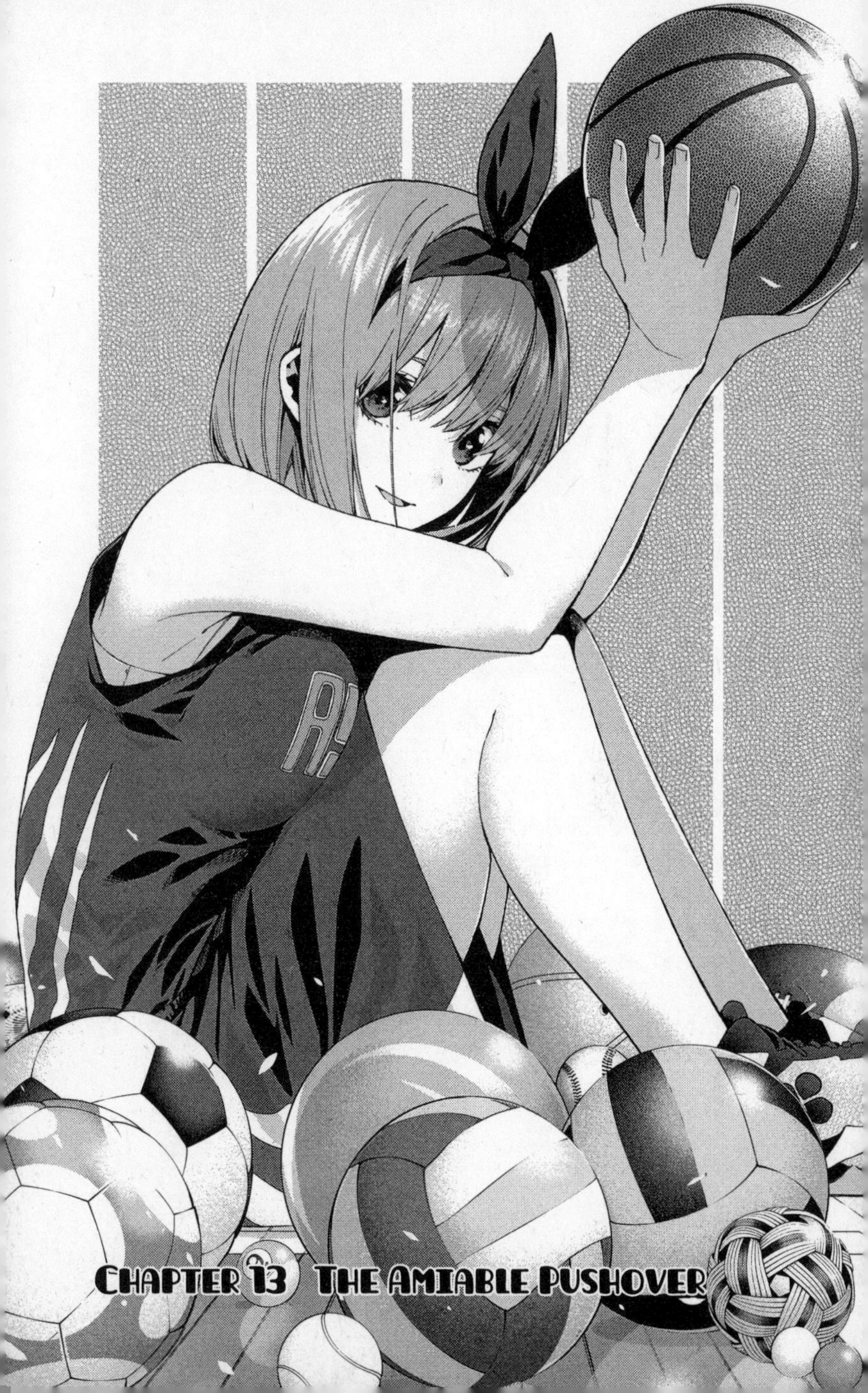

Chapter 13 The Amiable Pushover

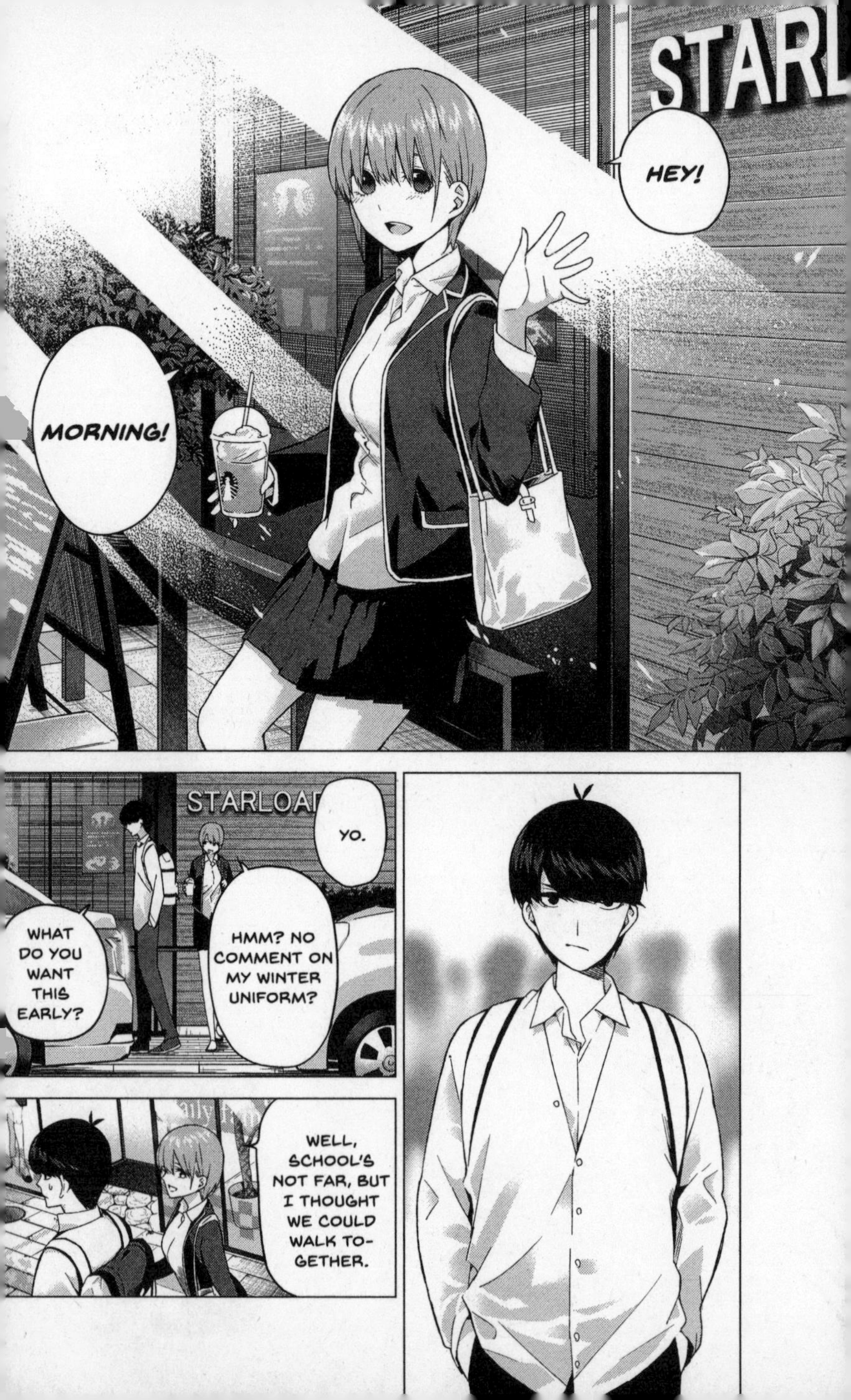
STARL
HEY!
MORNING!
STARLOAD
YO.
HMM? NO COMMENT ON MY WINTER UNIFORM?
WHAT DO YOU WANT THIS EARLY?
WELL, SCHOOL'S NOT FAR, BUT I THOUGHT WE COULD WALK TO-GETHER.

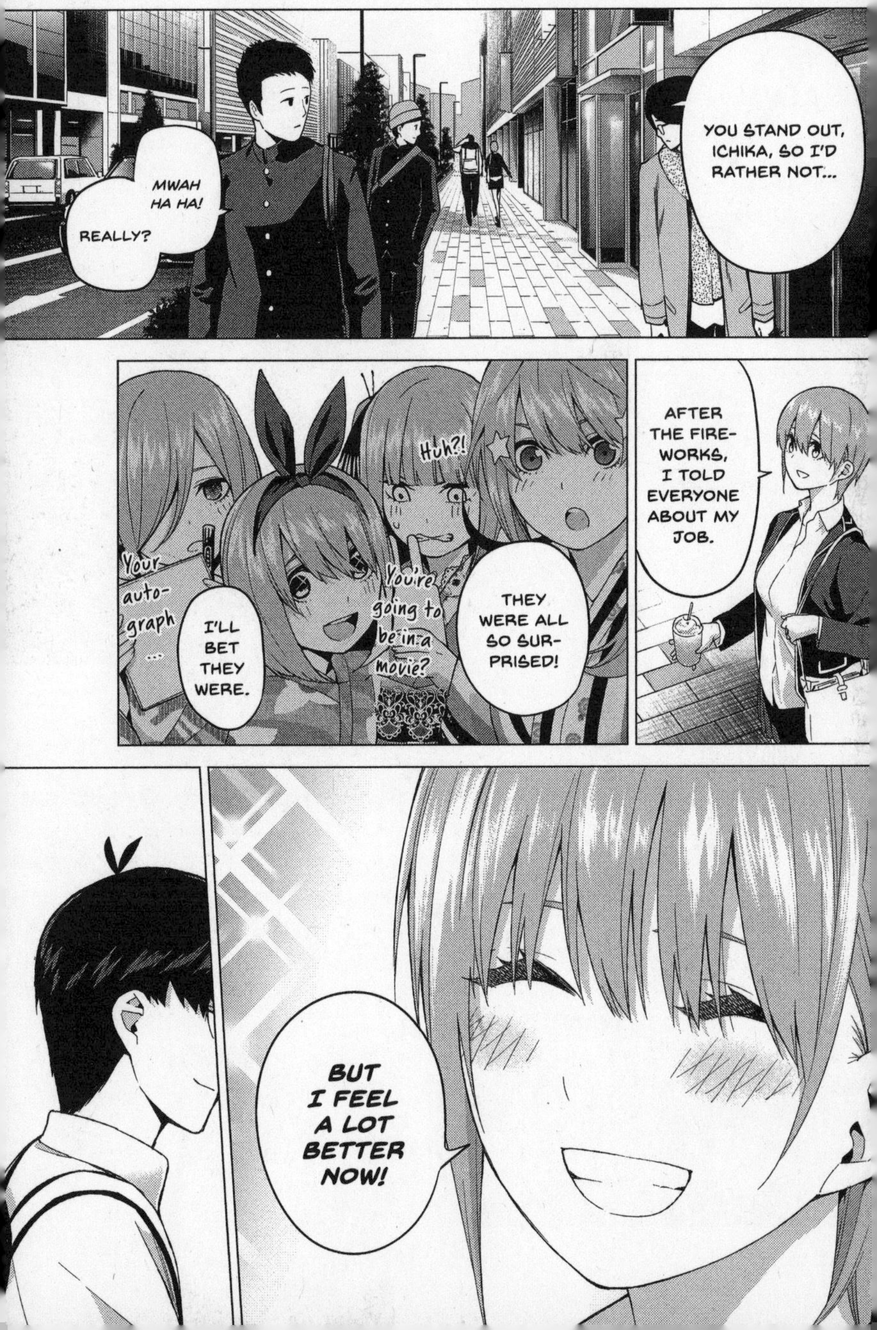
YOU STAND OUT, ICHIKA, SO I'D RATHER NOT...
MWAH HA HA!
REALLY?
AFTER THE FIRE-WORKS, I TOLD EVERYONE ABOUT MY JOB.
THEY WERE ALL SO SUR-PRISED!
Huh?!
You're going to be in a movie?
I'LL BET THEY WERE.
Your auto-graph...
BUT I FEEL A LOT BETTER NOW!

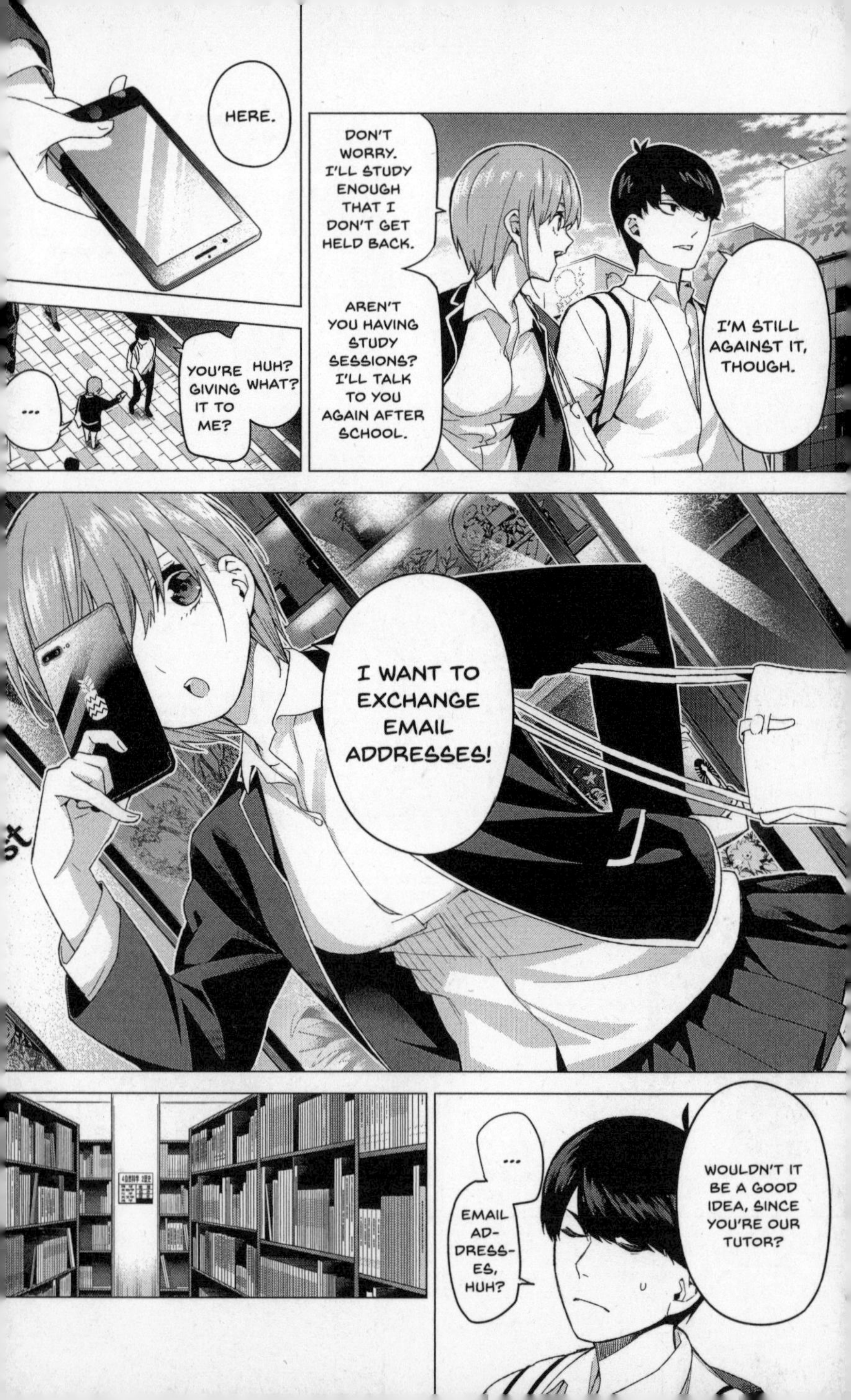
I'M STILL AGAINST IT, THOUGH.
DON'T WORRY. I'LL STUDY ENOUGH THAT I DON'T GET HELD BACK.
AREN'T YOU HAVING STUDY SESSIONS? I'LL TALK TO YOU AGAIN AFTER SCHOOL.
HERE.
YOU'RE GIVING IT TO ME? HUH? WHAT?
...
I WANT TO EXCHANGE EMAIL ADDRESSES!
WOULDN'T IT BE A GOOD IDEA, SINCE YOU'RE OUR TUTOR?
...
EMAIL AD-DRESS-ES, HUH?

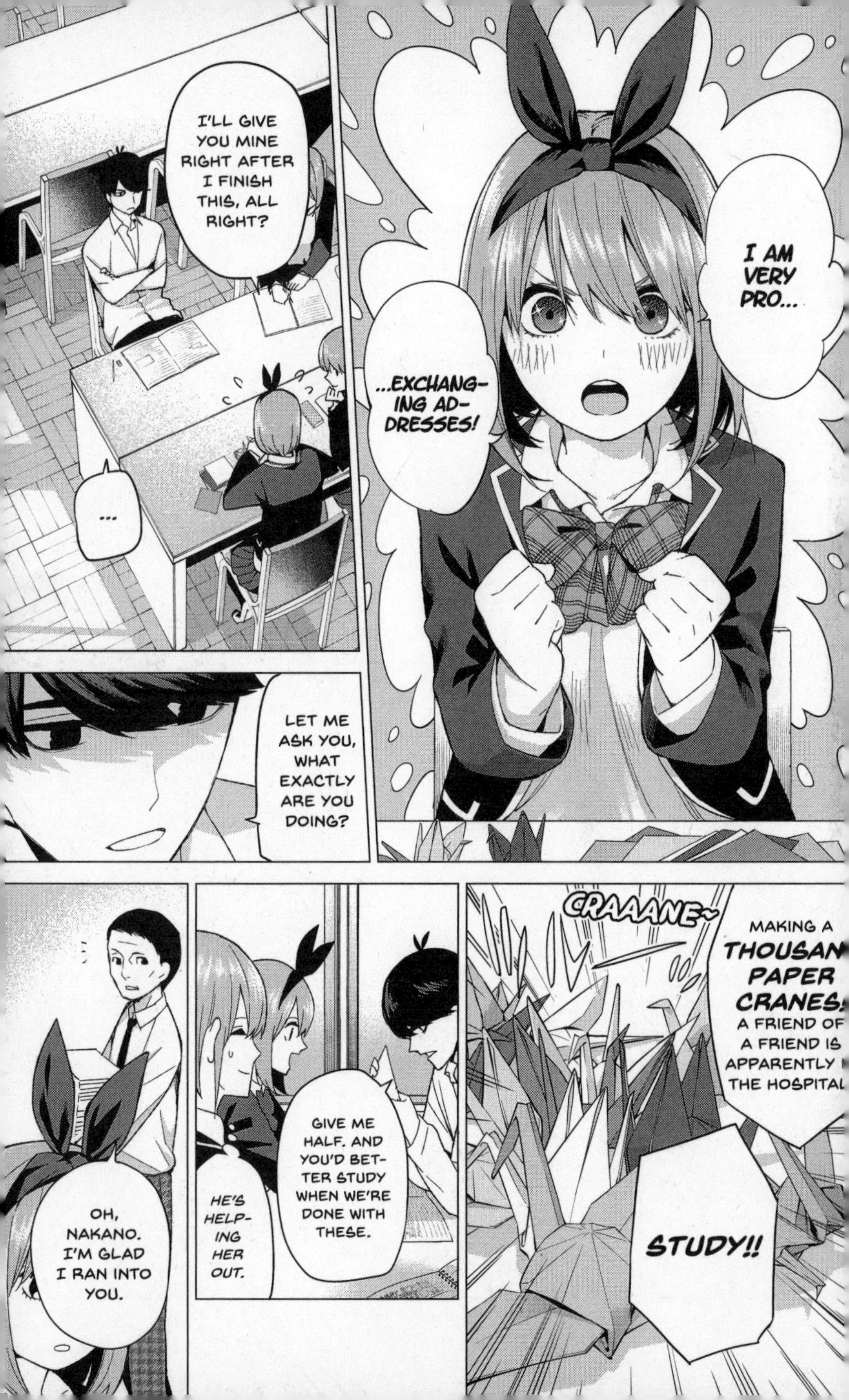

I AM VERY PRO...
...EXCHANGING ADDRESSES!
I'LL GIVE YOU MINE RIGHT AFTER I FINISH THIS, ALL RIGHT?
...
LET ME ASK YOU, WHAT EXACTLY ARE YOU DOING?
CRAAANE~
MAKING A THOUSAN PAPER CRANES! A FRIEND OF A FRIEND IS APPARENTLY THE HOSPITAL
STUDY!!
GIVE ME HALF. AND YOU'D BETTER STUDY WHEN WE'RE DONE WITH THESE.
HE'S HELPING HER OUT.
OH, NAKANO. I'M GLAD I RAN INTO YOU.

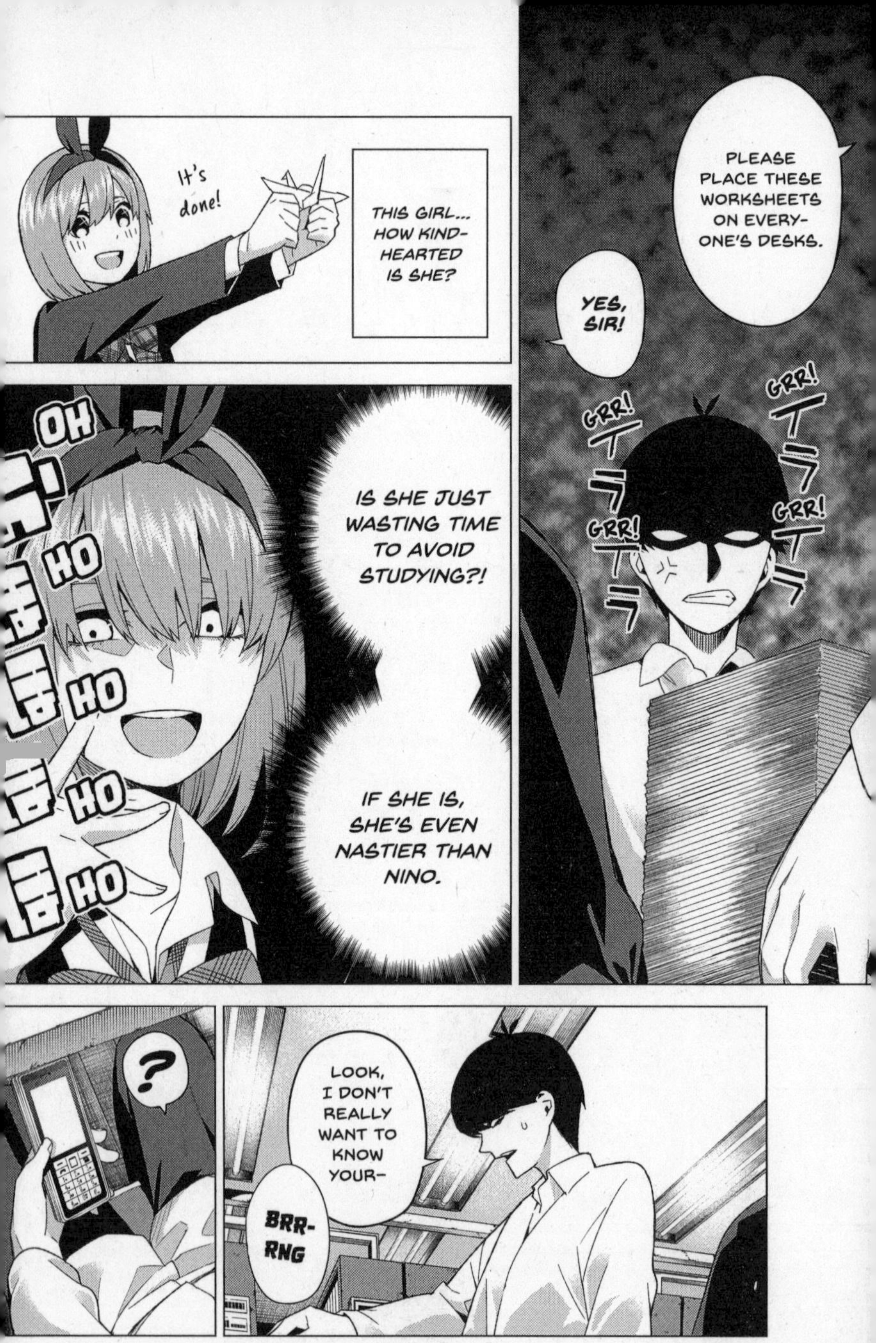
PLEASE PLACE THESE WORKSHEETS ON EVERY-ONE'S DESKS.
YES, SIR!
GRR!
GRR!
GRR!
GRR!
It's done!
THIS GIRL... HOW KIND-HEARTED IS SHE?
IS SHE JUST WASTING TIME TO AVOID STUDYING?!
IF SHE IS, SHE'S EVEN NASTIER THAN NINO.
OH
HO
HO
HO
HO
LOOK, I DON'T REALLY WANT TO KNOW YOUR-
BRR-RNG
?

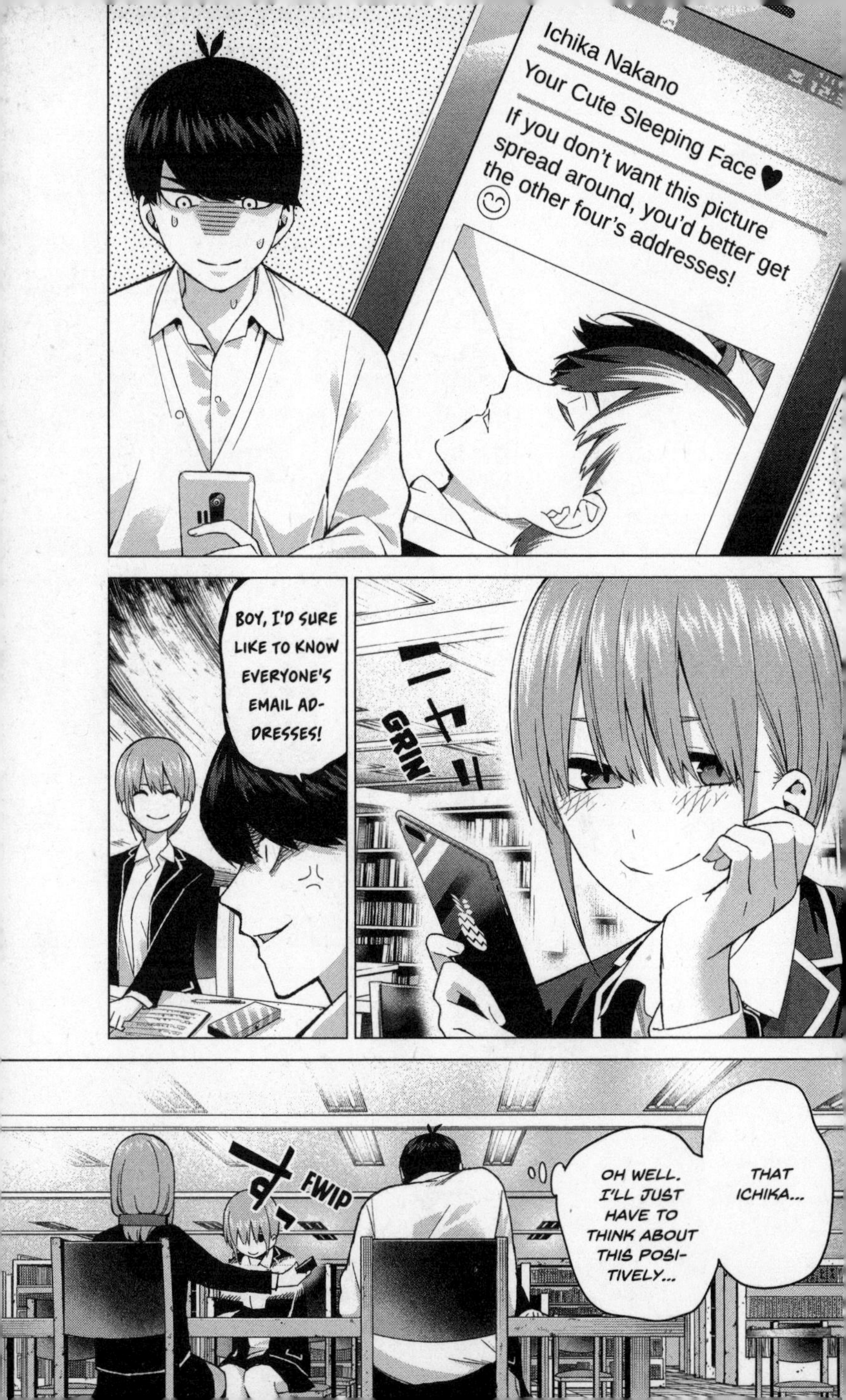
Ichika Nakano
Your Cute Sleeping Face ♥
If you don't want this picture spread around, you'd better get the other four's addresses! 😊
GRIN
BOY, I'D SURE LIKE TO KNOW EVERYONE'S EMAIL AD-DRESSES!
THAT ICHIKA...
OH WELL. I'LL JUST HAVE TO THINK ABOUT THIS POSI-TIVELY...
FWIP

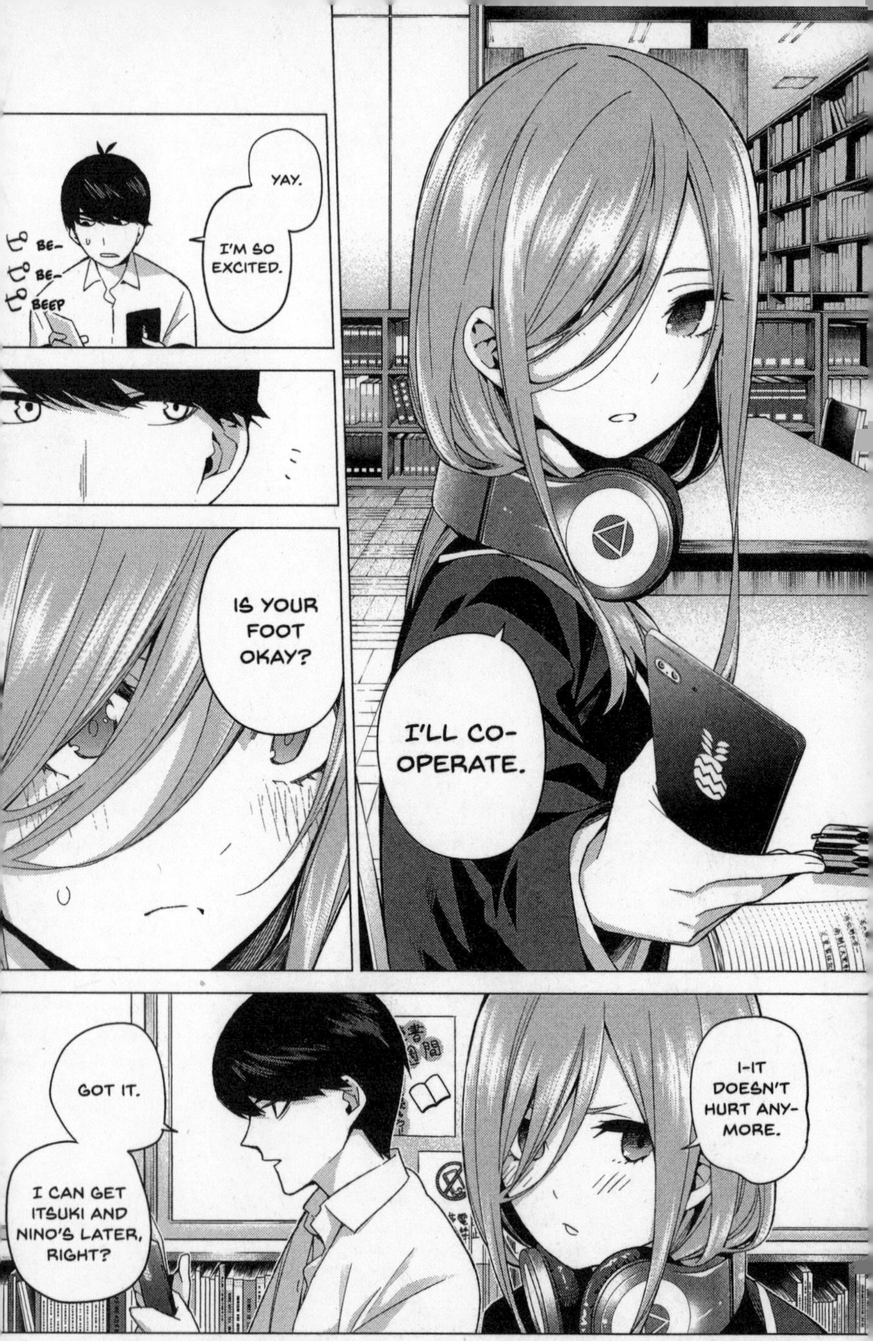

I'LL CO-OPERATE.
YAY.
I'M SO EXCITED.
ピピピ
BE- BE- BEEP
IS YOUR FOOT OKAY?
I-IT DOESN'T HURT ANYMORE.
GOT IT.
I CAN GET ITSUKI AND NINO'S LATER, RIGHT?

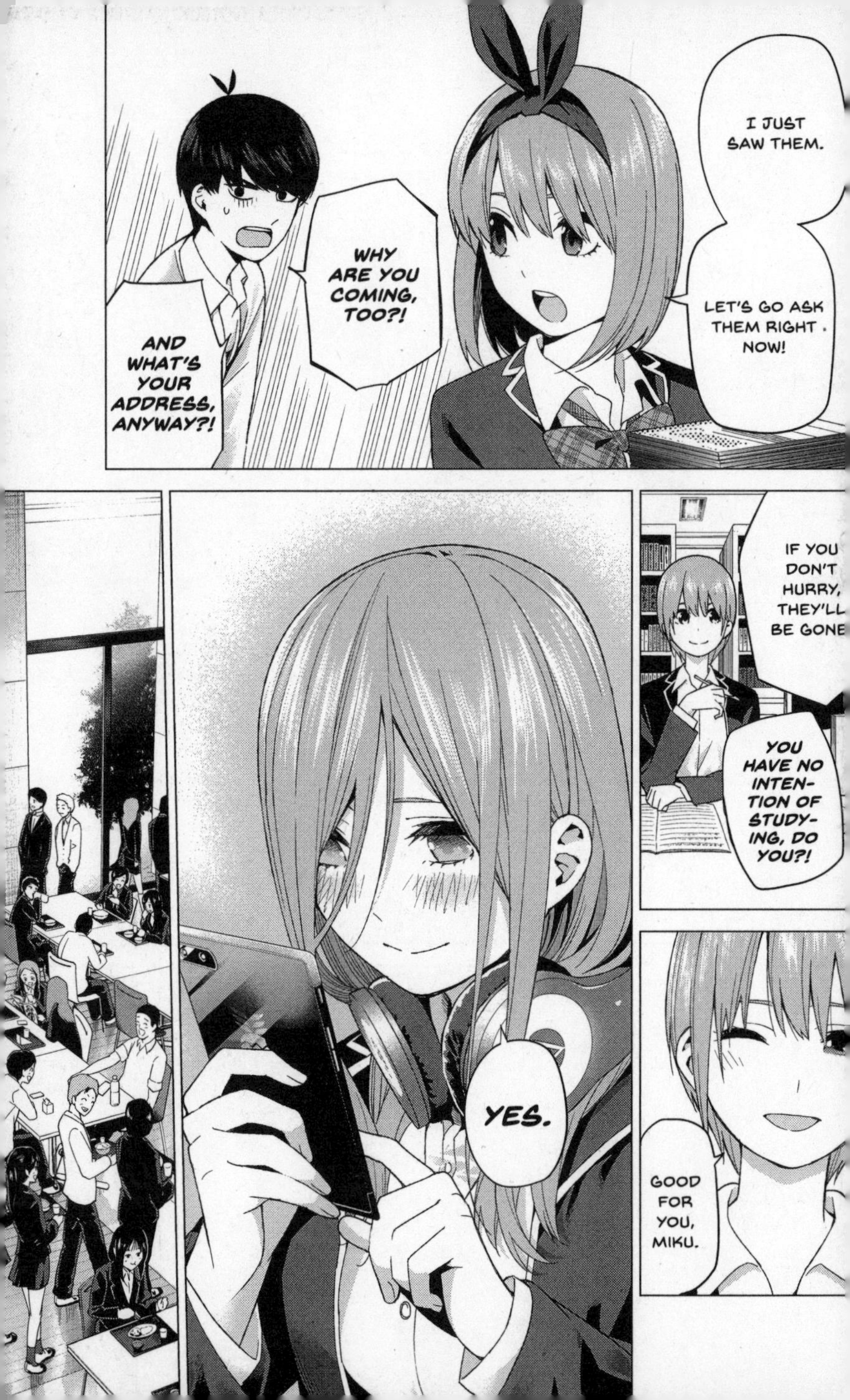
I JUST SAW THEM.
LET'S GO ASK THEM RIGHT NOW!
WHY ARE YOU COMING, TOO?!
AND WHAT'S YOUR ADDRESS, ANYWAY?!
IF YOU DON'T HURRY, THEY'LL BE GONE
YOU HAVE NO INTENTION OF STUDYING, DO YOU?!
GOOD FOR YOU, MIKU.
YES.

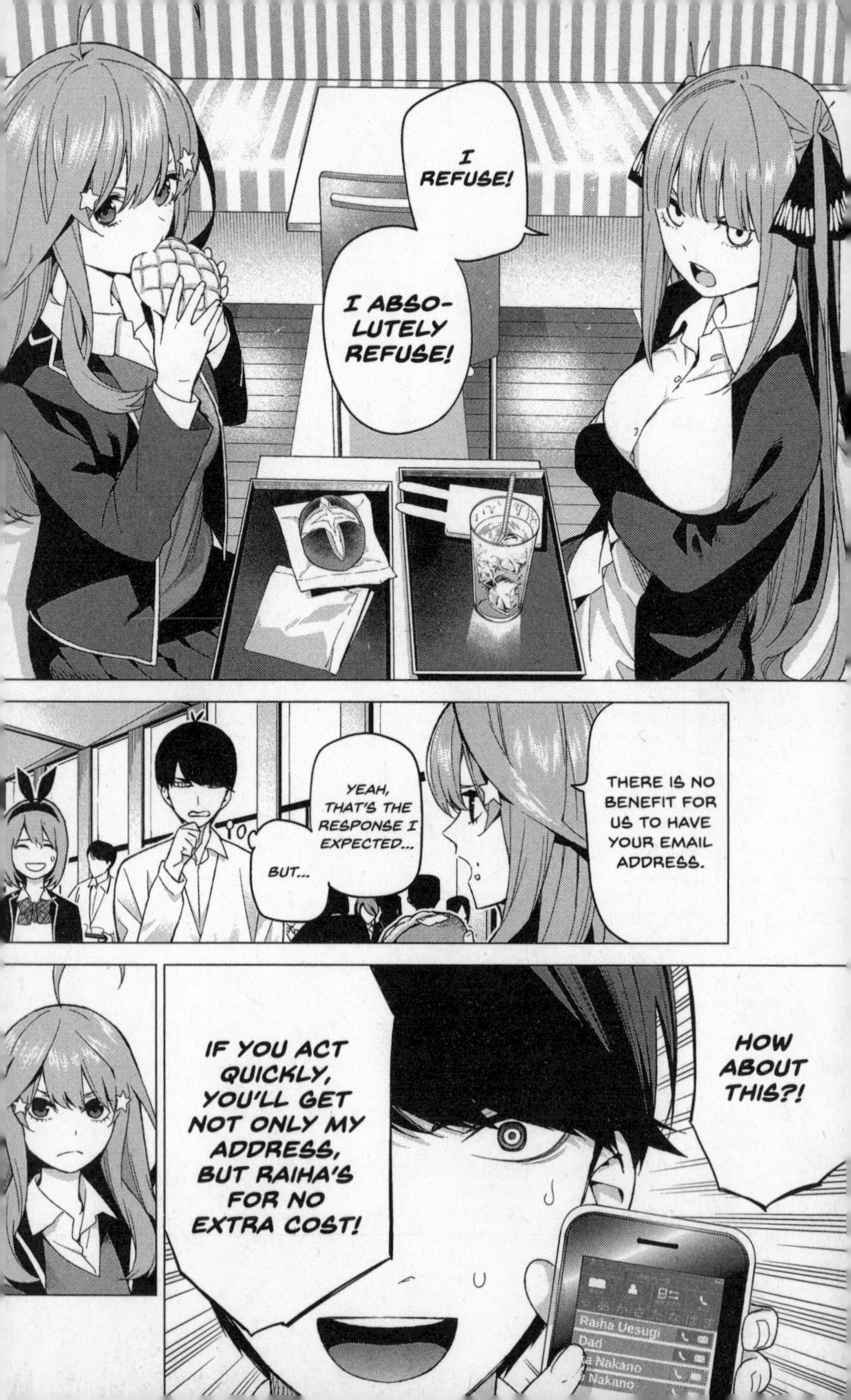
I REFUSE!
I ABSOLUTELY REFUSE!
THERE IS NO BENEFIT FOR US TO HAVE YOUR EMAIL ADDRESS.
YEAH, THAT'S THE RESPONSE I EXPECTED...
BUT...
HOW ABOUT THIS?!
IF YOU ACT QUICKLY, YOU'LL GET NOT ONLY MY ADDRESS, BUT RAIHA'S FOR NO EXTRA COST!
Raiha Uesugi
Dad

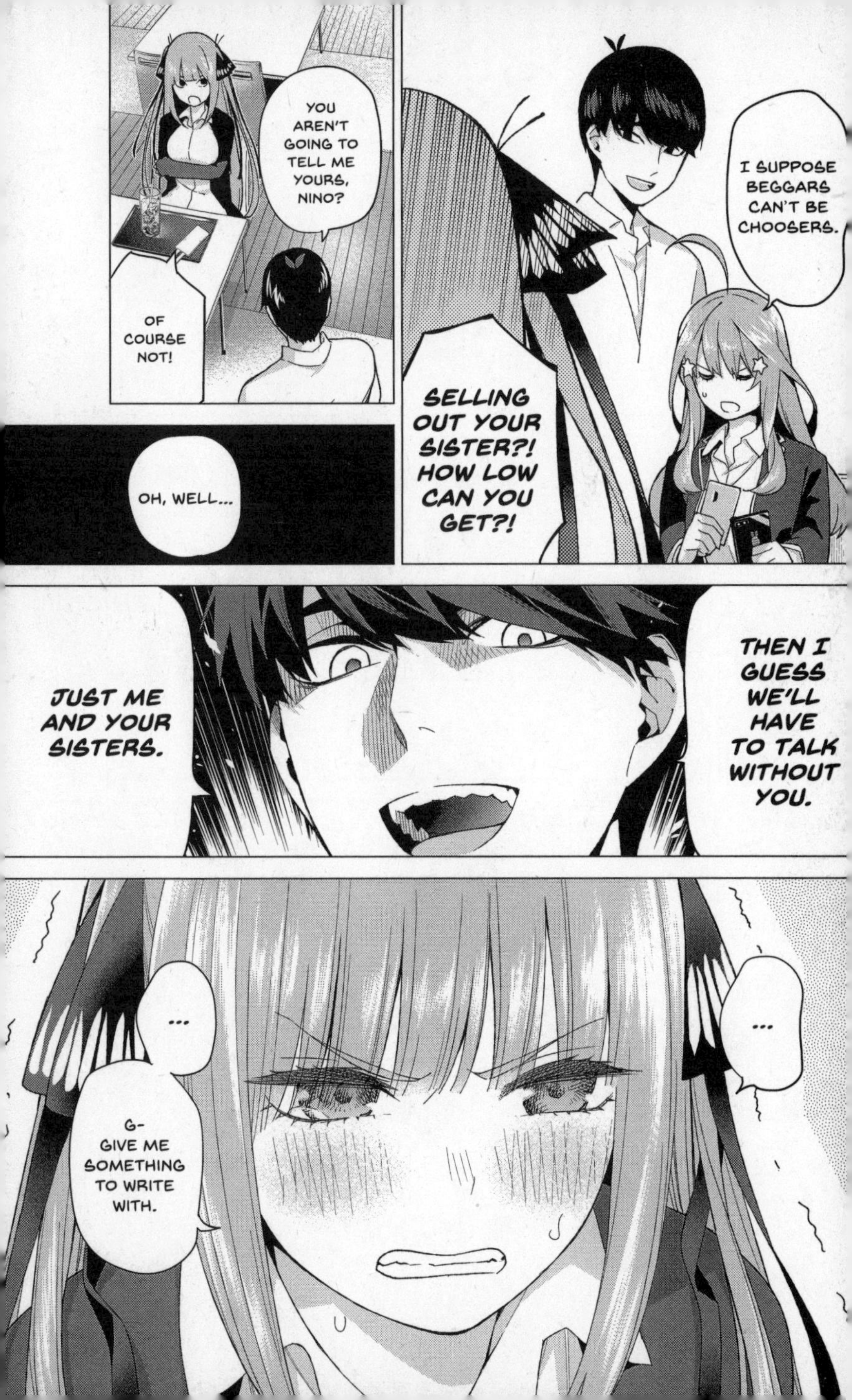
I SUPPOSE BEGGARS CAN'T BE CHOOSERS.
SELLING OUT YOUR SISTER?! HOW LOW CAN YOU GET?!
YOU AREN'T GOING TO TELL ME YOURS, NINO?
OF COURSE NOT!
OH, WELL...
THEN I GUESS WE'LL HAVE TO TALK WITHOUT YOU.
JUST ME AND YOUR SISTERS.
...
...
G- GIVE ME SOMETHING TO WRITE WITH.

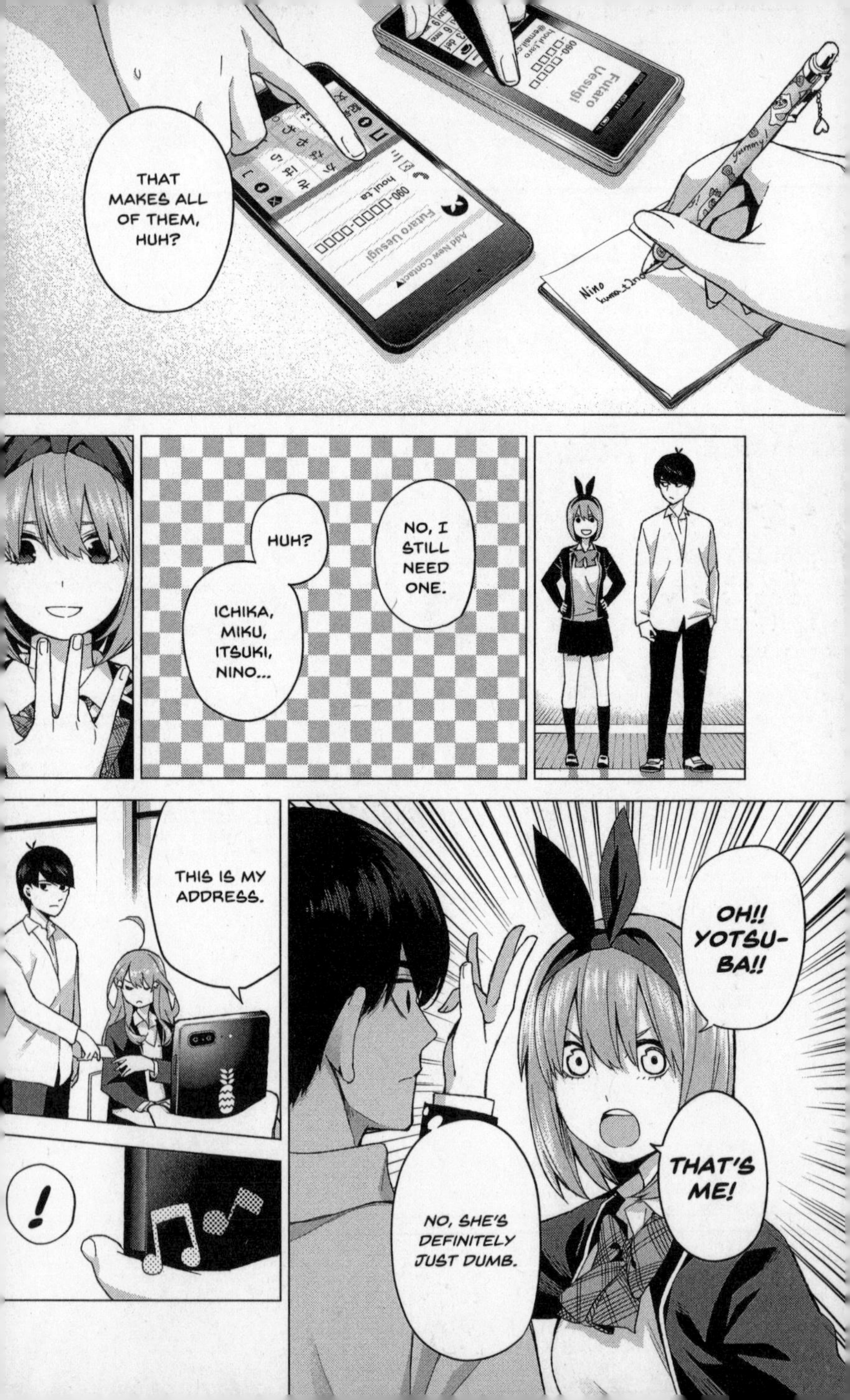
THAT MAKES ALL OF THEM, HUH?
Add New Contact
Futaro Uesugi
NO, I STILL NEED ONE.
HUH?
ICHIKA, MIKU, ITSUKI, NINO...
OH!! YOTSU-BA!!
THAT'S ME!
NO, SHE'S DEFINITELY JUST DUMB.
THIS IS MY ADDRESS.
!

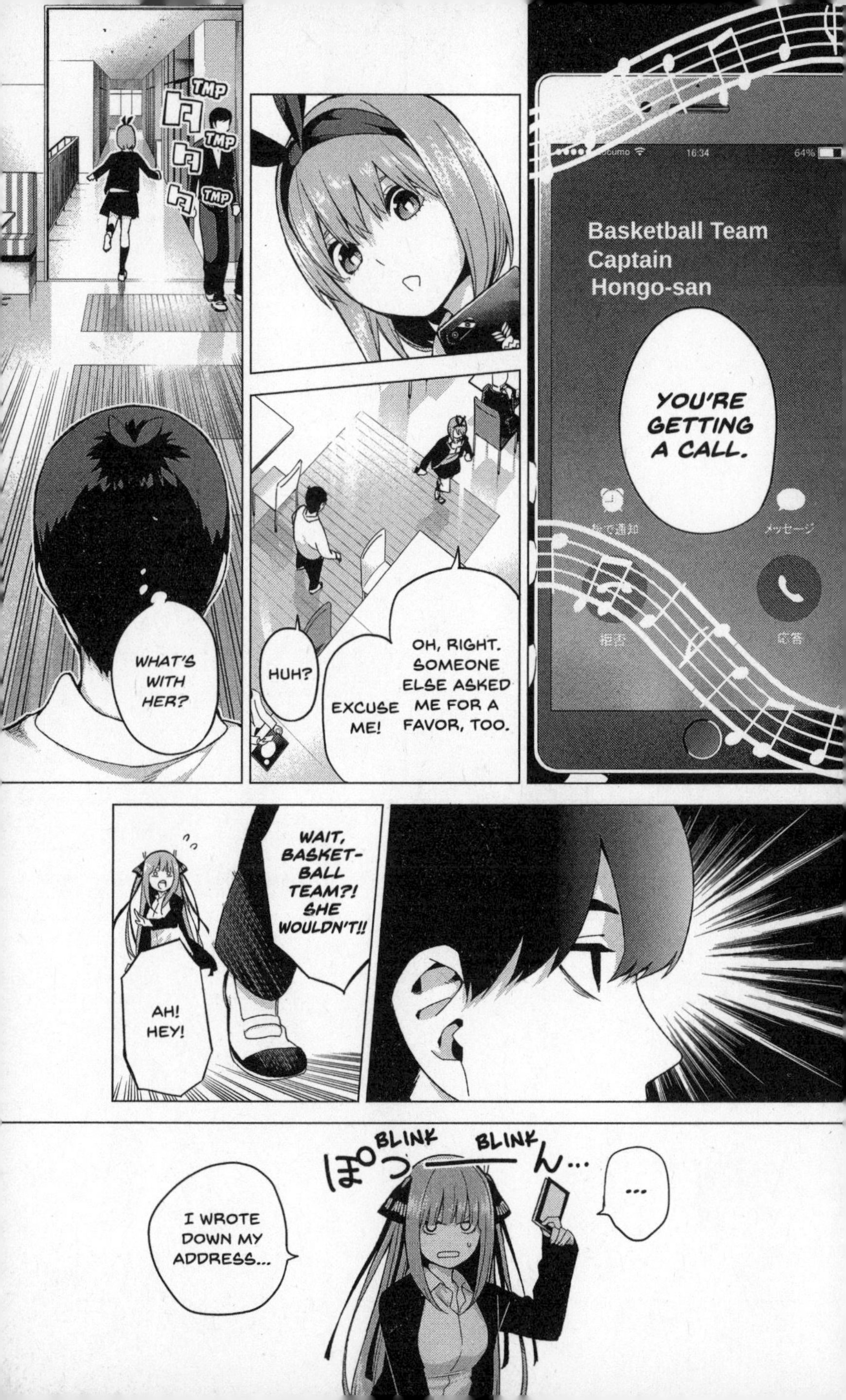
16:34
64%
Basketball Team Captain Hongo-san
YOU'RE GETTING A CALL.
メッセージ
応答
OH, RIGHT. SOMEONE ELSE ASKED ME FOR A FAVOR, TOO.
EXCUSE ME!
HUH?
TMP
TMP
TMP
WHAT'S WITH HER?
WAIT, BASKET-BALL TEAM?! SHE WOULDN'T!!
AH! HEY!
...
ぽつーーん...
BLINK BLINK
I WROTE DOWN MY ADDRESS...

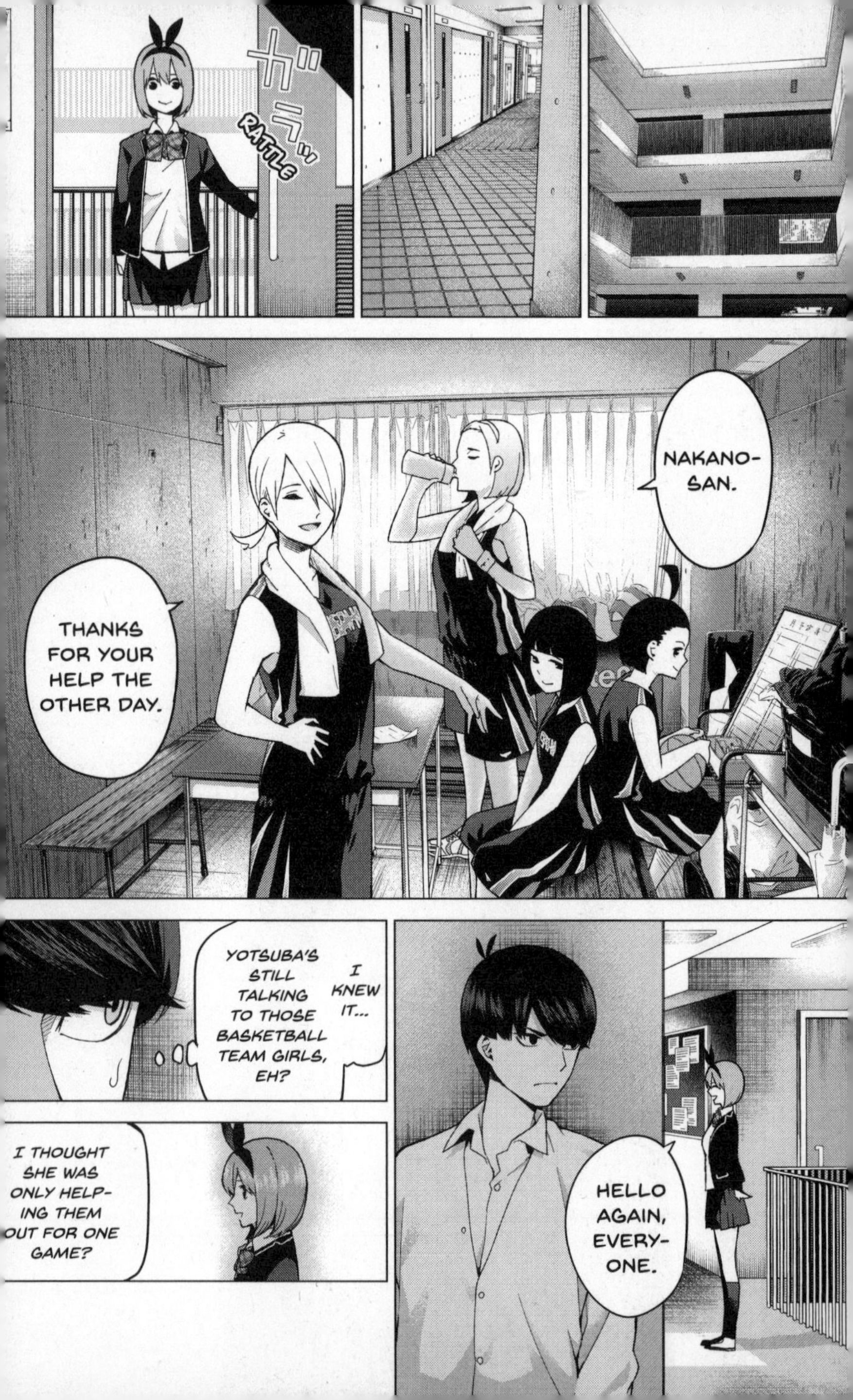
ガラッ
RATTLE
NAKANO-SAN.
THANKS FOR YOUR HELP THE OTHER DAY.
HELLO AGAIN, EVERY-ONE.
I KNEW IT...
YOTSUBA'S STILL TALKING TO THOSE BASKETBALL TEAM GIRLS, EH?
I THOUGHT SHE WAS ONLY HELP-ING THEM OUT FOR ONE GAME?

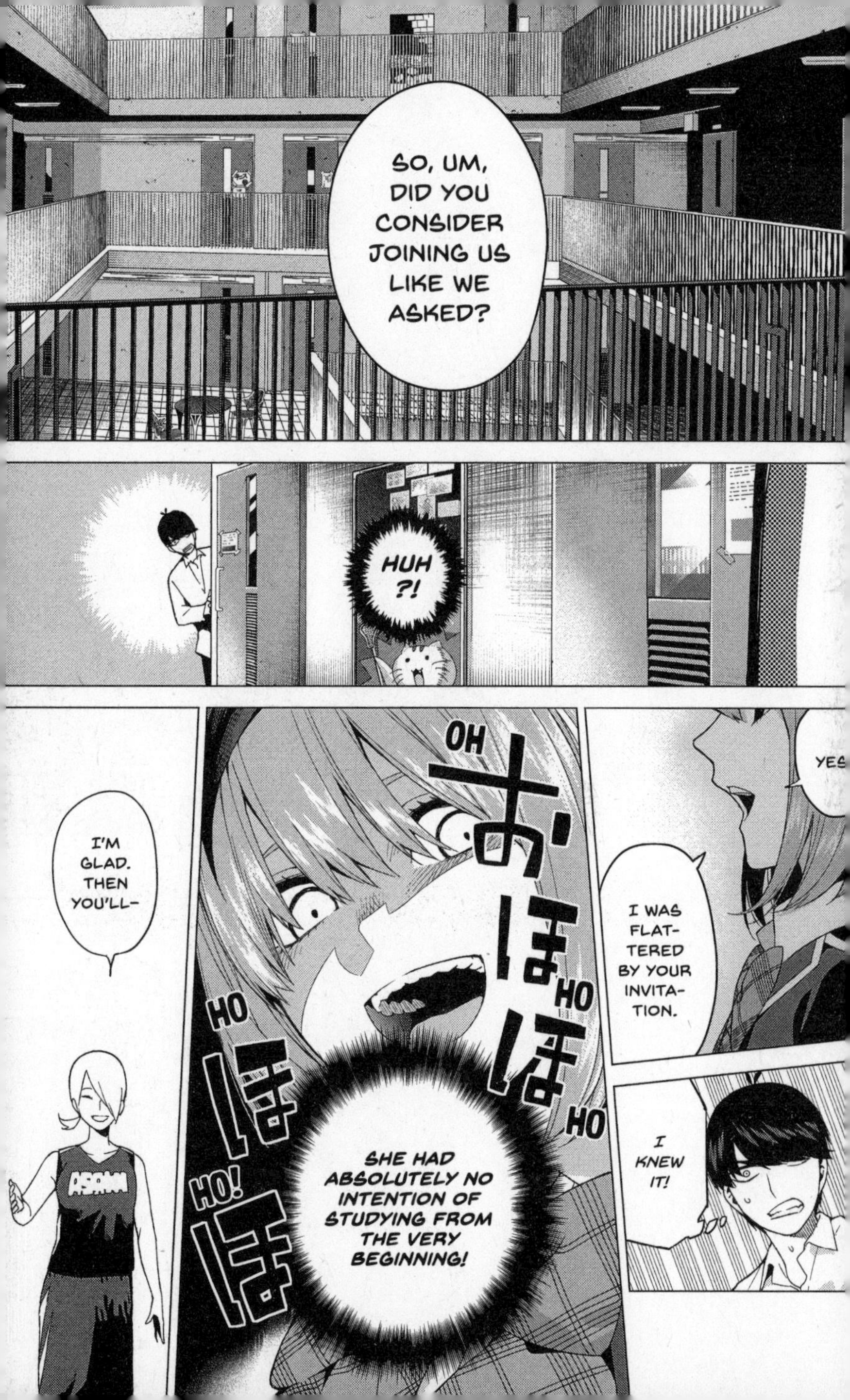
SO, UM, DID YOU CONSIDER JOINING US LIKE WE ASKED?
HUH ?!
YES
I WAS FLATTERED BY YOUR INVITATION.
I KNEW IT!
おほほほほ
OH HO HO HO HO!
SHE HAD ABSOLUTELY NO INTENTION OF STUDYING FROM THE VERY BEGINNING!
I'M GLAD. THEN YOU'LL-

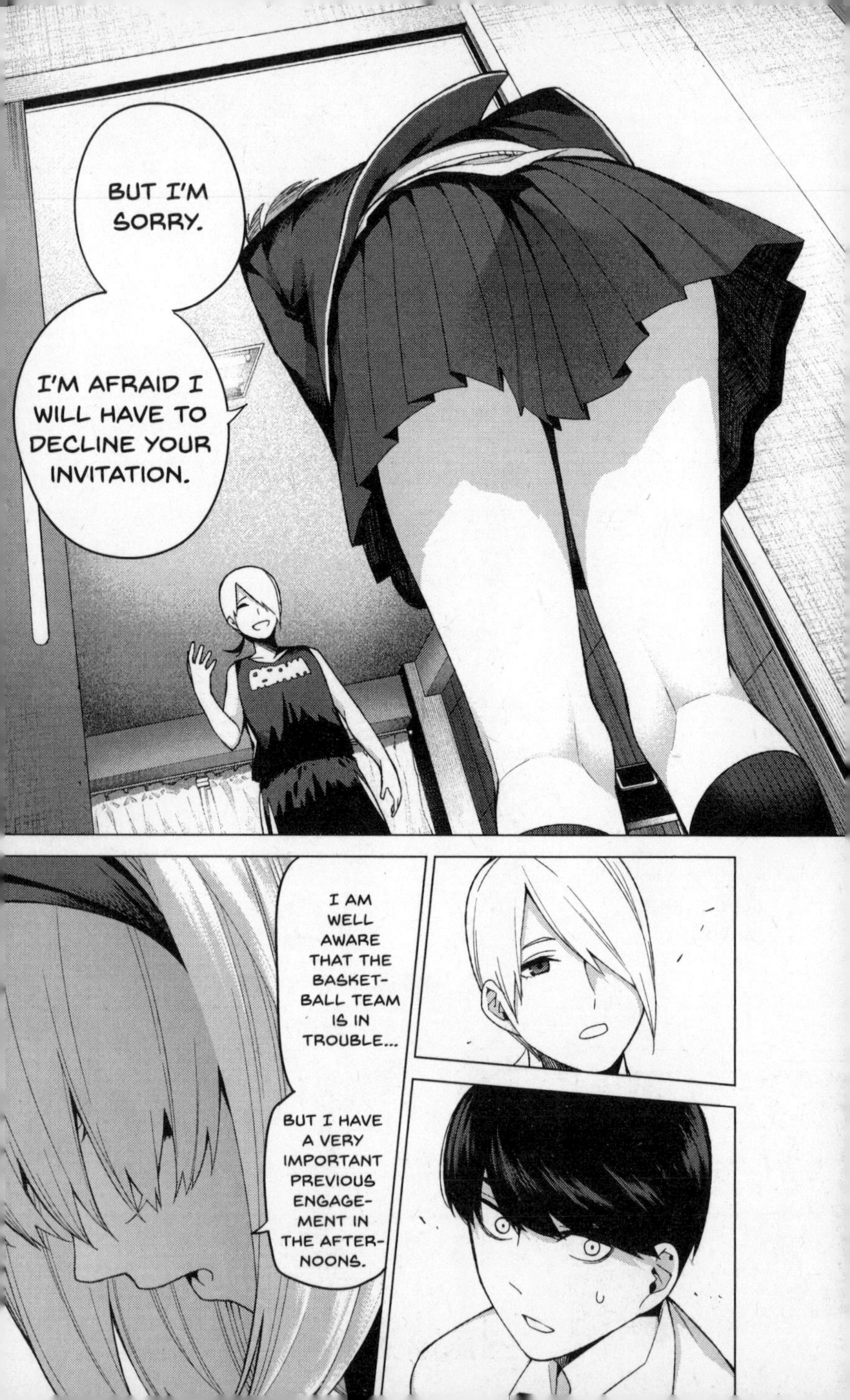
BUT I'M SORRY.
I'M AFRAID I WILL HAVE TO DECLINE YOUR INVITATION.
I AM WELL AWARE THAT THE BASKET-BALL TEAM IS IN TROUBLE...
BUT I HAVE A VERY IMPORTANT PREVIOUS ENGAGE-MENT IN THE AFTER-NOONS.

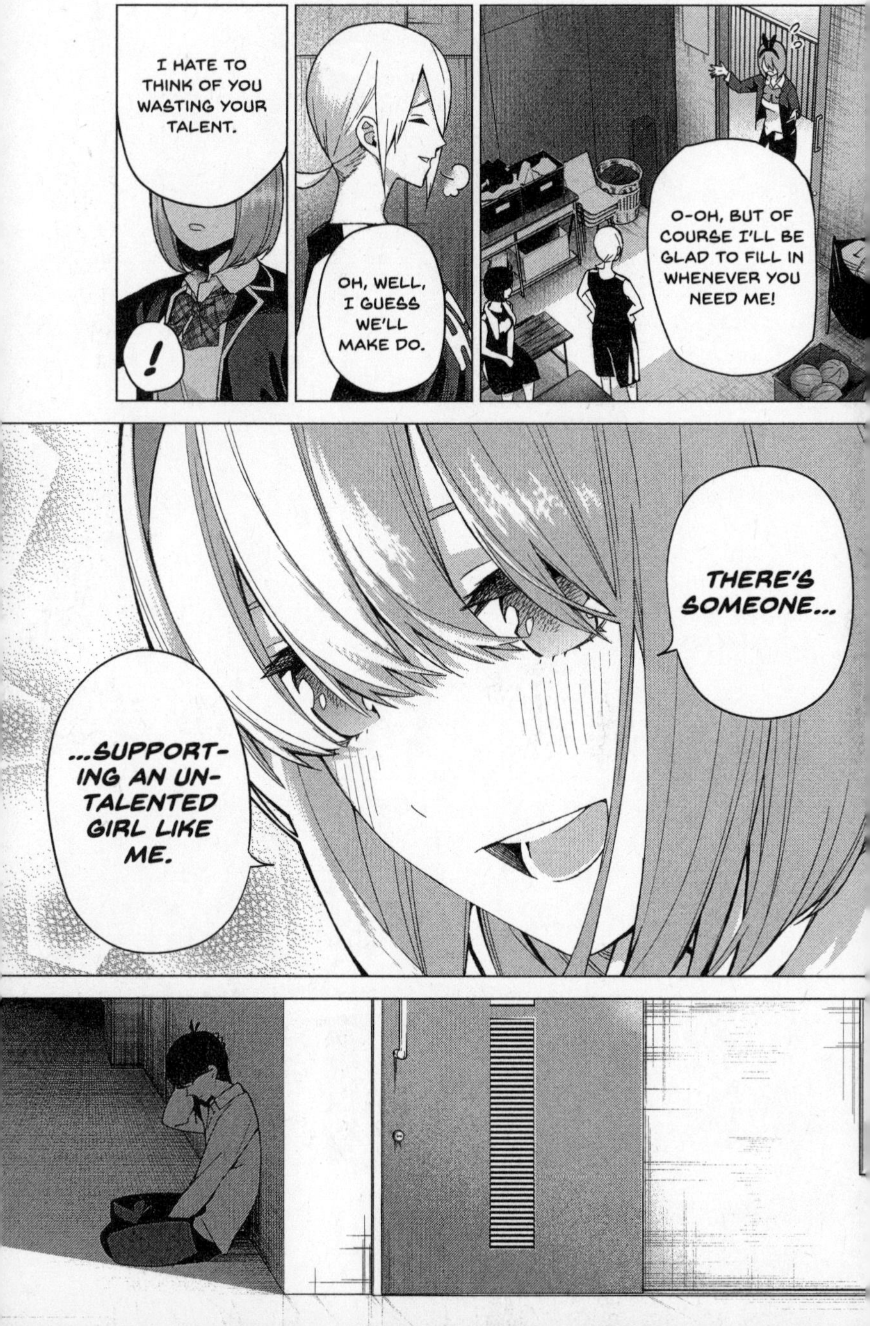
O-OH, BUT OF COURSE I'LL BE GLAD TO FILL IN WHENEVER YOU NEED ME!
OH, WELL, I GUESS WE'LL MAKE DO.
I HATE TO THINK OF YOU WASTING YOUR TALENT.
!
THERE'S SOMEONE...
...SUPPORT-ING AN UN-TALENTED GIRL LIKE ME.

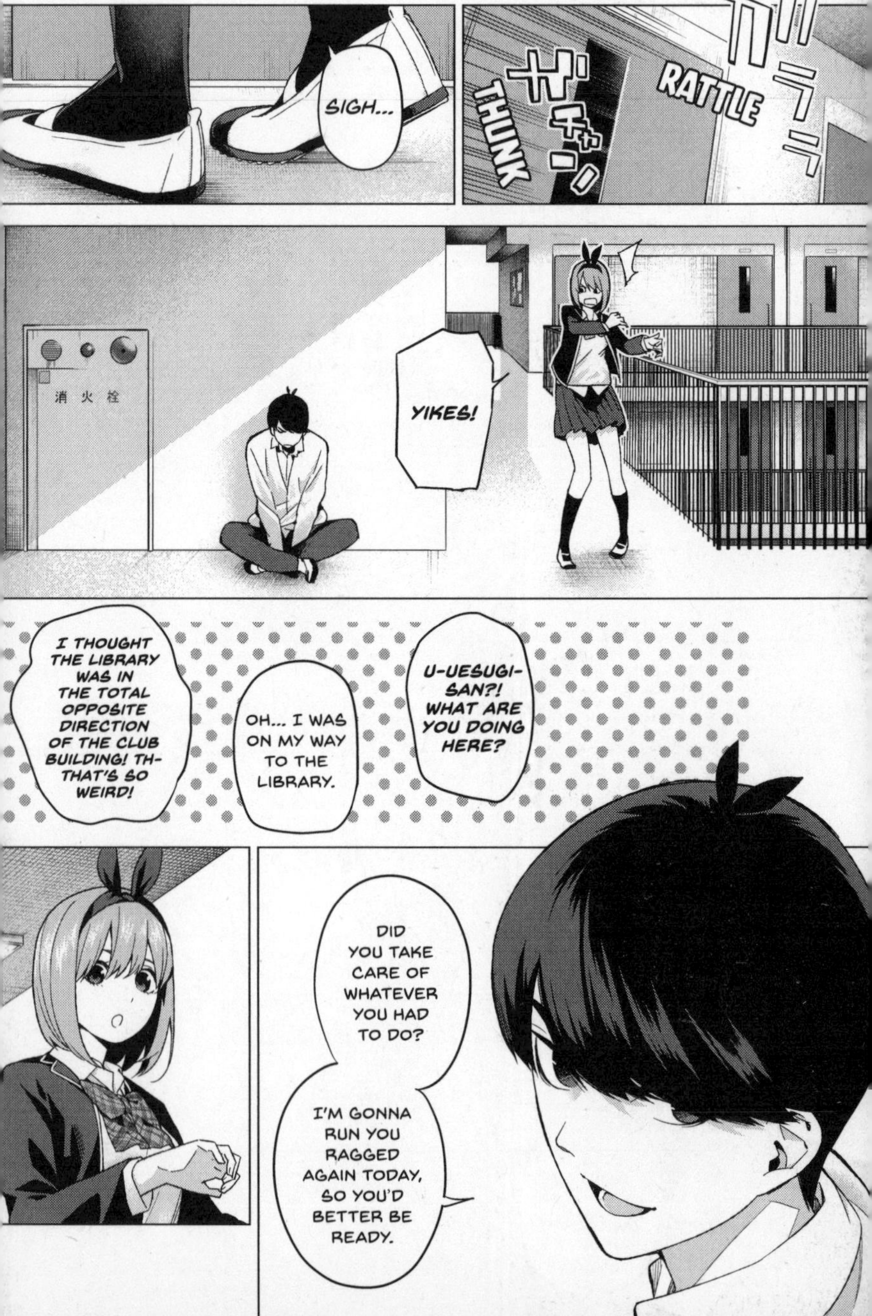
RATTLE
THUNK
SIGH...
消火栓
YIKES!
U-UESUGI-SAN?! WHAT ARE YOU DOING HERE?
OH... I WAS ON MY WAY TO THE LIBRARY.
I THOUGHT THE LIBRARY WAS IN THE TOTAL OPPOSITE DIRECTION OF THE CLUB BUILDING! TH-THAT'S SO WEIRD!
DID YOU TAKE CARE OF WHATEVER YOU HAD TO DO?
I'M GONNA RUN YOU RAGGED AGAIN TODAY, SO YOU'D BETTER BE READY.

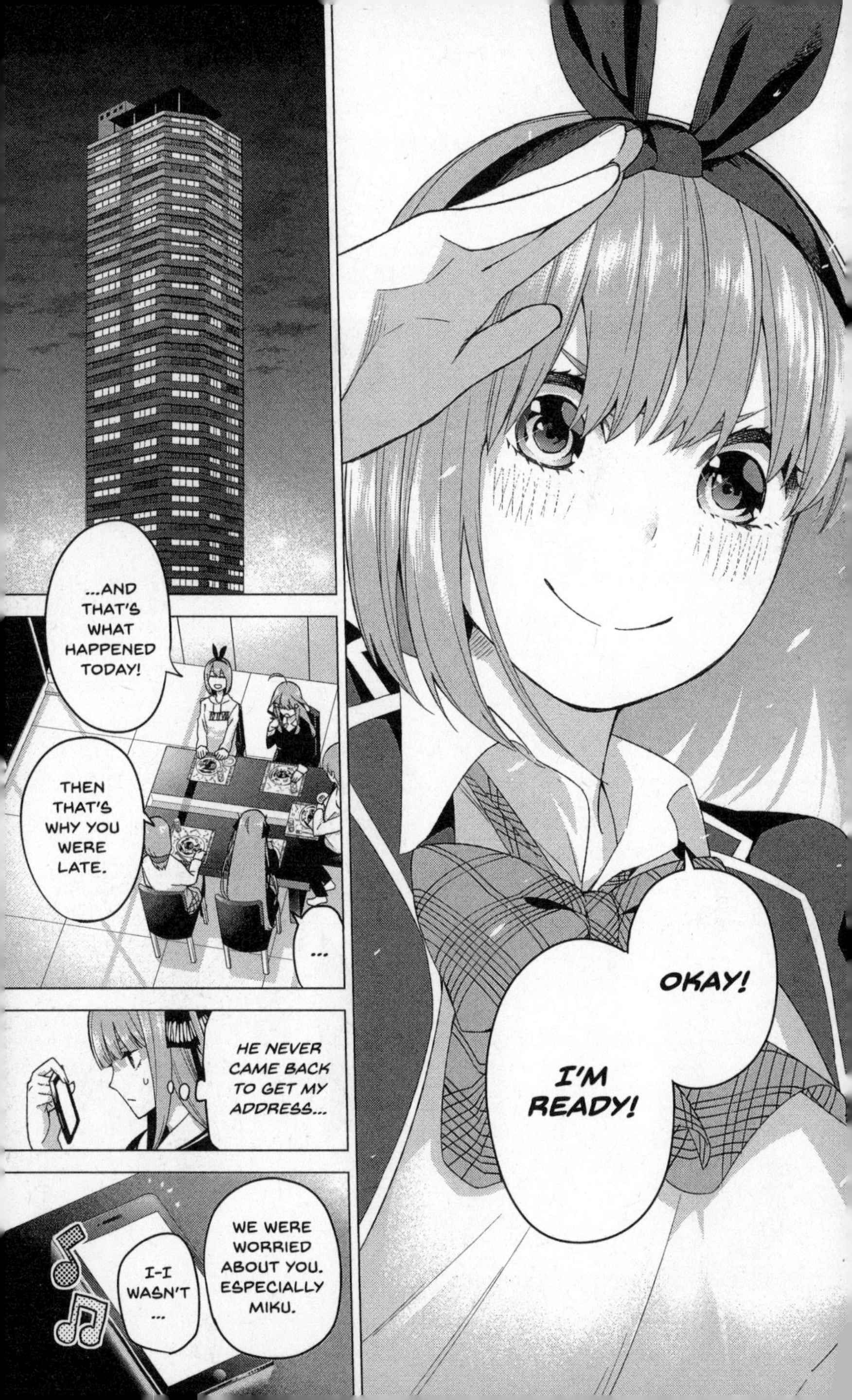
OKAY!
I'M READY!
...AND THAT'S WHAT HAPPENED TODAY!
THEN THAT'S WHY YOU WERE LATE.
...
HE NEVER CAME BACK TO GET MY ADDRESS...
WE WERE WORRIED ABOUT YOU. ESPECIALLY MIKU.
I-I WASN'T ...

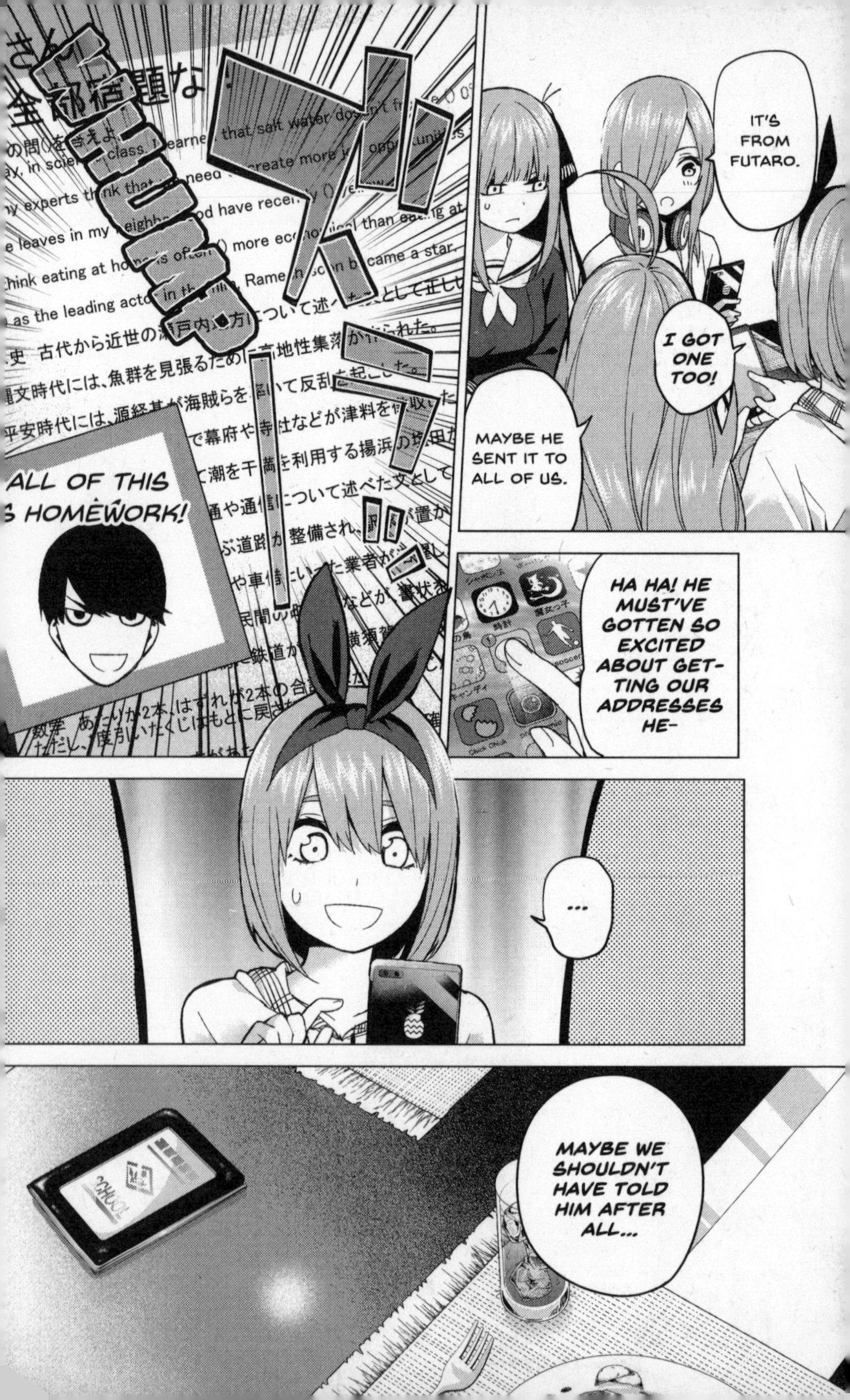
IT'S FROM FUTARO.
I GOT ONE TOO!
MAYBE HE SENT IT TO ALL OF US.
HA HA! HE MUST'VE GOTTEN SO EXCITED ABOUT GET-TING OUR ADDRESSES HE-
ALL OF THIS
S HOMEWORK!
...
MAYBE WE SHOULDN'T HAVE TOLD HIM AFTER ALL...

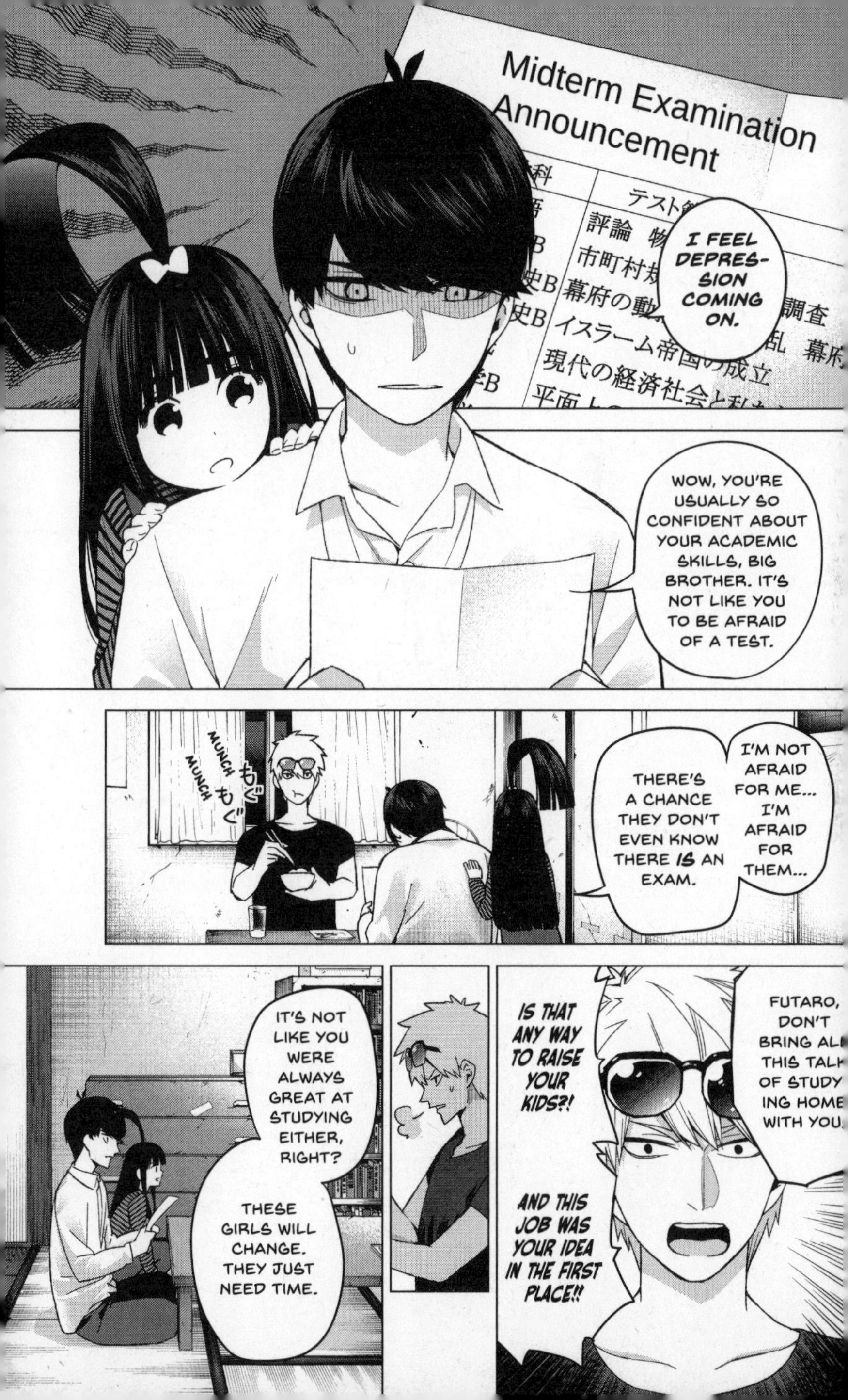
Midterm Examination Announcement
I FEEL DEPRES-SION COMING ON.
WOW, YOU'RE USUALLY SO CONFIDENT ABOUT YOUR ACADEMIC SKILLS, BIG BROTHER. IT'S NOT LIKE YOU TO BE AFRAID OF A TEST.
I'M NOT AFRAID FOR ME... I'M AFRAID FOR THEM...
THERE'S A CHANCE THEY DON'T EVEN KNOW THERE *IS* AN EXAM.
もぐ もぐ
MUNCH MUNCH
FUTARO, DON'T BRING AL THIS TALK OF STUDY ING HOME WITH YOU.
IS THAT ANY WAY TO RAISE YOUR KIDS?!
AND THIS JOB WAS YOUR IDEA IN THE FIRST PLACE!!
IT'S NOT LIKE YOU WERE ALWAYS GREAT AT STUDYING EITHER, RIGHT?
THESE GIRLS WILL CHANGE. THEY JUST NEED TIME.

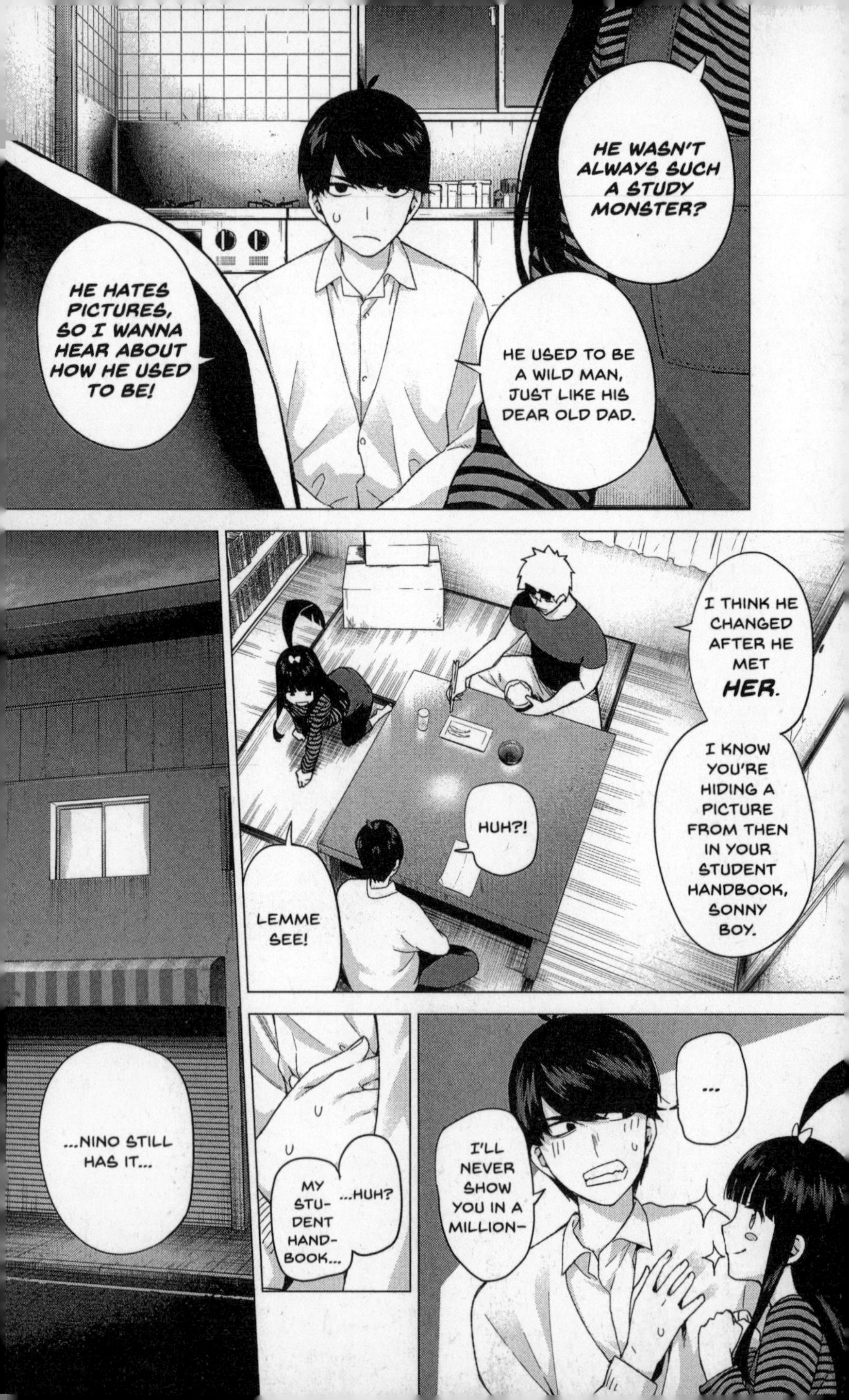
HE WASN'T ALWAYS SUCH A STUDY MONSTER?
HE USED TO BE A WILD MAN, JUST LIKE HIS DEAR OLD DAD.
HE HATES PICTURES, SO I WANNA HEAR ABOUT HOW HE USED TO BE!
I THINK HE CHANGED AFTER HE MET HER.
I KNOW YOU'RE HIDING A PICTURE FROM THEN IN YOUR STUDENT HANDBOOK, SONNY BOY.
HUH?!
LEMME SEE!
...
I'LL NEVER SHOW YOU IN A MILLION-
...HUH?
MY STU-DENT HAND-BOOK...
...NINO STILL HAS IT...

Chapter 14 The Picture That Started It All

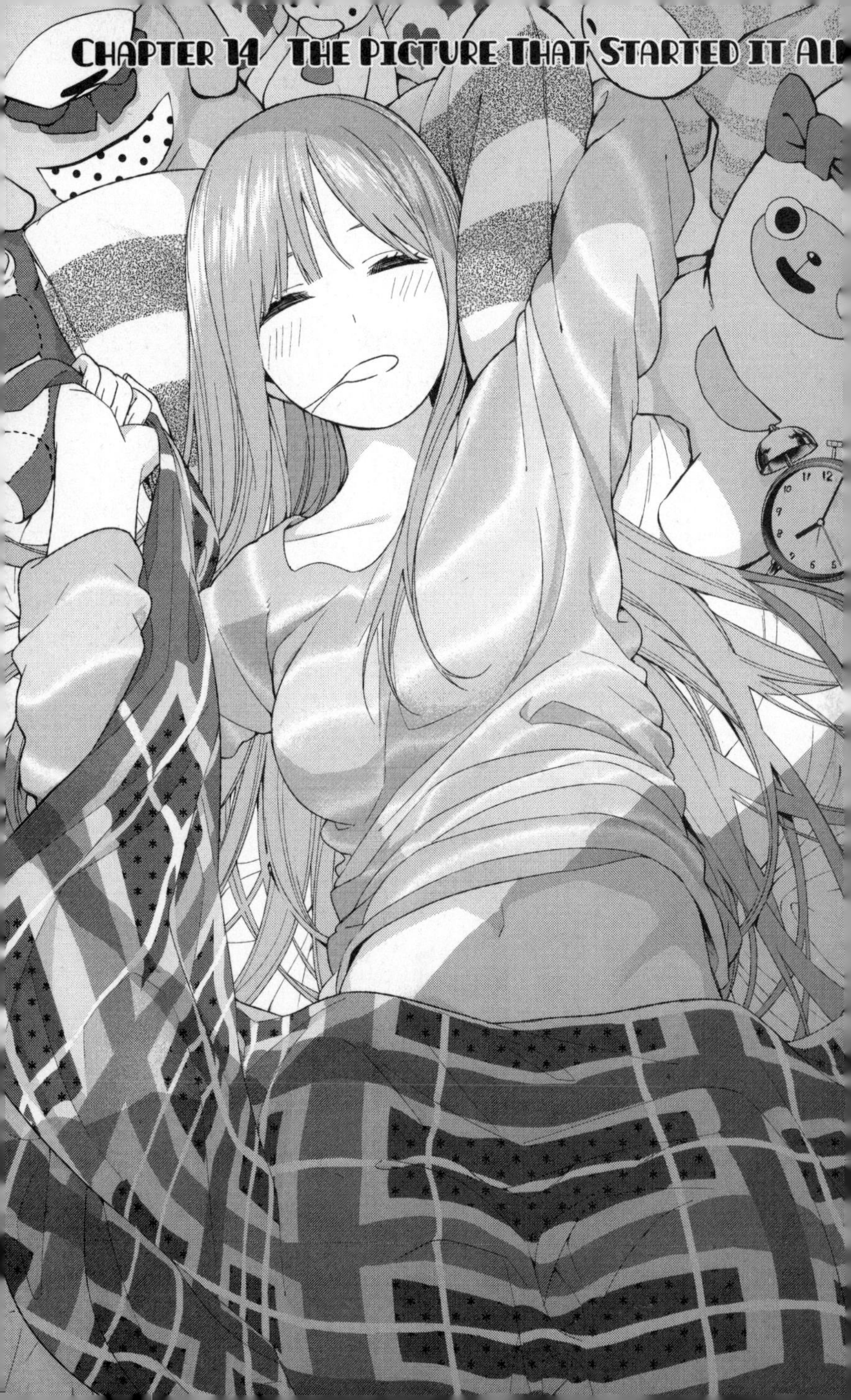

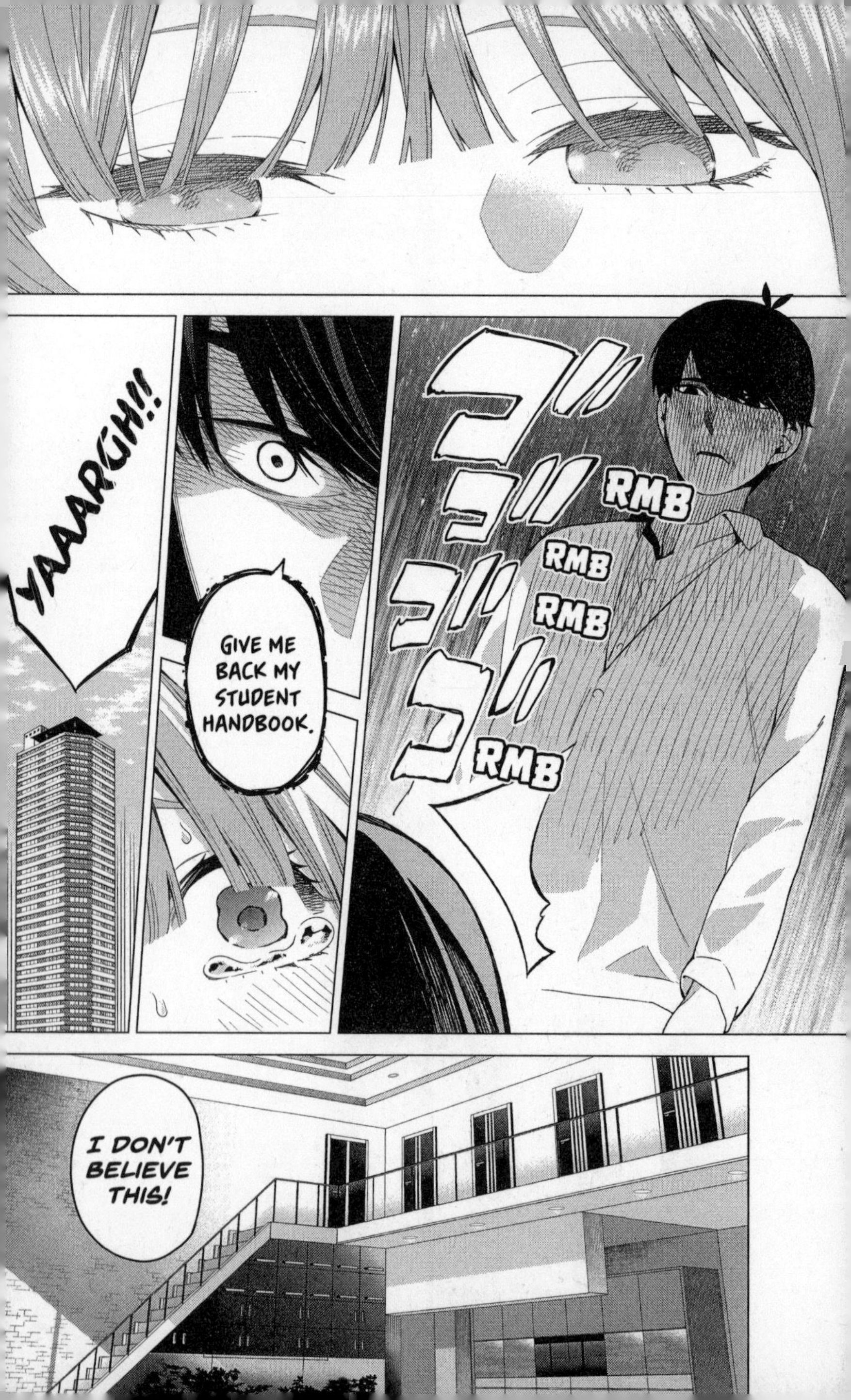
RMB
RMB
RMB
RMB
GIVE ME BACK MY STUDENT HANDBOOK.
YAAARGH!!
I DON'T BELIEVE THIS!

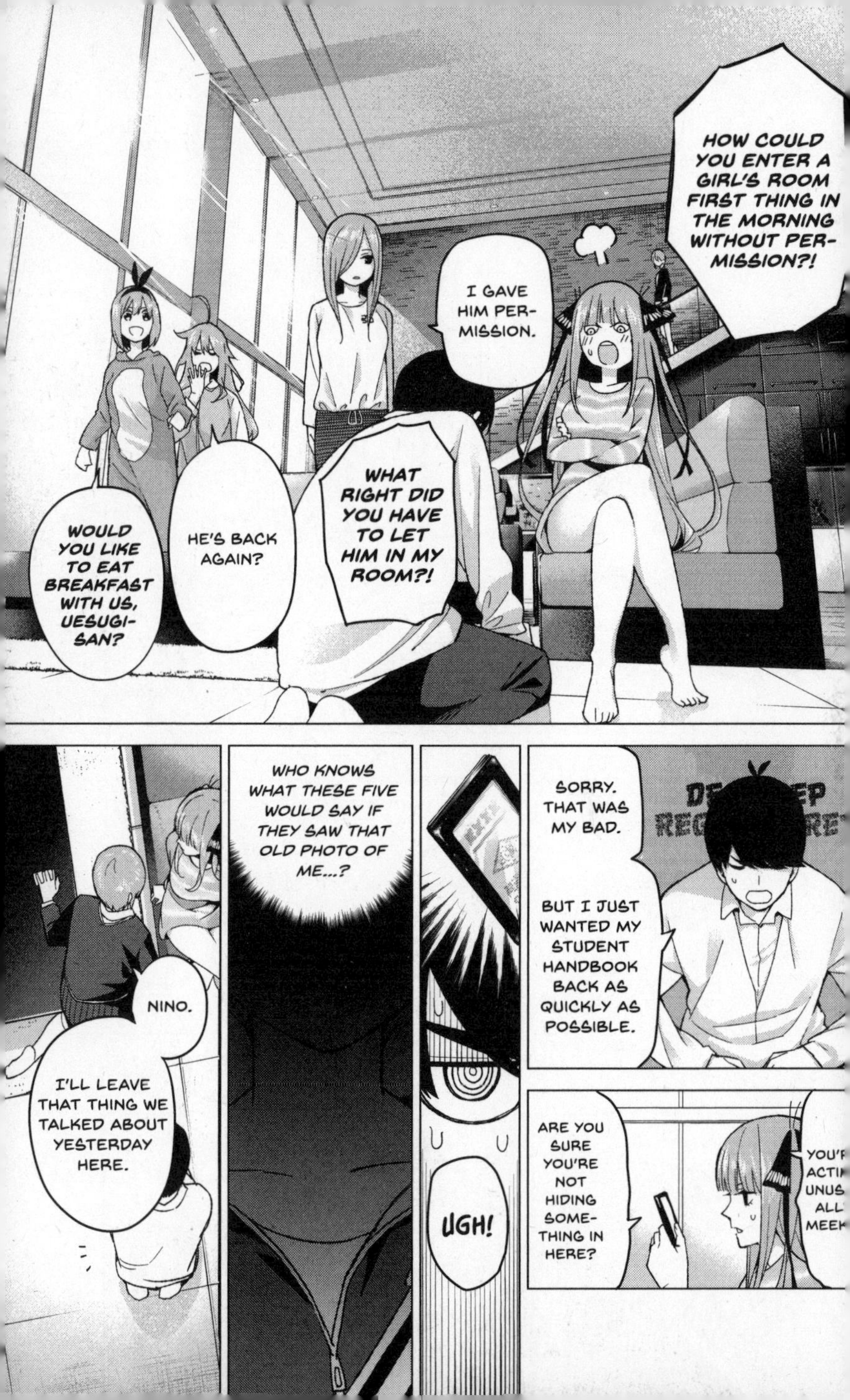
HOW COULD YOU ENTER A GIRL'S ROOM FIRST THING IN THE MORNING WITHOUT PER-MISSION?!
I GAVE HIM PER-MISSION.
WHAT RIGHT DID YOU HAVE TO LET HIM IN MY ROOM?!
HE'S BACK AGAIN?
WOULD YOU LIKE TO EAT BREAKFAST WITH US, UESUGI-SAN?
SORRY. THAT WAS MY BAD.
BUT I JUST WANTED MY STUDENT HANDBOOK BACK AS QUICKLY AS POSSIBLE.
YOU'R ACTI UNUS ALL MEEK
ARE YOU SURE YOU'RE NOT HIDING SOME-THING IN HERE?
UGH!
WHO KNOWS WHAT THESE FIVE WOULD SAY IF THEY SAW THAT OLD PHOTO OF ME...?
NINO.
I'LL LEAVE THAT THING WE TALKED ABOUT YESTERDAY HERE.

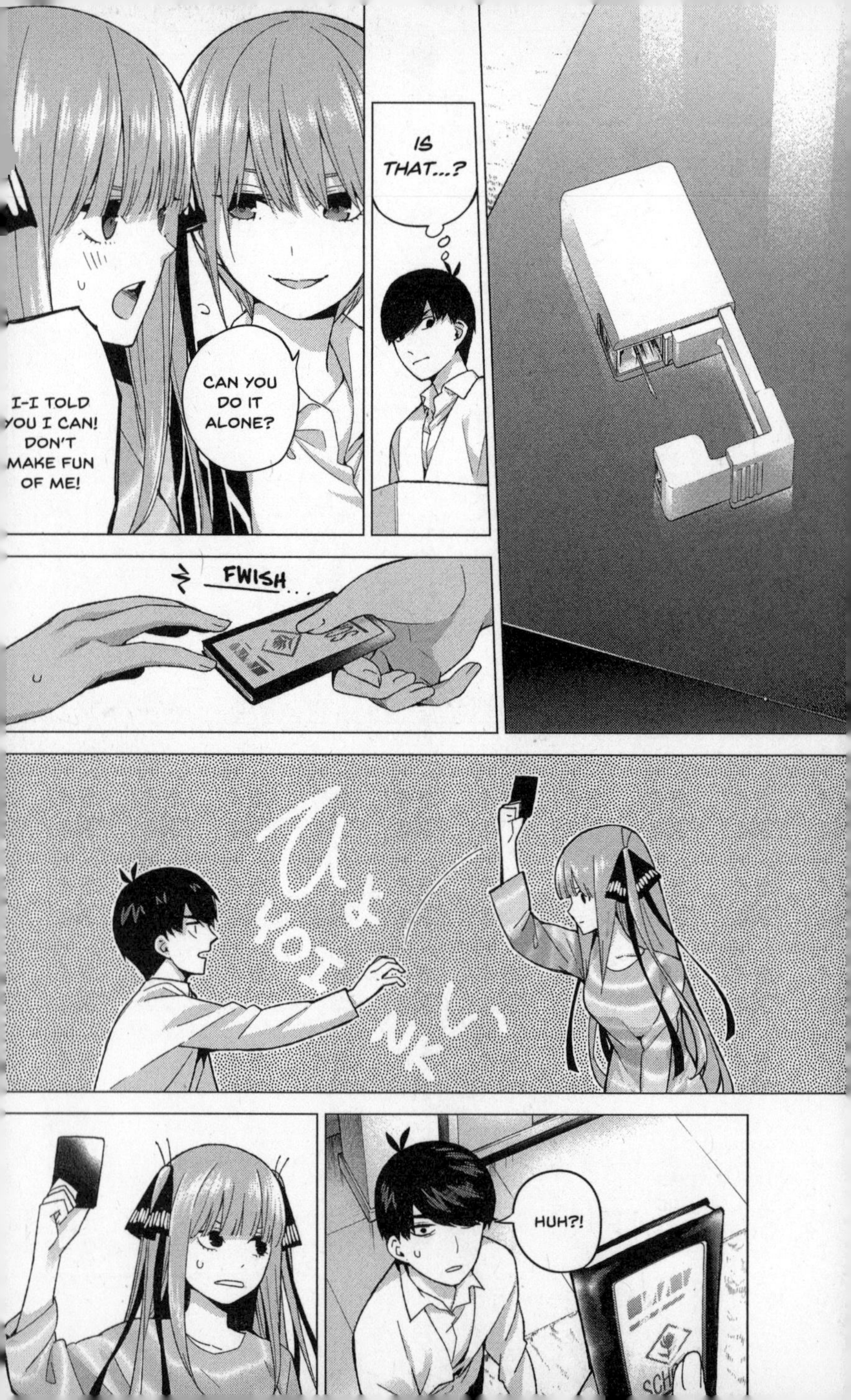
IS THAT...?
CAN YOU DO IT ALONE?
I-I TOLD YOU I CAN! DON'T MAKE FUN OF ME!
FWISH...
YOINK
HUH?!

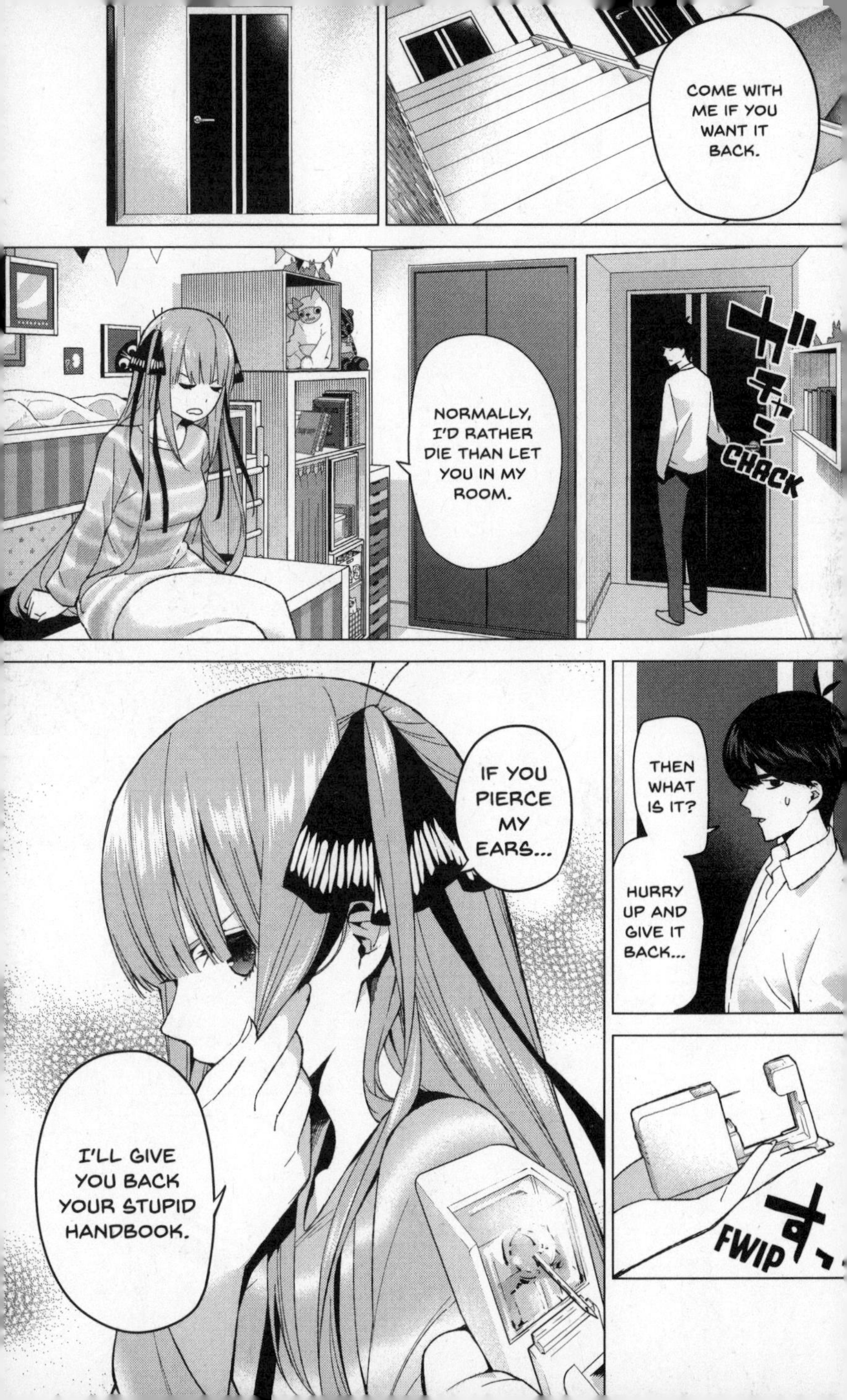
COME WITH ME IF YOU WANT IT BACK.
ガチャ
CHACK
NORMALLY, I'D RATHER DIE THAN LET YOU IN MY ROOM.
THEN WHAT IS IT?
HURRY UP AND GIVE IT BACK...
すっ
FWIP
IF YOU PIERCE MY EARS...
I'LL GIVE YOU BACK YOUR STUPID HANDBOOK.

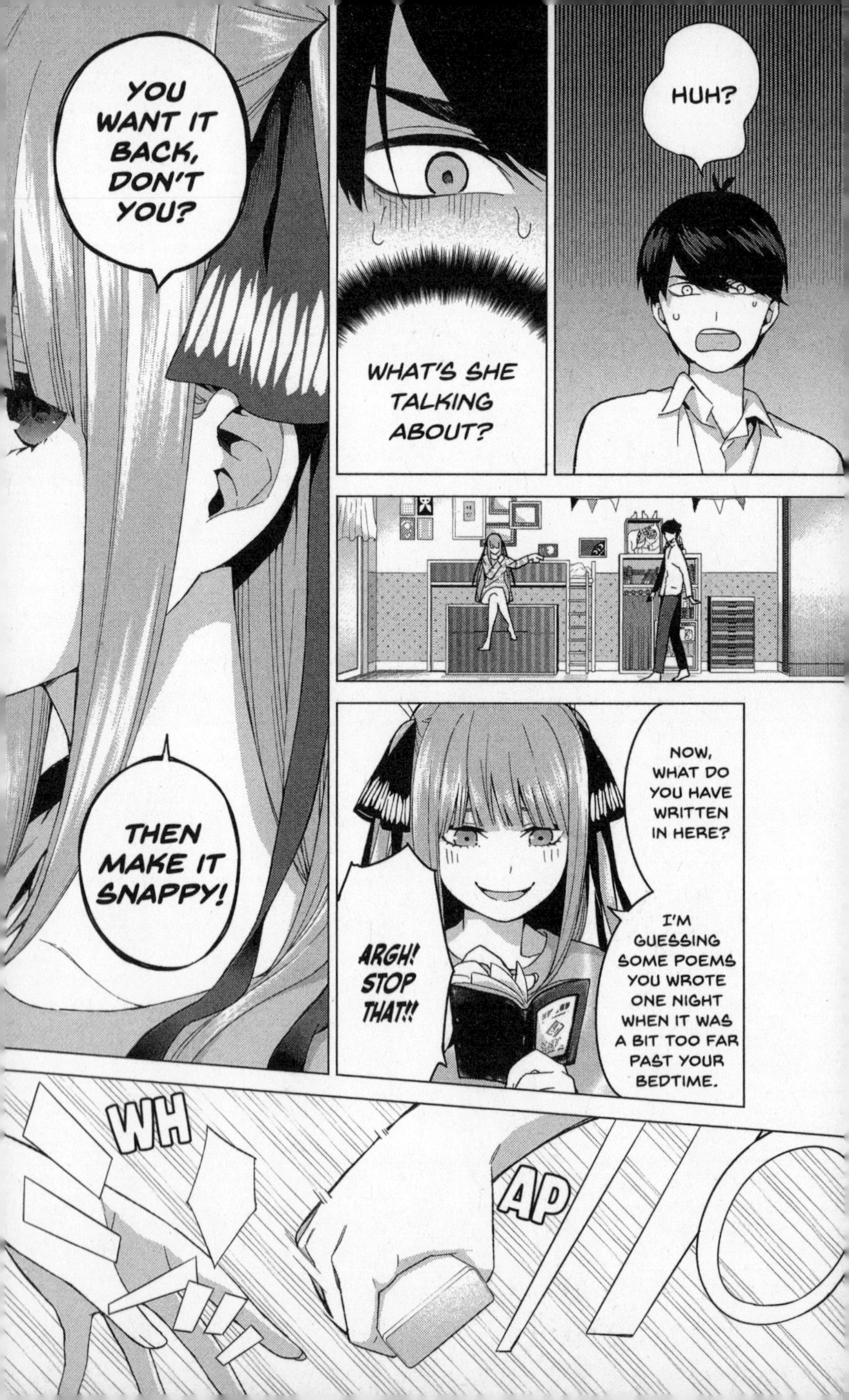
HUH?
WHAT'S SHE TALKING ABOUT?
NOW, WHAT DO YOU HAVE WRITTEN IN HERE?
I'M GUESSING SOME POEMS YOU WROTE ONE NIGHT WHEN IT WAS A BIT TOO FAR PAST YOUR BEDTIME.
ARGH! STOP THAT!!
YOU WANT IT BACK, DON'T YOU?
THEN MAKE IT SNAPPY!
WH
AP

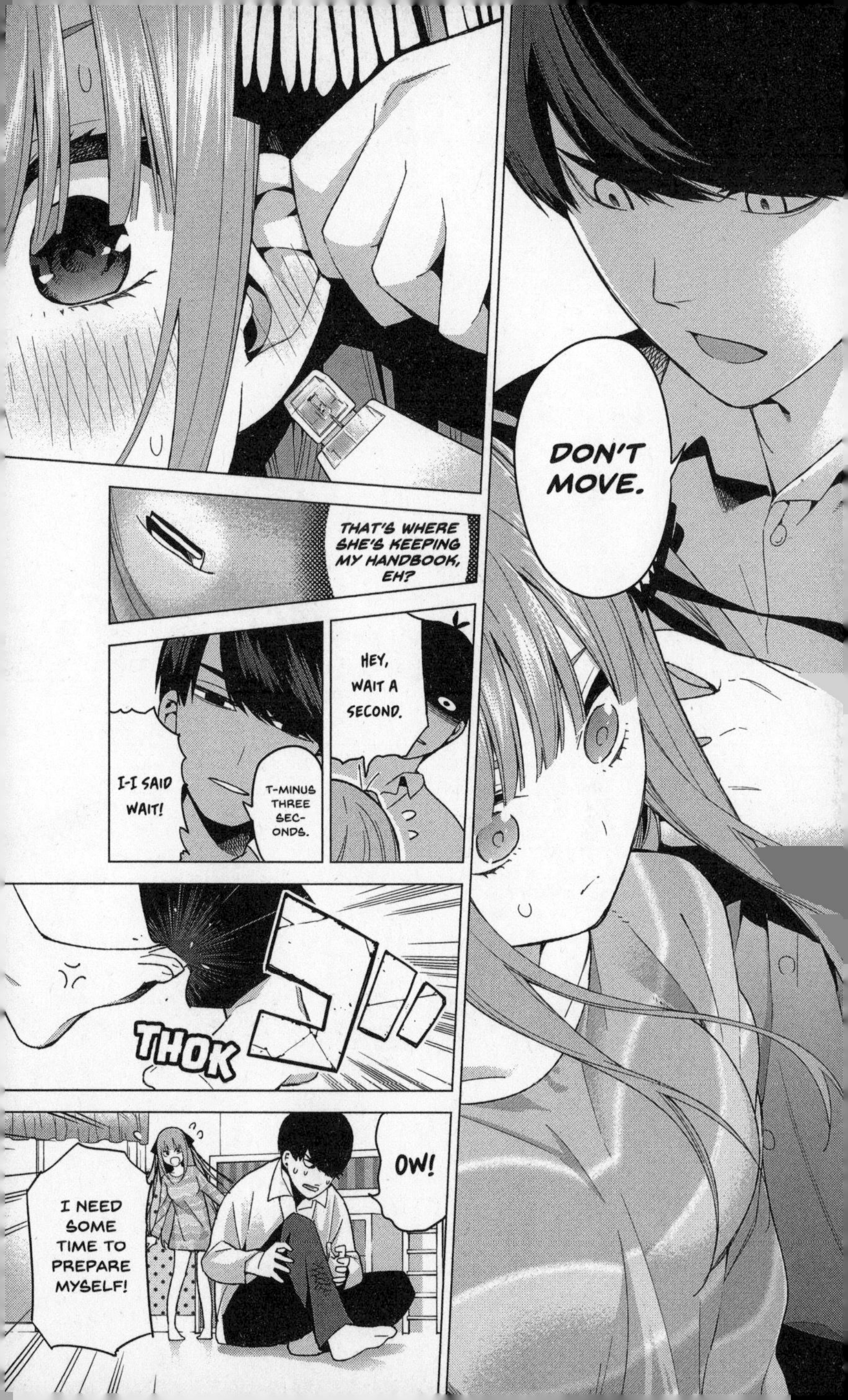
DON'T MOVE.
THAT'S WHERE SHE'S KEEPING MY HANDBOOK, EH?
HEY, WAIT A SECOND.
T-MINUS THREE SEC-ONDS.
I-I SAID WAIT!
THOK
OW!
I NEED SOME TIME TO PREPARE MYSELF!

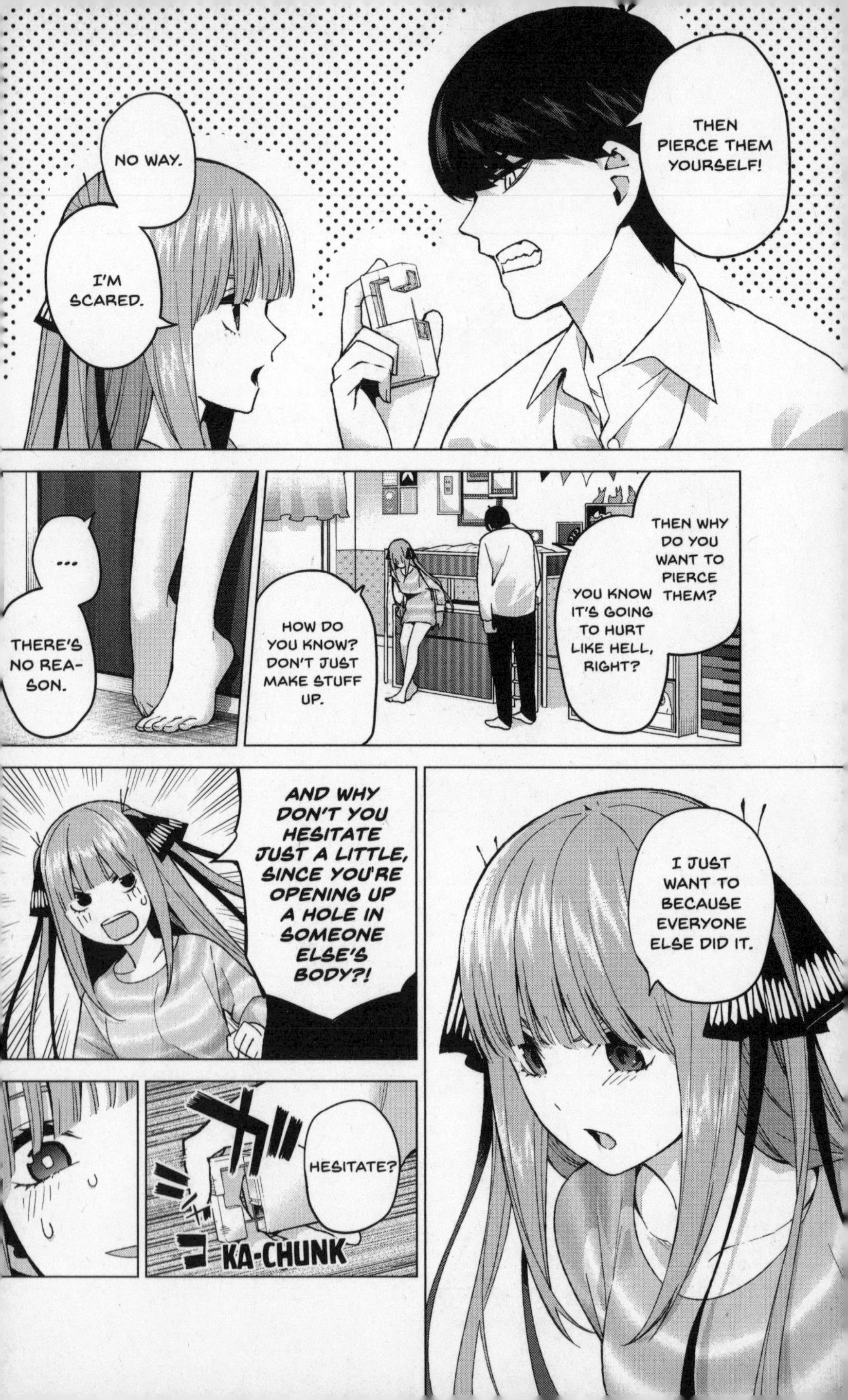
THEN PIERCE THEM YOURSELF!
NO WAY.
I'M SCARED.
THEN WHY DO YOU WANT TO PIERCE THEM?
YOU KNOW IT'S GOING TO HURT LIKE HELL, RIGHT?
HOW DO YOU KNOW? DON'T JUST MAKE STUFF UP.
...
THERE'S NO REA-SON.
I JUST WANT TO BECAUSE EVERYONE ELSE DID IT.
AND WHY DON'T YOU HESITATE JUST A LITTLE, SINCE YOU'RE OPENING UP A HOLE IN SOMEONE ELSE'S BODY?!
HESITATE?
KA-CHUNK

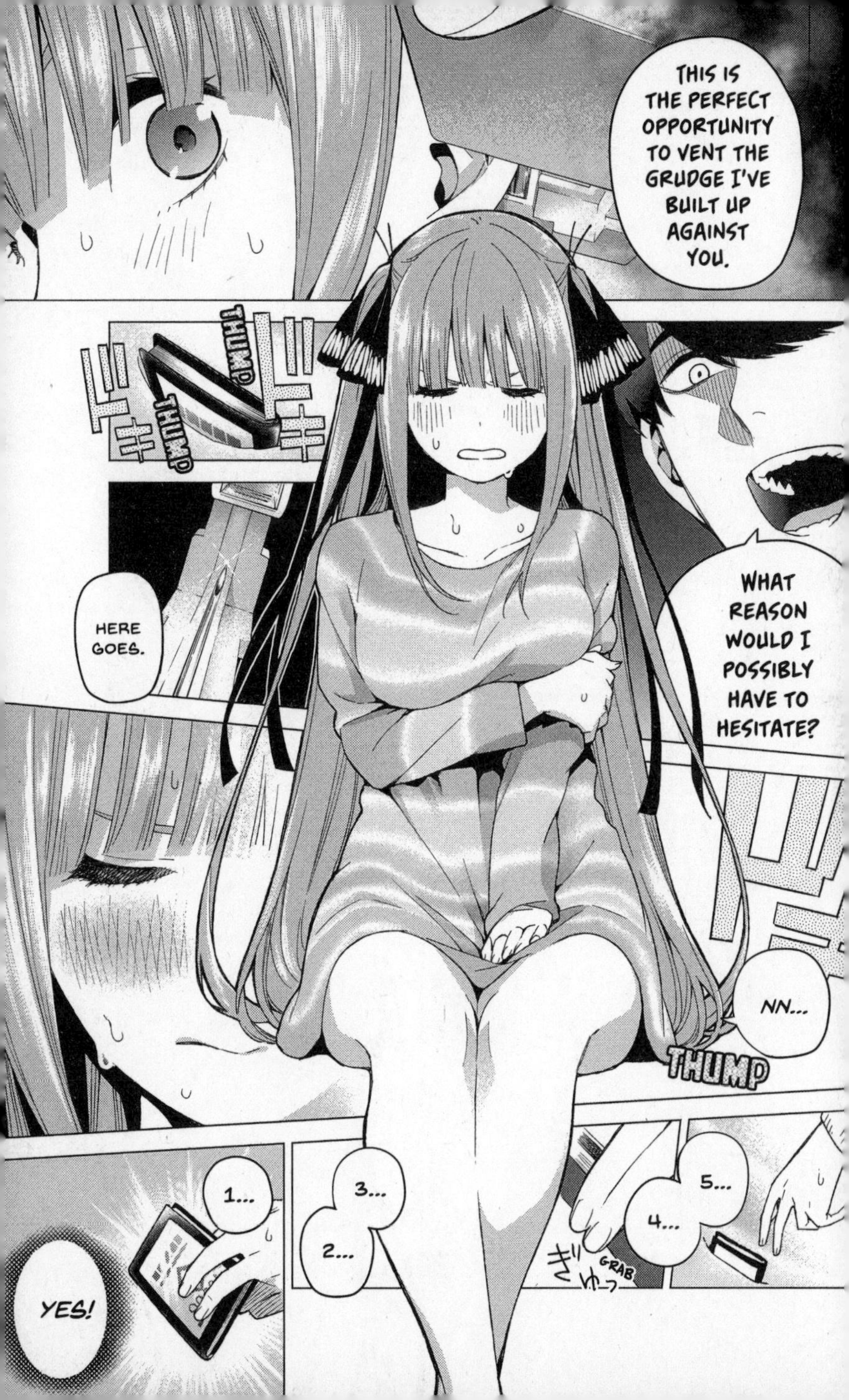
THIS IS THE PERFECT OPPORTUNITY TO VENT THE GRUDGE I'VE BUILT UP AGAINST YOU.
WHAT REASON WOULD I POSSIBLY HAVE TO HESITATE?
THUMP
THUMP
HERE GOES.
NN...
THUMP
5...
4...
GRAB
3...
2...
1...
YES!

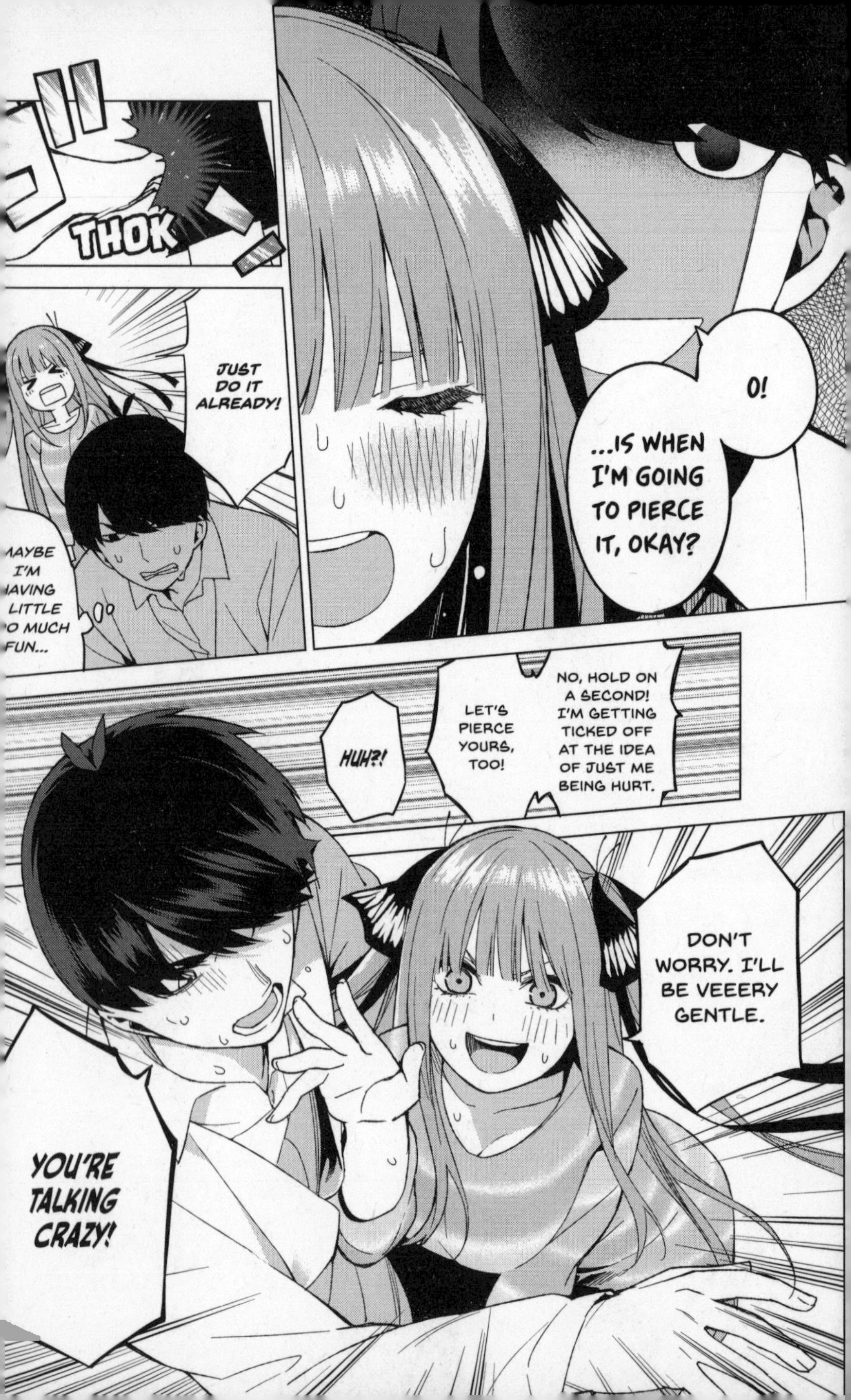
O! ...IS WHEN I'M GOING TO PIERCE IT, OKAY?
THOK
JUST DO IT ALREADY!
MAYBE I'M HAVING LITTLE O MUCH FUN...
NO, HOLD ON A SECOND! I'M GETTING TICKED OFF AT THE IDEA OF JUST ME BEING HURT.
LET'S PIERCE YOURS, TOO!
HUH?!
DON'T WORRY. I'LL BE VEEERY GENTLE.
YOU'RE TALKING CRAZY!

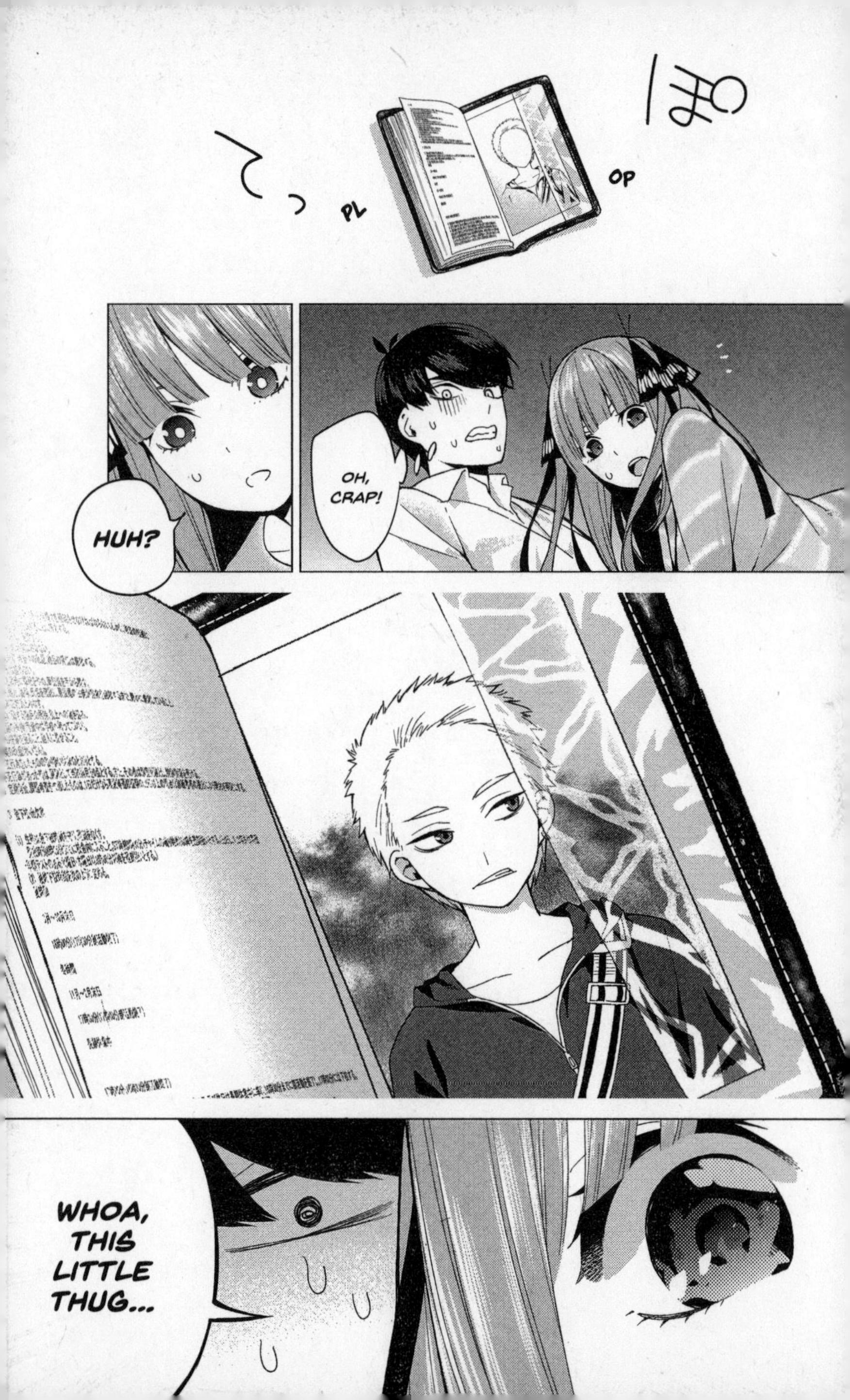
ぽ
OP
てっ
PL
OH, CRAP!
HUH?
WHOA, THIS LITTLE THUG...

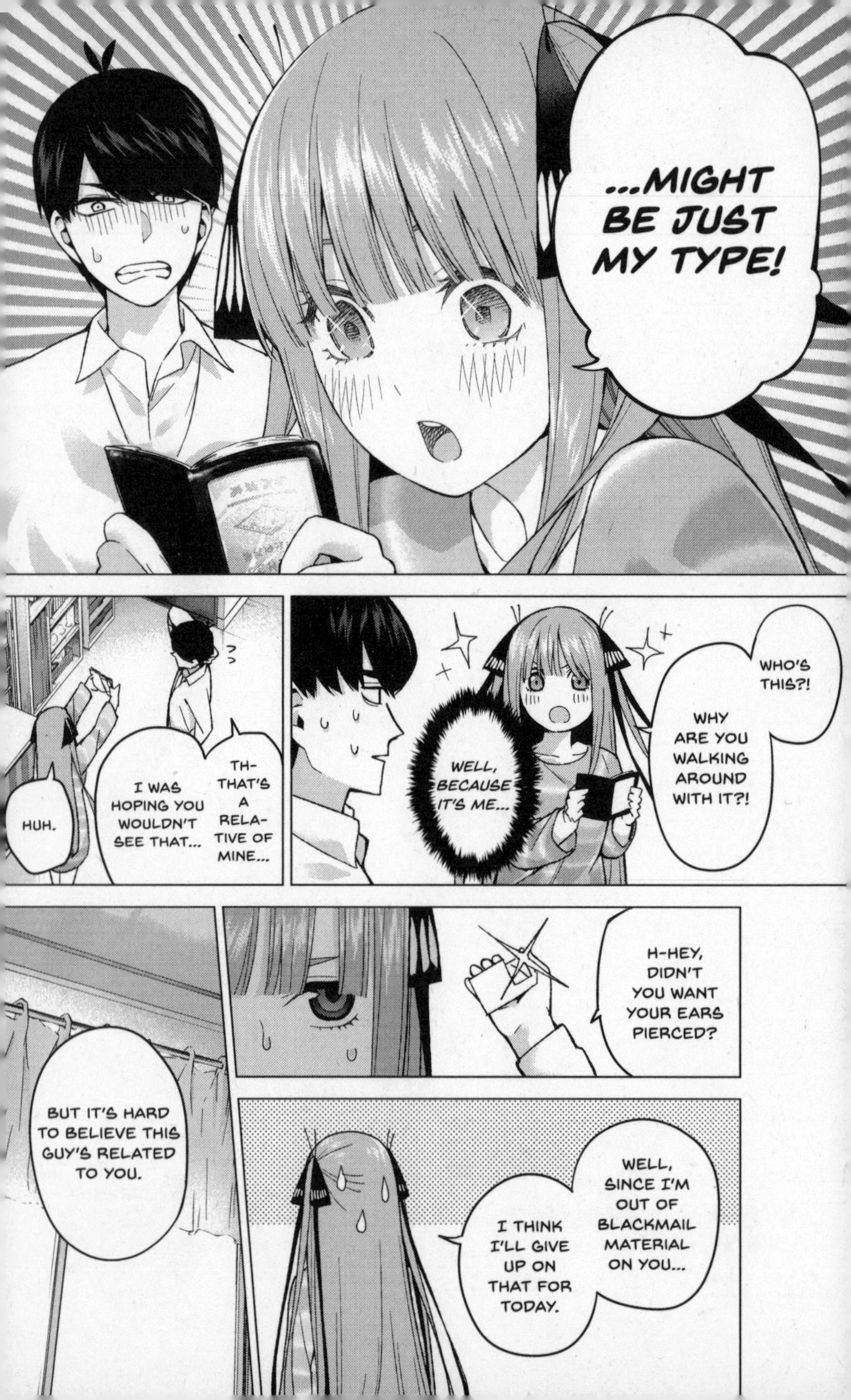
...MIGHT BE JUST MY TYPE!
WHO'S THIS?!
WHY ARE YOU WALKING AROUND WITH IT?!
WELL, BECAUSE IT'S ME...
TH-THAT'S A RELA-TIVE OF MINE...
I WAS HOPING YOU WOULDN'T SEE THAT...
HUH.
H-HEY, DIDN'T YOU WANT YOUR EARS PIERCED?
WELL, SINCE I'M OUT OF BLACKMAIL MATERIAL ON YOU...
I THINK I'LL GIVE UP ON THAT FOR TODAY.
BUT IT'S HARD TO BELIEVE THIS GUY'S RELATED TO YOU.

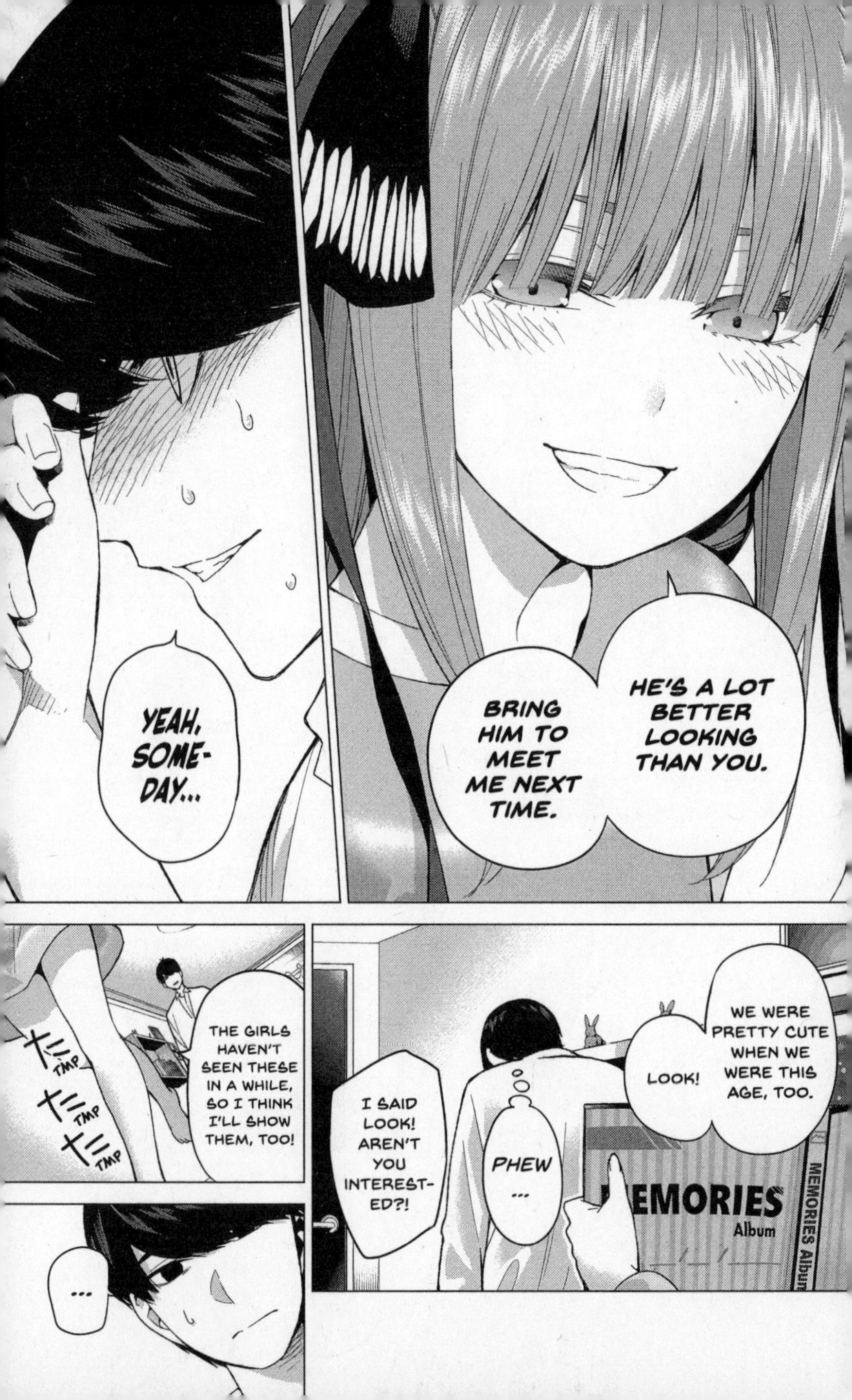
HE'S A LOT BETTER LOOKING THAN YOU.
BRING HIM TO MEET ME NEXT TIME.
YEAH, SOME-DAY...
WE WERE PRETTY CUTE WHEN WE WERE THIS AGE, TOO.
LOOK!
PHEW...
I SAID LOOK! AREN'T YOU INTEREST-ED?!
MEMORIES Album
MEMORIES Album
THE GIRLS HAVEN'T SEEN THESE IN A WHILE, SO I THINK I'LL SHOW THEM, TOO!
TMP
TMP
TMP
...

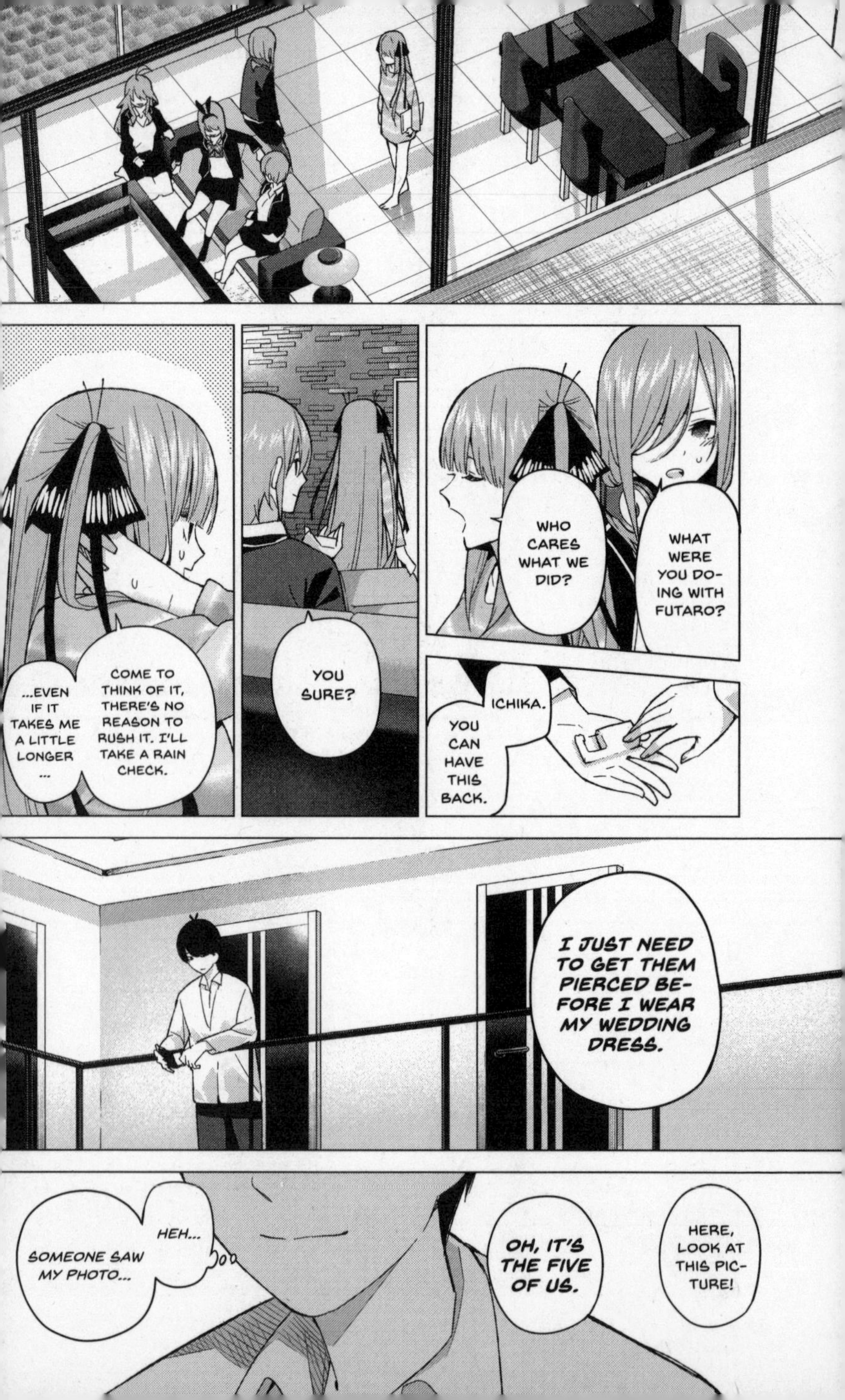
WHAT WERE YOU DOING WITH FUTARO?
WHO CARES WHAT WE DID?
ICHIKA.
YOU CAN HAVE THIS BACK.
YOU SURE?
COME TO THINK OF IT, THERE'S NO REASON TO RUSH IT. I'LL TAKE A RAIN CHECK.
...EVEN IF IT TAKES ME A LITTLE LONGER ...
I JUST NEED TO GET THEM PIERCED BEFORE I WEAR MY WEDDING DRESS.
HERE, LOOK AT THIS PICTURE!
OH, IT'S THE FIVE OF US.
HEH...
SOMEONE SAW MY PHOTO...

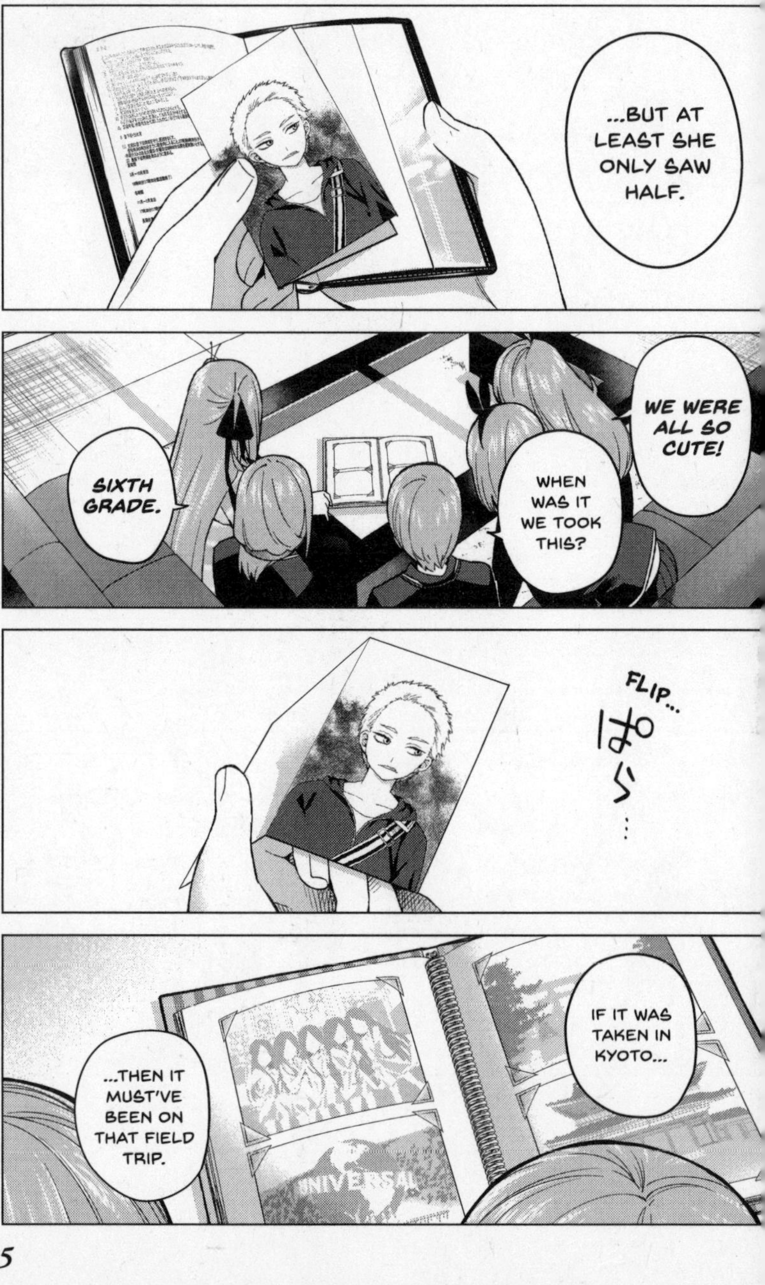
...BUT AT LEAST SHE ONLY SAW HALF.
WE WERE ALL SO CUTE!
WHEN WAS IT WE TOOK THIS?
SIXTH GRADE.
FLIP...
ぱら…
IF IT WAS TAKEN IN KYOTO...
...THEN IT MUST'VE BEEN ON THAT FIELD TRIP.
UNIVERSAL

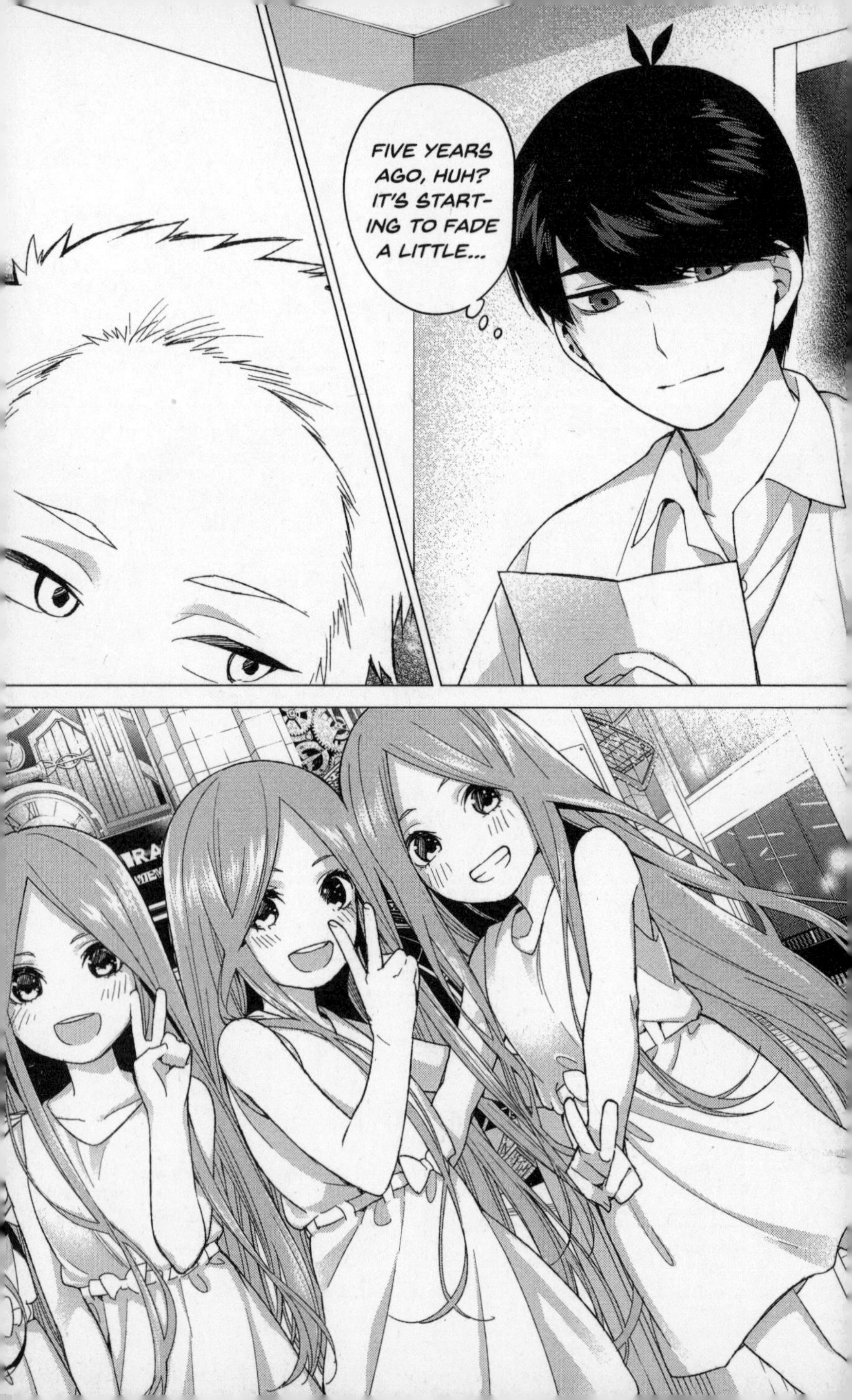
FIVE YEARS AGO, HUH? IT'S STARTING TO FADE A LITTLE...

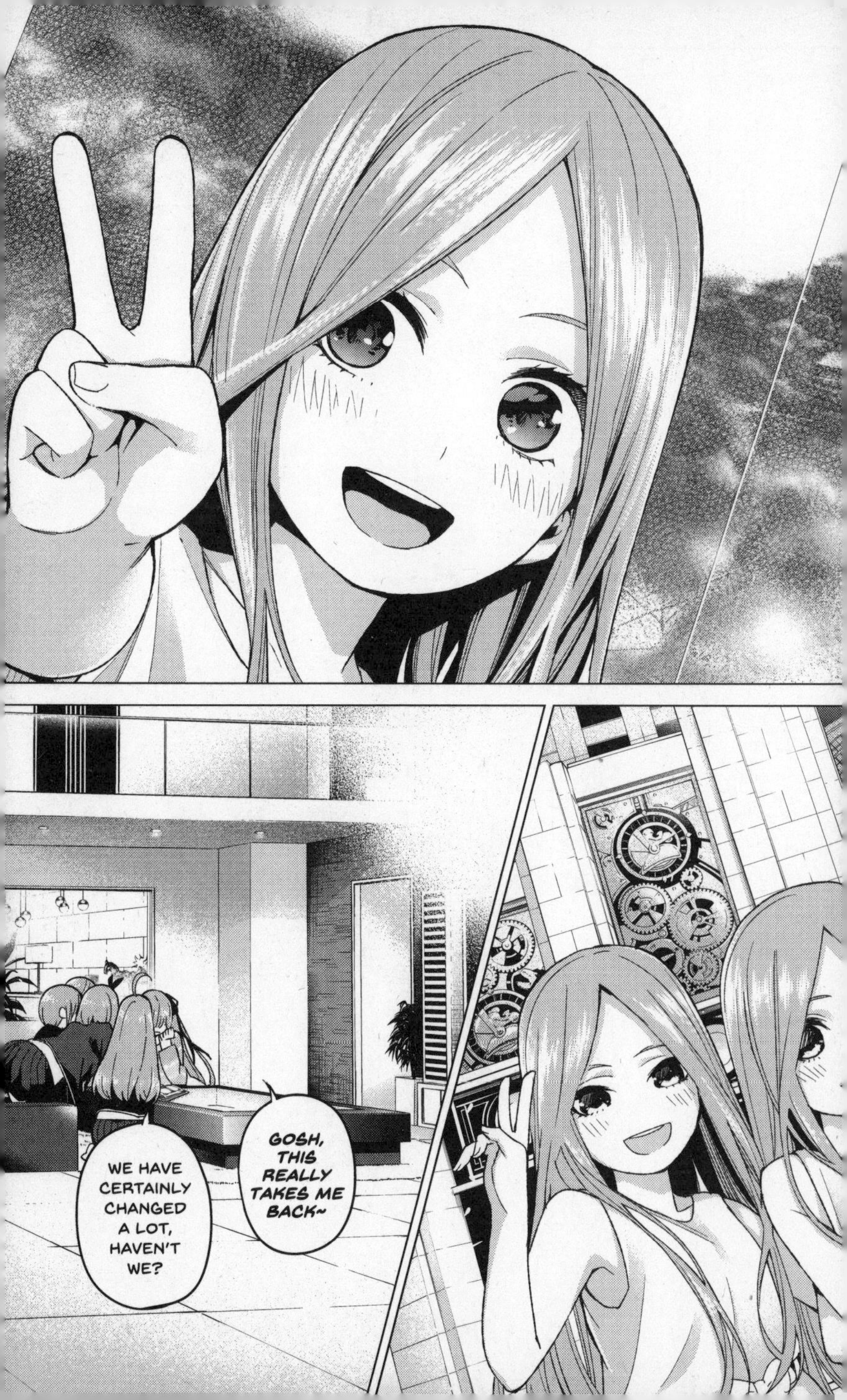
GOSH, THIS REALLY TAKES ME BACK~
WE HAVE CERTAINLY CHANGED A LOT, HAVEN'T WE?

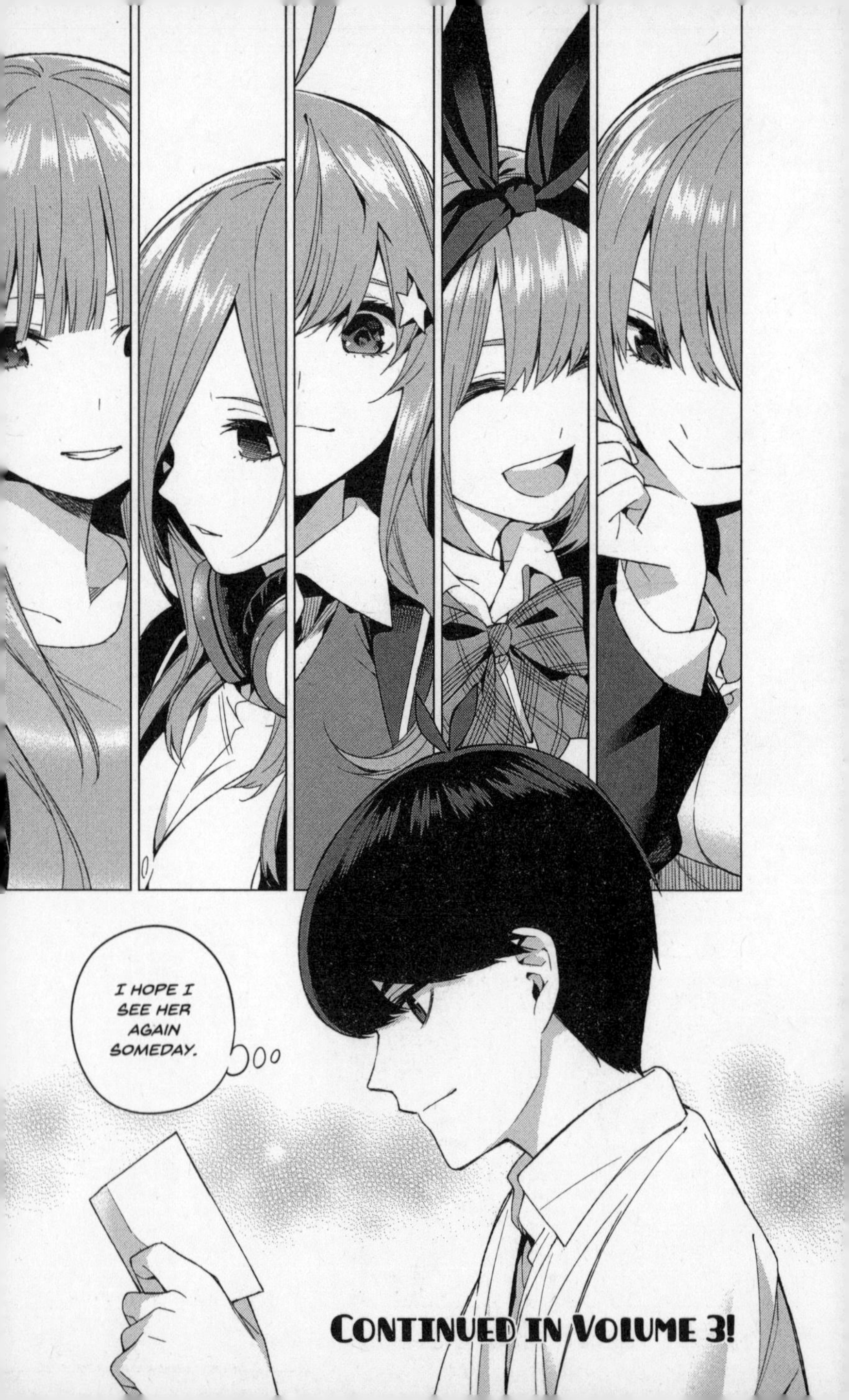
I HOPE I SEE HER AGAIN SOMEDAY.
CONTINUED IN VOLUME 3!

EXTRA BONUS COMI

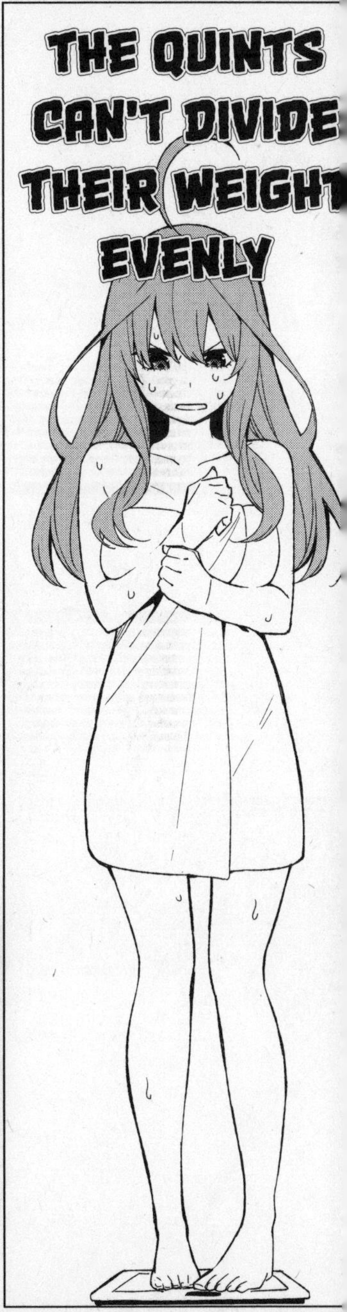
THE QUINTS CAN'T DIVIDE THEIR WEIGHT EVENLY

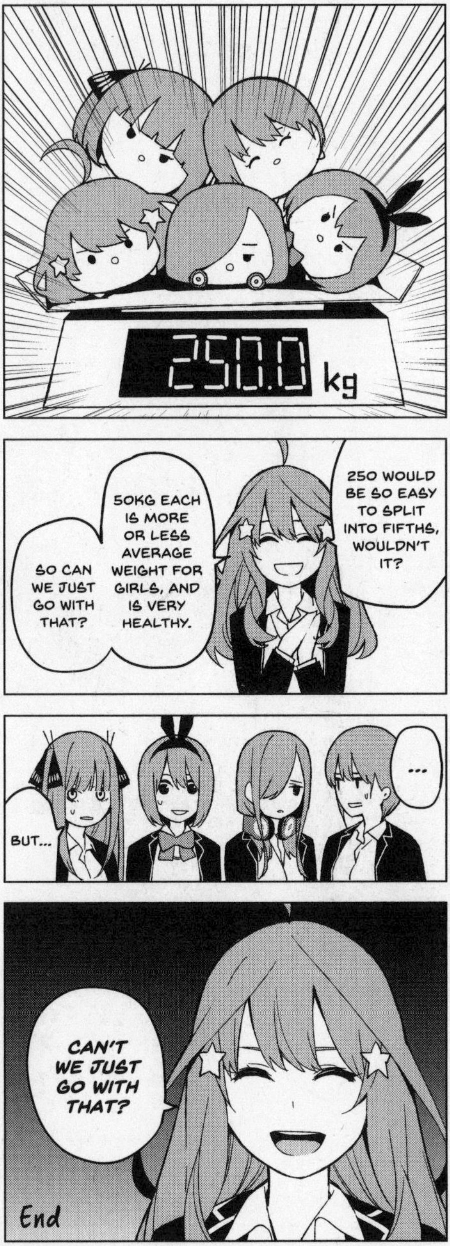
250.0 kg
250 WOULD BE SO EASY TO SPLIT INTO FIFTHS, WOULDN'T IT?
50KG EACH IS MORE OR LESS AVERAGE WEIGHT FOR GIRLS, AND IS VERY HEALTHY.
SO CAN WE JUST GO WITH THAT?
...
BUT...
CAN'T WE JUST GO WITH THAT?
End

Staff Ueno Hino Ogata

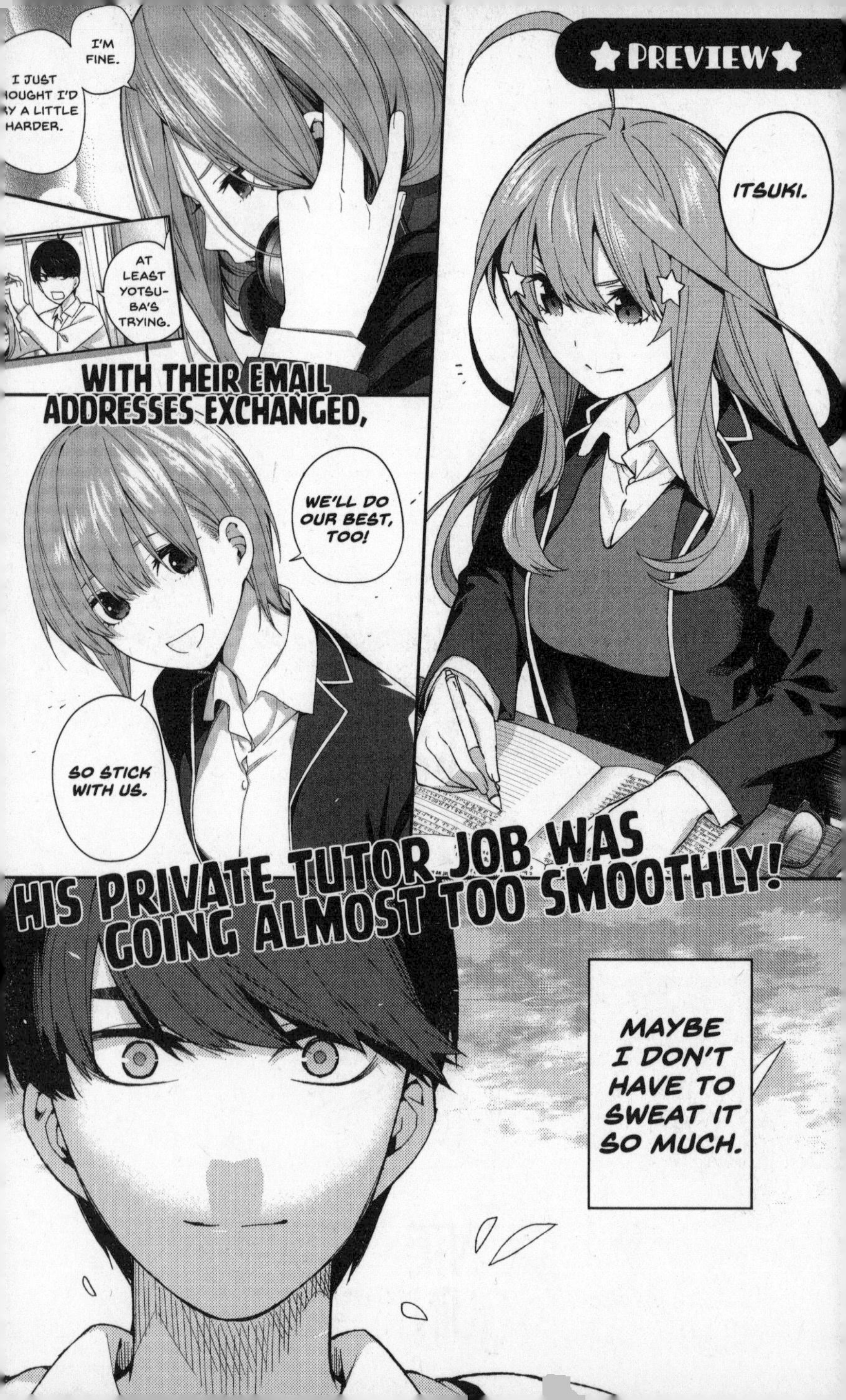
★PREVIEW★
ITSUKI.
I'M FINE.
I JUST
OUGHT I'D
Y A LITTLE
HARDER.
AT LEAST YOTSU-BA'S TRYING.
WITH THEIR EMAIL ADDRESSES EXCHANGED,
WE'LL DO OUR BEST, TOO!
SO STICK WITH US.
HIS PRIVATE TUTOR JOB WAS GOING ALMOST TOO SMOOTHLY!
MAYBE I DON'T HAVE TO SWEAT IT SO MUCH.

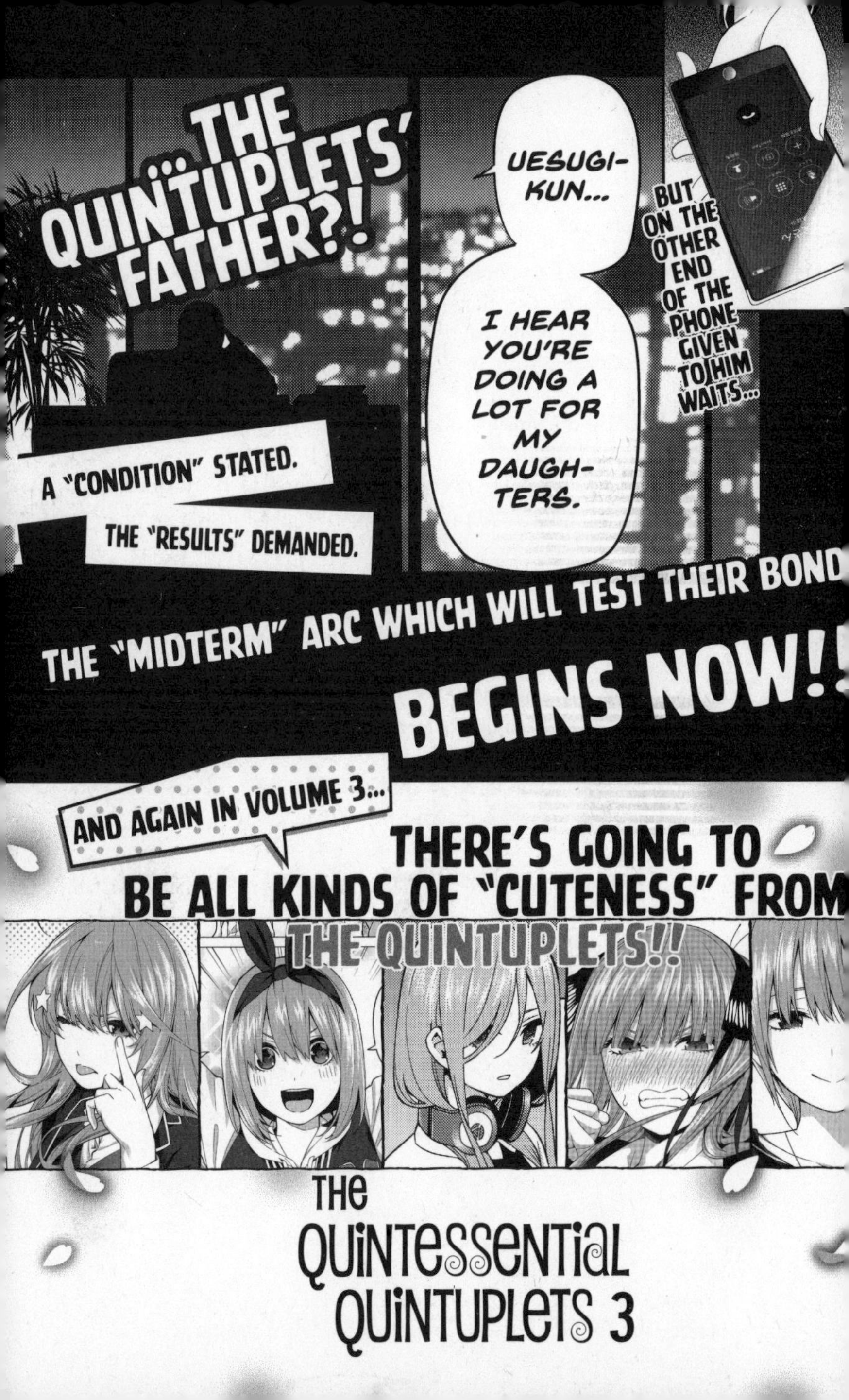
BUT ON THE OTHER END OF THE PHONE GIVEN TO HIM WAITS...
UESUGI-KUN...
I HEAR YOU'RE DOING A LOT FOR MY DAUGHTERS.
...THE QUINTUPLETS' FATHER?!
A "CONDITION" STATED.
THE "RESULTS" DEMANDED.
THE "MIDTERM" ARC WHICH WILL TEST THEIR BOND
BEGINS NOW!!
AND AGAIN IN VOLUME 3...
THERE'S GOING TO BE ALL KINDS OF "CUTENESS" FROM THE QUINTUPLETS!!
THE QUINTESSENTIAL QUINTUPLETS 3

A Kodansha Comics Trade Paperback Original.

The Quintessential Quintuplets volume 2 copyright © 2017 Negi Haruba
English translation copyright © 2019 Negi Haruba

Published in the United States by Kodansha Comics,
an imprint of Kodansha USA Publishing, LLC, New York.

Publication rights for this English edition arranged through Kodansha Ltd., Tokyo.

First published in Japan in 2017 by Kodansha Ltd., Tokyo,
as *Gotoubun no Hanayome* volume 2.

Cover Design: Saya Takai (RedRooster)

ISBN 978-1-63236-775-4

Printed in the United States of America.

www.kodanshacomics.com

9 8 7 6 5 4 3 2 1

Translation: Steven LeCroy
Lettering: Jan Lan Ivan Concepcion
Additional Layout: Belynda Ungurath
Editing: David Yoo, Thalia Sutton
Editorial Assistance: YKS Services LLC/SKY Japan, INC.
Kodansha Comics Edition Cover Design: Phil Balsman